55.00

P9-CAO-187

History of American Presidential Elections

Supplemental Volume
1972–1984

History of American Presidential Elections
1789–1984

Arthur M. Schlesinger, jr.
Editor
Albert Schweitzer Chair in the Humanities
City University of New York

Fred L. Israel
Associate Editor
Department of History
City College of New York

William P. Hansen
Managing Editor

1986
CHELSEA HOUSE PUBLISHERS
New York
New Haven   Philadelphia

Excerpt from *Stand Up For America* (Description of
Assassination Attempt) by George Wallace. Copyright ©
1976 by George Wallace. Reprinted by permission of
Doubleday & Co., Inc.

First Printing

Library of Congress Cataloging in Publication Data
Main entry under title:

History of American presidential elections, 1789–1984.

    Includes index.
      1. Presidents—United States—Election—History.
2. United States—Politics and government.   I. Schlesinger,
Arthur Meir, 1917–   II. Israel, Fred L.
III. Hansen, William P.
E183.H58   1985   324.973'09   84-23166
ISBN 0-87754-492-1

Chelsea House Publishers
Harold Steinberg, Chairman & Publisher
Susan Lusk, Vice President
A Division of Chelsea House Educational Communications, Inc.

Chelsea House Publishers
133 Christopher Street, New York, NY 10014

345 Whitney Avenue, New Haven, CT 06510

5014 West Chester Pike, Edgemont, PA 19028

Prefatory Note

In the twelve years that spanned the reelections of Richard Nixon (1972) and Ronald Reagan (1984), the United States experienced profound political and social change. The widespread dissent and confrontational radicalism of the 1960s and early 1970s was replaced by an acceptance of more conservative and traditional values. In the late 1960s, there was seemingly no end to the causes to which protesters rallied in an attempt to restructure American society. But the staying power of these "rebels" proved brief. Indeed, by the presidential election of 1984, the dominant society had succeeded in absorbing both the rebels and their rebellion. Ronald Reagan clearly had a mandate. In fact, the 1984 landslide was a culmination of political patterns which had begun to emerge in 1972.

An analysis of the 1972 election vote by major population groups shows that the Democratic coalition forged during the New Deal had fallen into disarray. One third of registered Democrats voted for Richard Nixon. This defection rate far exceeded that recorded in any of the previous five presidential elections. The nation's manual workers, representing more than a third of the electorate and the core vote for all Democratic aspirants since the 1930s, went heavily for Nixon over George McGovern (57% to 43%). The most dramatic switch in voting behavior, however, occurred among labor union people. For the first time since the mid-1930s, a majority (54%) of labor union families voted the Republican ticket.

In 1984, Reagan totally destroyed what little was left of the New Deal coalition. The vote among Catholics and Protestants was exactly the same (61% for Reagan and 39% for Walter Mondale). For the previous three decades, Catholics had voted, on average, 20 points more Democratic than their Protestant counterparts. Likewise, after voting more Democratic than their elders in the previous five presidential elections, voters under age 30 were as Republican in 1984 as persons 30 and older.

In 1964, following Lyndon Johnson's rout of Barry Goldwater, there had been talk of the possible demise of the Republican party. In just 20 years the cycle had come full swing, showing once again the ever-changing nature of forces at play in modern American politics.

In organizing this volume, Professor Schlesinger and I have incurred many agreeable debts of gratitude. Our first is to the four contributors—Richard C. Wade, Betty Glad, Jules Witcover, and William V. Shannon—who generously agreed to participate in this project. We gratefully acknowledge the assistance of Philip Cohen, the President of Chelsea House Publishers and to Harold Steinberg, the Publisher. To Karyn G. Browne, who coordinated this project, we owe a very special thank you.

Fred L. Israel
Associate Editor

CONTENTS
Supplemental Volume
1972–1984

Editor's Note: The spelling, style, and punctuation of the documents following each essay have been retained as they appeared in the original sources.

A Time of Political Upheaval

by *Arthur M. Schlesinger, jr.*

The broad contours of American presidential politics changed little in the thirty years from the mid-1930s, when Franklin D. Roosevelt's New Deal coalition began its ascendancy, to the mid-1960s. In contrast, the sixteen years from Richard Nixon's election in 1968 to Ronald Reagan's reelection in 1984 were a time of political upheaval. New electronic technologies, new party rules, new forms of campaign management, and new sources of campaign finance gave the electoral process new shape and character. Extensive population shifts, both in residence (from city to suburb; from frostbelt to sunbelt) and in employment (from manufacturing to services and to high technology), created new constituencies and promised new political combinations. Republican victories in four of the five presidential elections after 1964 portended the breakup of the aging New Deal coalition and the reversal of the priorities that had dominated the republic since 1933. The four elections covered in this volume saw, in short, striking changes in the organization of presidential politics, in the structure of the electorate and in the goals of national policy.

I

Underlying the changes in the organization of presidential politics was the decay of the political party. This decay had been taking place for some time. The last half of the 19th century had been the age of party supremacy. Never were the major parties more in control of political life. Never were they more effective in mobilizing voters at elections. The American political party, as the

British observer James Bryce wrote in 1888, was characterized by a "sort of military discipline." Even as Bryce wrote, however, the long decline of the party was under way.

The corruption associated with political bosses had already brought the local party machine into increasing disrepute. The complacency of national party leadership provoked the rise of third parties pressing questions the major parties sought to forget. The Progressive movement of the early 20th century attacked boss control and gave voters a new voice through the primary system. The spread of a civil service based on merit began to dry up the reservoir of political patronage. The falling-off of mass immigration after the First World War deprived the city machine of its historic clientele. The growth of the welfare state during the Great Depression terminated the role of parties in ministering to the poor and helpless. As levels of education rose, voters ignored party leaders and insisted on making their own political choices. Parties thus lost their classical functions one after another and in time lost their control of the electorate. "The growing independence of voters," Franklin D. Roosevelt said in 1940, ". . . has been proved by the voters in every Presidential election since my childhood—and the tendency, frankly, is on the increase."

After the Second World War, party loyalty grew ever more tenuous. Ticket-splitting became common. The old-style political machine disappeared, even, finally, in Chicago. More and more voters described themselves as independents. The passage into the electronic age speeded the process of disintegration. The essential function of the party had been to serve as middleman between politician and voter, interpreting each to the other and supplying the link that held the system together. Then television, by presenting the politician directly to the voter, and computerized public opinion polls, by presenting the voter directly to the politician, took over the party's mediatorial function. Computers and the microchips soon appropriated tasks of research, communication and manipulation once performed by political organizations. The party was left to wither on the vine.

The electronic technologies gave presidential primaries new vitality and voters a new sense of entitlement in the nominating process. No presidential convention after 1952 dared reverse the verdict of the primaries, and no presidential candidate after 1952 required more than one ballot for nomination. Once nominated, candidates tended increasingly to run campaigns through personal organizations rather than through their party's national committee. The new technologies nourished a new breed of electronic specialists, who formed campaign-management firms, worked indifferently for one party or the other and usurped the role so long played by party professionals. In the electronic age, campaigns abandoned the traditional paraphernalia of mass democracy—volunteers, rallies, torchlight parades, leaflets, posters, billboards, bumper stickers—and relied increasingly on television, on computer-targeted mailings and phone banks and on paid help.

The party thus lost its command not only of lines of communication with the voter but of the presidential nominating process and of the management of presidential campaigns. It also saw its command of campaign finance greatly reduced. The Federal Election Campaign Act of 1974 not only provided for public funding of presidential elections but imposed limits both on political contributions and political spending. In limiting contributions to candidates, the law permitted larger contributions by non-party political action committees (PACs) than by individuals. The advantage thus conferred on PACs was greatly increased two years later when the Supreme Court in *Buckley* v. *Valeo* knocked out the spending ceilings in congressional campaigns, doing so on the bizarre ground that political spending was equivalent to speech and therefore protected by the First Amendment. The Court evidently had no doubt that money talks. This ill-considered decision not only stimulated the formation of PACs as well as the appetite of candidates but also sanctioned, even in publicly-financed presidential campaigns, "independent expenditures" by PACs—that is, political spending not coordinated with the favored candidate and campaign. No aggregate limit, moreover, was placed on the amount of money PACs could receive and disburse. With a freer hand to play, PACs lured an increasing share of political money from the parties. By the mid-1980s, PACs had increased sevenfold in number since 1974 (from 600 to more than 4000); the money they spent increased tenfold. PAC contributions accounted for 13 percent of congressional campaign funds in 1974; 41 percent in 1984. Because PACs typically represented special interests, many observers feared their distorting and corrupting effects on the political process.

The decline of the party as the organizing unit of American politics could be measured in the decline of voter turnout. In presidential elections between the Civil War and the end of the 19th century, despite the general absence of exciting candidates and issues, the proportion of eligible voters actually going to the polls never fell below 70 percent. In no presidential election after 1900 has turnout exceeded 65 percent, and in no presidential election after 1968 has it exceeded 55 percent. Doubtless the enlargement of the voting pool—women in 1920, blacks in 1965, 18-year-olds in 1971—contributed to the decline. But the basic reason was the growing ineffectuality of the party as an agent of voter mobilization.

The plight of the parties stimulated rescue movements. The reform of party rules, initiated by the McGovern Commission in the Democratic party and imitated up to a point by the Republicans, gave the national committees new autonomy and strength and sought to incorporate newly awakened constituencies, notably women and racial minorities, into the party framework. While some rule changes were justly criticized for enlarging citizen participation at the expense of party professionalism, excesses were soon corrected. In the longer run, the reform movements unquestionably modernized and strengthened the national party organizations. There was even hope that the new technologies, after having done so much to weaken the party system, might give parties a new lease on life. For, it was believed, the party organization could find a new function in providing candidates with an electronic base and computerized services too sophisticated and expensive for individuals to provide for themselves.

But party modernization was a holding action. It extended the parties' lease on life, but it did not reverse the deep-running tendency in the political culture to turn away from the single-minded party discipline and loyalty of earlier times. Even so popular a President as Ronald Reagan could not bring along a Republican Congress in the wake of his triumphant reelection.

The impact of party decay on presidential elections was to give new opportunity to contenders running against the party establishment—George McGovern in 1972, Jimmy Carter in 1976, Ronald Reagan in 1980, even (though he failed to win the nomination) Gary Hart in 1984. In the general elections, presidential candidates depended less on the party organization, professional politicians and historic party identity and more on television, media specialists, and their own personal appeal.

II

Population changes also affected presidential politics. The American people were growing older. In 1900 only 4 percent had been over 65. By the 1980s the proportion of old folks was approaching 9 percent. Demographers predicted that by the early 21st century it would be over 20 percent. It was hardly coincidental that the "graying of America" was accompanied by the election and reelection of the oldest President in the nation's history.

At the same time, Americans were moving out of the Northeast and the Middle West into the Sunbelt—the states below the 37th parallel from Virginia across to southern California. In 1964 California displaced New York as the nation's most populous state. Almost 90 percent of population growth in the 1970s took place away from the Northeast and Middle West. If that trend continued, 60 percent of the people would live in the Sunbelt by the year 2000.

The flight to the Sunbelt had strong political implications. Between the Civil War and the Second World War, only two men born outside the Northeast (defined to include Ohio) made it to the White House. Of the eight Presidents after 1945, only one—Kennedy—came from the Northeast. Each new decennial census gave the South and West further weight in the Electoral College. Since these two regions had become conservative in their politics, the drift of population enlarged the strongholds of the right. In particular, Republicans hoped that they had at last captured the "Solid South" that had sustained the Democrats for so many long years. Even within the Northeast and Middle West, movement from the city to the suburbs fostered conservative tendencies. By 1980 nearly 45 percent of Americans lived in suburbs as against less than 30 percent in central cities.

City dwellers had been key parts of the New Deal coalition. So too had been industrial workers in the mass-production industries. But by the 1980s only a third of American workers were in manufacturing. There were now twice as many white-collar and service workers as there were blue-collar workers. The increase in fast-food employment by the early 1980s was greater than the total employment in the once thriving automotive and steel industries. Third World competition, facilitated by the overvalued American dollar, led observers to speak of the "twilight of smokestack America" and even of the "deindustrialization of America."

Changes in the structure of employment also had political consequences. There were fewer trade union members than before, and they deferred less to their leaders. The number of poor people increased in the 1980s, but they were often disinclined to vote. The rise of aggressive black politics, as personified in 1984 by Jesse Jackson, hastened the movement of southern whites into the Republican party. The foundations of the New Deal coalition appeared to be in decay. Republican emphasis on economic opportunity, tax reduction and venture capital attracted the Yuppies of the high-technology age a good deal more than did Democratic emphasis on protecting the steel and automotive industries.

Of the population growth in the 1970s, about 40 percent was due to immigration. The annual rate of legal entry was higher than in any decade since the first of the 20th century. Hispanics, the fastest growing minority, increased by 60 percent during the 1970s, the result both of immigration, legal and illegal, and of a high birth rate. Some experts expected Hispanics to overtake blacks as the nation's predominant minority in the early 21st century. By the 1980s Hispanics were emerging as a political force, electing a governor in New Mexico and mayors in Denver, San Antonio, Miami, Tampa and Santa Fe. Mexicans and Puerto Ricans tended to be Democrats, Cubans Republicans; but Hispanics in general became a target of Republican solicitude in the Reagan years.

Changes in the composition of the electorate thus appeared to undermine the bases of party division that had prevailed in the half century since the New Deal had redrawn the political map of the republic. In the 1980s an administration bent on counterrevolution against the New Deal came to power. Its long-term purpose was to give the nation a new political map. Its hope was that Ronald Reagan would bring about a party realignment as fundamental and enduring as that brought about by Franklin Roosevelt in the 1930s.

III

The theory of periodic party realignment sees the American party system as consisting typically of a majority party and a minority party, both oriented around a particular set of problems. In time, exigent new problems emerge, cutting across party lines and confronting the established system with questions it struggles to ignore. Frustration produces voter restiveness, awakens new constituencies, and leads to ideological division and high-intensity politics. The realignment process culminates when a crucial event produces a fundamental shift in the pattern of voting and in the direction of national policy. The result is a new party system founded on a new lineup of political forces and a new rationale of party division.

Realignment theorists identify five party systems or electoral eras in American political history. These five systems began roughly in the 1790s, the 1820s, the 1850s, the 1890s and the 1930s. Over the last century and a quarter, each realignment cycle has run about forty years. The sixth party system is thus presumably overdue in the 1980s. Some analysts—Kevin Phillips, for example—think that the realigning election in fact took place in 1968, when Richard Nixon and George Wallace together won 57 percent of the popular vote, but that Watergate prevented the consolidation of a new conservative majority. Nevertheless, Phillips points out, the party ascending to power in 1968 controlled the White House, as in previous realignments, for sixteen of the twenty years after the critical election. According to this reading, the conservative period was in late middle age by the mid-1980s.

An alternative reading dates the start of realignment in 1981, with Reagan as the architect of the sixth party system. This reading finds sustenance in Reagan's remarkable success in capturing the policy agenda and in redefining the terms of political debate. It finds sustenance too in the demographic shifts and especially in the marked appeal of Reaganite ideology to younger voters. If this reading is correct, the Reagan coalition is replacing the Roosevelt coalition and can be expected to dominate the republic for forty years to come.

The question arises, however, whether realignment theory is not in conflict with the thesis of party decay. For the realignment cycle assumes the party to be the constitutive unit of American politics. But if the party as an institution is in serious trouble, then the operational premise of the realignment model is in trouble too. Some analysts doubt that either party can organize an enduring majority in the electronic age. The prospect for the future by this view appears to be not realignment but dealignment.

Realignment theory is also in conflict with another cyclical perspective on American politics—the theory of periodic alternations in the national mood between conservatism and liberalism, between periods dominated by private interest and periods dominated by public purpose. According to this model, the 1980s, with the Reaganite cult of private interest, was a replay of the 1950s, which was itself a replay of the 1920s. In the same way, eras of public purpose have come at thirty-year intervals: Theodore Roosevelt in 1901, Franklin D. Roosevelt in 1933, John Kennedy in 1961.

The generation is the mainspring of this cyclical interpretation, each generation when it arrives in power reenacting the ideals of its coming of political age thirty years before. So the young men and women whose values were molded by Theodore Roosevelt and Woodrow Wilson—Franklin and Eleanor Roosevelt, Harry Truman—produced the New and Fair Deals in their own maturity. The generation whose ideals were formed by FDR—Kennedy and Johnson— produced in their maturity the New Frontier and the Great Society. The age of Kennedy similarly touched and inspired a new generation. That generation's time is yet to come and, according to the political cycle, is due to begin shortly before or after 1990.

IV

These years of upheaval in American presidential politics thus conclude in a question mark. No one can doubt the significance of the changes in the organization of presidential elections, in the structure of the electorate and in the objectives of national policy. Whether the developments so ably recorded and analyzed in the essays that follow are a prelude to a new era of conservative ascendancy or to a renewal of liberal purpose remains for the voters to decide, which is as it should be in a democracy.

The answer will depend on the capacity of presidential leadership to deal with substantive issues. The republic faces staggering problems in the years ahead: the avoidance of nuclear war and the restraint of the nuclear arms race; the local explosions in the Third World; the widening disparities of income and opportunity in the national community; the multiplication of the poor and the underclass; the slowdown on racial justice; the mounting burden of public and private debt; the decline of heavy industry before competition abroad and the microchip at home; the unprecedented trade deficit; the deterioration of education; the rotting away of the great cities; the decay of infrastructure—roads, bridges, dams, harbors, waterways—and the pollution of the environment.

In the introduction to the first volume of the *History of American Presidential Elections,* I quoted President John Kennedy's statement of 1961: "Before my term is over, we shall have to test anew whether a nation organized and governed such as ours can endure. The outcome is by no means certain." The outcome seems no more certain a quarter of a century later.

Election of 1972

Richard C. Wade is Professor of History at the Graduate Center of the City University of New York. He is the author of The Urban Frontier: The Rise of the Western Cities, 1790–1830 *and* Slavery in the Cities: the South, 1820–1860. *He is the co-author of* Chicago: Growth of a Metropolis.

Election of 1972

by *Richard Wade*

In retrospect historians can always find significance in any presidential election. If the results of a given election are close, that in itself creates importance; if the margin is great, the landslide is given great meaning. And, regardless of the outcome of an election, the twists and turns of the campaign trail inevitably insure that no contest is devoid of historical importance or without interpretive possibilities.

The election of 1972 has its own unique dimensions. For example, it was the first election under newly instituted guidelines for delegate selection in the Democratic party, a change that drastically altered the selection process and ultimately affected Republican politics as well. The election illustrated the continuing decline of party dominance as independents became more important factors in national politics. For the first time, people between the ages of 18 and 21 could vote (following the passage of the 26th Amendment) and the election, as a result, measured the more lasting effects of the upheavals of the 1960s that had been produced by the Vietnam war and racial unrest at home. It was also the first presidential election after the Census Bureau noted in 1970 that more people lived in suburbs than cities, a finding that strongly influenced campaign strategies. But, most significantly, political corruption was epitomized that year by a gross breach of trust, perhaps the most deceitful act in American political history, which for the first time forced a President to resign in disgrace. In itself, Nixon's landslide victory would have sufficed to give the 1972 election historical noteworthiness, but underneath the surface churned powerful and

3

baffling forces which would not only present historians with dramatically new perspectives, but which would also dominate American society for decades to come.

The beginning of wisdom about the election of 1972 is an understanding of the 1960s, for the contest actually began on August 16, 1968, when Senator George McGovern stood at his fourth floor window of the Blackstone Sheraton Hotel in Chicago. Outside, thousands of demonstrators in and around Logan Park taunted a stiff, glaring blue line of helmeted police. Suddenly the tense scene erupted and a wild melee followed. Policemen wielded nightsticks while the demonstrators threw rocks and bottles. Cries and screams were heard above the sound of shattering glass. A few hours later the National Guard replaced the police and installed barbed wire to protect the string of hotels on Michigan Avenue. As the sour smell of tear gas seeped into the South Dakotan's room, the internal peace of the country had seldom seemed so fragile. It looked as though the country's social fabric might break apart and the ugly emotions produced by the present national conflicts would spill out over the nation. The flashing police clubs, the obscenities of the crowd, the sting of tear gas, the rumors of riots and racial war in other parts of the city, the sight of young national guardsmen pitted against agitated young students, showed that unless something could be done, America might not reach its two hundredth year in recognizable form. In the future loomed worsening race relations, the greater despair of the poor, the growing cynicism of the young, and the people's deepening disappointment with the quality of their lives. At the center of the nation's sickness was the perceived bankruptcy of its values and its leadership. The assassination of three of the country's most popular leaders, John and Robert Kennedy and Martin Luther King, shocked the American consciousness and symbolized the violent forces that were unleashed in this decade.

Five miles southwest of the Blackstone Hotel, the Democrats debated the Vietnam war—the issue that had drawn the angry crowds to Logan Park. America's involvement in the Southeast Asian conflict seriously divided the nation. The issue had shattered the incumbent President's hopes for reelection; now the party that had coasted to victory in the 1964 contest was feeling similar strains. The mood on the convention floor was volatile. At one point, Senator Abe Ribicoff accused host Mayor Richard J. Daley of using "gestapo tactics" to control the demonstrators, to which Daley responded with an obscene gesture. The war issue did, in fact, receive rational and orderly debate over national television before the delegates upheld the Johnson Administration's conduct of the war by 163 votes. There were even touching moments, as when many delegates tearfully sang the Battle Hymn of the Republic after viewing a film biography of John F. Kennedy.

In McGovern's view, the election of Richard M. Nixon, the Republican nominee, would mean continued violence at home and abroad. Nor did other public figures seem to offer the prospect of the kind of leadership that could harness the social forces swirling across the country. Certainly there were devoted statesmen who in ordinary times could occupy the Oval Office with intelligence and dignity. But the times were not ordinary, and there was scarcely any expectation that they soon would be.

George McGovern came to believe that he could provide the needed leadership. In fact, the convention had been a personal triumph for him. He had begun his candidacy only eighteen days before its opening. His decision to run stemmed from the dilemma of Robert Kennedy's delegates, now without a candidate following the assassination. Though many drifted to Humphrey or McCarthy, others found the primary wounds too deep and sought a more legitimate heir to the legacy they had just fought to secure. McGovern had supported JFK and later became head of his Food for Peace program. Moreover, the senator from South Dakota had been close to Robert Kennedy and shared his belief that the great priorities of the nation were ending the war in Vietnam and reconciling competing social groups at home. Indeed, RFK had given McGovern his finest testimonial when he called him "the most decent man in the Senate."

During the four turbulent days of the Chicago convention McGovern provided new leadership to his two hundred delegates, most of whom had never met him before. (Some, in fact, were not even sure where he came from. One supporter, when told the candidate was from South Dakota, cried in anguish, "Christ, I've been telling everyone he's from Iowa.") At every caucus McGovern pledged to support the nominee of the convention. He was always careful to tell some of his angriest followers that under no circumstances would he lead a walkout or entertain a third party candidacy. The night of Humphrey's victory, much against the wishes of his key advisers, he joined the Democratic candidate on the rostrum in a demonstration of support. George McGovern, alone among national figures, walked out of the convention a larger man than he went in.

As he left Chicago McGovern had turned to an aide and remarked, "If that's the competition, I can handle it." He was not thinking of 1968 at that moment, but of four years ahead. No doubt he had thought of the Presidency before. After all, he came from middle America, where mothers still dreamed of such miracles. More importantly, as a senator he came to know well the kind of individuals "mentioned" for the nomination; as an historian, he was unawed by the gauge of men who had dominated the public scene in the past.

Yet 1972 was four years away and the obstacles were formidable. The first was reelection to the Senate from South Dakota. As he began his senatorial campaign, McGovern was greeted by a poll showing his margin over his challenger at only four points, a sharp decline from the previous spring. The decline seemed foreboding since South Dakota was a Republican state and his own margin of victory in 1962 had been less than 500 votes. Hence it was essential to arrest the decline. The Senator went back to the kind of campaigning he liked best—face-to-face conversations with South Dakotans, small meetings and endless traveling across the plains. An inept opponent certainly helped the cause. Though Nixon handily carried the state in the 1968 presidential election, McGovern was reelected that year with 55 per cent of the vote, a performance unequalled by any Democrat in the history of South Dakota.

Richard Nixon's presidential victory, however, dampened the euphoria, for it meant that the man George McGovern most distrusted would occupy the White House for four years and would undoubtedly be the Republican nominee in 1972. This was particularly bitter since McGovern's early hero in American politics had been Adlai Stevenson, the man whom Nixon savaged in both 1952 and 1956. "That man is outside the breastworks," he once said, unconsciously repeating an earlier judgment made of Nixon by Sam Rayburn. Nixon had pledged to end the war if elected, but McGovern never believed him, reminding the voters that as early as 1954 Nixon had advocated the committing of American troops in Vietnam. Furthermore, the new President was a dedicated cold warrior who might well widen the war in the guise of ending it. What had been a personal desire to run in 1972 now took on a new urgency.

The experience of 1968, however, produced another imperative: there might not be a viable Democratic party, much less a McGovern nomination, if the system of delegate selection to the next convention was not changed. The system had grown up over a long period of time. In essence, the states determined delegate selection procedures under their own party rules or general statutes. Some had primaries, others called conventions, still others used complicated caucuses. In addition, there were wide variations from state to state, and every system was laced with unfairness, secrecy, and even chicanery. Part of the problem in Chicago had been the unrepresentativeness of a convention which largely reflected the party establishment without an adequate leavening of the new forces—blacks, Hispanics, women, and the young. "The lesson I would like to see our party learn," McGovern said in Chicago, "is that we have to open up the party once again to the voice of all our people and break these repressive procedures" so that "the average citizen in this land can have a voice in the selection of our presidential nominees and in the writing of the platform." In fact, the convention had adopted this view by mandating a commission to reform party procedures for the 1972 convention.

A few months after the 1968 election Senator Fred Harris, the Democratic national chairman, appointed George McGovern to head a fifteen-member commission to do the job of party reform. At the time the position looked like no gift. Some of the Senator's closest associates advised him against accepting, arguing that it would only put him in the middle of factional infighting and that no document, however skillfully contrived, could satisfy everyone. Yet McGovern felt a duty to try. He had always been an organization man and believed that the Democratic party was the best available instrument for responsible and liberal government. It now faced internal divisions that might destroy it. As an historian he could look back to Baltimore in 1856 and Chicago in 1912 to know that the two-party structure proved fragile under prolonged stress. His risk was undoubtedly high; but what would the nomination of a divided party be worth?

In addition, the offer was important in itself. The fact that the National Committee had turned to him indicated that McGovern had come out of Chicago with the respect of people from both the "old" and "new" political camps. He was also convinced that the demand for reform was so widespread that sensible recommendations would be accepted by nearly all segments of the party. Nor was he oblivious to the openings into all factions that the chairmanship involved, since hearings would take him to every part of the country and bring him into contact with local leaders and reporters. In short, McGovern thought the assignment necessary, feasible, and opportune.

Two central matters needed resolution: first, the procedures of delegate selection should be made fair and clear; second, there had to be a guarantee of adequate representation of the aggrieved groups within the Democratic party. The first problem required a great deal of work, but involved little controversy; the latter, the representation issue, contained dangers of the highest magnitude.

"Adequate representation" was hard to define. Did it mean that the convention itself was to mirror the party's constituents? Or did it merely require that all groups have equal access to the machinery that produced delegates? The commission trod warily through this mine field, and finally adopted the phrase "reasonable representation" to each group's share of the population. The members insisted unanimously that quotas were not intended. Yet they had unwittingly placed a thorn in the party's side that has since irritated and festered. McGovern himself patiently, if not persuasively, asserted that the object was to open up the process, not to exclude anyone. Somebody, however, would ultimately have to decide what "reasonable respresentation" was.

A few months after the commission had unanimously approved the "equal representation" guidelines, the National Committee ratified the new regulations without dissent. A quiet revolution had been accomplished with little notice and scarcely a tremor. Nearly every state had to change its rules to qualify for convention seats; now ordinary party members had a sporting chance to occupy them. In December 1970, Senator McGovern stepped down as chairman of the commission amidst the thanks of the party leaders and a firm commitment to support the guidelines by the new national chairman, Lawrence O'Brien, who observed wryly, "they are my survival kit."

By this time, too, the general argument for a McGovern candidacy had been fashioned. More than any other possible nominee, with the exception of Senator Edward Kennedy, he could hold together the antiwar movement within the Democratic party. In the gloomy and angry aftermath of 1968, some disappointed McCarthy supporters broached the idea of a new party, and they kept this threat alive during the intervening years. If 1972 turned into another Chicago, they warned, there would be a fourth party in the field (George Wallace was expected to lead a third-party challenge). The continuing ambiguity of Eugene McCarthy's own statements and the on-and-off flirtation of Senator Harold Hughes of Iowa with the prospect strengthened this strategy. Only McGovern's nomination promised to keep this sizable, if loosely organized, element within the party because his peace and reform credentials were unassailable.

In addition, his loyalty to the party reassured the regulars. He might be a liberal on the issues, but he was no organizational maverick. His performance in 1968 had demonstrated that. Moreover, his career in South Dakota marked him as a party professional. In 1956 he took a state that had two Republican senators, a Republican governor, and 100 Republican legislators out of 102, and within a decade made it broadly Democratic. Regular politicians could relate to that, especially because South Dakota was such a conservative state. McGovern had good personal relations with many party leaders who respected his candor as well as his success. Mayor Richard Daley, for example, encouraging him after 1968, observed, "The good Lord sometimes opens another door when He closes the first one."

Beyond the nomination, of course, lay the broader electorate, and here the case seemed even more persuasive. The country was drifting to the right as it recoiled from the upheavals of the 1960s. Yet the Democratic party's tradition was clearly liberal. McGovern's entire career had been based on selling progressive ideas to essentially conservative voters in South Dakota. He had never fudged on the issues at home, but his low-key, prudent manner had made new trends acceptable in his own state. Would not 1972 require a Democratic candidate who could sustain his party's historic liberalism while making needed changes palatable to a cautious public?

At this time there was virtually no discussion of the general election. It was assumed that Richard Nixon would be renominated and would be more vulnerable than in 1968. A further supposition was that Wallace would also be in the race and take roughly the same 13.5 percent of the votes. The Democratic goal was 45 percent, or a few points higher than Humphrey's performance. McGovern, it was argued, would hit the President in his Achilles' heel—character. The contrast between the candid, open, and honest senator and a dissembling, secretive, "Tricky Dick" Nixon would be compelling, notwithstanding the traditional advantages of incumbency.

The route to the nomination seemed at least possible, even if formidable. Ever since Estes Kefauver had forced Adlai Stevenson into a few contests in 1956, primaries assumed an increasing importance in the selection of the Democratic nominee. JFK disposed of the Catholic issue through a string of primary victories, and in 1968 President Johnson's experience in New Hampshire and Wisconsin prompted his withdrawal from the race. Each year more states dispensed with old and usually unrepresentative convention and caucus systems, until by 1972 nearly half had primaries, choosing well over half the delegates who would attend the convention.

For McGovern, the primaries were the key to victory. Their number, however, posed real problems. Where would the money come from? How could he recruit a staff large enough to organize twenty states? The solution was clear: enter wherever there was enough support to warrant a dignified showing, but concentrate on key states. Previous experience had created what one strategist called the "historic corridor"—that set of primaries that had been crucial in previous elections. The corridor contained the first and the last primaries, New Hampshire and New York; between lay Wisconsin, Nebraska, Oregon, California, and perhaps West Virginia. Anyone who carried these seven could not be denied the nomination without the risk of an irreparably divided party.

Even this limited activity, however, required money. Staff projections ran into the millions, though they varied widely. In the long run McGovern's innocence of large election costs proved a great asset. His presidential bid in 1968 had cost only $80,000 and his successful reelection campaign for the Senate only slightly more. He came to the conclusion that if there was a candidacy there would be money; if not, none. To start down a two-year road without foreseeable financing seemed lunacy to some. It was, to be sure, arrogant; it also led to a remarkable innovation in American politics.

McGovern explained his decision to run to the people of his home state in a television address on January 18, 1971, and with a national press conference in Washington, D.C. the next day. His message was that all of the issues that had racked the nation in 1968 remained. The war in Vietnam continued; race relations had worsened; the number of poor had increased; the young remained alienated. Indeed, the Nixon Administration had irritated the exposed nerves of American society in a most calculated manner for four years. But McGovern's central concern from the beginning was the decreasing confidence of the American people in their leaders. "The most painful new phrase in the American political vocabulary," he told his fellow South Dakotans, "is the 'credibility gap'—the gap between rhetoric and reality. Put bluntly it means people no longer believe what their leaders tell them." He promised a campaign that would "rest on candor and reason."

The second part of the announcement scenario was a long letter to antiwar activists detailing the reasons for the early candidacy. It frankly asserted that he had no substantial financial support and would have to rely on modest contributions to run. Signed by McGovern himself, it launched a new technique of campaigning, later widely adopted by both parties (and, ironically, exploited especially by the New Right), where the candidate reached over party organizations to their membership by direct mail. Observers later emphasized its success in fund-raising, yet more significant was the way it tied a McGovern constituency to the Senator in a personal sense. As the mailing lists multiplied, they contained the names of the troops for the primaries.

Other potential candidates came largely from the liberal wing of the party—a long list that included Senators Edmund Muskie of Maine, Birch Bayh and Vance Hartke of Indiana, former Senator Fred Harris of Oklahoma, 1968 presidential candidate Eugene McCarthy of Minnesota, and former Attorney General Ramsey Clark. An unexpected factor arose in New York when Mayor John Lindsay changed party affiliation as a prelude to a bid for the presidential nomination on the Democratic ticket. Of all, the Kennedy possibility was always the most complex problem for McGovern. He had "stood in," so to speak, for the RFK delegates in 1968; he was personally close to Edward Kennedy, and a large portion of his active supporters came from earlier Kennedy campaigns. In retrospect, the Kennedy shadow was helpful because it emphasized McGovern's connection to the party's central figure, and so long as it remained, other candidates were seriously handicapped. Kennedy's neutrality was always benevolent, permitting old JFK and RFK veterans to move to the South Dakotan or sit it out.

The conventional wisdom calculated that the most likely candidate was Edmund Muskie. The January 1972 Gallup Poll showed him leading even Senator Kennedy, 32 to 27, with McGovern barely visible at 3 per cent. The Democratic "establishment," or what was left of it, assumed the inevitability of his nomination. Muskie had the proper liberal voting record; he had favorable public exposure as Hubert Humphrey's running mate in 1968; though clearly cautious, he quietly exuded a solid composure and thoughtfulness; and, in a fractured party, he made few enemies during the charter years of the preceding decade. Throughout 1971 he put together a veteran organization and lined up an impressive string of endorsements that read like a "Who's Who" of elected officials. Labor maintained its historic formal neutrality. Indeed, its leadership may have preferred Senator Henry "Scoop" Jackson, but some international unions and many AFL-CIO locals were quite active for Muskie. And no one worried about money. Only some unforeseen event or blunder of his own separated Muskie from the 1972 nomination.

Actually, Muskie's formidable backing concealed two landmines. The first was the continuing war in Vietnam. As the year began, its intensity continued unabated. The nightly news put the fighting into every living room. The "body count" designed to show the United States winning the conflict inevitably included an increasing number of Americans. President Johnson had once observed that support for the war would wane when "the caskets start coming home." The prolonged conflict, with no "light at the end of the tunnel," embittered both its advocates and opponents. Muskie had been deeply troubled by American policy, but his ambivalence created an opening for the more resolute antiwar forces.

The second event affecting Muskie's chances was the adoption of the 26th Amendment to the Constitution. This extended the vote to those between 18 and 21 years old. Women had been enfranchised in 1919 and the Voting Rights Act of 1965 secured for blacks what the post-Civil War amendments had originally intended. Now those "old enough to shoot" would be able to vote. Many of those who could now vote were not anxious to enlist in an unpopular war. Large numbers of college students finessed the draft and transformed their antiwar sentiments into a larger attack on American institutions, beginning with university governance. Campuses across the nation mixed the mutiny against college regulations with protest against American involvement in the Vietnam war. Student activity was highlighted on the nightly news and provided excitement and a good environment for Democratic presidential aspirants. In a flush of enthusiasm, young people registered in significant numbers. It was no small matter; the "26ers," as the regulars called them, provided McGovern with his margin of victory in key primary states.

The Muskie campaign, despite its logical grounding and its traditional support, never quite caught on with Democratic voters. It was suddenly aborted in New Hampshire, the first primary state. The *Manchester Times-Union* published a bogus letter claiming the Senator's wife once referred to Canadian-Americans as "Cannucks." Muskie responded with a tearful defense of his wife. In itself the episode was inconsequential, in fact, movingly human. But since he had been projected as cool and restrained, the event contradicted expectations. The cadence of the Muskie parade was broken and could not be restored. Actually, the senator from Maine won the New Hampshire primary with 46 percent of the vote, yet the media converted McGovern's 37 percent into a virtual victory. The Muskie effort unravelled, and it finally ended with the Wisconsin primary three weeks later.

In the days between New Hampshire and Wisconsin, a political Halley's Comet streaked across the sky, lighting up the landscape for a brief moment and then disappearing almost as rapidly. John Lindsay, the mayor of New York, a Republican, handsome and articulate, elected without the support of either party, the spokesman for cities beleaguered by violence and decay, announced in the spring that he was changing his party affiliation and would seek the Presidency through the Democratic primaries. His strategy was transparent: skip the early primaries and enter Florida, with its large concentration of retired New Yorkers, and then Wisconsin, with its sizable antiwar student population and the antiparty tradition of the La Follettes.

The Lindsay campaign, however, had a more important dimension than the candidate himself. It was the first campaign for the Presidency conducted entirely through the media. It sought to invent a serious candidacy through television exposure. The youthful mayor of the nation's largest city was above all things telegenic. New York had survived the worst disorders of the 1960s; as a Republican turned Democrat he could attract independents; and he was the preeminent representative of the party's urban base. Moreover, David Garth, a pioneer in media politics who had engineered the Mayor's reelection, took total control of the campaign. An astute mix of the evening news and paid commercials, it was argued, could make John Lindsay a household name in the primary states. It was a "state-of-the-art" candidacy, yet it proved no more substantial than the evanescent images on the television screen. After a humiliating defeat in Wisconsin, Lindsay withdrew.

The other candidates floundered from the outset. Typically they began with bold announcements, firm assurances of financial support, and many staff appointments. Soon, however, the entrance fee to the presidential sweepstakes became too high and most had to find a graceful way out. Of the marginal liberal aspirants, only Hartke made it into New Hampshire. One by one, as the ill-starred ships went down, the life rafts drifted toward McGovern. The serious field narrowed to McGovern and Muskie as the Wisconsin primary approached.

The Badger State was important in other ways. Everyone was in the contest—Muskie, Humphrey, Wallace, Lindsay, and McGovern. The state comprised a cross section of the country, though not in precise proportions. It had a tradition of heavy voting in the primaries; indeed, the law encouraged voters of both parties to participate in the contest. It was also perfect for McGovern. His best organizers had been there for fifteen months; like Humphrey, he was a neighbor, enjoying a close psychological connection with the voters, particularly in the farm districts. The state university with its scattered branches provided a ripe recruiting ground for campaign volunteers. And Wisconsin's historical tradition, including as it did both Robert La Follette and Joe McCarthy, was profoundly independent. Only Milwaukee with its ethnic enclaves presented a problem, though the burgeoning suburbs promised to balance off any substantial losses in the city.

As Muskie hobbled into Wisconsin, Wallace charged in. Fresh from a victory in Florida and drawing on the nagging discontent of ordinary Americans, he suddenly became McGovern's most serious opponent. He had little organization and his campaign had gotten a late start, but he had done well four years earlier and had come to Wisconsin several times in 1968. In addition, he could draw from Republicans as well as from disenchanted Democrats in the primary. As the other contenders faded away, the Alabama governor grew more prominent. On primary day he ran a strong second to McGovern.

It had been expected that Wallace's impact in the general election in 1972 would be the same as it had been four years before when he won over 13 percent of the vote as an independent candidate. But Florida and Wisconsin thrust him into the race inside the Democratic party. In addition, the Alabama governor's candidacy had firmer roots than the other, more conventional candidates. No less than McGovern, Wallace represented those alienated by traditional party politics. He appealed to what the press liked to refer to as "middle Americans"— southern whites, blue-collar and skilled workers, low level clerks and small businessmen, portions of the emerging immigrant groups, and all who resented the upward surge of the blacks and the young. His broader constituency was among those who felt, often vaguely, that too much power had moved to Washington. The first of a long line of "outsiders" to seek the office, Wallace attacked the bureaucracy, the elites, the intellectuals, and the leaders of both parties. His outrageous language and caustic wit actually softened his indictment, but his slogan, "send them a message," became part of the nation's political vocabulary.

Suddenly, on May 15, an assassin's bullet ended George Wallace's candidacy. Campaigning in a Maryland shopping center, he was gunned down by a young man wearing a Wallace hat and sporting other campaign paraphernalia. Though not killed, Wallace was hospitalized and permanently paralyzed from the waist down. A stunned nation remembered again the grim days of 1963 and 1968. Violence clearly knew no ideological bounds, nor did the sympathy of the American public. In Michigan the voters gave Wallace a sweeping victory in the primary, and for weeks the country's most prominent leaders were photographed at his bedside.

The removal of Wallace did not alter the race for the nomination, but it governed the outcome in the general election. Liberal Democrats, especially McGovern, had assumed that an independent Wallace candidacy in November would attract from 10 to 14 percent of the vote, mostly from those who would otherwise have voted for Nixon. With Wallace removed, Nixon had a plush cushion, permitting him to sit out the campaign and forcing McGovern into a clumsy and unsuccessful attempt to win Wallace votes. The South Dakotan was so firmly rooted in his party's liberal tradition that the reach to the right had an awkward and artificial air. Worse still, it dampened the enthusiasm of his earlier supporters, most of whom viewed Wallace as racist and reactionary. The bullet that wounded George Wallace in May killed the McGovern candidacy in November.

With Wallace out of the picture Humphrey moved in to take up the slack in a narrowing field. Though Nebraska and Oregon came next in the historical corridor, he fixed on California, the second largest delegation and a winner-take-all primary. If McGovern could be ambushed there, he would be denied a first ballot victory, and a deadlocked convention would conceivably turn to Humphrey. Intraparty bitterness had been increasing from primary to primary, though it never reached the savage level of 1968. Suddenly the latent divisions erupted in California. Humphrey, McGovern's old friend and neighbor, headed for the jugular with uncharacteristic ferocity. He particularly attacked McGovern's proposals for a deep cut in the defense budget and cash payments to all taxpayers, calling them reckless and irresponsible. McGovern's wide lead in the California primary plummeted; his eventual margin of victory was a thin five percent. Worse still, the closeness of the results prompted a raucous credentials fight on the convention floor a month later in Miami.

McGovern's larger problems were obscured by a resounding sweep in New York two weeks later. He not only picked up 241 delegates (25 more would be added later from the at-large bonus), but his delegates had defeated 60 out of 62 county chairmen, including the state chairman. Only the Albany machine prevailed—and that by the thinnest margin in half a century.

Just before the New York primary, early on the morning of June 17, five men broke into the Democratic National Committee headquarters in the Watergate Hotel in Washington, D.C. to replace already installed surveillance devices. Though equipped with all the latest gadgets, they bungled the job badly and were caught. American politics had never known this kind of activity before, and no one really knew how to judge it. Surely it seemed farfetched to think that the Republican party, much less the President, had anything to do with it. The most probable explanation was that overzealous Nixon supporters had decided to help out their candidate in their own way. The fact that some were anti-Castro Cubans encouraged the "uncontrolled fanaticism" theory. Only a handful of observers connected the episode with the GOP, and fewer still with the Oval Office.

One of these was George McGovern. From the outset he was convinced that what came to be called Watergate was a part of a broader pattern of official corruption fully in keeping with his low opinion of Richard Nixon. While most Democrats running for office or addressing party affairs delighted in making fun of the bizarre event, McGovern held a dark and grim view of the break-in, which he articulated again and again during the campaign. The President, however, separated himself from the break-in with such surgical dispatch that he remained untouched by the consequences until the next year.

By June the historical corridor had been secured, with New Hampshire, Wisconsin, Nebraska, Oregon, California, and New York witnessing an impressive string of McGovern victories. Results elsewhere had been mixed or worse, but the public assumed that the senator from South Dakota had earned the nomination. Yet these states in themselves did not comprise enough delegates, and the candidates hoping to stop McGovern now turned to other areas for assistance. When the tabulations began, however, it was clear that McGovern had done surprisingly well in the convention and caucus states, and their delegates, added to the primary harvest, brought him within hailing distance of a first ballot decision.

McGovern's victories in the nonprimary states stemmed directly from the new regulations surrounding delegate selection, which assured a fair process and representative results. His Washington staff always understood this and quietly and efficiently picked up delegates all over the country. They found support in such unlikely places as Louisiana and South Carolina, and did well in Georgia and Texas. By midyear McGovern had become a national candidate, drawing delegates from all parts of the country and nearly every state.

A last minute "stop McGovern" coalition inevitably arose at the convention, which opened in Miami on July 10. The crucial moments came in the seating of the California and Illinois delegations, where the contest involved the rules of delegate selection. With California it was, ironically, the issue of proportional representation; Humphrey had taken over 40 percent of the vote without winning a single delegate. The issue with Illinois was whether the Cook County delegation had been properly elected. In both cases McGovern turned back the challenges. Indeed, they were futile as well as desperate. If the candidate who had won most of the primaries had been denied the nomination, there would have been a massive walkout and the Democratic party would have been hopelessly, and perhaps permanently, divided.

The convention itself stood in marked contrast to previous ones. The number of women delegates had risen to nearly 40 percent; young people amounted to another quarter; blacks and Hispanics were represented above their share of the population but below their portion of enrolled Democrats. In the New York delegation 250 of the 278 representatives had never attended a convention before. Who was not at Miami was significant too. Governors, mayors, senators, and congressmen accustomed to participation were onlookers, if they came at all. Labor leaders who used to be automatic delegates from the big industrial states watched the proceedings on television in their hotel suites. Those prominent in the old ethnic politics—Irish, Italians, Eastern Europeans—complained of their "exclusion." In fact, it was not categories of voters, but their established leaders who were absent. Ethnic proportions were not greatly altered, but it was housewives, teachers, and students who represented them rather than prominent spokesmen. Of course the participation of youth was new, a direct result of the 26th Amendment. Moreover, under the reformed Democratic National Committee rules, the convention conducted its business in serious fashion, not closing up shop each day until the early hours of the morning. A national poll later showed that 67 percent of the voters held a positive opinion of the whole affair.

To some extent McGovern's nomination was anticlimactic. He had established his control over the convention during the credentials contests the first night and was never seriously challenged again. The party platform contained few surprises. Basically it extended the positions the party had held since 1960. The Vietnam plank, to be sure, was sharper and crisper; crime received the attention it demanded; revenue sharing became more explicit; and tax reform was elevated to a critical level. Floor fights highlighted the growing concern over the social issues of abortion, drugs, and amnesty for Vietnam war resisters that had previously lain outside political discussion. These debates contributed to the general notion that the convention was dominated by radical elements, even though moderates won all of the roll call votes.

With the nomination secured McGovern turned to the task of choosing a running mate. His first choice was Edward Kennedy, who would have brought strong connections with organized labor, Catholics, and party regulars, as well as the formidable family name and resources. When the Massachusetts Senator refused, the selection became something of a lottery. The criteria were clear: the vice presidential candidate ought to be from a large state, acceptable to labor and traditional party leaders, and preferably a Catholic. A long list was whittled down to a half dozen, and at the last moment McGovern announced that Senator Thomas Eagleton of Missouri was the man. Though unknown to most of the delegates, Eagleton had all the required credentials and more— he came from a border state, as a former attorney general he could handle the "law and order" issue, and he had demonstrated appeal to suburban voters.

The delegates had scarcely gone home when the bombshell exploded. Newspaper reporters discovered that Senator Eagleton had a history of "nervous exhaustion" and had been hospitalized three times. Once, at the Mayo Clinic in Minnesota, doctors had used shock treatment as part of their therapy. Unfortunately, Eagleton had not revealed these facts to McGovern at the time of the nomination. The two called a joint press conference (appropriately, it turned out, at Custer, South Dakota) to disclose the facts in an orderly and sober fashion and avoid a sensational exposé by the press. But nothing could minimize the impact of the revelations, and McGovern was forced to seek out a new running mate.

The damage had been done—those seven days shook the campaign and it was never the same again. Though McGovern had acted deliberately and decently, it seemed to many that he lacked decisiveness. Worse still, debate over the issue only lessened; it did not disappear. Even staff members, eager to escape blame, kept the question alive by contradictory statements about the conversation with Eagleton in the hectic hours before the fatal decision to choose him as a running mate. The intense round of campaign planning never took place, and throughout the next few months the effort had an air of improvisation rather than clear direction.

Finding another running mate was not a simple matter. McGovern offered the spot to six others, including Senators Humphrey and Muskie, before deciding on R. Sargent Shriver. The irreverent charged he was a "second string Kennedy," but Shiver had impressive credentials of his own. As former chairman of the Chicago School Board he had gained firsthand knowledge of the crisis in education; his tenure as the first director of the Peace Corps had given him invaluable experience in foreign affairs; and as head of President Johnson's war on poverty he had been a pioneer in the difficult world of urban revival. In addition, he was known to be an articulate and energetic campaigner.

The whole delay, however, had cost the Democrats the advantage they had gained with an early convention. McGovern's next step was to reach out to those elements in the party that he had defeated in order to get the nomination. Well publicized meetings with Lyndon Johnson, George Wallace, Richard

Daley, and southern governors demonstrated that to win he had to put together what the primaries had pulled apart. Overtures to George Meany and the AFL-CIO high command were less successful, and he finally had to rely on a Labor for McGovern Committee comprised of many of the larger and more effective unions, but without the formal labor endorsement usually accorded a Democratic presidential candidate.

This strategy distracted McGovern from the media campaign which increasingly dominated the entire effort. Since the media had replaced the party as the means of communication with the voters, it was believed that McGovern's central concern should not be with traditional campaigning, but rather with television, particularly the news spots at six and eleven. These required "visuals" showing the candidate at a shopping mall, a hospital, or a factory, talking with ordinary people about their problems and concerns. Schedules were built around this strategy, requiring the candidate to fly from one time zone to another to accommodate the demands of television. Thus, it was argued, millions of people could be exposed to the candidate instead of the thousands who attended even the best organized rallies. On the last day of the campaign, McGovern flew from New York and ended up in South Dakota, but not before touching down in Pennsylvania, Kansas, and California in between— fitting summary of the new "media politics."

The logistics of the media strategy did, however, isolate the candidate from the voters. Every day the routine was a morning "visual" and perhaps a press conference, then "wheels up" for a flight to another city where the sequence would be repeated for the local cameras. Each stop required clumsy disembarking while the candidate waited for 200 reporters to get off their plane and be bussed to the next "event." It was not unusual to be airborne for three or four hours, with another four hours eaten up coming and going to airports. This left little time for more intimate conventional campaigning—street rallies, luncheons with the party faithful, or private meetings where McGovern could get a sense of the voters' thinking. At the end, the "people's candidate" was a picture on a screen, almost as isolated as the President. And the press, with nothing much else to do, took to writing damaging stories about internal staff differences. The authors of this strategy had intended to manipulate the media, but instead the needs of the camera governed the campaign.

While McGovern's campaign from the start featured surprise and uncertainty, the incumbent President had little turmoil on his path to renomination. The Watergate break-in occurred in June; the Republican convention was in August. The full dimension of the affair was not known until after the election, and during the campaign the incumbent was wreathed in the authority of the office. There was no overt party opposition, nor any "historical corridor" to the nomination. He was free to choose the themes for the general election.

To be sure, the press continued to nag at his heels (though newspapers editorially supported him, with 753 for him as against only 56 for McGovern) and he was never able to shake off the image of "Tricky Dick." Moreover, the war continued and indeed widened, and a Democratic Congress thwarted his domestic programs. Yet even his constraints enlarged his area of maneuverability by turning his attention to foreign affairs. In February 1972 he visited China; later he blockaded Haiphong and bombed Hanoi; next he was in Moscow. All these initiatives overshadowed the Democratic party's complicated primaries and caucuses. And public opinion polls indicated that each move was popular. Moreover, he and his aides masterfully exploited the communications system— television, radio, and the press. He avoided questions about his policies by simply not having press conferences. (His predecessors, from Roosevelt to Johnson, had averaged between 24 and 36 press conferences a year while Nixon had a total of seven in the election year, about the same number as in each of his first three years in the White House.) Daily communications were left to official surrogates who deflected or absorbed criticism and obscured the President's intentions. This aloofness contrasted sharply with the persistent and bitter conflict within the Democratic party, and especially George McGovern, who was anxious, often indiscreetly so, to court the media.

Neither did Nixon have to worry about a formally divided party. The GOP was clearly the minority party in 1972 whether measured in voter enrollment or officeholders. Yet it had the brass ring, the White House. The party's historic moderate wing was crippled, the right was not so disaffected as to launch a campaign against an incumbent president. Hence, he decided to run his campaign outside the party altogether. Very early on he established the Committee to Re-elect the President (CREEP). He located its headquarters across the street from the White House and staffed it with people loyal to himself, not the party. The Committee would organize and direct the campaign, raise the money, and alone would have direct access to the Oval Office. Though two years later this arrangement proved troublesome, it indicated that even after a quarter of a century within the GOP, Nixon was as much of an outsider as George McGovern. Both won their party's nomination, but neither had any important relationship to his party's national committee or establishment. Nixon had trouble finding someone to take the position of national chairman of the Republican party. McGovern's choice was a woman who would reflect the rising influence of feminism. But leadership in both campaigns came from outside the national committees.

Mercifully protected from any primary challenge, Nixon had only to bask in the enthusiasm of his own convention. The location was the same as the Democrats had chosen, Miami, but the conventions could not have been more different. The mechanics of the Republican operation were a model of efficiency and precision directed to television's prime time. Nixon's acceptance speech was only two minutes late; McGovern's was five hours behind schedule. A brief scuffle over rules early in the gathering was easily defeated; the Democrats had engaged in endless roll calls. The seats in the Republican convention were filled by middle America, successful and middle aged, mostly white and male. The genial chaos of the Democrats gave way to an orchestrated celebration of Nixon's first term; the slogan that rang through the hall was "Four More Years."

Nixon's acceptance speech, like the GOP platform, was hardly arresting, but did include the broad themes of the campaign. He attacked the Democrats for supporting quotas, asserted that McGovern was the spokesman for a party that had lost its legitimate past and embraced a radical future, waged an assault on "paternalism" and planners; and made a strong statement on the Vietnam war that would become his centerpiece. "There are three things" that we will never do, he said, "abandon our prisoners of war . . . join our enemies in imposing a communist government on our allies . . . or stain the honor of the United States." He also said he was happy to run again with his Vice President, Spiro T. Agnew, adding in a reference to the Eagleton affair, "I am not going to change my mind tomorrow."

By Labor Day it was clear that the Nixon strategy was working wonderfully. The President remained aloof and inaccessible. He refused to debate, kept away from the press, and used short radio speeches to explain his record, with no chance for interruption or rebuttal. His extraordinary fund-raising permitted extensive and repetitive commercials in the big media markets of the large industrial states. Direct mail was targeted to crucial political districts while phone banks brought the message to special groups of voters. Nixon might complain that the Democrats cynically exploited "interest groups," but Theodore H. White identified some new ones working for Nixon, including the Hairdressers Committee, the Veterinarians Committee, the Motorcyclists Committee, and the Indians-Aleuts-Eskimos Committee. This was the first fully electronic campaign in history, complete with television and radio commercials, phone banks, labeled direct mail, and, as Watergate would reveal, electronic surveillance of the opposition. In despair, Teddy White, the chronicler of many campaigns, observed wryly that "It was easier to cover the President on campaign in 1972 by staying home and watching television—which was the way the President wanted it."

Yet all this organization, efficiency, and money did not ease the public's increasing impatience and frustation with the war in Southeast Asia. This had always been McGovern's special issue. As early as 1963, in his maiden speech on the floor of the Senate, he had warned about the consequences of American involvement. It was the antiwar issue that galvanized the students; it was the same issue that financially floated his campaign. Then on October 28, ten days before the election, Henry Kissinger announced that "peace is at hand" as a result of some negotiations in Paris. It turned out, of course, not to be true, but the last remaining thin thread of hope snapped. Big crowds in the closing days for both candidates kept some interest alive, but not even George McGovern, son of a Methodist minister, thought any miracle was on the way.

By November it was clear that McGovern was hopelessly behind and that the surge that brought Humphrey almost abreast of Nixon in 1968 would not develop in 1972. Though McGovern's crowds were large and enthusiastic, the polls persistently showed a spread of twenty or more points. The results confirmed their prediction. Nixon won over 60.7 percent of the popular vote and nearly swept the electoral college. McGovern carried only Massachusetts and the District of Columbia. The Wallace vote had obviously moved to the President *en masse,* and the defection of the traditional white Democrats, a trend that had been visible for over a decade, intensified. Only the blacks by a large margin and the young by a narrow one remained firm. But unlike the Goldwater rout in 1964, state and local slates usually escaped the presidential landslide.

The overwhelming Nixon victory led to a search for an explanation within the Democratic party. Regular leaders, still smarting from their primary defeats, quickly blamed the "McGovern people" who had presumably excluded them from the convention in Miami and then from the campaign. Columnists tended to emphasize the broken momentum which began perhaps as early as the California primary and certainly became critical with the Eagleton episode in July. Others dwelt on the staff problems that persistently plagued the Senator's entourage. Still other voices asserted that Nixon's tactics of isolation and aloofness prevented any contest, much less a rational choice for the electorate.

Yet none of these analyses explained the more than twenty-point difference between the candidates. No doubt the Eagleton affair cost votes; the disaffection of the regulars accounted for more; a better disciplined staff would at least have saved some embarrassment; and Nixon's strategy did indeed make a genuine choice difficult. Any one of these factors might explain a close election, but not even all of them together account for the extraordinary gap in the popular vote.

Rather, what lay beneath the surface was a massive national backlash against the tumultuous events of the 1960s. The Nixon years may have been uninspiring and tinged with irregularity and fraud, but they had not seen cities in flames or campuses in turmoil. Television screens no longer featured the violent rhetoric or ugly confrontations that dominated President Johnson's second term. Moreover, the war, which agonized even those who supported it, had seemingly "wound down." Somehow, voters in 1972 believed, or at least hoped, that the country had returned to "normalcy." Underneath, all the vexing questions remained—race, injustice, war, and a new, impatient generation—but the daily upheavals of the previous decade had all but disappeared. The tide that had swelled in 1968 had receded, and though most of the wreckage lay in full view across the beach, most Americans preferred to look beyond to a more tranquil sea.

Richard Nixon, of course, had little to do with the fact that the tide was going out, but he was the President, and the public associated four years of relative social calm with the man who presided over it. Similar comfort could be found in foreign affairs, where Nixon's new *détente* with China and the Soviet Union relieved international tensions and quieted anxieties about future wars. Furthermore, the end of the draft in the spring of 1972 took the immediacy of foreign policy away from the campuses and the family dinner tables. To be sure, there was no peace, but there was less war.

The Nixon campaign shrewdly capitalized on the national uneasiness that underlay the calm. By refusing to campaign conventionally, by attacking bussing without disclaiming civil rights, by replacing the debate about poverty with a restatement of the "work ethic," and by blaming much of the unrest on "permissiveness," he at once reassured people about the things that bothered them, while himself appearing to be a moderate rather than an archconservative. At the same time, voters equated the McGovern campaign with the disturbing events of the 1960s. His peace theme, for example, conjured up ugly memories of student unrest and the Chicago convention. Among his followers were the blacks, Hispanics, and young people who had been the rough cutting edge of the decade of demonstrations. Added to this was the emergence of militant feminism, with its unsettling tactics and unpredictable consequences. It was to preserve a fragile social tranquility that so many voted for a man whose own political career, ironically, had been built around the most divisive events of the previous twenty years and who would later be forced from office in disgrace.

Even so, McGovern ran only three percentage points behind Hubert Humphrey's total in 1968. The nearly ten million Wallace votes of the previous election went over almost completely to Nixon. No liberal Democrat could have won or done measurably better. Wallace had offered a convenient halfway house for disgruntled Democrats leaving the party, an exodus which began in the Fifties and continued unabated except for the brief Kennedy years. This movement was difficult to gauge in national elections, but it surfaced continuously in state and local contests and party primaries.

Working class whites comprised the largest contingent of the refugees. Enjoying better jobs and higher pay, they had just enough money to move to more pleasant neighborhoods and to see their children have a chance for a college education. Yet, they had little financial security. Economic forces—recession or inflation—affected them first and most damagingly, and prolonged illness could wipe out everything. Behind these anxieties lay the ultimate fear of unemployment and the knowledge that there was a thin line separating what the economists called "full employment" and the handout.

Recently a new breed of political analyst has tried to tie this phenomenon to an ethnic base. Second- and third-generation Americans made up much of the emergent working class in the northern cities and, at least since the Depression, they had voted heavily Democratic. Overwhelmingly Catholic, the Irish, Italians, and Poles began to drift away from the party mooring even as they moved to the suburbs. One reason was clearly economic, for as a group they had benefited from the almost continuous prosperity since World War II. In addition, the G.I. Bill of 1944 gave them an opportunity for college that their parents had never dreamed of. Though they hesitated to join the GOP, which they equated with hard times and Herbert Hoover, they no longer felt they needed the party of Franklin Roosevelt.

But another, deeper cause for their disaffection lay in the problem of race. The better neighborhoods on the edge of the city or nearby suburbs pulled them, and the enormous growth of the urban black population gave them a push. Swarming into the northern cities from the South, blacks increasingly occupied the residential center of the metropolis. Desperate for housing and jobs, they crowded into old working-class areas. Here they competed for the neighborhood; at the factory gate they competed for employment. Both groups had been voting Democratic for generations, but now this elemental collision fractured the party. Blue-collar whites, feeling that the national leadership was too committed to the blacks, drifted away. In the late 1960s the ghettos erupted, accelerating the flight. The elections of 1960 and 1964 concealed the attrition on the national level. The rioting and confrontations brought the schism into the open and into the Democratic party. George Wallace's surprising surge in the 1968 primaries and his early victories in 1972 came from a shrewd exploitation of this widening fissure.

Analyses of this new trend in voting preferences of the white ethnic groups emphasized the immigrant background of many of these working-class voters and tied their recent "independence" to a heightened consciousness of Old World traditions and values now adapted to the American experience. The argument is sometimes merely a thin cover for bigotry. But in its more serious form this view asserted the primacy of ethnicity over both race and class. It is supposedly the "Irishness" or "Italianness" or "Polishness" that best explains their political behavior, with Catholicism providing another link among immigrant groups that had previously been bitter rivals. This theory arose largely from election statistics drawn from the urban North. As convenient and compelling as this analysis may seem for New York, Chicago, or Boston, it does not explain why blue-collar voters of older, Protestant stock reacted the same way. The blue-collar exodus from the party occurred everywhere. The west end of Louisville and the south side of Atlanta, each with only a trace of immigrant background, witnessed the same development as Cleveland and Chicago, with their endless layers of ethnicity.

The volatility of the blue-collar workers showed just one dimension of the growing independence of the American electorate. Every poll indicated that voters in general were drifting away from the old parties, and a disturbing number were dropping out of electoral politics altogether. The sources of the disaffection varied, but they touched every age, race, and income group. The result was that neither party could gain a majority. Or, to put it differently, the United States contained an increasingly antiparty electorate operating within the framework of a traditional two-party system. In the past the unattached, called "independents," had been thought to be liberal; they probably were until the 1930s and still were in 1972 in a few places. By the 1970s, however, that large indeterminate group had clearly become conservative, particularly fearful of the changes portended by the radical mutiny of the 1960s. The Wallace candidacy of 1968 ought to have sent that message; in fact it concealed its importance because party leaders and political commentators considered the 13.5 percent Wallace vote as indicative of a lack of enthusiasm for either party's nominee. The 1972 election, with its clear choice, defined the independents as cautious voters who had deep forebodings about the future, hence neither party could depend on their support.

The election of 1972 also presaged the suburban captivity of American politics. The 1970 census that revealed that, for the first time in history, more people lived in suburbs than cities, also showed that the suburbanites voted in greater percentages than their urban neighbors. The result was an inevitable shift of power to the outer parts of metropolitan areas. This tidal change in voting strength had been concealed in the presidential elections of the previous decade, but was abundantly clear on the local level. Indeed, in 1972 Nixon's largest majorities came from the crabgrass country. The Democrats retained their urban base, but it had shrinking significance. Moreover, the suburbs were no longer the exclusive preserve of the well-to-do, but rather the habitat of the white post-war generation. Suburbs were now as representative of the nation as the cities had been in the days of the New Deal. Surely their power would stretch well beyond 1972.

The election of 1972 gained more importance in retrospect than it seemed to have on the morning after Nixon's victory. In the next months the *Washington Post* revealed the broader dimensions of the Watergate scandal. The break-in at the Democratic headquarters was not just an act of excessive enthusiasm by Nixon supporters; but was instead only a small part of a larger web of corruption that extended beyond the Committee to Re-elect the President and reached into the center of the whole Administration. The President, of course, left Washington in shame, and indictments were also handed down against three former cabinet members, including two attorney generals; two of the President's assistants quit when faced with court charges; officers of CREEP were indicted for perjury; and corporate officials awaited judicial action: ultimately testimony before congressional committees and grand juries disclosed manipulations that made the Grant and Harding Administrations seem almost virtuous. Congress itself moved to impeach the President, who escaped this fate by resigning. The "mandate of 1972" had quickly evaporated, and Nixon's triumphant reelection was followed by the most serious constitutional crisis since the Civil War.

Appendix

Candidacy Announcement by Senator George McGovern
Washington, D.C., January 19, 1971

In announcing his candidacy for President, Senator George McGovern promised that, if elected, he would end the Vietnam War "quickly" and "in terms that are both acceptable to the American people and in the interest of the suffering peoples of Southeast Asia."

Two and a half years ago I asked you to gather in this Capitol to hear my announcement as a candidate for the Democratic presidential nomination. You will recall that I made that announcement only a few days before the 1968 Democratic National Convention in the wake of the tragic death of the late Robert Kennedy. I undertook that last-minute effort at the urging of many of his committed delegates who knew that I deeply shared the twin ideals for which the late Senator Kennedy gave his life—an end to the war in Vietnam and the healing of injustice and trouble in our own land. I am most grateful for the opportunity that brief effort gave me to address the nation in a unique way.

Since 1968, the war in Vietnam has widened into Cambodia and Laos, and a serious economic recession has seized the nation.

Our cities and ghettos seem to be quieter today than they were a few years ago. But it is a stillness born more of resignation and despair than from any confidence in progress or the future. Despite all the discussions, despite the speeches and commissions, the poor remain poor, the oppressed dwell amid their oppression, the environment continues to deteriorate, our rural areas decline, and life in our great cities is steadily dehumanized.

Americans have never believed that simply to talk about problems was to solve them. We need action, and I intend action.

But surely our failure to act must also reflect a larger loss of spirit and confidence—almost as if citizens felt that the conditions and quality of their lives were beyond their influence. And it is this, in my judgment, that is the heart of the matter. From participatory democracy to women's liberation and citizens' conservation councils, we see an increasing assertion of the individual, a desire not simply to have things done, but to do them.

We want to matter as individuals—all of us. The task of future leadership is not to rule people's lives. It is to change the institutions of our society so the citizens may shape their own lives.

I do not intend to assert that these are simple problems or that the answers are obvious. I do know that we must look for new policies and procedures rather than rush to enact new programs which are simply modified versions of old failures. But we cannot begin even this task unless we reverse the growing corruption of public life which views individuals as objects to be deceived or manipulated, and which regards the art of leadership as a capacity to follow the latest public-opinion poll.

I now seek the presidency as a public servant whose career has been devoted from the beginning to the conditions of peace abroad and a humane society at home. I have reached this decision only after a growing conviction that I could bring to the presidency the sense of values, the toughness of mind, and the compassionate spirit which the times demand.

I begin this quest early because I want to travel the land, listening to the concerns and aspirations of the American people and refining my own views on the issues that beset us.

I shall not rely primarily on task-force studies by the experts or on travel to foreign capitals. Rather, I shall make every effort to share a full and honest dialogue with the people of America.

I believe that the American people today want above all else a sense of confidence in themselves and in their leaders. Our people feel a mounting sense of powerlessness to shape their own lives and control their own destiny. The purpose of my candidacy is to assist in the recovery of public confidence and a new pride in our national purpose.

I undertake this quest for the presidency primarily to call the nation home to the liberating ideals that gave us birth.

We need a new dedication to the claims of life over death, to the claims of liberty over oppression, and to the pursuit of happiness over the blight of racism, division, and despair. I know that there is a glorious future for the American people if we are faithful to the ideas of Paine and Madison, of Jefferson and Lincoln.

I do not propose at this time to spell out a detailed blueprint of my positions, but all of you know of my long fight to stop a war in Southeast Asia which has brought such a grievous burden to the American people in the loss of their sons, the inflation of their economy, and the division of their country. I have no doubt that as president, I could end that war quickly on terms that are both acceptable to the American people and in the interest of the suffering peoples of Southeast Asia.

You know, too, that for many years I have called for the development of conversion planning to divert excessive outlays to the urgent needs of our society.

In the months ahead, I shall be speaking more in depth to the various steps I think our country must take in developing an enlightened foreign policy and a common-sense public agenda here at home.

As for today, let me begin with one pledge above all others—to speak the truth about the hard questions fully and openly.

Announcement of Candidacy for Renomination and Reelection by President Richard M. Nixon
January 7, 1972

In this letter to Lane Dwinell, who headed the New Hampshire Committee to Re-elect the President, Richard Nixon pledged "to bring peace and progress both abroad and at home."

Dear Lane:

Thank you for your generous letter, and for the petitions you have filed entering my name in the New Hampshire primary.

It was in New Hampshire that I began my campaign for the Presidency four years ago, and I remember well the opportunity that campaign provided to visit so much of the State and to meet so many of its people. I have tried to be true to the trust they expressed, and to carry forward the effort we began in New Hampshire in 1968: to bring peace and progress both abroad and at home, and to give America the leadership it needs for a new era of national greatness.

We have made significant beginnings in these past three years. I want to complete the work that we have begun, and therefore I shall be a candidate for renomination and reelection. I deeply appreciate the confidence expressed by those who signed the petitions, and I shall do all in my power to be worthy of that confidence.

In addition to New Hampshire, I shall also permit my name to be entered in the other primaries. As I am sure you will understand, however, it will not be possible for me to campaign actively and personally in any of the primary elections. I feel it is essential, particularly in this year when events of such importance to the world's future are taking place, that at least until the Republican Convention the President should refrain from public partisan activities in order to conduct the business of government with the minimum intrusion of purely political activity.

On my behalf, therefore, please express to the people of New Hampshire my warm greetings, my gratitude for their past courtesies, and my hope that together we can work toward a national renewal that will make the anniversary year of 1976 as proud a milestone for America as was 1776.

Description by Governor George Wallace of the Assassination Attempt Upon Him on May 15, 1972, in Laurel, Maryland

The shooting and subsequent paralysis of George Wallace had a significant impact on the election of 1972. Here the Alabama governor provides a dramatic account of the attempted assassination.

The primary campaign in Maryland should have closed in Frederick on May 13, 1972. We were carrying the same message that had produced such encouraging prospects for Michigan, where it was obvious that workers were fed up with the pseudoliberal philosophies of the Democratic regulars.

I hadn't varied my speeches much, because people seemed anxious to hear me hit the hard themes that had touched a popular chord in Florida, where it first became apparent that my support was much more extensive than any of the professional political analysts had imagined. I blasted federal government interference in state affairs, the asinine system of busing school children to Kingdom Come and back, legislation by court ruling, ruinous taxation and bloated bureaucracy, and loopholes in tax laws that permitted tax refuges in the big foundations.

I knew I was voicing the real grievances of the grass roots, and this conviction was reinforced when opposing candidates in both parties began to echo my views about busing and taxation. They could see that millions of Americans were in agreement with me, and it was throwing a scare into them. Even political commentators in the newspapers and on the radio and TV networks began to admit reluctantly that George Wallace was the front-runner.

It was gratifying to know we were running strong and that Michigan and Maryland primary voters would probably put me far out ahead of the field. But it had been a grueling campaign, and I was glad to see it reaching a pause. Frederick was the real windup, and every report indicated I would have little trouble coming out on top in Maryland. After Frederick, a rally was scheduled in Annapolis for the night of the fifteenth, and it was decided to add Wheaton and Laurel to the route. But this was just frosting on the cake. Frederick was the clincher.

It was a good meeting. The crowd was big, boisterous, and responsive. The usual groups of hecklers stayed on the fringes and were fairly quiet. I had had them with me all through the campaign, but I think I bothered them more than they bothered me. They were always disappointed in my speeches, because they always hoped I would say something really extreme and were frustrated when I stuck to the issues.

When the meeting ended, the Secret Service men told me there was a hostile gang waiting near the automobile. I called Cornelia over and told her to leave the hall first, alone or with someone else, so she wouldn't be recognized.

"I'll go out with you," she insisted. I tried to persuade her that there could be unpleasantness and danger, but she said firmly, "My place is with you."

We left together, through a cordon of helmeted police. There was a crowd shouting and throwing small objects—apple cores, sticks, some small stones, and bricks. Just as I was getting into the car a brick hit me in the chest—a glancing blow that caused no damage. I got in and we drove off, with the hecklers screeching invectives and obscenities.

We flew back to Montgomery that same night. The next day was Mother's Day, and I enjoyed a relaxed schedule. There were just a few political chores to attend to, and I had most of the day with my mother and mother-in-law and Cornelia, and the children. Later we went to visit Lurleen's grave.

Glen Curlee came over that night, and we had a long chat. We discussed things we had never talked about before, such as how much insurance I carried, what provisions I had made for the financial security of my family. I told Glen I had been saving in a limited way ever since I was elected judge, in 1952. It wasn't a large sum, but enough to provide for my family, for a limited time in case anything happened to me.

"Glen, you should do some systematic saving or investment," I urged.

He snorted. "There's a big difference between what you make and what I earn. I have to spend mine almost as fast as it comes in."

Glen later insisted that I must have had some premonition about what was going to happen, because these topics had never come up before, even in our most intimate conversations. But it wasn't premonition. I think it was just part of the letdown after intensive campaigning.

The nearest thing to premonition was a dream my son George had about a week before, during the Michigan tour. He usually traveled in a separate plane, but one morning he insisted on riding with Cornelia and me. He was quite upset and explained that he dreamed that he saw a lot of people gathered around me, as though I was lying in state. The whole thing affected him so much that he didn't do his usual singing stint with his band that night.

I didn't pay too much attention to it, either then or later. For weeks I had been too busy to think about much except the campaign and the problems that kept arising in Alabama. It was like the old bombing missions in the Pacific. You were assigned a target, but you didn't really have time to worry about consequences or danger. The night before we flew a mission, there was a cruise-control plan to be carefully calculated and plotted so as to squeeze the last mile out of every gallon of limited fuel. Then, in flight, there were all those instruments staring at you out of the panels: pressure gauges, tachometers, altimeters, airspeed indicators, oil temperature gauges, cylinder head temperature gauges, the mixture control settings, fuel transfer switches—a thousand details that kept eyes and mind busy. There was no time to think about danger.

It was the same with the bombing run and the race back to base. It wasn't until later that the heavy thoughts began to run through one's mind, thoughts about what could have happened but didn't.

For years I had lived with the possibility of assassination. I had made enemies, and others had been made for me by people who had consistently and deliberately misrepresented my political and racial philosophies. To say that I was indifferent to the existence of danger would be incorrect. The eternal presence of the Secret Service agents was a constant reminder of what had happened to the late president John F. Kennedy, Senator Robert Kennedy and Reverend Martin Luther King. But events moved too fast to permit much time for morbid reflections.

With the campaign just about over, however, the thoughts that had been inhibited came to the surface. It wasn't premonition, just the normal reaction of a tired mind.

When Cornelia joined us, the conversation took a lighter turn. She knows how to turn off my darker moods. We commented on the Frederick crowd and what might have happened if the one who threw the brick had possessed more zip and accuracy with his high, hard one.

"The hecklers don't really bother me," I commented. "But I often wonder whether someone out there might try something foolish."

"George, you've been lucky for a long time," said Glen, "and I'm sure your luck will hold out one more day. That's all you need—one more day."

The repartee and relaxation helped, although I was tired of campaigning. I asked Glen why we couldn't stay right in Montgomery and call off the next day's schedule in Maryland.

"After all, if we can believe the reports, we're doing well and should carry the state," I explained. "Going to Annapolis won't affect the results—it's too late."

Glen agreed that the next day's schedule wouldn't influence the voting, but he pointed out that arrangements had already been made with the local people, and it wouldn't look good to let them down.

He was right, of course. But lethargy, not premonition, was prompting me to stay home.

A night's sleep didn't help much, because I woke up the next morning in an irritable mood—something that, fortunately for my family and friends, doesn't happen too often. We were due at the airport at 9 A.M. and when I went in to see how Cornelia was coming along, I found her talking on the telephone, her hair still uncombed.

"Who's that on the phone?" I snapped.

"It's Bobbie Jo," she explained. "They want me to appear on the Bonnie Angelo show in Washington tonight."

I almost jerked the phone out of her hand and told Bobbie Jo there would be no show—that as a matter of fact I wasn't even sure Cornelia would be going along on the trip. I handed the phone back to Cornelia and said, "If you don't hurry and get ready, I'll go off and leave you here."

It was an inexcusable performance, and I knew it, but I was jumpy and tense. Cornelia put up with it meekly. She had often told me that I should feel free to let off steam with her, because she was the only person I didn't have to put on a front with. She insisted it was good therapy for me to unwind my tensions occasionally.

I remained uptight on the ride to the airport. We got there on time, only to find that the plane wasn't ready. There had been a mix-up. Someone had neglected to advise the crew that Wheaton and Laurel had been added to the schedule and that take-off would be at nine rather than ten. There was no one to fly the plane. Calls were made to the crew, but it would mean a delay of at least an hour.

"That will make us late at Wheaton," I said almost hopefully. "Perhaps we should just get in touch with the organizers and cancel out."

We couldn't agree on what to do, so I resigned myself to the inevitable and sat quietly while we waited for the pilots to show up. They arrived about 10 A.M. and we took off for Washington. As we were boarding, Cornelia turned to me and grinned.

"Honey, I'm sorry I made you late."

My surly mood didn't break until after we had left National Airport and were driving to Wheaton. Then I reached over and squeezed Cornelia's hand and winked at her. She smiled, and both of us recognized that the incident was over and forgotten.

There were hostile elements in the Wheaton crowd, and the Secret Service wouldn't let Cornelia go on stage as she usually did before I was introduced. Objects were flying: tomatoes, eggs, soap with nails. But apart from the hecklers it was a fine, large crowd, and I realized it would have been unfair to disappoint them. I hit all the issues hard, and the audience was responsive and friendly.

There was only one unpleasant note. The heckling group, present at all my speeches, was close to the platform, just to my right. I had faced hecklers all through the campaign and was more or less used to them. They rarely had anything new to say, and I could usually play them for laughs from the sympathetic crowds—stock quips like "I see some members of the audience are still undecided."

I asked this group, if they didn't want me, who were they for. They shouted, "McGovern! McGovern!"

They began using abusive language, about as foul as any I had ever heard in any army latrine. It was conduct I am sure a decent person like George McGovern would have repudiated.

I think what bothered me most—and saddened me—was the spectacle of a sweet-faced girl about seventeen or eighteen mounted on the shoulders of one of the messy-bearded hecklers. She wasn't really pretty, but she had a pleasant, childish face that seemed all innocence until she contorted her mouth and started spewing some of the worst obscenities I have ever heard. I glanced at her from time to time and kept thinking, "How can there be so much hate behind such a sweet-looking face?"

But all I said was, "Is that what they teach you at the college you attend?"

I remember wondering about her family, and if they knew where she was and what she was doing and the language she was using. Her accent—and that of her companions—was definitely not Maryland. Every time she shouted something especially vile, she turned to the rest of the heckling group and waited expectantly for their approving laughter. It didn't hurt me. But it saddened me.

There was someone else in the crowd at Wheaton, but I never noticed him. Photos taken show Arthur Bremer up near the front, although not among the hecklers. I probably saw his face from time to time as I glanced out over the crowd, but it meant nothing to me and I have no memory of it.

I put everything into my delivery, and the crowd roared its approval. I wound up with a slightly raspy throat, which I was sure would clear up after lunch and before the Laurel meeting.

We drove to Howard Johnson's in Laurel after the Wheaton rally broke up. Lunch turned out to be a banquet arranged by the management in a special room set apart for me and my staff and all the Secret Service personnel. A couple of the agents stayed outside, but Cornelia went out and invited them to join us. She left early, saying she wanted to go over to Montgomery Wards, just around the corner from the shopping center, to get her hair combed. She didn't get back in time, so we had to go on to the shopping center. It was a much bigger gathering than I had anticipated, in view of the improvised facilities. Again it was a good crowd—strangely enough, with no hecklers.

I was about ten minutes into my speech when my voice began to crack. It was only momentary, and I was able to resume at almost normal pitch. Someone passed up a cup full of honey (I learned later that Cornelia had sent over to a grocery store nearby and bought it to ease my sore throat). I never did take it.

The rally ended, and I started for the car. The people in the crowd began to shout:

"We want to shake hands with the governor!"

"Come on, George, let's shake the hand of the next President!"

I turned and looked inquiringly at the Secret Service agents with me. They shook their heads. But the crowd kept shouting—friendly, good people. And there's something in me that handshaking satisfies. I like the touch of hand to hand, because I receive a pleasant sensation of confidence and force. So I waved my finger in a negative at the agents, took off my coat, handed it to one of the agents, and started back.

"Don't go, Governor," one of them told me. "It isn't wise."

"I'll be all right," I insisted. "I'll take the responsibility."

I went to the fringe of the crowd and one by one grasped the outstretched hands and listened to the words of encouragement.

"God bless you, Governor!"

"Keep telling it like it is, George!"

I nodded and thanked them. Then I heard a voice from my right.

"Hey, George, let me shake hands with you!"

I turned and started to extend my hand. Suddenly I heard five sharp reports. I spun around to the left. My knees buckled and I dropped to the ground. There was no pain, but I knew I had been hit—and hit badly. I lay on the ground as turmoil took over around and above me. I saw a circle of confused faces with helpless expressions. I tried to move my legs, but nothing happened. It was as though they didn't belong to me at all.

"This must be the end," I thought to myself. "I'll start feeling faint and pass out, and that will be the end." I thought, I will never see Cornelia and the family again.

I looked around and saw I wasn't the only one hit. There was E. C. Dothard bleeding, and so was one of the Secret Service men (Nick Zarvos). Suddenly

Cornelia, whom I had seen only fleetingly since the luncheon, loomed above me and threw herself over me in a protective gesture. If there were any more bullets coming she was determined to stop them before they hit me. She winced as she saw the wounds, then murmured, "You're going to be all right, honey. I'm going to get you out of this. I'm going to take you home and out of all this."

I wasn't too sure what she meant at the time, but her idea was to give up the whole thing—to get out of national politics and back to the safety of Montgomery.

Someone pulled Cornelia back, although it took a lot of effort. Then someone else, a doctor I suppose, put a handkerchief on the wound in my stomach to test the bleeding pattern.

One of my staff members kneeled beside me and told me, "Don't worry, Governor. You'll be all right. It's nothing. Nothing at all."

I looked at him incredulously and said, "My goodness, Emmett, you say it's nothing. You'd better take another look."

There were nine holes, because the bullets had gone through me, hitting Dothard and the agent. Pain was starting to set in as I looked up and saw a man standing beside me, pistol in one hand. He kneeled to take my pulse, and the pistol was pointing right at my head.

"Who are you?" I gasped.

"Secret Service," was the answer.

I nodded recognition. "Well, agent, I wish you'd point that gun in some other direction. I've been shot enough for one day."

The agent looked abashed and said, "Oh, my goodness!" He quickly moved the gun. He was a clean-cut young fellow, intent on protecting me, and didn't realize where his gun was pointing. The incident was picked up by the TV cameras, and I wouldn't be surprised if the tape is shown to the other Secret Service agents as an example of what not to do in such circumstances.

By this time the pain was getting to me. It grew in intensity until it took all my will power to keep from screaming. I prayed, "My God, if You're going to take me, do it quick and stop this suffering."

The pain was so excruciating that I barely remember being picked up, put into the station wagon, transferred to an ambulance, and sped off. I did not lose consciousness at any time, although the pain made me oblivious to just about everything that was going on around me. I was convinced I was fatally wounded, and I was trying to be as gritty as possible to the end. I prayed to God to spare me but if it were not his will that he not let me suffer any longer.

A collage of images rushed through my mind: Cornelia, my mother, the children, Lurleen. Then I thought of that baby-faced girl back in Wheaton.

I thought of the two Kennedys and Martin Luther King. I remember thinking how stupid it all was, how impossible that this sort of thing could happen in a country full of such fine people. Were the hate and violence of the few going to make a martyr out of me along with the others? The pain that possessed me made me sure of it.

"What a sorry way for it all to end!" was the thought that raced through my mind. There was so much left undone, so much unsaid, so much torn fabric in the country to be mended. I tried to put the pain out of my mind by thinking back, not as they say dying people do, but trying to piece together the important things that had happened to me. My thoughts turned to Clio, the town where I grew up. Strangely, the most distant memories came back in poignant clearness.

The distant memories of my life and family ran through my mind in a clear flash: Bobbie Jo and her husband; Jimbo, my only grandson; Peggy Sue; George, Jr., my only son and namesake; my little Lee—only eleven years old; my step-sons, Jim and Josh—only seven and eight; and my mother, brothers, and sisters.

I remember praying to God, "Please let me live to see them again." My mind flashed the memories of the last few lucid moments of my first wife's life when with her weak, tired voice she reminded me, "We will all meet in heaven."

Acceptance Speech by Senator George McGovern
Miami, July 13, 1972

In a memorable acceptance speech at the Democratic convention, George McGovern promised that, if elected President, within 90 days of his inauguration every American soldier would be out of Vietnam. Unfortunately for the Democratic nominee, his speech was delivered at 3 a.m., long after most Americans had gone to bed.

With a full heart I accept your nomination.

My nomination is all the more precious in that it is the gift of the most open political process in our national history. It is the sweet harvest cultivated by tens of thousands of tireless volunteers—old and young—and funded by literally hundreds of thousands of small contributors. Those who lingered on the edge of despair a brief time ago have been brought into this campaign—heart, hand, head, and soul.

I have been the beneficiary of the most remarkable political organization in American history—an organization that gives dramatic proof to the power of love and to a faith that can move mountains. As Yeats put it: "Count where man's glory most begins and ends, and say my glory was I had such friends."

This is a people's nomination. And next January we will restore the government to the people. American politics will never be the same again.

We are entering a new period of important, hopeful change in America comparable to the political ferment released in the eras of Jefferson, Jackson, and Roosevelt.

I treasure this nomination especially because it comes after vigorous competition with the ablest men and women our party can offer: my old and treasured friend and neighbor, Hubert Humphrey; that gracious and good man from Maine, Ed Muskie; a tough fighter for his beliefs, Scoop Jackson; a brave and spirited woman, Shirley Chisholm; a wise and powerful lawmaker from Arkansas, Wilbur Mills; the man from North Carolina who opened new vistas in education and public excellence, Terry Sanford; the leader who in 1968 combined the travail and the hope of the American spirit, Gene McCarthy.

And I was as moved as all of you by the appearance at this convention of the governor of Alabama, George Wallace. His votes in the primaries showed the depth of discontent in this country, and his courage in the face of pain and adversity is the mark of a man of boundless will. We all despise the senseless act that disrupted his campaign. Governor, we pray for your speedy and full recovery, so you can stand up and speak out forcefully for all of those who see you as their champion.

In the months ahead, I covet the help of every Democrat and every Republican and independent who wants America to be the great and good land it can be.

33

This is going to be a national campaign carried to every part of the nation—north, south, east, and west. We are not conceding a single state to Richard Nixon. I want to say to my friend, Frank King, that Ohio may have passed a few times at this convention but *I'm* not going to pass Ohio. Governor Gilligan, Ohio may be a little slow counting the votes, but when they come in this November, they are going to show a Democratic victory.

To anyone in this hall or beyond who doubts the ability of Democrats to join together in common cause, I say never underestimate the power of Richard Nixon to bring harmony to Democratic ranks. He is our unwitting unifier and the fundamental issue of this campaign. And all of us together are going to help him redeem the pledge he made ten years ago: Next year you won't have Richard Nixon to kick around any more.

We have had our fury and our frustrations in these past months and at this convention.

Well, I frankly welcome the contrast with the smug, dull, and empty event which will take place here in Miami next month. We chose this struggle. We reformed our party and let the people in.

And we stand today not as a collection of back-room strategists, not as a tool of ITT or any other special interest, but as a direct reflection of the public will.

So let our opponents stand on the status quo, while we seek to refresh the American spirit.

Let the opposition collect their $10 million in secret money from the privileged. And let us find one million ordinary Americans who will contribute $25 each to this campaign—"A Million-Member Club" with members who will expect, not special favors for themselves, but a better land for us all.

In Scripture and in the music of our children we are told: "To everything there is a season, and a time to every purpose under heaven."

And for America, the time has come at last.

This is the time for truth, not falsehood.

In a democratic nation, no one likes to say that his inspiration came from secret arrangements behind closed doors. But in a sense that is how my candidacy began. I am here as your candidate tonight in large part because during four administrations of both parties, a terrible war has been charted behind closed doors.

I want those doors opened, and I want that war closed. And I make these pledges above all others—the doors of government will be opened, and that brutal war will be closed.

Truth is a habit of integrity, not a strategy of politics. And if we nurture the habit of truth in this campaign, we will continue to be truthful once we are in the White House. Let us say to Americans, as Woodrow Wilson said in his first campaign: ". . . let me inside (the government) and I will tell you everything that is going on in there."

The destiny of America is safer in the hands of the people than in the conference rooms of any elite. Let us give our country the chance to elect a government that will seek and speak the truth, for this is a time for truth in the life of our nation.

And this is a time, not for death, but for life.

In 1968, Americans voted to bring our sons home from Vietnam in peace—and since then, twenty thousand have come home in coffins.

I have no secret plan for peace. I have a public plan.

As one whose heart has ached for ten years over the agony of Vietnam, I will halt the senseless bombing of Indochina on Inauguration Day.

There will be no more Asian children running ablaze from bombed-out schools.

There will be no more talk of bombing the dikes or the cities of the north.

Within ninety days of my inauguration, every American soldier and every American prisoner will be out of the jungle and out of their cells and back home in America where they belong.

And then let us resolve that never again will we shed the precious young blood of this nation to prop up a cruel and corrupt dictatorship ten thousand miles from our shores.

Let us choose life, not death. This is the time.

This is also the time to turn away from excessive preoccupation overseas to rebuilding our own nation.

America must be restored to her proper role in the world. But we can do that only through the recovery of confidence in ourselves. The greatest contribution America can make to our fellow mortals is to heal our own great but deeply troubled land. We must respond to the ancient command: "Physician, heal thyself."

It is necessary in an age of nuclear power and hostile ideologies that we be militarily strong. America must never become a second-rate nation. As one who has tasted the bitter fruits of our weakness before Pearl Harbor, 1941, I give you my sacred pledge that if I become president of the United States, America will keep its defenses alert and fully sufficient to meet any danger. We will do that not only for ourselves, but for those who deserve and need the shield of our strength—our old allies in Europe and elsewhere, including the people of Israel, who will always have our help to hold their promised land.

Yet we know that for thirty years we have been so absorbed with fear and danger from abroad that we have permitted our own house to fall into disarray. We must now show that peace and prosperity can exist side by side—indeed, each now depends on the other.

National strength includes the credibility of our system in the eyes of our own people as well as the credibility of our deterrent in the eyes of others abroad. National security includes schools for our children as well as silos for our missiles, the health of our families as much as the size of our bombs, the safety of our streets and the condition of our cities and not just the engines of war. And if we someday choke on the pollution of our own air, there will be little consolation in leaving behind a dying continent ringed with steel.

So while protecting ourselves abroad let us "form a more perfect union" here at home. This is the time.

And we must make this a time of justice and jobs for all.

For more than three years, we have tolerated stagnation and a rising level of joblessness, with more than five million of our best workers unemployed. Surely this is the most false and wasteful economics. Our deep need is not for idleness, but for new housing and hospitals, for facilities to combat pollution and take us home from work, for products better able to compete on vigorous world markets.

The highest domestic priority of my administration will be to ensure that every American able to work has a job to do. This job guarantee will and must depend upon a reinvigorated private economy, freed at last from the uncertainties and burdens of war. But it is our commitment that whatever employment the private sector does not provide, the federal government will either stimulate, or provide itself. Whatever it takes, this country is going back to work.

America cannot exist with most of our people working and paying taxes, to support too many others mired in a hopeless welfare mess. Therefore, we intend to begin by putting millions back to work; and after that is done, we will assure to those unable to work an income adequate to a decent life.

Beyond this, a program to put America back to work demands that work be properly rewarded. That means the end of a system of economic controls in which labor is depressed, but prices and corporate profits run sky-high. It means a system of national health insurance, so that a worker can afford decent health care for himself and his family. It means real enforcement of the laws so that the drug racketeers are put behind bars for good and our streets are once again safe for our families.

Above all, honest work must be rewarded by a fair and just tax system. The tax system today does not reward hard work; it penalizes it. Inherited or invested wealth frequently multiplies itself while paying no taxes at all. But wages earned on the assembly line, or farming the land—these hard-earned dollars are taxed to the last penny. There is a depletion allowance for oil wells, but no allowance for depleting the farmer who feeds us or the worker who serves us all.

The Administration tells us that we should not discuss tax reform in an election year. They would prefer to keep all discussion of the tax laws in closed rooms, where they, their powerful friends, and their paid lobbyists can turn every effort at reform into a new loophole for the rich. But an election year is the people's year to speak; and this year, the people are going to ensure that the tax system is changed so that work is rewarded and so that those who derive the highest benefits will pay their fair share rather than slipping through the loopholes at the expense of the rest of us.

So let us stand for justice, and jobs, and against special privilege. This is the time.

We are not content with things as they are. We reject the view of those who say: "America—love it or leave it." We reply: "Let us change America, so we can love it the more."

And this is the time. It is the time for this land to become again a witness to the world for what is noble and just in human affairs. It is the time to live more with faith and less with fear—with an abiding confidence that can sweep away the strongest barriers between us and teach us that we truly are brothers and sisters.

So join with me in this campaign. Lend me your strength and your support—and together, we will call America home to the ideals that nourished us in the beginning.

From secrecy, and deception in high places, come home, America.

From a conflict in Indochina which maims our ideals as well as our soldiers, come home, America.

From military spending so wasteful that it weakens our nation, come home, America.

From the entrenchment of special privilege and tax favoritism—

From the waste of idle hands to the joy of useful labor—

From the prejudice of race and sex—

From the loneliness of the aging poor and the despair of the neglected sick, come home, America.

Come home to the affirmation that we have a dream.

Excerpts from Senator Thomas Eagleton's News Conference
Rapid City, South Dakota, July 25, 1972

Senator Eagleton, the Democratic nominee for Vice President disclosed that he had voluntarily hospitalized himself three times between 1960 and 1966 for "nervous exhaustion and fatigue." Since 1966, said the 42-year old candidate, he had "experienced good, solid, sound health."

In political campaigning it is part and parcel of that campaigning that there will be rumors about candidates. Rumors have followed me during my political career, dating back when I first ran for office in 1956 . . . there have been some rumors circulating as to my health. Thus, today I wish to give you as complete a picture as I possibly can as a layman about my personal health.

I charge no one with malice as far as spreading these rumors, but I think it is a legitimate question the press has to ask me about whether my health is such that I can hold the high office of Vice President of the United States.

On three occasions in my life I have voluntarily gone into hospitals as a result of nervous exhaustion and fatigue. A few in this room know me well . . . and they know me to be an intense and hard-fighting person.

I sometimes push myself too far. In 1960, John F. Kennedy was running for President and I was a Democratic nominee for Attorney General [for Missouri] . . . I was in many instances my own car driver. The day of Secret Service escorts wasn't my cup of tea in 1960, and I pushed myself, terribly hard, long hours, day and night.

After that campaign was over I did experience exhaustion and fatigue. I was on my own volition hospitalized in Barnes Hospital in St. Louis, Mo. . . . The period of that hospitalization, as best I can recall it, was probably four weeks. It started around Dec. 1 and culminated perhaps the first day of January or soon afterwards in 1961.

The second experience was perhaps four days in length. I went to Mayo Clinic in Rochester, Minn., between Christmas, Dec. 25, 1964, and New Year's Day, Jan. 1, 1965. During that week, the holiday week, I was in Mayo's for four days for physical examination. Part of the manifestation of my fatigue and exhaustion relates to the stomach. I am like the fellow in the Alka-Seltzer ad who says I can't believe I ate the whole thing.

But I do get, when I do overwork and tire myself, kind of a nervous stomach situation. It's one of the physical manifestations of what I have experienced.

The third and final time, ladies and gentlemen, was in perhaps middle or late September of 1966 when I once again went back to Mayo clinic, once again for exhaustion and fatigue. The length of that stay, I think, was approximately three weeks.

One could ask and should ask well, in light of that history, have you learned anything. All of us live our lives, I guess, in the attempt to learn more about ourselves . . . in many respects we are our own worst enemies and it took these experiences, these tough experiences, for me to learn a little bit about myself.

I still am an intense person, I still push very hard. but I pace myself a great deal better than I did in earlier years. The past six years, from 1966 to date, I've experienced good, solid, sound health. I make it a regular practice to be as idle as I can on Sundays . . . in the winter months that's my day to lie on the couch and watch the Redskins and the St. Louis football Cardinals and the Kansas City Chiefs, the last two being by favorite teams.

So I believe and I have every confidence that at age 42 I've learned how to pace myself and learned how to measure my own energies and know the limits of my own endurance. Insofar as this campaign is concerned I intend to give it all I have but on a measured basis, and not to repeat the experiences that I have experienced as heretofore mentioned. So as far as the initial exposition is concerned I've about said all I can and now I'll take questions from the press on any matter that they feel pertinent to what I have just said.

Questions and Answers

Q: Was Senator McGovern aware of these things . . . before he decided on you as a candidate?

EAGLETON: No, he was not. He was made aware of it on the weekend or the Monday after the convention.

Q: How did Senator McGovern react to it?

MCGOVERN: Well let me say, Mr. Schumacher, that when I talked to Senator Eagleton about my decision to ask him to go as my running mate, I asked if he had any problems in his past that were significant or worth discussing with me. He said no and I agree with that.

I am fully satisified on the basis of everything I've learned about these brief hospital visits that what is manifested in Senator Eagleton's part was the good judgment to seek out medical care when he was exhausted. I have watched him in the U.S. Senate for the past four years. As far as I am concerned, there is no member of that Senate who is any sounder in mind, body and spirit than Tom Eagleton. I am fully satisfied and if I had known every detail that he discussed this morning . . . he still would have been my choice for Vice President.

Q: At the risk of being indelicate, did you find during these periods of exhaustion that it affected your ability to make rational judgments.

EAGLETON: No, I was in a position to make rational judgments and decisions. I was depressed. My spirits were depressed. This was one of the manifestations, along with the stomach upset, of the exhaustion and fatigue I heretofore described.

Q: Was alcohol at all involved?

A: Alcohol was not involved in any iota, in any way, shape or form whatsoever, I can assure you—categorically and without hesitation, unequivocal— there's been no trace, no hint, not one iota of alcoholism as part of these rumors—as part of the actual facts.

Q: During these periods, did you receive any psyschiatric help?

A: Yes, I did.

Q: What kind of treatment?

A: As I entered the hospitals, voluntarily as I have described, my physician was an internist, Dr. William Perry of St. Louis. He's still practicing in St. Louis and he's no longer my physician since I moved to Washington. I used the services of the Senate, which is Dr. Pearson and his staff. Parenthetically, not to avoid your questions, I have received a Senate exam and another one at Bethesda Naval Hospital and all the doctors have found so far is that I'm two pounds overweight and have half a hemorrhoid . . . I was treated by a psychiatrist, Dr. Frank Shobez.

Q: Can you tell us what type of psychiatric treatment you received?

A: Counselling from a psychiatrist, including electric shock.

Q: Any drugs?

A: Sleeping pills.

Q: Was the electric shock treatment at all three hospitals?

A.: No. Barnes in 1960 and Mayo's in 1966, not at Mayo's in 1964.

Q: What were the purposes of the electric shock treatment?

A: At that time it was part of the prescribed treatment for one who is suffering from nervous exhaustion and fatigue and manifestations of depression.

Q: Do you intend to make public the documentation of this history?

A: Medical reports are matters between one doctor and another doctor. They're not written in laymen's language. . . . I know of no situation where any candidate for any office has made public records of any communication between doctors and other doctors pertaining to a particular patient.

Q: Would you release your doctors from the traditional doctor-patient relationship?

A: I'm sure Dr. Perry will make a statement. I haven't talked to Dr. Perry but he'll make a summary statement of what his findings were. He is not really the most important one because I haven't seen Dr. Perry as a patient for, I guess, over four years . . .

Q: What doctors did you see at Rochester?

A: I don't remember the names of the physicians. If you know how the Mayo operation is, you're more or less treated by a group of physicians . . . you're sort of the patient of the entire group.

Q: Why did you decide to address yourself to the problem now when you did not decide to do so in your previous political career?

A: In seeking the second highest office in the land, it is only natural that one's life becomes more and more of an open book. It's quite obvious that I haven't relished being under these lights, before 30 or 40 newsmen, describing my health. It isn't a joyous undertaking and I think it is natural that, until it is necessary to respond to rumors that were circulating, the natural tendency would be to keep one's peace.

Q: If you had this to do over again, would you have consulted Senator McGovern before you formally accepted the Vice-Presidential choice?

A: Senator McGovern's staff was aware, I believe, the night before my name was put in nomination, of the rumors . . . that were circulating on the floor of the convention and they were satisfied as to my health as to permit me to be the Vice-Presidential candidate.

Q: Senator McGovern, can you give us your assessment of your running mate's health?

McGOVERN: Well, I think Tom Eagleton is fully qualified in mind, body and spirit to be the Vice President of the United States and, if necessary, to take on the Presidency on a moment's notice. . . . I know fully the whole case history of his illness, I know what his performance has been in the Senate over the last four years and I don't have the slightest doubt about the wisdom of my judgment in selecting him as my running mate, nor would I have any hesitance at all trusting the U. S. Government to his hands. I wouldn't have hesitated one moment if I had known everything Senator Eagleton said here today.

Senators McGovern and Eagleton's Statements on Eagleton's Withdrawal as the Democratic Vice Presidential Nominee, July 31, 1972

Under pressure, Senator Eagleton was forced to withdraw as his party's vice presidential nominee. Eagleton had revealed that he had been hospitalized three times during the 1960s for nervous exhaustion and depression and that he had been treated with electric shocks and tranquilizers.

Senator McGovern

Sen. Eagleton and I have met to discuss his vice presidential candidacy.

I have consistently supported Sen. Eagleton. He is a talented United States senator whose ability will make him a prominent figure in American politics for many, many years.

I am fully satisfied that his health is excellent. I base that conclusion on my conversations with his doctors and my close personal and political association with him. In the joint decision we have reached, health was not a factor.

But the public debate over Sen. Eagleton's past medical history continues to divert attention from the great national issues that need to be discussed.

I have referred to the growing pressures to ask for Sen. Eagleton's withdrawal. We have also seen growing vocal support *for* his candidacy.

Sen. Eagleton and I agree that the paramount needs of the Democratic Party in 1972 are unity and a full discussion of the real issues. Continued debate between those who oppose his candidacy and those who favor it will serve to further divide the party and the nation.

Therefore, we have jointly agreed that the best course is for Sen. Eagleton to step aside.

I wish nothing but the best for Sen. Eagleton. He is and will remain my good friend. Further, he has generously agreed to campaign for the Democratic ticket this fall. I can assure you I welcome his strong help.

Senator Eagleton

As Sen. McGovern has stated, he and I are jointly in agreement that I should withdraw as the Democratic candidate for vice president.

Needless to say this was not an easy decision for Sen. McGovern or for me. Literally thousands and thousands of people have phoned, telegramed or written to me and Sen. McGovern urging me to press on.

I will not divide the Democratic Party, which already has too many divisions.

Therefore I am writing to the chairman of the Democratic Party tomorrow morning, withdrawing my candidacy.

My personal feelings are secondary to the necessity to unify the Democratic Party and elect George McGovern the next President of the United States.

My conscience is clear. My spirits are high.

This is definitely NOT my last press conference, and Tom Eagleton is going to be around for a long, long time.

I'm for George McGovern, and I'm going to continue working to see him elected President of the United States.

Statement by President Richard M. Nixon Concerning the Selection of Spiro Agnew as Running Mate
July 27, 1972

Although Vice-President Spiro Agnew's sometimes harsh rhetoric and outspokenness had alienated many of his countrymen, President Nixon decided to keep him as his running mate in 1972.

Q: Mr. President, on the subject of the Vice President, of your selection of Mr. Agnew, could you tell us if you considered anybody else for the job and who they were?

THE PRESIDENT: No. My thoughts with regard to Vice President Agnew were expressed at rather great length in this very room in an interview with one of the other networks. I think it was CBS.

On that occasion, I expressed my confidence in the Vice President. I won't go over those matters that I covered at considerable length then now, except to say that I reaffirm that confidence as expressed then.

Under the circumstances, I believe that the choice I made 4 years ago is one that should now be reaffirmed by asking him to run for the office again.

Now, there has been speculation, I would hasten to say, about other people for the Vice Presidency. That is inevitable. The Vice President could get sick or the Vice President might decide not to run, all of these things. I don't think he is going to get sick. He is also in excellent health, better than I. He plays tennis. But, in any event, there has been a lot of speculation. Secretary Connally's name comes to mind.

I should point out that a really great injustice was done to Secretary Connally in the suggestion, I think, on one of the news reports to the effect that I gave Secretary Connally the "bad news" that he was not going to be the Vice Presidential candidate when I saw him Friday night.

This was not bad news to him. As a matter of fact, it was not news at all. He and I had discussed this problem when he came to California after his world trip. At that time, I discussed the Vice Presidency. After all, not only from the standpoint of ability to hold the office of Vice President but from the standpoint of ability to win the election, Secretary Connally, whose political judgment I respect very much, strongly urged that Vice President Agnew be continued on the ticket.

Acceptance Speech by President Richard M. Nixon
Miami, August 23, 2972

In his acceptance speech President Richard Nixon hammered away at George McGovern's pledge to end the Vietnam War. Alluding to the Democratic nominee's peace proposals, Nixon insisted that he as President, would never "ask an enemy for peace on terms that would betray our allies and destroy respect for the United States."

Mr. Chairman, delegates to this convention, my fellow Americans:

Four years ago, standing in this very place, I proudly accepted your nomination for President of the United States.

With your help and with the votes of millions of Americans, we won a great victory in 1968.

Tonight, I again proudly accept your nomination for President of the United States.

Let us pledge ourselves to win an even greater victory this November, in 1972.

I congratulate Chairman Ford. I congratulate Chairman Dole, Anne Armstrong and the hundreds of others who have laid the foundation for that victory by their work at this great convention.

Our platform is a dynamic program for progress for America and for peace in the world.

Speaking in a very personal sense, I express my deep gratitude to this convention for the tribute you have paid to the best campaigner in the Nixon family—my wife Pat. In honoring her, you have honored millions of women in America who have contributed in the past and will contribute in the future so very much to better government in this country.

Again, as I did last night when I was not at the convention, I express the appreciation of all of the delegates and of all America for letting us see young America at its best at our convention. As I express my appreciation to you, I want to say that you have inspired us with your enthusiasm, with your intelligence, with your dedication at this convention. You have made us realize that this is a year when we can prove the experts' predictions wrong, because we can set as our goal winning a majority of the new voters for our ticket this November.

I pledge to you, all of the new voters in America who are listening on television and listening here in this convention hall, that I will do everything that I can over these next 4 years to make your support be one that you can be proud of, because as I said to you last night, and I feel it very deeply in my heart: Years from now I want you to look back and be able to say that your first vote was one of the best votes you ever cast in your life.

Mr. Chairman, I congratulate the delegates to this convention for renominating as my running mate the man who has just so eloquently and graciously introduced me, Vice President Ted Agnew.

I thought he was the best man for the job 4 years ago.

I think he is the best man for the job today.

And I am not going to change my mind tomorrow.

Finally, as the Vice President has indicated, you have demonstrated to the Nation that we can have an open convention without dividing Americans into quotas.

Let us commit ourselves to rule out every vestige of discrimination in this country of ours. But my fellow Americans, the way to end discrimination against some is not to begin discrimination against others.

Dividing Americans into quotas is totally alien to the American tradition.

Americans don't want to be part of a quota. They want to be part of America. This Nation proudly calls itself the United States of America. Let us reject any philosophy that would make us the divided people of America.

In that spirit, I address you tonight, my fellow Americans, not as a partisan of party, which would divide us, but as a partisan of principles, which can unite us.

Six weeks ago our opponents at their convention rejected many of the great principles of the Democratic Party. To those millions who have been driven out of their home in the Democratic Party, we say come home. We say come home not to another party, but we say come home to the great principles we Americans believe in together.

And I ask you, my fellow Americans, tonight to join us not in a coalition held together only by a desire to gain power. I ask you to join us as members of a new American majority bound together by our common ideals.

I ask everyone listening to me tonight—Democrats, Republicans, independents, to join our new majority—not on the basis of the party label you wear in your lapel, but on the basis of what you believe in your hearts.

In asking for your support I shall not dwell on the record of our Administration which has been praised perhaps too generously by others at this convention.

We have made great progress in these past 4 years.

It can truly be said that we have changed America and that America has changed the world. As a result of what we have done, America today is a better place and the world is a safer place to live in than was the case 4 years ago.

We can be proud of that record, but we shall never be satisfied. A record is not something to stand on; it is something to build on.

Tonight I do not ask you to join our new majority because of what we have done in the past. I ask your support of the principles I believe should determine America's future.

The choice in this election is not between radical change and no change. The choice in this election is between change that works and change that won't work.

I begin with an article of faith.

It has become fashionable in recent years to point up what is wrong with what is called the American system. The critics contend it is so unfair, so corrupt, so unjust, that we should tear it down and substitute something else in its place.

I totally disagree. I believe in the American system.

I have traveled to 80 countries in the past 25 years, and I have seen Communist systems, I have seen Socialist systems, I have seen systems that are half Socialist and half free.

Every time I come home to America, I realize how fortunate we are to live in this great and good country.

Every time I am reminded that we have more freedom, more opportunity, more prosperity than any people in the world, that we have the highest rate of growth of any industrial nation, that Americans have more jobs at higher wages than in any country in the world; that our rate of inflation is less than that of any industrial nation, that the incomparable productivity of America's farmers has made it possible for us to launch a winning war against hunger in the United States, and that the productivity of our farmers also makes us the best-fed people in the world with the lowest percentage of the family budget going to food of any country in the world.

We can be very grateful in this country that the people on welfare in America would be rich in most of the nations of the world today.

Now, my fellow Americans, in pointing up those things, we do not overlook the fact that our system has its problems.

Our Administration, as you know, has provided the biggest tax cut in history, but taxes are still too high.

That is why one of the goals of our next Administration is to reduce the property tax which is such an unfair and heavy burden on the poor, the elderly, the wage earner, the farmer, and those on fixed incomes.

As all of you know, we have cut inflation in half in this Administration, but we have got to cut it further. We must cut it further so that we can continue to expand on the greatest accomplishment of our new economic policy: For the first time in 5 years wage increases in America are not being eaten up by price increases.

As a result of the millions of new jobs created by our new economic policies, unemployment today in America is less than the peacetime average of the sixties, but we must continue the unparalleled increase in new jobs so that we can achieve the great goal of our new prosperity—a job for every American who wants to work, without war and without inflation. The way to reach this goal is to stay on the new road we have charted to move America forward and not to take a sharp detour to the left, which would lead to a dead end for the hopes of the American people.

This points up one of the clearest choices in this campaign. Our opponents believe in a different philosophy.

Theirs is the politics of paternalism, where master planners in Washington make decisions for people.

Ours is the politics of people—where people make decisions for themselves.

The proposal that they have made to pay $1,000 to every person in America insults the intelligence of the American voters.

Because you know that every politician's promise has a price—the taxpayer pays the bill.

The American people are not going to be taken in by any scheme where Government gives with one hand and takes it away with the other.

Their platform promises everything to everybody, but at an increased net in the budget of $144 billion, but listen to what it means to you, the taxpayers of the country. That would mean an increase of 50 percent in what the taxpayers of America pay. I oppose any new spending programs which will increase the tax burden on the already overburdened American taxpayer.

And they have proposed legislation which would add 82 million people to the welfare rolls.

I say that instead of providing incentives for millions of more Americans to go on welfare, we need a program which will provide incentives for people to get off of welfare and to get to work.

We believe that it is wrong for anyone to receive more on welfare than for someone who works. Let us be generous to those who can't work without increasing the tax burden of those who do work.

And while we are talking about welfare, let us quit treating our senior citizens in this country like welfare recipients. They have worked hard all of their lives to build America. And as the builders of America, they have not asked for a handout. What they ask for is what they have earned—and that is retirement in dignity and self-respect. Let's give that to our senior citizens.

Now, when you add up the cost of all of the programs our opponents have proposed, you reach only one conclusion: They would destroy the system which has made America number one in the world economically.

Listen to these facts: Americans today pay one-third of all of their income in taxes. If their programs were adopted, Americans would pay over one-half of what they earn in taxes. This means that if their programs are adopted, American wage earners would be working more for the Government than they would for themselves.

Once we cross this line, we cannot turn back because the incentive which makes the American economic system the most productive in the world would be destroyed.

Theirs is not a new approach. It has been tried before in countries abroad, and I can tell you that those who have tried it have lived to regret it.

We cannot and we will not let them do this to America.

Let us always be true to the principle that has made America the world's most prosperous nation—that here in America a person should get what he works for and work for what he gets.

Let me illustrate the difference in our philosophies. Because of our free economic system, what we have done is to build a great building of economic wealth and money in America. It is by far the tallest building in the world, and we are still adding to it. Now because some of the windows are broken, they say tear it down and start again. We say, replace the windows and keep building. That is the difference.

Let me turn now to a second area where my beliefs are totally different from those of our opponents.

Four years ago crime was rising all over America at an unprecedented rate. Even our Nation's Capital was called the crime capital of the world. I pledged to stop the rise in crime. In order to keep that pledge, I promised in the election campaign that I would appoint judges to the Federal courts, and particularly to the Supreme Court, who would recognize that the first civil right of every American is to be free from domestic violence.

I have kept that promise. I am proud of the appointments I have made to the courts, and particularly proud of those I have made to the Supreme Court of the United States. And I pledge again tonight, as I did 4 years ago, that whenever I have the opportunity to make more appointments to the courts, I shall continue to appoint judges who share my philosophy that we must strengthen the peace forces as against the criminal forces in the United States.

We have launched an all-out offensive against crime, against narcotics, against permissiveness in our country.

I want the peace officers across America to know that they have the total backing of their President in their fight against crime.

My fellow Americans, as we move toward peace abroad, I ask you to support our programs which will keep the peace at home.

Now, I turn to an issue of overriding importance not only to this election, but for generations to come—the progress we have made in building a new structure of peace in the world.

Peace is too important for partisanship. There have been five Presidents in my political lifetime—Franklin D. Roosevelt, Harry Truman, Dwight Eisenhower, John F. Kennedy, and Lyndon Johnson.

They had differences on some issues, but they were united in their belief that where the security of America or the peace of the world is involved we are not Republicans, we are not Democrats. We are Americans, first, last, and always.

These five Presidents were united in their total opposition to isolation for America and in their belief that the interests of the United States and the interests of world peace require that America be strong enough and intelligent enough to assume the responsibilities of leadership in the world.

They were united in the conviction that the United States should have a defense second to none in the world.

They were all men who hated war and were dedicated to peace.

But not one of these five men, and no President in our history, believed that America should ask an enemy for peace on terms that would betray our allies and destroy respect for the United States all over the world.

As your President, I pledge that I shall always uphold that proud bipartisan tradition. Standing in this Convention Hall 4 years ago, I pledged to seek an honorable end to the war in Vietnam. We have made great progress toward that end. We have brought over half a million men home, and more will be coming home. We have ended America's ground combat role. No draftees are being sent to Vietnam. We have reduced our casualties by 98 percent. We have gone the extra mile, in fact we have gone tens of thousands of miles trying to seek a negotiated settlement of the war. We have offered a ceasefire, a total withdrawal of all American forces, an exchange of all prisoners of war, internationally supervised free elections with the Communists participating in the elections and in the supervision.

There are three things, however, that we have not and that we will not offer.

We will never abandon our prisoners of war.

Second, we will not join our enemies in imposing a Communist government on our allies—the 17 million people of South Vietnam.

And we will never stain the honor of the United States of America.

Now I realize that many, particularly in this political year, wonder why we insist on an honorable peace in Vietnam. From a political standpoint they suggest that since I was not in office when over a half million American men were sent there, that I should end the war by agreeing to impose a Communist government on the people of South Vietnam and just blame the whole catastrophe on my predecessors.

This might be good politics, but it would be disastrous to the cause of peace in the world. If, at this time, we betray our allies, it will discourage our friends abroad and it will encourage our enemies to engage in aggression.

In areas like the Mideast, which are danger areas, small nations who rely on the friendship and support of the United States would be in deadly jeopardy.

To our friends and allies in Europe, Asia, the Mideast, and Latin America, I say the United States will continue its great bipartisan tradition—to stand by our friends and never to desert them.

Now in discussing Vietnam, I have noted that in this election year there has been a great deal of talk about providing amnesty for those few hundred Americans who chose to desert their country rather than to serve it in Vietnam. I think it is time that we put the emphasis where it belongs. The real heroes are 2 1/2 million young Americans who chose to serve their country rather than desert it. I say to you tonight, in these times when there is so much of a tendency to run down those who have served America in the past and who serve it today, let us give those who serve in our Armed forces and those who have served in Vietnam the honor and the respect that they deserve and that they have earned.

Finally, in this connection, let one thing be clearly understood in this election campaign: The American people will not tolerate any attempt by our enemies to interfere in the cherished right of the American voter to make his own decision with regard to what is best for America without outside intervention.

Now it is understandable that Vietnam has been a major concern in foreign policy. But we have not allowed the war in Vietnam to paralyze our capacity to initiate historic new policies to construct a lasting and just peace in the world.

When the history of this period is written, I believe it will be recorded that our most significant contributions to peace resulted from our trips to Peking and to Moscow.

The dialogue that we have begun with the People's Republic of China has reduced the danger of war and has increased the chance for peaceful cooperation between two great peoples.

Within the space of 4 years in our relations with the Soviet Union, we have moved from confrontation to negotiation, and then to cooperation in the interest of peace.

We have taken the first step in limiting the nuclear arms race.

We have laid the foundation for further limitations on nuclear weapons and eventually of reducing the armaments in the nuclear area.

We can thereby not only reduce the enormous cost of arms for both our countries, but we can increase the chances for peace.

More than on any other single issue, I ask you, my fellow Americans, to give us the chance to continue these great initiatives that can contribute so much to the future of peace in the world.

It can truly be said that as a result of our initiatives, the danger of war is less today than it was; the chances for peace are greater.

But a note of warning needs to be sounded. We cannot be complacent. Our opponents have proposed massive cuts in our defense budget which would have the inevitable effect of making the United States the second strongest nation in the world.

For the United States unilaterally to reduce its strength with the naive hope that other nations would do likewise would increase the danger of war in the world.

It would completely remove any incentive of other nations to agree to a mutual limitation or reduction of arms.

The promising initiatives we have undertaken to limit arms would be destroyed.

The security of the United States and all the nations in the world who depend upon our friendship and support would be threatened.

Let's look at the record on defense expenditures. We have cut spending in our Administration. It now takes the lowest percentage of our national product in 20 years. We should not spend more on defense than we need. But we must never spend less than we need.

What we must understand is, spending what we need on defense will cost us money. Spending less than we need could cost us our lives or our freedom.

So tonight, my fellow Americans, I say, let us take risks for peace, but let us never risk the security of the United States of America.

It is for that reason that I pledge that we will continue to seek peace and the mutual reduction of arms. The United States, during this period, however, will always have a defense second to none.

There are those who believe that we can entrust the security of America to the good will of our adversaries.

Those who hold this view do not know the real world. We can negotiate limitation of arms, and we have done so. We can make arrangements to reduce the danger of war, and we have done so.

But one unchangeable rule of international diplomacy that I have learned over many, many years is that, in negotiations between great powers, you can only get something if you have something to give in return.

That is why I say tonight: Let us always be sure that when the President of the United States goes to the conference table, he never has to negotiate from weakness.

There is no such thing as a retreat to peace.

My fellow Americans, we stand today on the threshold of one of the most exciting and challenging eras in the history of relations between nations.

We have the opportunity in our time to be the peacemakers of the world, because the world trusts and respects us and because the world knows that we shall only use our power to defend freedom, never to destroy it; to keep the peace, never to break it.

A strong America is not the enemy of peace; it is the guardian of peace.

The initiatives that we have begun can result in reducing the danger of arms, as well as the danger of war which hangs over the world today.

Even more important, it means that the enormous creative energies of the Russian people and the Chinese people and the American people and all the great peoples of the world can be turned away from production of war and turned toward production for peace.

In America it means that we can undertake programs for progress at home that will be just as exciting as the great initiatives we have undertaken in building a new structure of peace abroad.

My fellow Americans, the peace dividend that we hear so much about has too often been described solely in monetary terms—how much money we could take out of the arms budget and apply to our domestic needs. By far the biggest dividend, however, is that achieving our goal of a lasting peace in the world would reflect the deepest hopes and ideals of all of the American people.

Speaking on behalf of the American people, I was proud to be able to say in my television address to the Russian people in May: We covet no one else's territory. We seek no dominion over any other nation. We seek peace not only for ourselves, but for all the people of the world.

This dedication to idealism runs through America's history.

During the tragic War Between the States, Abraham Lincoln was asked whether God was on his side. He replied, "My concern is not whether God is on our side, but whether we are on God's side."

May that always be our prayer for America.

We hold the future of peace in the world and our own future in our hands. Let us reject therefore the policies of those who whine and whimper about our frustrations and call on us to turn inward.

Let us not turn away from greatness.

The chance America now has to lead the way to a lasting peace in the world may never come again.

With faith in God and faith in ourselves and faith in our country, let us have the vision and the courage to seize the moment and meet the challenge before it slips away.

On your television screen last night, you saw the cemetery in Leningrad I visited on my trip to the Soviet Union—where 300,000 people died in the siege of that city during World War II.

At the cemetery I saw the picture of a 12-year-old girl. She was a beautiful child. Her name was Tanya.

I read her diary. It tells the terrible story of war. In the simple words of a child she wrote of the deaths of the members of her family. Zhenya in December. Grannie in January. Then Leka. Then Uncle Vasya. Then Uncle Lyosha. Then Mama in May. And finally—these were the last words in her diary: "All are dead. Only Tanya is left."

Let us think of Tanya and of the other Tanyas and their brothers and sisters everywhere in Russia, in China, in America, as we proudly meet our responsibilities for leadership in the world in a way worthy of a great people.

I ask you, my fellow Americans, to join our new majority not just in the cause of winning an election, but in achieving a hope that mankind has had since the beginning of civilization. Let us build a peace that our children and all the children of the world can enjoy for generations to come.

Address by President Richard M. Nixon
Washington, D.C., November 2, 1972

In one of his most effective speeches as President, Richard Nixon looked to the future and liked what he saw under continued Republican leadership.

Good evening:

I am speaking to you tonight from the Library of the White House. This room, like all the rooms in this great house, is rich in history.

Often late at night I sit here thinking of the crises other Presidents have known—and of the trials that other generations of Americans have come through.

I think, too, of the Presidents who will be sitting here a generation from now, and how they will look back on these years. And I think of what I want to accomplish in these years. I would like to share some of those thoughts with you this evening.

Above all, I want to complete the foundations for a world at peace—so that the next generation can be the first in this century to live without war and without the fear of war.

Beyond this, I want Americans—all Americans—to see more clearly and to feel more deeply what it is that makes this Nation of ours unique in history, unique in the world, a nation in which the soul and spirit are free, in which each person is respected, in which the individual human being, each precious, each different, can dare to dream and can live his dreams.

I want progress toward a better life for all Americans—not only in terms of better schools, greater abundance, a cleaner environment, better homes, more attractive communities, but also in a spiritual sense, in terms of greater satisfaction, more kindness in our relations with each other, more fulfillment.

I want each American—all Americans—to find a new zest in the pursuit of excellence, in striving to do their best and to be their best, in learning the supreme satisfaction of setting a seemingly impossible goal, and meeting or surpassing that goal, of finding in themselves that extra reserve of energy or talent or creativity that they had not known was there.

These are goals of a free people, in a free nation, a nation that lives not by handout, not by dependence on others or in hostage to the whims of others, but proud and independent—a nation of individuals with self-respect and with the right and capacity to make their own choices, to chart their own lives.

That is why I want us to turn away from a demeaning, demoralizing dependence on someone else to make our decisions and to guide the course of our lives.

That is why I want us to turn toward a renaissance of the individual spirit, toward a new vitality of those governments closest to the people, toward a new pride of place for the family and the community, toward a new sense of responsibility in all that we do, responsibility for ourselves and to ourselves, for our communities and to our communities, knowing that each of us, in every act of his daily life, determines what kind of community and what kind of a country we all will live in.

If, together, we can restore this spirit, then 4 years from now America can enter its third century buoyant and vital and young, with all the purpose that marked its beginning two centuries ago.

In these past 4 years, we have moved America significantly toward this goal. We have restored peace at home, and we are restoring peace abroad.

As you know, we have now made a major breakthrough toward achieving our goal of peace with honor in Vietnam. We have reached substantial agreement on most of the terms of a settlement. The settlement we are ready to conclude would accomplish the basic objectives that I laid down in my television speech to the Nation on May 8 of this year:

—the return of all of our prisoners of war, and an accounting for all of those missing in action;

—a cease-fire throughout Indochina; and

—for the 17 million people of South Vietnam, the right to determine their own future without having a Communist government or a coalition government imposed upon them against their will.

However, there are still some issues to be resolved. There are still some provisions of the agreement which must be clarified so that all ambiguities will be removed. I have insisted that these be settled before we sign the final agreement. That is why we refused to be stampeded into meeting the arbitrary deadline of October 31.

Now, there are some who say: "Why worry about the details? Just get the war over!"

Well, my answer is this: My study of history convinces me that the details can make the difference between an agreement that collapses and an agreement that lasts—and equally crucial is a clear understanding by all of the parties of what those details are.

We are not going to repeat the mistake of 1968, when the bombing halt agreement was rushed into just before an election without pinning down the details.

We want peace—peace with honor—a peace fair to all and a peace that will last. That is why I am insisting that the central points be clearly settled, so that there will be no misunderstandings which could lead to a breakdown of the settlement and a resumption of the war.

I am confident that we will soon achieve that goal.

But we are not going to allow an election deadline or any other kind of deadline to force us into an agreement which would be only a temporary truce and not a lasting peace. We are going to sign the agreement when the agreement is right, not one day before. And when the agreement is right, we are going to sign, without one day's delay.

Not only in America, but all around the world, people will be watching the results of our election. The leaders in Hanoi will be watching. They will be watching for the answer of the American people—for your answer—to this question: Shall we have peace with honor or peace with surrender?

Always in the past you have answered "Peace with honor." By giving that same answer once again on November 7 you can help make certain that peace with honor can now be achieved.

In these past 4 years, we have also been moving toward lasting peace in the world at large.

We have signed more agreements with the Soviet Union than were negotiated in all the previous years since World War II. We have established the basis for a new relationship with the People's Republic of China, where one-fourth of all the people in this world live. Our vigorous diplomacy has advanced the prospects for a stable peace in the Middle East. All around the world, we are opening doors to peace, doors that were previously closed. We are developing areas of common interest where there have been previously only antagonisms. All this is a beginning. It can be the beginning of a generation of peace—of a world in which our children can be the first generation in this century to escape the scourge of war.

These next 4 years will set the course on which we begin our third century as a nation. What will that course be? Will it have us turning inward, retreating from the responsibilities not only of a great power but of a great people—of a nation that embodies the ideals man has dreamed of and fought for through the centuries?

We cannot retreat from those responsibilities. If we did America would cease to be a great nation, and peace and freedom would be in deadly jeopardy throughout the world.

Ours is a great and a free nation today because past generations of Americans met their responsibilities. And we shall meet ours.

We have made progress toward peace in the world, toward a new relationship with the Soviet Union and the People's Republic of China, not through naive sentimental assumptions that good will is all that matters, or that we can reduce our military strength because we have no intention of making war and we therefore assume other nations would have no such intention. We have achieved progress through peace for precisely the opposite reasons: because we demonstrated that we would not let ourselves be surpassed in military strength and because we bargained with other nations on the basis of their national interest and ours.

As we look at the real world, it is clear that we will not in our lifetimes have a world free of danger. Anyone who reads history knows that danger has always been part of the common lot of mankind. Anyone who knows the world today knows that nations have not all been suddenly overtaken by some new and unprecedented wave of pure good will and benign intentions. But we can lessen the danger. We can contain it. We can forge a network of relationships and of interdependencies that restrain aggression and that take the profit out of war.

We cannot make all nations the same, and it would be wrong to try. We cannot make all of the world's people love each other. But we can establish conditions in which they will be more likely to live in peace with one another. Tonight I ask for your support as we continue to work toward that great goal.

Here at home, as we look at the progress we have made, we find that we are reaching new levels of prosperity.

We have cut inflation almost in half. The average worker has scored his best gains in 8 years in real spendable earnings. We are creating record numbers of new jobs. We are well on the way to achieving what America has not had since President Eisenhower lived here in the White House: prosperity with full employment, without inflation and without war.

We have lowered the level of violence, and we are finally turning the tide against crime.

I could go on with what we have done—for the environment, for the consumer, for the aging, for the farmer, for the worker, for all Americans—but now we must not look backward to what we have done in the past, but forward to what we will do in the future.

It is traditional for a candidate for election to make all sorts of promises about bold new programs he intends to introduce if elected. This year's Presidential campaign has probably established an alltime record for promises of huge new spending programs for just about anything and everything for everybody imaginable. I have not made such promises in this campaign. And I am not going to do so tonight. Let me tell you why.

In the first place, the sort of bold new programs traditionally promised by candidates are all programs that you—the taxpayer—pay for. The programs proposed by our opponents in this campaign would require a 50-percent increase in Federal taxes, in your taxes. I think your taxes are already too high. That is why I oppose any new program which would add to your tax burden.

In the second place, too many campaign promises are just that—campaign promises. I believe in keeping the promises I make, and making only those promises I am confident I can keep. I have promised that I will do all in my power to avoid the need for new taxes. I am not going to promise anything else in the way of new programs that would violate that pledge.

In the third place, my own philosophy of government is not one that looks to new Federal dollars—your dollars—as the solution of every social problem.

I have often said that America became great not because of what government did for people, but because of what people did for themselves. I believe government should free the energies of people to build for themselves and their communities. It should open opportunities, provide incentives, encourage initiative—not stifle initiative by trying to direct everything from Washington.

This does not mean that the Federal Government will abdicate its responsibilities where only it can solve a problem.

It does mean that after 40 years of unprecedented expansion of the Federal Government, the time has come to redress the balance—to shift more people and more responsibility and power back to the States and localities and, most important, to the people, all across America.

In the past 40 years, the size of the Federal budget has grown from $4.6 billion to $250 billion. In that same period, the number of civilian employees of the Federal Government has increased from 600,000 to 2,800,000. And in just the past 10 years, the number of Federal grant-in-aid programs has increased from 160 to more than 1,000.

If this kind of growth were projected indefinitely into the future, the result would be catastrophic. We would have an America topheavy with bureaucratic meddling, weighted down by big government, suffocated by taxes, robbed of its soul.

We must not and we will not let this happen to America. That is why I oppose the unrestrained growth of big government in Washington. That is why one of my first priorities in the next 4 years will be to encourage a rebirth and renewal of State and local government. That is why I believe in giving the people in every community a greater say in those decisions that most directly affect the course of their daily lives.

Now, there will be those who will call this negative, who call it a retreat from Federal responsibilities.

I call it affirmative—an affirmation of faith in the people, faith in the individual, faith in each person's ability to choose wisely for himself and for his community.

I call it an affirmation of faith in those principles that made America great, that tamed a continent, that transformed a wilderness into the greatest and strongest and freest nation in the world.

We have not changed. The American people have not grown weak. What has grown weak is government's faith in people. I am determined to see that faith restored.

I am also determined to see another kind of faith restored and strengthened in America. I speak of the religious faith, the moral and spiritual values that have been so basically a part of our American experience. Man does not live for himself alone, and the strength of our character, the strength of our faith, and the strength of our ideals—these have been the strength of America.

When I think of what America means, I think of all the hope that lies in a vast continent—of great cities and small towns, of factories and farms, of a greater abundance, more widely shared, than the world has ever known, of a constant striving to set right the wrongs that still persist—and I think of 210 million people, of all ages, all persuasions, all races, all stations in life.

More particularly, I think of one person, one child—any child. That child may be black or brown or white, rich or poor, a boy whose family came here in steerage in 1920, or a girl whose ancestors came on the Mayflower in 1620. That one child is America, with a life still ahead, with his eyes filled with dreams, and with the birthright of every American child to a full and equal opportunity to pursue those dreams.

It is for that one child that I want a world of peace and a chance to achieve all that peace makes possible. It is for that one child that I want opportunity, and freedom, and abundance. It is for that one child that I want a land of justice, and order, and a decent respect for the rights and the feelings of others.

It is for that one child that I want it said, a generation from now, a century from now, that America in the 1970's had the courage and the vision to meet its responsibilities and to face up to its challenges—to build peace, not merely for our generation but for the next generation; to restore the land, to marshal our resources, not merely for our generation but for the next generation; to guard our values and renew our spirit, not merely for our generation but for the next generation.

It is for that one child that I want these next 4 years to be the best 4 years in the whole history of America.

The glory of this time in our history is that we can do more than ever before—we have the means, we have the skills, we have an increasing understanding of how the great goals that we seek can be achieved.

These are not partisan goals. They are America's goals. That is why I ask you tonight, regardless of party, to join the new American majority next Tuesday in voting for candidates who stand for these goals. That is why I ask for your support—after the election—in helping to move forward toward these goals over the next 4 years.

If we succeed in this task, then that one child—all of our children—can look forward to a life more full of hope, promise, than any generation, in any land, in the whole history of mankind.

Thank you, and good evening.

Address by Senator George McGovern
November 3, 1972

Shortly before the presidential election of 1972 Secretary of State Henry Kissinger announced that peace in Vietnam was "at hand." Senator McGovern argued loudly that this was merely a political ploy and in a speech to the nation traced the history of the Nixon Administration's conduct of the war.

I want to talk with you tonight about two events that occurred last night. The first was President Nixon's paid political broadcast, in which he discussed the Vietnam negotiations. He admitted that he has rejected the settlement his own negotiator accepted nearly a month ago. He did not say when there would be an agreement. And he withdrew the latest promise of peace.

So this past week has become another week when the war was not ended. We were told that peace was at hand. But then the hand that could have signed that peace pushed it aside.

The second event last night occurred in Michigan. I was on television answering questions from people who called on the phone. After the program, we received a call from Mr. Charles Stewart of Gladstone, Michigan.

His son, an Army enlisted man, was killed in Vietnam two days ago. He died on the day the peace was supposed to be signed. He was nineteen. He died on the day Mr. Nixon decided to continue fighting the war, while fighting over what he calls the "details" of peace.

Charles Stewart, Jr., died for those "details." And he was not alone. This week twenty-two other Americans died for the same "details."

For the sake of those "details," the bombs still fall, the guns still fire, and the terrible pain goes on.

Even as I speak to you, human lives are being lost in a war that is wrong. More parents learn each week the terrible sorrow of burying their own sons.

But now we have learned something else.

Charles Stewart, Jr., and all the others are not really dying for details, but for a deception.

The President may say peace, peace—but there is no peace, and there never was.

For it is not the details, but the central issues that are still in dispute.

I know that many Americans were struck by the coincidence that after four years of fighting and dying, the Administration announced just twelve days before the election that peace was in reach. We wondered why a settlement that was unsatisfactory until now was embraced at the end of this campaign.

But, like you, I wanted deeply to believe what we were told. If you know my record of opposition to this war for more than nine years, through both Democratic and Republican administrations, then you also know that I would rather have peace than a campaign issue.

60

So I welcomed Dr. Kissinger's announcement last Thursday. I welcomed the news that an agreement was just a few minor matters away.

But now this hope is betrayed. We see now that when the President's most important adviser announced that peace had come, it was actually a deception designed to raise our hopes before we went to vote on Tuesday.

This is blunt language and a strong accusation. I am sorry to say it, but I believe it to be true.

I ask you to judge for yourselves. I ask you to hear Mr. Nixon's own words, to heed his record, and then to decide if he has been fair and open with the people.

In 1968, the American people voted to end the war. Mr. Nixon was elected on a promise of peace. And since then, every measure of public opinion has carried a rising cry for peace.

In 1969, the central issue was whether to seek a military victory for General Thieu or peace for the American people.

The basis for successful negotiations was already there.

The other side wanted elections, conducted not by General Thieu but by an independent coalition group.

General Thieu wanted continued war, to preserve his power unchallenged. He said he would never accept a deadline, that he would never allow a coalition, and that he would never permit peace until he had won.

Mr. Nixon chose General Thieu. And he began his term with the same discredited policy that had failed before—that had failed for the French and failed for us. He thought peace could be won through more war, through invasions and incursions, through bombs and bullets and blood.

With Senator Hatfield and other members of the Congress, Republicans and Democrats alike, I sponsored legislation to bring the peace that was promised. We proposed a deadline to end the bombing and to bring our troops and prisoners home, to leave Vietnam, and to leave it to the Vietnamese to work out their own peace.

This proposal had the support of three-quarters of the American people. But when it appeared that it might pass, Mr. Nixon disclosed that he was engaged in secret discussions with the North Vietnamese. He told us he was searching for peace in the conference room, and that Congress should not interfere.

That disclosure did not hasten an agreement in Paris. All it did was to stifle the demand for peace at home. And that is why it was made.

Mr. Nixon's policy did not change. He involved Cambodia to capture a central Vietcong commander center that did not exist. He sent armies into Laos that were hurled back in defeat and despair. He bombed more relentlessly than ever. He mined North Vietnamese harbors, seeking an impossible victory through reckless acts of war.

But to placate the American people, he pretended he was making peace. As the bombs kept falling, Dr. Kissinger kept traveling. The secret meetings suddenly became highly publicized meetings, to make sure you knew they were taking place as the election approached.

We have challenged that charade in this campaign. We have reminded candidate Nixon of his own words in 1968—that "those who have had a chance for

four years, and could not produce peace, should not be given another chance."
And I have set before the American people, not a secret plan, but an open plan
to end the war.

Mr. Nixon apparently feared that challenge. So on October 8, Dr. Kissinger
agreed in a closed meeting to accept the settlement the other side wanted—on
almost the same terms they offered four years ago.

North Vietnamese forces would stay in the South.

Elections would be arranged by a coalition—by Communists, by neutralists,
and by representatives of the Saigon regime—to assure that General Thieu could
not dictate the results.

American bombing would stop, American forces would leave, and American
prisoners would be freed—all within a period of sixty days.

Mr. Nixon's representative agreed to all of this on October 8. And he agreed,
too, on when the settlement would be signed—October 31, one week before
the election.

That was no arbitrary deadline, as Mr. Nixon pretended last night.

It was an agreed-upon deadline, set by both sides together. Now it had passed.

And there was no "major breakthrough" for peace, as Mr. Nixon also pretended last night.

Instead, there has been a fatal breakdown on the central issues. Now this
chance for an agreement is gone.

Dr. Kissinger took the agreement to General Thieu. And General Thieu said no.

Dr. Kissinger took the agreement to President Nixon. And President Nixon
said no.

What Dr. Kissinger accepted and what Mr. Nixon and General Thieu rejected
was a coalition to set up the elections, and American withdrawals without a
mutual withdrawal by North Vietnam.

Those are the conditions General Thieu has always rejected. And because
they are not resolved, as Mr. Nixon admits, we have changed nothing in the
last four years.

Now someone must answer for 20,000 more American dead, for 110,000 more
wounded, for 550 more captured or missing, for $60 billion more wasted in the
last four years.

And now someone must answer for the cruel political deception of these past
several weeks.

On October 11, when the agreement was still secret, I addressed the nation
on Vietnam.

I spelled out what I saw as the greatest single roadblock to peace—Mr. Nixon's
unfailing acceptance of General Thieu's orders; his willingness to place the power
of this corrupt dictator ahead of freedom for our prisoners, life for our soldiers,
and an end to the war.

I also outlined my program for peace. It called for an end to the bombing,
an end to the shelling, and withdrawal in ninety days' time. It accepted the
North Vietnamese offer to free our prisoners as we withdraw.

Republican politicians ridiculed that proposal. They said it was "unrealistic,"
and they called it "surrender."

But that was not true, and they knew it.

Three days before I spoke, Dr. Kissinger had already embraced the same principles in private, in discussion with North Vietnam. But they called that "peace with honor"—the same results they called "surrender," just a few days before.

So what can we conclude today?

After four years of war, Mr. Nixon has closed the door to peace once again. If he escapes his responsibility now, do you think he will end the war after the election, once he is free from the will of the American people?

We know, too, that the war can be ended in a matter of hours, on the terms I have already proposed. If General Thieu says we cannot dictate peace to him, we need a president who will reply: "General Thieu, you are not going to dictate any more war for us."

Mr. Nixon will never say that. I will.

Mr. Nixon will never sign the agreement. I will.

Mr. Nixon will not end the war. It will be my very first act.

Now we must draw the painful conclusion that the events of recent weeks were not a path to peace, but a detour around Election Day. The officials who are sworn to serve you instead have sought to mislead you for their own political gain. Their strategy was designed to create the illusion of peace from Thursday, October 26—when Dr. Kissinger made his announcement—until Tuesday, November—when you will make your decision about the next president of the United States.

In a campaign marked by falsehood, sabotage, secret funds, special-interest deals, and criminal activity, this is the worst deceit of all. They have played politics with the Justice Department, the FBI, the Supreme Court, and even the Constitution. Now they play politics with our prisoners and our soldiers and life itself. It is they who treat our men like toy soldiers, to be knocked over by the hand that should protect them.

What we are seeing in this campaign is the manipulation of our hopes by men who know how to get power and want to keep it, but do not know what it is for. In politics, there are some things more precious than victory. One of them is truth.

But these men will say anything to win.

They will say that there is peace even in the midst of war. They will say that inflation is cut in half when in fact it is as high as it was before. They will say that the tide has been turned against crime when crime is at the highest tide in history.

But the truth is all around us. Ask the families of our prisoners if the fighting has ended. Ask a housewife if the cost of living is under control. Ask yourselves if you feel safe on a city street at night.

And ask yourselves if you really believe the incredible attacks on the Democratic Party in 1972. They are part of the same technique of fear and innuendo Mr. Nixon has used so often before—against Harry Truman, Congressman Voorhees, Helen Gahagan Douglas, and Adlai Stevenson, against Lyndon Johnson and Hubert Humphrey, and John and Robert Kennedy. This year, for example, Mr. Nixon tells you that the programs I have proposed would mean a 50 percent increase in federal taxes. That is a lie—and the President knows it.

He made the same charge at the Republican Convention—and when the press asked Administration officials to prove it, they could not even explain it.

I am tired of answering the same old lies.

I am tired of the lie that my economic proposals will put half the country on welfare. The truth is that they will reduce welfare by 30 percent and put the nation back to work.

I am tired of answering the lie that my tax reform will increase the taxes of working people and ordinary citizens, when the truth is that it will not take a single penny more from Americans who live on wages or salaries. Indeed, it will cut your property taxes at least by a third.

Mr. Nixon knows what my positions really are. But he does not want you to know. Why do you think he is so afraid to come out of the White House and meet me like a man, in face-to-face debate? Why is he so anxious to falsify my views? Why is he so unwilling to make his charges in front of me, where no distortion will go unchallenged?

The answer is clear. Mr. Nixon and his campaigners are trying to trick you into voting against yourself. They understand how you will vote when you learn what I want to do, and what they have done.

And what they have done with the war in Vietnam is the worst of their deeds.

That is why peace remains the overriding issue. For without peace, there will be no reduction in the cost of living. There will be no full employment. There will be no renewal of our purpose as a nation. And there will be no life at all for so many among us.

If Mr. Nixon disagrees with the main thrust of my remarks here this evening, I urge that we go together before the American people and clarify our differences on the issues tomorrow or Sunday, or even Monday, evening.

At this late stage of the campaign, it is past time he quit hiding behind his so-called surrogates or aides like Mr. Kissinger. Mr. Nixon is responsible for his own policies. He is the one who should reply on these crucial issues—not Mr. Kissinger. He is the one who should defend and clarify the issues in public debate with me—not Mr. Kissinger or some other aide.

I do not honestly know whether the war weighs as deeply on the minds of the American people as it does on mine. I do not honestly know whether the blunt words I have said tonight will help me or hurt me in this election. I do not really care.

For almost a decade, my heart has ached over the fighting and the dying in Vietnam. I cannot remember a day when I did not think of this tragedy. I can remember every picture of a bombed-out school or a napalmed child, and every letter from a family in South Dakota who lost their son. I remember the campaign of 1968, when we heard of a promise of peace. And I worry that unless this country votes for peace now, in the next campaign, in 1976, we will still be working out the "details" of a war that has gone on four more years.

I think of the words of Valerie Kuschner, whose husband has been a prisoner since 1967. "My husband," she said, "has already had his four more years."

Yet many of you wonder whether there really is another choice. Millions are confused and doubtful and suspicious of any candidate who pledges peace.

What can I tell you?

I can only say that there is no way I could continue a war I have hated from the beginning.

And this is the sharpest difference between Mr. Nixon and me. He has always supported that war. I have opposed it.

He has called Vietnam our finest hour. I have called it the saddest chapter in our national history.

He will not set a date for peace. As president, I will bring all of our troops and all of our prisoners home within ninety days of my inauguration.

This Tuesday will be a day of reckoning for America.

It will be the day when we decide between war and peace.

The Scripture says: "I have set before you life and death, blessing and cursing; now choose life so that thou and thy seed may live."

Thank you and God bless you.

Pre-Election Day Announcements by
President Richard M. Nixon
November 4–6, 1972

As the election campaign of 1972 drew to a close, President Nixon repeatedly emphasized the foreign policy achievements of his Administration.

Radio Address on Foreign Policy, November 4, 1972

Good afternoon:

Through the long years of America's involvement in Vietnam, our people's yearning for peace has largely been focused on winning an end to that difficult war. As a result, there has often been a tendency to lose sight of the larger prospects for peace in the rest of the world. As peace in Vietnam comes closer, we can look to the larger world and the long-term future with hope and satisfaction.

Four years ago I promised that we would move from an era of confrontation to an era of negotiation. I also said that we would maintain our own strength and work to restore that of our alliances, because the way to make real progress toward peace is to negotiate from strength and not from weakness. Because we have done so, the world today is more peaceful by far than it was 4 years ago. The prospects for a full generation of peace are brighter than at any time since the end of World War II.

In the past 4 years, we have concluded more—and more significant—agreements with the Soviets than in all the previous years since World War II. We have ended nearly a quarter century of mutual isolation between the United States and the People's Republic of China. All over the world, the tide toward negotiation is moving. North and South Korea are negotiating with one another. East and West Germany are negotiating with one another. A cease-fire has been in effect for more than 2 years in the Middle East. The leaders of India and Pakistan are talking with one another. The nations of Europe, of NATO, and of the Warsaw Pact are preparing to meet next year in a European Security Conference, and preparations are underway for negotiations on mutual and balanced reduction of armed forces in Central Europe.

All this is evidence of solid progress toward a world in which we can talk about our differences rather than fight about them.

Nineteen hundred seventy-two has been a year of more achievement for peace than any year since the end of World War II. This progress did not just happen by itself.

In my Inaugural Address nearly 4 years ago, I said that the greatest honor history can bestow is the title of peacemaker, but I also pointed out that peace does not come through wishing for it, that there is no substitute for days and even years of patient and prolonged diplomacy.

For the past 4 years this Nation has engaged in patient and prolonged diplomacy in every corner of the world, and we have also maintained the strength that has made our diplomacy credible and peace possible. As a result, we are well on the way toward erecting what I have often referred to as a structure of peace, a structure that rests on the hard concrete of common interests and mutual agreements, and not on the shifting sands of naive sentimentality.

That term, "a structure of peace," speaks an important truth about the nature of peace in today's world. Peace cannot be wished into being. It has to be carefully and painstakingly built in many ways and on many fronts, through networks of alliances, through respect for commitments, through patient negotiations, through balancing military forces and expanding economic interdependence, through reaching one agreement that opens the way to others, through developing patterns of international behavior that will be accepted by other powers. Most important of all, the structure of peace has to be built in such a way that all those who might be tempted to destroy it will instead have a stake in preserving it.

In the past 4 years, my efforts to build that structure of peace have taken me to 22 countries, including four world capitals never visited by an American President before—Peking, Moscow, Warsaw, and Bucharest. Everywhere I have traveled I have seen evidence that the times are on the side of peace, if America maintains its strength and continues on course. For example, ever since World War II, the world's people and its statesmen have dreamed of putting the nuclear genie back in the bottle, of controlling the dreaded nuclear arms race, but always that race remained unchecked until this year.

In Moscow last May, we and the Soviet Union reached the first agreement ever for limiting stategic nuclear arms. We signed that agreement last month in Washington. This was an historic beginning. It moved back the frontiers of fear. It helped check the dangerous spiral of nuclear weapons. It opened the way to further negotiations on further limitations on nuclear arsenals which will soon begin.

As we pursue these negotiations, however, let us remember that no country will pay a price for something that another country will give up for nothing. If we had scrapped the ABM missile system, as many advocated, we would never have achieved the first arms agreement with the Soviets. If we unilaterally slashed our defenses now as our opponents in this election advocate, the Soviets would have no incentive to negotiate further arms limitations.

Or take another example. After 10 years of recurring international monetary crises, we took bold actions a year ago to strengthen the dollar and to bring about a reformed international monetary system that would be fair to the United States and fair to the world. The result of these actions has been a solid and substantial beginning on just such a system, and the stage is now set for an international effort to achieve some of the most important monetary and trade reforms in history. As we complete these reforms in the years ahead, we can usher in a new age of world prosperity, a prosperity made even greater by the rapid expansion of peaceful trade that is now taking place, not only with our traditional trading partners but also with nations that have been our adversaries.

I cite these simply as examples of the broad, unfinished agenda of peace that now lies before us, the agenda of new starts made, of negotiations begun, of new relationships established, which now we must build on with the same initiative and imagination that achieved the initial breakthroughs. As we move forward on this agenda, we can see vast areas of peaceful cooperation to be explored.

We agreed in Peking to pursue cultural, journalistic, educational, and other exchanges, so that the world's most prosperous nation and its most populous nation can get to know one another again.

We agreed in Moscow to cooperate in protecting the environment, explore in space, fight disease. This means the day is fast approaching when a Russian cosmonaut and an American astronaut will shake hands in space, when a Russian chemist and an American biologist will work side by side to find a cure for cancer. And each time our nations join hands in the works of peace, we advance the day when nations will no longer raise their hands in warfare.

Throughout the world today America is respected. This is partly because we have entered a new era of initiative in American foreign policy, and the world's leaders and its people have seen the results. But it is also because the world has come to know America. It knows we are a nation of peaceful intentions, of honorable purposes, true to our commitments. We are respected because for a third of a century under six Presidents we have met the responsibilities of a great and free nation. We have not retreated from the world. We have not betrayed our allies. We have not fallen into the foolish illusion that we could somehow build a wall around America, here to enjoy our comforts, oblivious to the cries or the threats of others. We have maintained our strength.

There are those today who condemn as a relic of a cold war mentality the idea that peace requires strength. There are those who ridicule military expenditures as wasteful and immoral. Our opponents in this campaign have even described the great bipartisan tradition of negotiating from strength as one of the most damaging and costly cliches in the American vocabulary. If the day ever comes when the President of the United States has to negotiate from weakness, that will be a dangerous day, not only for America but for the whole world.

Those who scoff at balance of power diplomacy should recognize that the only alternative to a balance of power is an imbalance of power, and history shows that nothing so drastically escalates the danger of war as such an imbalance. It is precisely the fact that the elements to balance now exist that gives us a rare opportunity to create a system of stability that can maintain the peace, not just for a decade but for a generation and more.

The years ahead will not be easy. The choices will not be simple. They will require an extra measure of care in distinguishing between rhetoric and reality, between the easy temptation and the hard necessity. We will be told that all the things we want to do at home could be painlessly financed if we slashed our military spending. We will be told that we can have peace merely by asking for it, that if we simply demonstrate good will and good faith, our adversaries will do likewise, and that we need do no more. This is dangerous nonsense.

A heavy responsibility lies on the shoulders of those who hold or seek power in today's world, a responsibility not to court the public favor by fostering illusions that peace can be either achieved or kept without maintaining our responsibilities.

As we approach the end of the war in Vietnam, the great question is whether the end of that war will be only an interlude between wars or the beginning of a generation of peace for the world.

Five months ago, I delivered the first television address to the Soviet people ever made by an American President. I tried to tell them something about America, about the people of America, about our hopes, our desire for peace and progress, not only for ourselves but for all the people of the world. In that talk, I repeated an old story told in Russia about a traveler who was walking to another village, who stopped and asked a woodsman how long it would take him to get there. The woodsman replied he did not know. The traveler was angry, because he was sure the woodsman lived in the village and knew how far it was. But then as soon as he had gone a few steps further down to the road, the woodsman called out to him to stop. "It will take you 15 minutes," the woodsman said. "Why didn't you tell me that in the first place?" the traveler demanded. And the woodsman answered, "Because then I didn't know the length of your stride."

In these past 4 years, we and the other nations of the world have had a chance to measure the length of our strides. At last we are traveling in the same direction toward a world of peace, toward an era of negotiation, and of expanding cooperation. In the next 4 years, the President of the United States, whoever he is, will negotiate with the leaders of many nations on a broad range of issues vital to America, vital to the world. As we cast our ballots next Tuesday, the world will see whether we have changed the length of our stride.

If you approve the beginnings we have made, then your vote on election day to support those policies will be a message to the leaders of all other nations that the American people are not going to retreat, are not going to surrender. It will strengthen the President's hand immensely as we continue to move from confrontation to negotiation to cooperation all around the world as we build toward a generation of peace.

Thank you, and good afternoon.

*   *   *

Statement About Conclusion of Campaign, November 4, 1972

This election eve visit to California is not only the last rally in a long campaign, it is also my last such campaign appearance as a candidate for public office. It is fitting that it should be here, in California. This is my native State, and the State in which I began my political career 26 years ago.

This moment calls forth many memories. But what is most important to me is the fact that this campaign road is ending on a positive note—a note of hope and optimism for America. With election day fast approaching, Americans can stand united in the knowledge that, more than at any time in this century, the hope for a full generation of peace burns bright.

The world is a calmer, more rational place today than it was 4 years ago. After so much sacrifice, patience, and endurance, the American people can finally rejoice in the confidence that a fair and honorable peace in Vietnam can soon be achieved. In the world at large, 1972 has been a year of greater achievement for peace than any since the end of World War II.

I am proud that my Administration was able to make such great progress for peace, and I am determined that just as we have worked resolutely to achieve a peace with honor and without surrender, we will also achieve peace with prosperity.

And that prosperity must be real prosperity—a prosperity free of rampant inflation and ever-higher taxes. To this goal my Administration and I are pledged.

The signs are hopeful. The new economic figures announced this week give us fresh evidence that a strong tide of real prosperity is rising across the Nation. The latest employment statistics reveal that 82,500,000 Americans were at work in the month of October, nearly 300,000 more than a month earlier and more than 5 million more than when this Administration took office.

Jobs are still increasing at the fastest rate since 1956—at a rate twice as fast as the rate of growth of the population. While unemployment remains a serious concern, the strength and thrust of this progress promises to make strong inroads into this problem in the near future.

As for the cost of living, adjusted wholesale prices rose only one-tenth of one percent in October, the lowest increase since March. And our overall rate of inflation is now the lowest of any major industrial nation in the free world.

As citizens of the number one agricultural State of the Union, Californians will also be glad to know that we have some good news for the American farmer this week. Secretary of Agriculture Earl Butz has announced that farm exports will reach our $10 billion goal during this fiscal year—a goal once scoffed at by our opponents. This high level of farm sales was made possible, in part, by our improved relations with the People's Republic of China and the Soviet Union.

All of these indicators tell us that we have been on the right course, that the support the people have consistently expressed for this Administration's policies to keep inflation, taxes, and prices down, and the American economy growing and expanding, have been right on target.

The political voices of gloom who were so quick to give up, the political prophets of doom who said that American society was falling apart, and the American economy along with it—these misguided pessimists have been proven wrong.

We are a strong country, militarily and economically. The fibers of our social fabric are strong. Our spirit is strong. It is because we are strong that we have been able to work successfully for peace in the world and prosperity at home.

As I conclude the last campaign visit of my last campaign for public office, I see a strong, respected America, and a proud, united American people. None of this could have been achieved merely by government; it was done by the people.

When it comes down to the important things, Americans still stand together—that we are one America in conscience, in purpose, and in inspiration.

This campaign—my last campaign—will be over in a few short days. But the work of building a better America goes on. The work of building an honorable peace and a real prosperity goes on. And much remains to be done. We must continue to move justly and firmly in the second round of SALT disarmament talks, in our efforts to achieve balanced, mutual troop reductions in Europe, in our efforts to keep the peace in the volatile Mideast.

We must continue the transition of the American economy from a wartime to a peacetime footing by effective means such as this Administration's technical mobilization and reemployment program, which has already relocated more than 17,000 displaced aerospace engineers and is part of our overall strategy that has successfully provided workers with 2.3 million real jobs—not government make-work jobs—in the past year alone.

I promise that in the next 4 years I will continue to use every resource at my disposal to keep us building, to keep us leading the way, and to keep America strong, decent, and united.

*   *   *

Address on Election Eve, November 6, 1972

Good evening:

Tomorrow, 100 million Americans will have an opportunity to participate in a decision that will affect the future of America and the future of the world for generations to come.

Regardless of how you vote, I urge each of you to vote. By your vote, you can make sure that this great decision is made by a majority of Americans eligible to vote, and not simply left to the minority who bother to vote.

I am not going to insult your intelligence tonight or impose upon your time by rehashing all the issues of the campaign or making any last-minute charges against our opponents.

You know what the issues are. You know that this is a choice which is probably the clearest choice between the candidates for President ever presented to the American people in this century.

I would, however, urge you to have in mind tomorrow one overriding issue, and that is the issue of peace—peace in Vietnam and peace in the world at large for a generation to come.

As you know, we have made a breakthrough in the negotiations which will lead to peace in Vietnam. We have agreed on the major principles that I laid down in my speech to the Nation of May 8. We have agreed that there will be a ceasefire, we have agreed that our prisoners of war will be returned and that the missing in action will be accounted for, and we have agreed that the people of South Vietnam shall have the right to determine their own future without having a Communist government or a coalition government imposed upon them against their will.

There are still some details that I am insisting be worked out and nailed down because I want this not to be a temporary peace. I want, and I know you want, it to be a lasting peace. But I can say to you with complete confidence tonight that we will soon reach agreement on all the issues and bring this long and difficult war to an end.

You can help achieve that goal. By your votes, you can send a message to those with whom we are negotiating, and to the leaders of the world, that you back the President of the United States in his insistence that we in the United States seek peace with honor and never peace with surrender.

I will not go into the other issues tonight, except to say that as we move to peace, we will open doors to progress on many fronts here at home. It means that we can have something we haven't had since President Eisenhower was President 15 years ago—prosperity without war and without inflation.

It means we can have progress toward better education, better health—in all the areas that I have presented to the American people over these past 4 years.

It means that we can move toward a goal that every American wants: that is, opportunity for each person in this great and good land to go to the top in whatever particular activity he chooses regardless of his background.

Those, then, are the issues you will have in mind.

Let me say, finally, I want to thank you for the honor of serving as President for the past 4 years, and, regardless of your decision tomorrow, I can assure you that I shall continue to work for a goal that every American has: Let's make the next 4 years the best 4 years in America's history.

Thank you. Good evening.

Summary of the Guidelines of the Commission on Democratic Party Structure and Delegate Selection (the McGovern-Fraser Commission)

Following the raucous 1968 Democratic convention in Chicago, the party appointed a special commission to make future delegate selection more representative. The commission was chaired by South Dakota Senator George McGovern from 1969 to 1971 and by Representative Donald Fraser of Minnesota from 1971 to 1972.

A–1 Discrimination on the Basis of Race, Color, Creed, or National Origin

Requires that the six basic elements from the Special Equal Rights Committee be added to all state party rules

Requires affirmative steps to overcome past discrimination, including minority presence in the state delegation in reasonable relationship to group presence in the state as a whole

A–2 Discrimination on the Basis of Age or Sex

Requires affirmative steps to overcome past discrimination, including presence of young people (ages 18–30 and women in reasonable relationship to their province in the state as a whole)

Requires state parties to allow Democrats aged 18–30 to participate in all party affairs

A–3 Voter Registration

Urges each state party to assess the burdens of state law, custom, or practice, as outlined in the report of the Grass Roots Subcommittee, and to remove or alleviate such barriers

A–4 Costs and Fees; Petition Requirements

Urges removal of all costs and fees in the delegate selection process; requires removal of all fees over $10, of all mandatory assessments on delegates and alternates, and of all fees which would constitute a strain on the individual

Requires removal of all petition requirements in excess of 1% of the standard for measuring Democratic strength for any delegate candidacies

A–5 Existence of Party Rules

Requires state parties to adopt and make readily available rules which describe the delegate selection process with detail and clarity; lists seven specific aspects which such rules should include

Requires rules which will facilitate maximum participation

Requires explicit written rules with uniform dates and times for all meetings in the delegate selection process; exempts rural areas if dates and times are uniform within the geographic area

B–1   Proxy Voting

Requires state parties to forbid the use of proxy voting in all procedures for delegate selection

B–2   Clarity of Purpose

Requires state parties to make clear to voters how any given party process contributes to the presidential nomination

Requires state parties to designate the delegate selection process as distinct from other party business

B–3   Quorum Provisions

Requires that state parties adopt a quorum of not less than 40% for all committees involved in the delegate selection process

B–4   Selection of Alternates; Filling of Delegate and Alternate Vacancies

Requires state parties to prohibit the selection of alternates by the delegate himself or by the state chairman

Requires state parties to fill all vacancies through a timely and representative party committee, a reconvening of the original selection body, or the selection of the delegation itself

B–5   Unit Rule

Requires state parties to forbid the unit rule and the practice of instructing delegates to vote against their preferences at any stage of the delegate selection process

B–6   Adequate Representation of Minority Views on Presidential Candidates at Each Stage in the Delegate Selection Process

Urges each state party to provide for fair representation of minority views on presidential candidates; recommends that the 1972 Convention require such representation to the highest level of the process

Suggests that such representation be accomplished either by dividing delegate votes according to presidential strength or by selecting delegates from fairly apportioned districts; promises to stimulate additional discussion

B–7   Apportionment

Requires state parties to apportion delegates to the national convention on a formula giving equal weight to total population and prior Democratic vote for President

Requires convention states to select at least 75% of their delegates at the district
  level or below, requires convention states to apportion lower-level delegates
  by population and/or some measure of Democratic strength

C–1 Adequate Public Notice

Requires convention states to circulate a concise public statement of the relationship between ongoing party business and delegate selection
Requires primary states to identify the presidential preference of candidates for
  delegate and of candidates for any party committee which selects delegates;
  requires placement of "uncommitted" designation next to the names of those
  who do not reveal a preference

C–2 Automatic (Ex Officio) Delegates

Requires state parties to repeal rules which provide for ex officio delegates

C–3 Open and Closed Processes

Urges state parties to provide for easy access and frequent opportunity for party
  enrollment by unaffiliated voters and non-Democrats

C–4 Premature Delegate Selection (Timeliness)

Requires that all activities of delegate selection occur within the calendar year
  of the Convention
Requires state parties to prohibit officials elected or appointed before the calendar year from choosing nominating committees or proposing or endorsing
  a slate of delegates, even when challenge procedures exist

C–5 Committee Selection Processes

Requires state parties to publicize the delegate selection role (if any) of the
  state committee at the time of its election
Requires state parties to limit delegates chosen in this fashion to not more than
  10% of the state total; recommends that state parties not permit any part of
  the delegation to be selected by party committees

C–6 Slate Making

Requires state parties to extend to the process of nominating delegates all
  guarantees of full and meaningful opportunity to participate which apply to
  the delegate selection process
Requires any slate-making body to observe adequate public notice, easy access
  to participation, and right to challenge the result, with the proviso that a slate
  bearing the name of a presidential candidate be assembled with due consultation with that candidate or his representatives

THE VOTES IN THE 1972 ELECTION

CANDIDATES FOR PRESIDENT AND VICE PRESIDENT
Democratic—George S. McGovern; R. Sargent Shriver
Republican—Richard M. Nixon; Spiro T. Agnew

STATE	Total	Dem.	Rep.	ELECTORAL VOTE	
				D	R
Alabama	1,006,111	256,923	728,701	—	9
Alaska	95,219	32,967	55,349	—	3
Arizona	622,926	198,540	402,812	—	6
Arkansas	651,320	199,892	448,541	—	6
California........	8,367,862	3,475,847	4,602,096	—	45
Colorado	953,884	329,980	597,189	—	7
Connecticut......	1,384,277	555,498	810,763	—	8
Delaware........	235,516	92,283	140,357	—	3
Dist. of Col.	163,421	127,627	35,226	3	—
Florida	2,583,283	718,117	1,857,759	—	17
Georgia	1,174,772	289,529	881,496	—	12
Hawaii	270,274	101,409	168,865	—	4
Idaho	310,379	80,826	199,384	—	4
Illinois	4,723,236	1,913,472	2,788,179	—	26
Indiana.........	2,125,529	708,568	1,405,154	—	13
Iowa	1,225,944	496,206	706,207	—	8
Kansas	916,095	270,287	619,812	—	7
Kentucky........	1,067,499	371,159	676,446	—	9
Louisiana........	1,051,491	298,142	686,852	—	10
Maine...........	417,042	160,584	256,458	—	4
Maryland........	1,353,812	505,781	829,305	—	10
Massachusetts....	2,458,756	1,332,540	1,112,078	14	—
Michigan	3,489,727	1,459,435	1,961,721	—	21
Minnesota	1,741,652	802,346	898,269	—	10
Mississippi.......	645,963	126,782	505,125	—	7
Missouri.........	1,855,803	697,147	1,153,852	—	12
Montana	317,603	120,197	183,976	—	4
Nebraska	576,289	169,991	406,298	—	5
Nevada..........	181,766	66,016	115,750	—	3
New Hampshire ..	334,055	116,435	213,724	—	4
New Jersey	2,997,229	1,102,211	1,845,502	—	17
New Mexico	386,241	141,084	235,606	—	4
New York	7,165,919	2,951,084	4,192,778	—	41
North Carolina ...	1,518,612	438,705	1,054,889	—	13
North Dakota	280,514	100,384	174,109	—	3
Ohio............	4,094,787	1,558,889	2,441,827	—	25
Oklahoma	1,029,900	247,147	759,025	—	8
Oregon..........	927,946	392,760	486,686	—	6
Pennsylvania.....	4,592,106	1,796,951	2,714,521	—	27
Rhode Island	415,808	194,645	220,383	—	4
South Carolina ...	673,960	186,824	477,044	—	8
South Dakota	307,415	139,945	166,476	—	4
Tennessee	1,201,182	357,293	813,147	—	10
Texas	3,471,281	1,154,289	2,298,896	—	26
Utah...........	478,476	126,284	323,643	—	4
Vermont.........	186,947	68,174	117,149	—	3
Virginia	1,457,019	438,887	988,493	—	11*
Washington......	1,470,847	568,334	837,135	—	9
West Virginia	762,399	277,435	484,964	—	6
Wisconsin	1,852,890	810,174	989,430	—	11
Wyoming........	145,570	44,358	100,464	—	3
Total...........	77,718,554	29,170,383	47,169,911	17	520

*A Republican elector voted for John Hospers

Election of 1976

BETTY GLAD is Professor of Political Science at the University of Illinois, Urbana. Her publications include Charles Evans Hughes and the Illusion of Innocence *and* Jimmy Carter: In Search of the Great White House.

Election of 1976

by *Betty Glad*

The race for the Democratic nomination in 1976 was one of the more extraordinary in American history. Jimmy Carter, a former one-term governor of Georgia barely known to the country at the beginning of the campaign, raced to the front after the first caucus and never seriously lost momentum during the following three and one-half months of primaries. By summer, it seemed he had acquired almost magical powers. Opposition faded after the last primaries, and the Democratic convention seemed more like a coronation than a contest. Theodore H. White, a journalist who has spent his professional life covering political leaders, told the *American Time Recorder* on August 15, "I think Jimmy Carter has a chance to become the first candidate ever to win all fifty states in an election."

The remarkable aspect of Carter's rise was that he had not come in on the wave of a clearly articulated protest movement, as had Democrats William Jennings Bryan in 1896 and George McGovern in 1972. Nor was he the choice of the leaders of his own party. Even on his home turf in Georgia, most Democratic officeholders failed to endorse him until it became apparent that he could not be stopped.

Carter won because his campaign was best geared to the new primary system, because the media provided the fuel to sustain him, and because he understood the mood of the country, now disillusioned by the loss of the Vietnam War and by Watergate. He met the people's need for a President who could restore their confidence in themselves and in the political process. Ironically, the very fact that the public had little perception of what Carter was really like enabled him to shape his image to meet the demands of new circumstances.

There were nine candidates at the opening of the presidential campaign in January 1976. The most prominent was Senator Henry Jackson of Washington. Throughout his thirty years in the Congress, Jackson had shown himself to be an old-style New Deal liberal on domestic issues; on foreign affairs, however, he was perceived as a conservative, having backed the war in Vietnam, a strong defense buildup, and a tough line against the Soviet Union. Also, he opposed busing as a means to racial integration. Lloyd M. Bentsen, Jr., of Texas, with only two years in the Senate, was the other middle-of-the-road contender.

To their right stood Alabama's governor George Wallace, who had based his political career on opposing Washington and the federal attempt to integrate schools in the South. He had received 10 million votes as the American Independent party candidate in 1968 and was ahead in the popular vote in the 1972 Democratic primaries until he was shot in a Maryland shopping center. Although confined to a wheelchair, by 1976 he had recovered to the point where he was ready once again to try for the Presidency.

The liberal field was crowded with Senator Birch Bayh of Indiana; seven-term congressman Morris Udall of Arizona; R. Sargent Shriver, Jr., former director of the Peace Corps and Anti-Poverty program and George McGovern's running mate in 1972; Governor Milton J. Shapp of Pennsylvania; Fred Harris of Oklahoma, a southern populist without the racist accoutrements; and Terry Sanford, the president of Duke University and a former governor of North Carolina.

Standing in the wings was Senator Hubert H. Humphrey of Minnesota. In the late fall of 1975, Humphrey had told Congressman Paul Simon of Illinois that he was available, although he would not lift a finger to obtain the nomination. Throughout the campaign, Humphrey hinted he would come in at the end if there was no other clear choice, but still declined actively to seek the nomination. His strategy was to be everyone's second choice in case of a deadlock at the convention.

Carter defied categorization. It was clear from his rhetoric and earlier career that he rejected Wallace's racism. But it was also clear to those who looked at his record that he was not a traditional, big-spending, old-line Democrat. His support of Jackson in the 1972 Democratic primaries and of a strong national defense, along with his stand against busing, suggested that he would be no flaming liberal in the White House. But Carter refused to apply political labels to himself and obscured his stands on controversial issues.

According to R. W. Apple of *The New York Times,* the frontrunners at the campaign's outset were Jackson, Bayh, Humphrey, and Carter. The inclusion of Carter was certainly not based on his standing in the polls. He had not even been mentioned in the Gallup polls as a presidential possibility until the spring of 1975, when he secured approximately 1 percent of the Democratic and independent vote. In December, Carter ranked only in the 8 percent of "all others" category among Democratic voters. Nor was he popular with political leaders. Early polls of regional Democratic meetings in the Northeast and Mid-west showed Carter as having practically no party support. The December Gallup poll found that only 17 percent of a national elite sample (drawn from leaders in business, government, and education) thought Carter would make a good President. A majority (52 percent) of the respondents felt they knew too little to judge whether or not Carter would make a good President.

Three days before his formal announcement, Carter said on "Meet the Press" that he would run in every state primary. Seventy percent of the delegates, Carter later told Tom Ottenad of the *St. Louis Post Dispatch,* would be chosen in these primaries, and weights were assigned to each state based on the delegates to be chosen, the potential media impact of a victory, and the relative strength of the opposition. Carter's plan was to apportion the 250 days available for campaigning the next year in accordance with these weights. The highest priority was given to New Hampshire, though Hamilton Jordan, Carter's campaign manager, thought it best to play down their effort. A strong showing would have more impact if it came as a surprise. "The press," Jordan pointed out, "shows an exaggerated interest in the early primaries as they represent the first confrontation between candidates, their contrasting strategies and styles." Flor-ida and Illinois ranked second and third. Iowa, which turned out to be the first caucus state, initially ranked behind the others.

In organizing the early primary states, Carter did not rely on local party leaders. Much like John F. Kennedy in 1960, Carter built up his own personal organization in a few key states. What was unique about the Carter effort was that he accomplished it with little money, a small personal following, and only a handful of aides.

Because he had no official responsibilities, Carter could campaign early and full time. By June 1975, according to his staff's figures, he had traveled more than 50,000 miles, visited 37 states, given over 200 speeches, and appeared on 93 radio and TV shows. He accepted invitations that better-known politicians would have ignored. His first trip to Iowa, for example, was in response to an invitation to attend a retirement party in Le Mars for Marie Jahn, an official of Plymouth County. Flattered that a candidate for the Presidency would bother to attend such a small event, she and several of her friends immediately com-mitted themselves to his campaign. Though he did recruit a few public officials and political activists, Carter mainly relied on family, friends, and Georgia volunteers to bear the brunt of the canvassing. In January 1976, for example, the Peanut Brigade, a plane-load of Georgians, paid $150 each for a chartered jet flight to New Hampshire to canvass for Carter.

In addition to his strategic and organizational skills, Carter showed finesse in managing the media. By fall of 1975 the national press was looking for any straw in the wind to mark the leaders in the presidential race, and Carter aides knew exactly how to promote Carter into that category. Early qualification for federal matching funds under the new campaign finance law—$5,000 in each of twenty states—was the first hurdle. After some unexpected difficulties (due to the requirement that candidates report their contributions minus fundraising costs), Carter was able to pass the qualifying test by September. Secret Service protection, which was offered after he qualified for federal matching funds, was accepted with alacrity.

Polls showing where party leaders were leaning were used to Carter's advantage. When Tim Kraft, who was handling the Iowa effort, learned that the *Des Moines Register and Tribune* planned a poll at a party dinner on October 25, he mobilized Carter supporters. Although only about a quarter of the 4,000 diners bothered to vote, Carter came in first. On November 16, in the presidential preference poll at the Florida Democratic state convention, Carter won a "whopping" 697 of the 1,035 votes cast. Milton Shapp, the only other candidate to attend the convention, came in second with 60 votes. Carter said, "This vote in Florida was the first major test of strength in the South . . . a good indication of what's going to happen in 1976."

Knowing that first impressions are apt to be lasting, the Carter people took other steps to influence the media's initial perception of their candidate. Carter's autobiography, *Why Not the Best?,* came out in 1975. With its idyllic portrait of his roots and his religious and political life, the book suggested that he was a new kind of political leader who could heal the country's wounds. When reporters interviewed him, Carter would invariably ask: "Have you read my book?" Moreover, his chief aides—Hamilton Jordan, Jody Powell, Peter Bourne, and Patrick Caddell—influenced the interpretation of the campaign by taking reporters into their confidence, sometimes giving them peeks at strategy memos. The impact of information thus leaked was heightened by its confidentiality. By the time journalist Kandy Stroud was allowed to see the Jordan memorandum of November 1974, it was treated like the Magna Carta. As she wrote in her book, *How Jimmy Won,* "The original was kept under lock and key. . . . And anyone wishing to read the memo was required to make a special appointment in Jordan's office and any excerpts were to be approved by Jordan himself. . . . No exact quotes were to be used."

To obtain steady, often complimentary, copy Carter presented a drama with a continuing storyline and a colorful cast of supporting family characters. Lillian, Billy, Ruth, Gloria, Uncle Alton, and Cousin Hugh were all interesting in their own right, as well as tangible proof of how close Jimmy was to many American types. The decision to base the campaign in Carter's hometown of Plains, Georgia, despite the problems of accessibility, was a master stroke. Big-city reporters could see for themselves the virtues of a friendly small town, unspoiled by urban blight, smog, and impersonality. Even the peanut became a symbol; after some hesitation, the staff decided that it would introduce a note of humility in the campaign. As one aide noted, "Humility was not our long suit."

Carter's handling of the media paid off. After that "silly poll on Iowa" (as Morris Udall called it), R. W. Apple noted that Carter "appears to have taken a surprising but solid lead" in Iowa's delegate race. Major newspapers and syndicated columnists began to take him seriously. Marquis Childs wrote on December 16, 1975, "Visionary as it seems, I believe Carter at the present moment has a better chance than any of the others to win the nomination."

On January 19, Carter "won" the caucuses in Iowa. Of those designating a favorite, 27.6 percent chose him—more than double the 13.1 percent of the votes Birch Bayh received. Afterwards UPI and *Time* marked him as the potential frontrunner, and he acquired the press retinue that assured him widespread coverage for his New Hampshire campaign. George Wallace's smashing victory over Carter in the Mississippi caucuses the next week and Harris's tie with him in the Oklahoma caucuses two weeks after that were not perceived as genuinely competitive contests and did not change these perceptions of Carter.

In the New Hampshire primary on February 24, 23,000 people voted for Carter, giving him 28.4 percent of the vote to Udall's 22.7 percent, Bayh's 15.2 percent, Harris's 10.8 percent, Shriver's 8.2 percent, and Humphrey's 5.6 percent. The liberal field took more than 60 percent of the total vote, and Carter had no competition from conservatives, with Jackson and Wallace bypassing the state. But Carter led each of the men in the race, and so he reaped the publicity bonanza Jordan had anticipated would go to the winner of the first primary. His face was on the covers of *Time* and *Newsweek,* the stories totaling 2,630 lines, compared to 300 for all the others, of which 96 went to Udall, the second-place finisher. In the week following the New Hampshire primary, as the political scientist Thomas Patterson pointed out in *The Mass Media Election,* Carter received three times the television news coverage and four times the newspaper coverage of his competitors.

Once the press declared Carter the frontrunner, there was a subtle shift in the way it treated other candidates. They were now only the challengers. The Massachusetts primary on March 2, the first in which all candidates were running, could have been disastrous for Carter. He ran a poor fourth (13.9 percent) behind Jackson (22.3 percent), Udall (17.7 percent), and Wallace (16.7 percent). Only Harris (7.6 percent), Shriver (7.2 percent), and Bayh (4.8 percent) ran behind Carter. But even that did not cause Carter to lose frontrunner status. Most media saw it as *Time* did: Massachusetts had "slowed the momentum" for Carter and to "recapture that forward thrust" he had to "run strongly (not win) against Wallace" in Florida, Illinois, and North Carolina.

The Carter people had proposed Florida—with its eighty-one delegates— as Carter's first crucial test. Riding the anti-busing wave, Wallace in 1972 had captured 42 percent of the vote and won every congressional district. Carter presented himself in 1976 as the man who could beat Wallace on his own turf and remove him as a factor in national politics. As a Southerner who had campaigned against Washington and the "big shots," Carter would appeal to potential Wallace voters. As a moderate on racial matters, he was the candidate for anti-Wallace liberals. When the liberal contenders were persuaded to stay out of Florida, labor and liberal activists fell in behind Carter—some only for the Florida race. The United Auto Workers, for example, campaigned for Carter in Florida in order to weaken Wallace before the Michigan primaries. What Carter understood—and many liberals did not—was that, if he beat Wallace in Florida, it might be too late for liberal voters to go to more congenial candidates later. With Wallace weakened, Carter would have a free run in the South, racking up delegates and gaining momentum.

On March 9, Carter edged out Wallace by a small margin of 34.3 to 30.6 percent, with Jackson taking 23.9 percent. He was aided by a silent issue that neither he nor Jackson (the only major northern candidate to enter the race) discussed. Wallace had to campaign in a wheelchair. "All they see is the spoke of my wheelchair, all humped over, saying the same thing," Wallace told one journalist. "It's hard to beat." According to an NBC exit poll, over 50 percent of the voters said they agreed with George Wallace, but 19.5 percent of them had voted for someone else because they were concerned about Wallace's health.

After Carter's Florida win, the press provided the publicity that would keep his campaign going. Scarce on resources and personnel, the Carter people had not been able to organize past Florida. As Joel McCleary, Carter's national financial director, said: "After Florida it was NBC, CBS, and *The New York Times.*" Patrick Caddell noted: "After Florida, there was one serious candidacy—Carter's . . .; because the media had made it that way."

The run-everywhere strategy enabled Carter to enter the Illinois primary, without appearing to challenge Chicago Mayor Richard J. Daley. Aside from the uncommitted slate led by the mayor in Cook County (where Carter ran no delegates), the only real opposition was from a weakened George Wallace. The two liberal candidates on the ballot—Fred Harris and Sargent Shriver—never got their campaigns off the ground. In the vote on March 16, Carter led the popularity poll with 48.1 percent of the vote (to Wallace's 27.6 percent, Shriver's 16.3 percent, and Harris's 5 percent) and won fifty-five delegates.

Carter's impressive win in North Carolina on March 23 (53.6 to 34.7 percent for Wallace) was aided by the fact that former governor Terry Sanford had withdrawn from the race the day after the Mississippi caucuses. The other conservative southern alternative, Lloyd Bentsen of Texas, pulled out of the race after his poor showing in Oklahoma.

In New York on April 6, Jackson took 38 percent of the vote; Udall, 25.5 percent; and Carter, only 12.8 percent, while 23.7 percent of the vote remained uncommitted. The press could have raised questions about the viability of Carter's candidacy. This was the second major industrial state in the North where Carter had had real competition, and he was overwhelmed. Ben Wattenberg, then with the Jackson campaign, recalls how he woke up the morning after in a hotel room and saw the following on what he thought was the *Today Show:* " 'Well, it's now a showdown between Carter and Humphrey.' I literally fell off the bed. Instead of it finally being a head-to-head clash between Jackson and Carter, it was still Carter versus the pack, and the pack then was Udall and Jackson, symbolized by Humphrey."

Actually most newspapers and television stations that morning featured a photograph of a triumphant Carter, in a Harry Truman-like pose, reading the headlines of a Wisconsin paper that earlier in the evening had proclaimed Udall the winner in that state. Because the New York race had seemed a foregone conclusion, NBC and CBS had shifted their attention to Wisconsin where Carter was in a tight race with Morris Udall. When Carter's win became apparent later on election night, by 271,220 to 263,771 (a margin of 7,449 votes), he had a major press bonanza.

The ethnic purity flap was the only serious crisis Carter faced during the entire primary campaign. On April 2, in an interview with Sam Roberts of the New York *Daily News,* Carter responded to a question about scattered-site public housing by saying: "I see nothing wrong with ethnic purity being maintained. I would not force a racial integration of a neighborhood by government action. But I would not permit discrimination against a family moving into the neighborhood." Four days later, when Ed Rabel, the CBS correspondent traveling with Carter, asked Carter to explain this statement, Carter noted his opposition to governmental programs designed to "inject black families into a white neighborhood," and talked of not being opposed to ethnics and blacks who try to maintain the "ethnic purity of their neighborhood," and said he considered it a natural inclination to do so.

Astonished, the reporters with Carter gathered in the back of the press bus and played their tapes again, to see if they had heard Carter correctly. For all his black support, could Carter be a closet racist? When they pushed at Carter at later press conferences, he dug himself in even deeper, speaking of a "diametrically opposite kind of family," and "the intrusion of alien groups into a neighborhood." The whole issue was put to rest, however, on April 13 when Martin Luther King, Sr., at a rally in downtown Atlanta, assured a cheering audience that Carter's slip of the tongue did not represent his thinking, that all men make mistakes and that he personally forgave Carter.

By the time of the primary campaign in Pennsylvania, which Jordan had identified as the "make-or-break" state, Carter was receiving much better press coverage than either Jackson or Udall. One day when all three were in Philadelphia, the Philadelphia *Bulletin* featured two front-page stories on Carter and ran his picture twice in the first four pages. The other candidates were covered in brief paragraphs.

Jackson and Udall, moreover, were mortally wounded by the freeze on federal funding from March 22 to May 21, due to problems in the makeup of the Federal Election Commission. Both had counted on federal matching funds for Pennsylvania and had to curtail severely their advertising and travel. Carter, however, was able to take advantage of a loophole in the federal campaign finance law. The Supreme Court had ruled that a candidate could spend as much of his own money as he wanted. With his own personal wealth, friends in the banks of Georgia, and frontrunner status in the presidential lottery, Carter was able to secure large personal loans to fund the Pennsylvania and later campaigns. From March through May, Jimmy Carter and the Committee for Jimmy Carter borrowed a total of $775,000 from various Georgia banks.

On election day in Pennsylvania, April 27, Carter took 37 percent of the preferential vote to Jackson's 24.6 percent, Udall's 18.7 percent and Wallace's 11.3 percent. Carter took 64 of the delegates to Udall's 22, Jackson's 19, Shapp's 17, and Wallace's 3—with the rest to be appointed later on the basis of strength in the preferential context. A *Washington Post* exit poll showed that 46 percent of the voters would have preferred Humphrey, had he been a declared candidate. Organized labor and the political professionals who had rallied around Jackson, in an "Anyone But Carter" effort, had not been able to deliver this vote to the

Senator from Washington. Many people voted for Carter because he was the best known. According to Thomas Patterson, 25 percent of the voters by the time of the Pennsylvania primary knew only Carter, and most of these voted for him. Of those voters who knew all three candidates, Carter received half the votes cast.

After the Pennsylvania primary Carter acted as if his nomination were a foregone conclusion. He would cut back his campaigning pace, he said, in order to concentrate on unifying the party, identifying the issues, and preparing for the general election. Carter's aides began suggesting to tardy politicians that they should get on board the bandwagon before it was too late. At a breakfast fundraiser in New York, Carter supporter William van den Heuvel offended New York Governor Hugh Carey, who had not committed to any candidate, with the statement, "The train is leaving the station."

Certainly Carter seemed to have a clear field ahead. Birch Bayh had "suspended" his campaign on March 4 after his seventh-place finish in the Massachusetts primary. Shriver quit on March 22, and Harris followed on April 8. (Both needed the federal matching funds, so they technically remained in the race, leaving their names on the ballots in several states.) Before the Pennsylvania primary, Humphrey had said he would enter the race only if Carter seemed likely to enter the first ballot with fewer than 1,100 delegates. After the Pennsylvania primary, Carter appeared too strong, and Humphrey disappointed his followers by announcing on April 29 that he had insufficient time and organization to campaign actively for the nomination. "The one thing I don't need at this stage of life is to be ridiculous," he said with tears in his eyes. Shortly after this press conference, Jackson, out of money, flew home to Seattle where he announced that he would no longer actively pursue the nomination.

These withdrawals left Udall as the only one among the original starters who could possibly stop Jimmy Carter. A charming, intelligent man, Udall had run a good, issue-oriented campaign. Unlike the other starters, he held his personal following even as Jimmy Carter had built up momentum. Had he taken Wisconsin, he would have become a serious contender. But he never received the press attention that might have won him a state and brought him the money to win other states.

There were two late entries in the presidential sweepstakes. After the Illinois primary, Idaho's Senator Frank Church and California's Governor Edmund (Jerry) Brown, Jr., announced that they would seek the nomination. Brown, the youngest of the candidates at 38 and a proponent of the neo-liberal doctrine that Americans would have to lower their expectations of government, decided to enter the race after the Massachusetts primary. Frank Church, an old-style liberal who had opposed the Vietnam War, had planned to enter the race earlier, but his work as the head of the Senate committee investigating the CIA kept him out of the race longer than he intended. At the time he plunged in, he assumed that, as the only late entry in the race, he could clean up in the Western states, including California, and then pick up other votes at the convention.

Neither Brown nor Church, however, had much chance of stopping Carter. They were starting with zero delegates at a time when it was too late even to acquire field delegates and to build organizations in many of the remaining states. Moreover, Carter had momentum. Network exit polls suggested that Carter had broadly based support—the black vote, the Wallace vote, the labor vote, the business vote, the liberal and conservative vote. A *Time* poll showed that he was the candidate who could best beat Ford in the fall campaign. Voters began to regard Carter more favorably as he began to look like the winner. Money was pouring in. After the Florida primary, Carter began to surpass all his competitors in money received. With his Pennsylvania victory, Carter soared way above all the others. He reached a peak of $2.25 million by May 31, fully $1.5 million ahead of his closest competitor. Federal matching funds followed private money.

The first primary after Pennsylvania reinforced the impression that Carter was unstoppable. On May 1 in Texas, he beat Lloyd Bentsen, now running as a favorite son, winning 92 out of 98 delegates. On May 4 he won Indiana with 68 percent of the vote and his home state of Georgia with 83.4 percent. (The Georgia primary had been postponed from its original March 9 date, giving Carter time to get his bandwagon going.) On May 6 Carter took Tennessee by 77.6 percent, although he lost Alabama to Wallace, taking only 8.6 percent of the delegates.

Yet, beneath the surface Carter remained vulnerable. By May 4 he had 553 delegates according to the *New York Times*—slightly over one third of the 1,505 needed to nominate. And not all Democrats were happy with this rush to Carter. As a *Time* poll showed, Carter was the choice of 39 percent of Democratic voters, with 59 percent favoring other candidates. More Democrats would prefer Humphrey if they were voting solely on the basis of issues.

From mid-May Carter began to suffer reversals that, had they occurred earlier, might have knocked him out of the race. On May 11 Frank Church beat Carter in Nebraska (38.5 to 37.6 percent). Brown, who had been drawing enthusiastic crowds of the sort that Carter never attracted, won Maryland on May 18 (48.4 to 37.1 percent). On the same day, Udall ran only one percentage point behind Carter in Michigan (43.4 to 43.1 percent). Had it not been for the 5,738 votes that went to Shriver and 4,081 to Harris, Udall, who was only 2,425 votes behind Carter, might have won. Carter's victory was even less impressive considering he had the support of Henry Ford, UAW President Leonard Woodcock, and Detroit Mayor Coleman Young. On May 25 Carter lost Oregon and Idaho to Church, and Nevada to Brown. On June 1 he suffered a dismal defeat at the hands of Church in Montana, and Rhode Island went to a slate of ostensibly "uncommitted" delegates (really pledged to Brown or Humphrey) in an extremely close contest.

Carter's decision to run everywhere minimized the impact of these losses, for each was usually offset by a countervailing win. When Carter lost Nebraska on May 11 he achieved a narrow win over Udall in Connecticut. The night of his defeats in Idaho, Nevada, and Oregon, he had compensatory wins in Arkansas and Kentucky. The night he lost Rhode Island and Montana, Carter won in George McGovern's home state of South Dakota. Even when Brown and Church won, Carter picked up delegates. In late May, Carter told reporters in New York City that his wins in the three southern primaries and some caucus statcs had put him over the 1,000 mark. In Los Angeles in early June, Carter advised Jerry Brown to count delegates: "I would say that someone who has 1,000 delegates is ahead of someone who has 25."

To avoid a possible tailspin after the last primaries—California, New Jersey, and Ohio on June 8—Carter enlisted the support of Mayor Daley. Brown would almost certainly be victorious in California. The slate of uncommitted Brown/ Humphrey delegates in New Jersey had held together and now emerged as a fairly solid stumbling block for Carter. Only Ohio, where Udall and Church were both entered, looked promising for Carter. Governor John J. Gilligan was supporting him, and there was a sizable conservative vote in the southern part of the state. To focus attention on Ohio, Daley explained in a press conference on primary day that a Carter win there would be decisive. No one, Daley added in obvious allusion to Humphrey, should have the nomination handed to him after refusing to take part in the primaries.

That evening Carter lost big in California—Brown taking 59 percent of the vote to Carter's 20.4 percent. In New Jersey the uncommitted slate received 42 percent to Carter's 28 percent. But in Ohio Carter captured 52.3 percent of the vote against Udall's 21.2 percent and Church's 13.9 percent. Overall he won 218 delegates that day, bringing his total count up to 1,117—short of the 1,505 required for nomination.

Within the next few days everyone agreed with Daley about Ohio, and the opposition to Carter collapsed. Wallace, Humphrey, Jackson, Shapp, Church, and Harris all released their delegates and offered full support. Though Udall technically remained a candidate, he released his delegates to vote as they pleased. On June 25 Brown also conceded, saying: "Governor Carter appears certain to be nominated, and if he is, I will enthusiastically support his candidacy in the fall."

Humphrey's vacillation had contributed to the political vacuum through which Carter had driven to secure the Democratic nomination. Gallup polls showed Humphrey the first choice of Democratic voters from January through late May. According to the various exit polls, he could have won the Iowa caucuses and the Florida, Illinois, and Pennsylvania primaries had he entered. As it was, his shadow candidacy cast a pall over the other liberal candidates. Organized labor frittered away its influence, giving desultory support to a variety of candidates. Party leaders such as Joseph Crangle and Paul Simon dissipated their energies on draft Humphrey movements that went nowhere. Most important, Humphrey's apparent availability for a draft encouraged the media and the party not to take other liberal candidates too seriously. According to *The New York Times,* just before the Pennsylvania primary, Speaker of the House Thomas P. O'Neill, Jr., told friends that he preferred Humphrey to any of the candidates then in the race. Jackson was seriously weakened in Pennsylvania because he was widely perceived as a stalking horse for Humphrey. Brown's later victories, as *The New York Times* suggested on May 11, were generally viewed as a boost for Humphrey.

Ironically, Humphrey, the old-line professional, was less aware than Jimmy Carter, the supposed amateur, that the 1976 primaries were a new ball game. Since 1968 the percentage of delegates chosen in primaries had risen from 30 to 70 percent. This and the abolition of the winner-take-all primaries made it very unlikely that late entrants could win the race. Moreover, a decision at the convention to nominate someone who had avoided most of the primaries would have raised serious questions of legitimacy. "A whole lot worse things could happen to the country," the *Washington Post* said on April 29, "than for Hubert Humphrey to be his party's nominee. But it matters how he gets there."

Still, there was an outside chance of stopping Carter after Pennsylvania if his three remaining opponents had worked together. But ideological differences, divergent ambitions, and fears of being labeled as spoilers prevented this. Representatives from the three campaigns did meet to discuss the possibility of strategically dividing up the territory so that Carter would have to face each opponent one on one. Thus attempting a political power block, Udall stayed out of Nebraska, where Church had been campaigning, and Maryland, where Brown was ahead. The plan foundered, however, when self-interest took over and Brown ran a write-in campaign in Oregon where Church was competing with Carter, and Church competed with Udall in Ohio. To make matters worse, none of the previously withdrawn candidates would endorse Udall, Brown, or Church.

With the collapse of the opposition after June 8, Carter worked to solidify the party. As early as mid-April, he had solicited information on vice presidential possibilities. In early June, he made public a large list of candidates, drawing from all segments of the party. His designation of Walter Mondale was not announced until the convention, but in choosing the liberal Minnesota senator he threw out a line to the party professionals and liberals he had beaten in the primaries.

To avoid party divisiveness at the convention, Carter's aides began working on the platform in early June. A draft plank pledged to breaking up vertically integrated oil interests was reduced to a vague commitment to free competition in the crude oil industry. Red-flag issues such as decriminalization of marijuana and protection of homosexual rights were avoided altogether. Southerners agreed to sidestep the busing issue. Blacks agreed to a restricted welfare reform plank. Former anti-Vietnam war protesters agreed to a provision to permit the President to grant pardons to deserters on a case-by-case basis, dropping a previous plank pledging blanket pardons. Even organized labor accepted general statements on full employment and national health insurance, foregoing specific references to the Humphrey-Hawkins full-employment bill or the Kennedy-Corman national health insurance bill.

At the convention, the presentation of the platform was less an occasion for debate than a chance for a parade of leading Democrats to signify by their presence that the party was now a family. Four names were placed in nomination: Carter, Udall, Brown, and Ellen McCormack (the anti-abortion candidate committed to one side of an issue that had been brushed over in this extraordinary campaign). Carter won by 2,238 1/2 votes to Udall's 329 1/2, Brown's 300 1/2, Wallace's 57, and McCormack's 22, with a scattering of votes for others.

In his acceptance speech, Carter invoked the names of Roosevelt, Truman, Kennedy, and Johnson, saying he had always been a Democrat. But in his rhetoric he was still the outsider and the populist. "I have never met a Dem-

ocratic President," he said. And he proclaimed his opposition to "special influence and privilege." Carter saw "no reason why big shot crooks should go free
and the poor ones go to jail." He called for a fairer tax system and denounced
exclusive private schools, as well as the self-perpetuating alliance between money
and politics. "Too many have had to suffer at the hands of a political and
economic elite," he said.

It was unusual rhetoric coming from a man whose forces had successfully
blunted any radical edge in the platform. But the Democrats were in no mood
to note contradictions. After Carter's acceptance speech, party chairman Robert
Strauss invited the most important Democrats to the podium—Jackson, Udall,
Church, Brown, Wallace, Daley, Humphrey, Representative Barbara Jordan,
Senators Edmund Muskie and John Glenn, Mayor Abraham Beame of New
York, and Governor Reuben Askew of Florida. Linking arms and joining hands,
they sang "We Shall Overcome."

Carter won over the traditional party leaders because of his apparent appeal
to so many different voting groups. As Leonard Woodcock noted when he
endorsed Carter, "If a political genius had offered to produce a candidate who
could carry the working class as well as the crucial black, moderate, and liberal
vote in the North, and at the same time beat the strident segregationist of the
South, he would have been called a dreamer. And yet, that is what Jimmy
Carter has done."

He had done this, in part, by downplaying the role of issues in his campaign.
As Carter told a group of network executives, the only "Presidents he knew of
who [had] emphasized the issues were Dewey, Goldwater, and McGovern."
Instead, Carter affirmed principles to which few could object: Government
should be honest and open, rational, and efficient; laws should be administered
evenhandedly; and government officials should be chosen on the basis of merit
rather than of politics. His television commercials showed him pulling weeds in
a field or walking along the corn rows on his farm as he spoke of the work ethic
and recalled his experience in balancing budgets on the farm.

On controversial matters that could not be avoided, Carter would make
general statements designed to please one section of his audience, and then at
the end slip in conditions which would appeal to another. Thus he supported
the principle of the right-to-work provision in the Taft-Hartley Act, but would
not oppose legislative measures to do away with it. He was against abortion,
but he accepted the right of every woman to choose for herself what she would
do.

Carter's other major rhetorical technique consisted of the use of code
phrases to imply attitudes that he did not have to spell out and that would create
common ground between himself and his audience. In announcing his candidacy
in 1974 he identified himself as "a farmer, an engineer, a businessman, a planner,
a scientist, a governor, and a Christian." In *Why Not The Best?* he wrote: "I
am a Southerner and an American . . . a father and a husband . . . a naval
officer, a canoeist, and among other things, a lover of Bob Dylan's songs and
Dylan Thomas's poetry." Citing his born-again Christian faith and his work as
a lay missionary, he appealed to evangelical Christians. At the same time, he

quoted Reinhold Niebuhr, Søren Kierkegaard, Paul Tillich, and Karl Barth for the intelligentsia. The emphasis on his smalltown, agrarian, religious, and family roots convinced social conservatives that he was at one with them. But his close relationship with the Allman Brothers country rock band sent the message that he was no uptight Bible thumper and would not condemn partying, drinking, or even drug use. In proclaiming "Maggie's Farm" (which describes the burning resentment of a white farmhand towards his middle-class farm owners) his favorite Dylan song, Carter suggested that he might even be a closet radical.

Equally important was Carter's refusal to position himself within the conventional political spectrum. "I never characterized myself as a conservative, liberal, or moderate and this is what distinguishes me," he said in January 1976. Or, as he stated on *Face the Nation* in March, 1976, the voters "just feel that I'm the sort of person they can trust, and if they are liberal, I think I'm compatible with their views. If they are moderate, the same; and if the voter is conservative, I think they still feel that I'm a good President." In an interview after his speech accepting the Democratic nomination, Carter called the speech "uniformly populist in tone." But when pressed to explain what the term "populist" meant, Carter demurred. "I will let you define it." Indeed, one of Carter's political advisors, Charles Kirbo, remarked in July, 1976, that Carter had "a wide area of populism" in him, but "I'm not sure what, politically, he cares about. Right now, I imagine he's caring about being President more than anything else."

Actually the deeper issue in 1976, as Carter suggested, was "simply the desire of the American people to have faith in government, to want a fresh start." By his evocative use of what journalist Thomas Ottenad called the "three R's" (i.e., region, race, religion), Carter met this need. The South, as his own political career suggested, was leading the country in a movement to give outsiders an increasing role in government. Southerners, moreover, could draw on their traditional intimacy with blacks to show the rest of the country how the races really could relate. "I sometimes think," Carter said, "that a Southerner of my generation can most fully understand the meaning and impact of Martin Luther King's life. He and I grew up in the same South." In his unabashed discussions of his born-again religious experiences—in *Why Not the Best?*, at a fundraiser in North Carolina, and at his Sunday school classes at the Plains Baptist church each Sunday—Carter suggested that religion could be a healing force in American life. Plains, itself, evoked idyllic images of pre-industrial America where the sky was always blue, the water clear, the land unspoiled, and the people cared, really cared for each other.

As Jody Powell observed shortly after the election, "There was a tremendous yearning in the country this year for something of substance that you could put some faith in. . . . People all over the land were looking for something they thought they had known once and somehow had lost touch with. I think that pine trees and home towns said something even to people who have never seen a small town, because they suggested something that they wanted."

Carter's self-presentation, moreover, suggested that he had the power to accomplish important things. When asked to explain his audacity in running for

President, Carter had said that he "always had self-assurance" and that he was at "complete peace" with himself and the world around him. His toughness was evident in the extraordinary self-discipline and sangfroid he showed on the campaign trail. He set a brutal pace for himself and reporters traveling with him. While other candidates might start as late as 9 A.M. Carter began each day around 5 A.M. His campaign plane flew on time, leaving lagging reporters behind. Even the softball games in Plains gave evidence of his drive, his competitive streak.

Stories about his past—how he had read *War and Peace* three times when a boy, how he had been a candidate for a Rhodes scholarship, his work as a nuclear engineer—all hinted at scientific and intellectual depths. Carter's charm was evident in his ability to weave his magic before blacks, county sheriffs, children, college students, the aged. As Tom Wicker observed, anyone who doesn't understand "the mystical appeal of Jimmy Carter to the American people in 1976" should have attended the senior citizens' center gathering where he discussed America's problems with Vietnam and Watergate."

Any fears that he might misuse his power were allayed by the compassion he professed for those less fortunate than himself. Carter himself proclaimed his capacity to love anonymous people he met on factory lines. His rectitude, he suggested, would keep him from abusing power. "I don't want anything selfish out of government," he often said. "I think I want the same thing you do. And that is to have our nation once again with a government as good and honest and decent and truthful and fair and competent and idealistic and compassionate, and as filled with love as are the American people." In contrast to Nixon, Carter suggested he would have no all-powerful palace guard or shadow cabinet. Even his aides would be selected on the basis of merit rather than politics. Most important, he looked you in the eye and said "I'll never lie to you . . . never make a misleading statement . . . never betray your trust." Whatever uneasiness Carter observers might have felt at those times when he seemed rough or tough or manipulative, it could be put to rest by the conviction that here was a deeply religious man.

His perfection was always tempered with assurances that he was one of the people. "I think my greatest strength," he said, "is that I am an ordinary man, just like all of you, one who has worked and learned and loved his family and made mistakes and tried to correct them without always succeeding." And this ordinariness was shown in the many little things he did on the campaign trail. He carried his own luggage, washed his own clothes in hotel rooms, and made his own bed when he stayed in private houses. He even gave his phone number and address to campaign audiences, urging them to keep in touch.

Carter thus presented himself as self-confident but humble; tough but compassionate; intellectual but in no way snobbish; ambitious for justice but not for himself. He was, in essence, an extraordinary ordinary man.

His self-presentation was aided by eager and hopeful journalism. For Gary Wills, Carter was a "real Southerner," not just a frontman for northern liberals like Terry Sanford or Reuben Askew. His background gave him a "a southern respect for the military without the awe that naval amateurs like the two Roosevelts displayed." He might even respect his promise to never be compromised. "The scary thing is that he might have some way of keeping it." Other journalists affirmed Carter's passion for social justice, though the record suggested he was really fairly conservative. Anthony Lewis concluded in *The New York Times* that "he cares about the powerless in society—genuinely I am convinced." When Carter talked conservatively, Stanley Cloud of *Time* implied, he was simply doing what Roosevelt had done in 1932, i.e., hiding liberal views under a conservative cover in order to win an election.

At times these bigger-than-life projections of Carter were a function of the interests of the journalists involved. Generally reporters working and traveling and joking with a candidate come to have a shared interest in obtaining good publicity for him—to help the candidate win the election, and to help themselves advance their own careers. As David Jones, national news editor of *The New York Times* explained in 1976, "When our political reporters get on that campaign they get trapped; they're in a cocoon and it distorts their perception of everything that is happening in the campaign because they don't see the broader dimensions." This symbiotic relationship was intensified in Carter's case by another factor. Because he was not well known at the beginning, established reporters were not assigned to him. As he gained prominence, he gave younger reporters the opportunity to get ahead and to challenge their own establishment. As Richard Reeves later wrote:

> Jimmy Carter, it turned out, was my candidate. . . . He was, as I thought about it, the candidate of a frustrated generation of American political reporters. . . . For years, we had seen our business defined by a generation that came along with John F. Kennedy—the Hugh Sideys and Joe Krafts—who had been able to report politics as the institutionalized ambition of their candidates, the Kennedys, Nixon, Humphrey, and Rockefeller.
>
> Then *we* found someone *they* didn't know—an outsider. We began touting Jimmy Carter in early 1976; they began mocking him. To me, he was a transitional figure who understood symbolic communication in mediaworld; to James Reston, he was the slightly laughable "Wee Jimmy."

Basically, Carter and the press held out to Americans the hope that after Vietnam and Watergate they could find once again a President they could admire and trust. By 1973, polls showed that 75 percent of the people thought the government had lied to them to some extent. Carter's genius lay in sensing that underneath the prevailing cynicism a deep longing remained for the good authority in which Americans had once believed. Carter was smart, tough, and disciplined, and voters expected that he could exercise power as strong Presidents have traditionally done. But Carter was also anchored in religious and moral values, claiming inner constraints on behavior lacking in some recent Presidents. It was not simply that Carter said he would never lie, as American Civil Liberties Union leader Charles Morgan said, "He's the only candidate who's comfortable saying he won't lie."

Carter's opponent in the fall election was President Gerald Ford. Appointed Vice President under the 25th amendment to replace Spiro T. Agnew, Ford became President after Nixon's resignation on August 10, 1974. He then appointed Nelson Rockfeller of New York, a man much distrusted by right-wing Republicans, as Vice President. At first Ford brought the country relief from the tawdriness of the Nixon years. It seemed, as he said when taking the oath of office, that "our national nightmare is over." His pardon of Nixon one month later, however, dissipated much of the initial goodwill. A public trial of the ex-President would be excessively punitive, he explained, and the country could not stand such an ordeal. Whatever might be said about the substance of his decision, the way he made it evoked memories of Watergate and concern that he might have made a deal with Nixon. When Ford's press secretary, Jerry ter Horst, heard the news, he resigned.

With his credibility undermined, Ford's plain ways and slow speech contributed to a growing perception of him as a well-meaning bumbler. Every time that Ford tripped or fell or misspoke, the press reported it in full. In the White House press room, reporters joked that Ford "can't even play President with a helmet." Although no incumbent President had been denied his party's renomination since Chester Arthur in 1884, right-wing Republicans now began looking for a conservative alternative. At a meeting sponsored by the American Conservative Union and the Young Americans for Freedom in February, 1975, delegates talked of a third party effort behind Ronald Reagan and formed a committee under Jesse Helms to look into the matter. Reagan himself urged that conservative efforts be directed to transforming the GOP.

To stave off challenges from the right, Ford announced early, on July 8, 1975, that he would seek another term. He chose Howard H. Callaway of Georgia, a former Secretary of the Army, to head his campaign, and former Deputy Defense Secretary David Packard to oversee his finance committee. Henry Kissinger, whose detente policies had infuriated conservatives, was replaced as head of the National Security Council on November 2, 1975, by his deputy, Air Force Lieutenant General Brent Scowcroft. Ford was relieved of the Rockefeller problem when the Vice President announced he would not seek his post again. As Callaway had suggested on two occasions the previous summer, opposition to Rockefeller in the South was an extra political burden for the President. This message to the right, however, was blunted because Ford retained Kissinger as secretary of state; moreover the hawkish secretary of defense, James R. Schlesinger, was replaced by the moderate Donald Rumsfeld; and William E. Colby of the CIA was replaced by the centrist George Bush, the U.S. representative to the Peoples Republic of China.

Ronald Reagan had pretty much decided to make his bid for the Presidency in the spring of 1974, while Nixon was still in office. He announced his candidacy on November 20, 1975. "Our nation's capital," he said, "has become the seat of a buddy system that functions for its own benefit—increasingly insensitive to the needs of the American who supports it with his taxes."

Reagan had first captured the hearts of the right with a national television address supporting Barry Goldwater for President in 1964. His attacks on the welfare "cheats" and student radicals in his successful campaign for the governorship of California in 1966 made him a conservative hero. His pleasant manner and willingness to compromise on tax and welfare programs during his two terms as governor had softened potential opposition from moderates. His campaign for the Republican presidential nomination in 1968, though late and half-hearted, called attention to him as a presidential possibility. Out of office in January, 1975, he devoted himself full time to winning a following around the country through his syndicated radio show, news column, and public speeches. In late 1975 he was nearly 65 and facing an appointed, not an elected, President from his own party. His time for another crack at the Presidency had come and it was perhaps a proposition.

Ideologically, Reagan was an implacable opponent of the welfare state, a law-and-order man, a crusading anti-communist who saw the world as a struggle between pure good and pure evil, an opponent of all forms of affirmative action to promote racial equality. On these matters he was considerably to the right of the Republican moderates clustered around Ford.

The ideological battle was joined shortly before the New Hampshire primary. On February 10, Reagan lambasted the Ford-Kissinger detente policies in a speech at Phillips Exeter Academy in New Hampshire. "The balance of forces has been shifting gradually toward the Soviet Union since 1970," he said. "Let us not be satisfied with a foreign policy whose principal accomplishment seems to be our acquisition of the rights to sell Pepsi Cola in Siberia." Ford, in a press conference on February 17, claimed that Reagan was too far to the right to win the general election—pointing to Reagan's earlier statements that Social Security should be made voluntary and his more recent suggestion that Social Security funds be invested in the stock market and that $90 billion in federal expenditures be cut by transferring federal programs to the states.

Ford had the support of most party leaders. But Callaway had difficulties in setting up a good campaign organization, Packard had trouble raising the big dollars they thought would roll in, and Reagan won over key people in New Hampshire. Yet Ford took New Hampshire on February 24 by a razor-thin margin (50.6 to 49.4 percent), Massachusetts on March 2 (64.4 to 35.6 percent), Vermont on March 2 (84 to 15.2 percent), Florida on March 9 (52.8 to 47.2 percent), Illinois on March 16 (58.9 to 40 percent). The *Washington Post's* delegate count now gave Ford 166 delegates to Reagan's 54, with 51 uncommitted. With these losses the contributions to Reagan began to slow down. The Reagan people—running a net debt of nearly $1 million—trimmed their spending to barely half of what it had been in February. Nine Republican governors suggested that Reagan withdraw to promote party unity. On March 20, his campaign manager, John Sears, engaged in tentative talks with presidential counselor Rogers C. B. Morton to discuss the possible Ford contributions to the Reagan campaign debt should Reagan withdraw.

The next series of primaries, however, were in states where Barry Goldwater had shown his greatest strength in 1964. In North Carolina on March 23, Reagan beat Ford by 52.4 to 45.9 percent. The small turnout (40 percent) gave weight to Jesse Helm's right wing followers and to Reagan's television speeches, run in the last four days of the campaign. Twenty-seven percent of those who voted for Reagan, according to an NBC News poll, made up their minds in the last week.

In a national television address on March 31, Reagan elaborated on the foreign policy critique presented in his Exeter speech and raised $1.5 million. The cutoff of the Federal Election Commission payout on March 22—occasioned by conflicts over the makeup of the commission—had seriously crippled an already debt-ridden campaign. These fresh funds put Reagan back on track for the crucial Texas campaign.

Although Ford won Wisconsin (55.2 to 44.3 percent) on April 6, he was completely swamped in Texas on May 1. Reagan swept every congressional district and won all 96 delegates. Texas was the first open primary and, with Wallace out of the Democratic race as a real contender, thousands of Wallace supporters crossed over to vote for Reagan. Charges that the Ford administration was engaged in secret negotiations to "give away" the Panama Canal was an especially important factor in the Texas vote.

Three days later, on May 4, Reagan won in Indiana, Georgia, and Alabama. Reagan surged ahead in the delegate count, taking 357 to Ford's 297. It was a disastrous showing for a sitting President. Ford's run of losses had not been equalled since Theodore Roosevelt challenged President William Howard Taft in 1912. At Ford Committee headquarters that night Rogers Morton, who replaced Callaway as campaign manager on March 30, said: "I'm not going to rearrange the furniture on the deck of the Titanic." On March 11, Reagan beat Ford in Nebraska (54.6 to 45.4 percent), although Ford took West Virginia (56.6 to 43.4 percent).

On May 18, Ford was back in the running, defeating Reagan nearly two to one in his home state of Michigan. This time independents went heavily for Ford and thousands of Democrats, in a massive turnout, heeded the plea of Republican leaders in the state to cross over to vote for their native son. In Maryland the same day Ford beat Reagan (57.9 to 42.1 percent).

After this victory, Ford held his own in a tight race down to the June 8 primaries and through five weeks of caucuses. Ford won most of the traditionally moderate states of the Midwest and Northeast. On May 25, he took Kentucky, Oregon, and Tennessee in close races. (Reagan hurt himself in the latter primary when he told reporters in Knoxville that he would consider returning the TVA to the private sector.) On June 1 Ford won in Rhode Island. On June 8, he won New Jersey (where Reagan had entered no delegate candidates) and Ohio (where Ford had the support of the governor and the Republican congressional delegation). On May 24, the Ford campaign also received a big boost when 119 previously uncommitted New York delegates voted to endorse him. The vote was engineered by Nelson Rockefeller, who earlier in 1976 had flirted with the possibility that he might enter as a presidential candidate should the convention be deadlocked between Reagan and Ford.

Reagan took most of the more conservative West and South. He swamped Ford in Arkansas, Nevada, and Idaho on May 25, and Montana and South Dakota on June 1. Ford then tried to capitalize on Reagan's suggestion in Sacramento that the United States might have to send troops to Rhodesia. Three days before the California primary the Ford organization ran television ads stating: "When you vote on Tuesday, remember Governor Ronald Reagan couldn't start a war. President Reagan can." Despite that, Reagan won California on June 8, with 65.7 percent of the vote.

After the June 8 primaries the race was still wide open. Reagan had a total 863 delegates to 958 for Ford, according to the *Washington Post*. Some 260 additional delegates remained to be chosen in the remaining caucus states and about 164 remained uncommitted from earlier races. For the next five weeks party leaders and local party activists fought toe to toe for these 424 delegates. Ford secured a majority in Iowa, Delaware, Minnesota, and North Dakota. Reagan took the lion's share in Minnesota, Washington, New Mexico, Montana, and Colorado. In the last two caucuses on July 17 Ford took all of Connecticut's 35 delegates and Reagan all of Utah's 20. On July 6, in the midst of these battles, Reagan appealed to the white ethnic voter in a 60-minute broadcast over the ABC network, by characterizing affirmative action as a form of reverse discrimination. "I'd like an opportunity to put an end to this distortion of the principle of equal rights," he said. On July 17, when the final caucus was over, *The New York Times* saw Ford ahead by 1,102 to 1,063 delegates. But the President was still 28 delegates short of the 1,130 needed for nomination. Reagan needed 67.

The next battle was for the approximately ninety-four delegates who remained uncommitted. As the incumbent, Ford had several advantages. During the spring freeze on federal funding he had been able to draw on White House resources and access to credit, while Reagan had gone without funds. Now he invited whole delegations to dine and drink at the White House, while aides worked on influential politicians in Mississippi (which was holding to the unit rule against party rules) and other uncommitted delegations.

Reagan, on the advice of his strategist, John Sears, countered on July 26 by naming the liberal Republican senator from Pennsylvania, Richard Schweiker, as his prospective runningmate. The objective was to broaden Reagan's appeal for the fall campaign and to cut into the Pennsylvania delegation at the convention, where there were still uncommitted votes, and thus start the final bandwagon to Reagan.

Instead, the move enraged conservatives. Clarke Reed, a Reagan supporter and head of the uncommitted Mississippi delegation, announced his "personal" endorsement of Ford after that choice. "This kind of Vice President," he said, "is too big a price to pay for the nominations." Senator James L. Buckley of New York, supported by Jesse Helms and Illinois Congressman Dan Crane, stated on August 11 that he would be available as a presidential candidate should there be a deadlock at the convention between Reagan and Ford. His goal was to prevent a first ballot nomination and to bring pressure on Reagan to drop Schweiker on the second ballot. (Buckley's candidacy was dropped on August 16 after New York State Party Chairman Richard Rosenbaum warned him that if he persisted in his effort, he would lose the state organization support in his reelection bid that year.) Reagan's move did not even cut into the Pennsylvania delegation as intended. A *New York Times* poll of the Pennsylvania delegation in late July showed only one convert to the Reagan cause. A Gallup poll on August 12 indicated that the move neither hurt nor helped Reagan with Republican and independent voters at large.

Reagan's political strategist, John Sears, had one last move—a procedural challenge on the floor of the convention at Kansas City to show Reagan's purported second ballot strength. (The Rules Committee had adopted a rule requiring each delegate to vote on the first ballot as he was pledged to vote under state law and not according to his personal preference). The Reagan backed amendment, 16-C, would require Ford to name his vice presidential choice before the balloting began. If all Reagan supporters voted for 16-C, they might secure a majority that would start a rush to Reagan.

After a debate on August 17, punctuated by boos and scuffles on the floor, Reagan lost the vote on 16-C by 1,069 in favor to 1,180 against, with 10 abstentions. Earlier rumors that the Mississippi delegation would vote against the resolution may have induced some waverers to vote against it. The Mississippi delegation, however, passed on the first roll call and did not deliver its thirty votes against the resolution until after Florida's vote had already given it the coup de grace. A Reagan aide said, "This was the ballgame."

Shortly after that vote, the Ford people yielded to another challenge from the Reagan-Helms people and accepted the "morality in foreign policy" plank. A clear rejection of the Ford-Kissinger foreign policies, it commended the Soviet dissident Alexander Solzhenitsyn, criticized détente, the Helsinki agreement signed by Ford in 1975, and secret agreements—a slap at the Ford-Kissinger negotiations over the Panama Canal. (Even the platform coming to the floor of the convention reflected earlier concessions to the Reagan-Helms forces on the platform committee—including a call for U.S. military superiority over the USSR, the retention of a mutual defense treaty between the United States and Taiwan, and the endorsement of three constitutional amendments—to "protect unborn children," to bar the assignment of students to schools on the basis of race, and to permit nonsectarian prayers in public schools. A women's task force at the convention had blocked the Reagan-Helms effort to get the Platform Committee to drop the Republican commitment to the Equal Rights Amendment.)

Ford won on the first ballot late at night on August 18 by 1,187 to 1,070. Mississippi, once considered the key to nomination, finally dropped its unit rule before the balloting and gave Ford 16 votes to Reagan's 14.

Reagan came so close to winning the nomination because party rules gave western and southwestern states a disproportionate share of the delegates at the expense of the more populous states in the Northeast and Midwest. Ford was more popular with Republican voters as a whole than Reagan (e.g., a Gallup poll in early July 1976 showed the President leading among Republicans by 61 to 31 percent). Reagan was slightly more popular with conservative voters, as an NYT-CBS poll showed. But his strength was regional, that is, with Southerners and Westerners, and the apportionment provision under which the Republican National Convention operated in 1976 played to his strength.

The fight at the convention also reflected ideological differences. Few Republicans expected to win the election. After a Gallup poll showed either Ford or Reagan getting only 40 percent of the votes against Carter, delegates responded to the question of whether their man could win with a forlorn "I hope so." The Reagan delegates, considerably more conservative and ideological than the Ford delegates, were mainly interested in inscribing their views in the party platform and in winning control of the party organization. A CBS/*New York Times* poll reported on June 25 that as many as half of the Ronald Reagan supporters were prepared to defect to Carter or boycott the election should Ford win the nomination.

Ford's vice presidential choice was motivated by the need to heal these divisions. On August 18, shortly after he had won the nomination, Ford consulted Reagan on six vice presidential possibilities. They were Senator Robert J. Dole of Kansas; Senator Howard H. Baker, Jr. of Tennessee; Treasury Secretary William E. Simon; Commerce Secretary Elliot L. Richardson; former Deputy Attorney General William D. Ruckelshaus, and former Governor John B. Connally. Reagan spoke most warmly of Dole, a tough-talking, sarcastic senator with friends in the Reagan camp. At a press conference the next afternoon Ford announced Dole as his vice presidential choice. Jesse Helms allowed his name to be placed into nomination by his ultraright supporters, a move that allowed him to ventilate his ideas before announcing his withdrawal.

In his acceptance speech Ford attacked congressional Democrats, challenged Jimmy Carter to debate, and said that Washington had gotten away from the people. "You at home, listening tonight, you are the people who pay taxes and obey the law," he said. "It is from your ranks that I come and on your side I stand." At the end of the speech he invited Reagan to the podium to address the delegates. The party platform is a "banner of bold, unmistakable colors," Reagan said. "We have just heard a call to arms based on that platform." Calling upon the party to unite against the Democrats, he ended by telling the delegates, "There is no substitute for victory."

There were several third party candidates in 1976. On the right there was the segregationist ex-governor of Georgia, Lester Maddox, of the American Independent party; Tom Anderson of the American Party; and Roger L. Macbride of the Libertarian Party. On the left were Peter Camejo of the Socialist Workers Party and Julius Levin of the Socialist Labor Party. Lyndon M. LaRouche of the U.S. Labor Party tried to appeal to extremists on both the left and right.

The only third force candidate apt to attract a following large enough to have impact on the election was Eugene McCarthy—the former Democratic senator whose strong showing in the New Hampshire primaries in 1968 had paved the way for Robert Kennedy's campaign and the decision of President Lyndon B. Johnson not to seek reelection. Running as an Independent in 1976, McCarthy's hope was to prevent the major party candidates from winning a majority in the Electoral College. Republicans, he believed, would prefer to negotiate with other electors than to throw the decision to the Democratically controlled House. Idcologically, McCarthy appealed to what he considered a neglected center, raising basic questions about the need to reduce a bloated military establishment, to create stronger institutional checks on U.S. intelligence agencies, to protect natural resources, to refashion a foreign policy in accord with traditional American ideas, and to challenge the lockhold the two major parties have on the political system. With Senator James Buckley he had successfully challenged the Campaign Finance Law of 1974 in the case of Buckley v. Valeo; the 1976 Supreme Court decision had led to the reorganization of the commission and the temporary cessation of federal matching funds. McCarthy's subsequent experience showed the problems that third parties still had under the provisions the Supreme Court allowed to stand. Denied federal matching funds unless they received 5 percent of the vote in the last election, they were still subject to a spending limitation of $1,000 per person and $500 per committee.

In September, the Louis Harris poll showed McCarthy with about 7 percent of the vote in New York, Illinois, Pennsylvania, Ohio, Michigan, and California. As Democratic Party Chairman Robert Strauss noted, his threat was primarily to Carter, for he was drawing about 4 to 1 from the Democrats. The campaign finance law, however, severely limited his funds. Moreover, McCarthy had to spend most of his time mounting legal challenges to the ways in which state laws were enforced against him and also to the decision of the League of Women Voters and the networks to limit the presidential debates to Carter and Ford. Although he had expected to be on the ballot in at least 40 states, McCarthy finally appeared in only 29.

At the beginning of the fall campaign, Jimmy Carter seemed almost invincible. Although he had dropped in the polls since the Democratic national convention, he was still leading Ford by about 15 points. Victory seemed within easy reach, as Hamilton Jordan pointed out in memos of June 2 and August 9. The ten border and southern states were almost sure bets. By adding all states that usually voted Democratic, Jordan figured that Carter could win by taking a few major swing states in the North. Not a state would be conceded to the Republicans, although Carter would focus his efforts on the wing states.

Ford, however, had a plan that might work. According to the strategy memo John Sears gave him in early August, the way he might win was to "act presidential," to undertake a negative campaign against Jimmy Carter, and to hope that Carter would make enough mistakes to close the gap.

"Acting presidential" meant that Ford should rely on presidential announcements set against the backdrop of the Rose Garden or Oval Office, and should prove his superior knowledge and experience in debates with Carter. The negative campaign would exploit vulnerabilities in Carter's support that Robert Teeter had discovered in his polls for Ford. Most people had weak perceptions and uncertain feelings about Carter. The Ford campaign would emphasize Carter's liberalism and reinforce public concern that Carter was really an unknown.

To make the Ford organization more efficient there was a shakeup at the top shortly after the convention. James A. Baker III replaced Morton as head of the campaign organization. Douglas Bailey and John Deardourff were given complete control over the negative campaign commercials, with the proviso that their work be within the bounds of responsible political discourse.

Carter began on an upbeat note on Labor Day at Warm Springs, Georgia, where he called on all the old Democratic names and symbols and some new ones—pledging through efficient management to balance the federal budget. A few days later, however, he fell into a series of petty exchanges with Ford over FBI Director Clarence Kelley's use of an FBI carpenter to install window valences in Kelley's private apartment. In the midst of these exchanges, Carter, the anti-boss candidate, fell deep into the embrace of the biggest boss of all, Mayor Daley of Chicago. Participating in a Chicago torchlight parade on September 9, Carter greeted an enthusiastic Democratic state convention with a tribute to Richard Daley, his "very good friend." Then on September 18, he was put on the defensive by White House charges that Carter wanted to raise taxes for one half of all American families. An Associated Press interview with Carter released the previous day quoted him as saying his goal was to shift the tax burden "toward those who have higher incomes and reduce the income tax on the lower income and middle income taxpayers." The problem was resolved when Carter pointed out that his phrase "middle income" had been inadvertently dropped in the press release.

Two days later, Robert Scheer's interview with Carter, soon to be published in *Playboy,* was released to newspapers around the country. Carter had outlined his political views and compared himself to past Presidents. "But I don't think I would ever take on the same frame of mind that Nixon or Johnson did, lying, cheating, and distorting the truth," he said. What attracted the most attention, however, was Carter's statement that he often looked at women with "lust in his heart," and his use of such sexual colloquialism as "screw" and "shack up."

The reaction among Christian conservatives was strong. In Atlanta seventeen independent Baptist preachers denounced Carter as having "brought reproach to the Christian faith." The Reverend Bailey Smith, once a strong Carter supporter, spoke of an earlier visit with Carter in Oklahoma when "Carter the politician, got down on his knees and prayed heaven down. How could his present use of 'shack up' and 'screw' in *Playboy* be reconciled with this memory." On the press bus, disbelief washed over the reporters. A CBS correspondent declared, "The campaign is dying right under our feet."

On September 23, in the midst of this flurry, Carter met Ford in debate— the first between presidential candidates since the Nixon-Kennedy exchanges in 1960. Carter spoke of a bureaucratic mess and lack of leadership in Washington and emphasized the need to reorganize the government and to reduce unemployment. Ford stressed the need to hold the lid on federal spending to balance the budget and cited the lowering of unemployment as a major goal. Observers noted that, while Carter seemed nervous and did not look presidential, Ford was no better. When the power failed on the microphones, both men froze— standing without speaking to one another, and looking straight ahead into the air for 27 minutes until power was restored. Afterward, a *New York Times*/CBS poll showed Ford the winner in the debate by 37 to 24%, with 39% undecided.

The morning after the debate, Carter compounded his problems. Passing through Houston, he told a group of Texas journalists at the airport that *Playboy* had misinterpreted his remarks about Johnson. "My reference to Johnson was about the misleading of the American people; the lying and cheating part referred to President Nixon. And the unfortunate juxtaposition of these two names in the *Playboy* article grossly misinterprets the way I feel about him." On the press plane later that day, national reporters got into a shouting match with Jody Powell and accused Carter of trying to "wing one past the provincials" and themselves. Carter further compounded his problems in San Diego that evening by asking a dozen journalists for advice. Several reporters, already uneasy at having been singled out for this special meeting, saw this as an attempt to manipulate them into becoming part of his campaign. Martin Schram of *Newsday* told Carter that the press was not in the business of advising candidates.

Carter was saved from what could have been a precipitous decline when the media shifted attention to Ford. The President formally opened his campaign at his alma mater, the University of Michigan at Ann Arbor, on September 15. Six days later his problems began. First there were stories that Ford had accepted free weekends from U.S. Steel, Gulf Oil, and other lobbies, and that Charles Ruff, the Watergate special prosecutor, had subpoenaed Ford's campaign financial records. Then, for four days a vulgar, racist joke, by Secretary of Agriculture Earl Butz, dominated the media. After this issue was closed by Butz's resignation, the House International Affairs Committee issued a Government Accounting Office report critical of Ford's handling of the Mayaguez rescue mission in the spring of 1975.

In the second debate on October 6, Carter tried to put Ford on the defensive, echoing earlier Reagan critiques of Kissinger's shuttle diplomacy, the purported decline in U.S. strength and a fear of competing with the USSR. Carter also accused the Ford administration of participating in the overthrow of the elected government in Chile, and of attempts to start a new "Vietnam" war in Angola. Ford traded blow for blow—citing Carter's various proposals for cuts in defense spending and his purported willingness to accept a Communist government in NATO. But then, in response to questions about the Helsinki pact, Ford stated: "There is no Soviet domination of Eastern Europe, and there never will be under a Ford Administration."

Ford, initially perceived as having won the debate by a margin of 44 to 35 percent, was losing by 61 to 19 percent the following night after newspaper highlighting of his mistake regarding Eastern Europe. On the campaign trail Ford was pressed for clarification. The President's failure to admit his mistake until October 12, a week later, prolonged the agony. The final blow came on October 13, when John Dean, appearing on NBC's *Today Show,* suggested that Ford had aided the Nixon White House in an attempt to delay or stop an early Watergate investigation by the House Banking Committee. The bad news, however, came to an abrupt end on October 14, when Special Prosecutor Charles F. Ruff refused to go into the matter raised by Dean and cleared Ford of allegations that he had diverted political contributions for his personal use.

During these three weeks Carter could have formulated the issues of his campaign. Instead, he took after Ford with evident relish, insisting that Ford's

failure to fire Butz showed that no one was leading the nation, and that Ford
had been brainwashed while behind the Iron Curtain.

In the vice presidential debate on October 15—the first in U.S. history—
Mondale and Dole argued over whether the Democratic or Republican programs
would serve the nation best. Dole, whose sarcastic wit had been considered one
of his assets, went too far, however, when he argued that World War I, World
War II, and the Vietnam and Korean Wars were all Democratic wars. Afterward
conservative columnist George Will noted that "until Dole took wing in his
debate with Walter Mondale, it was unclear when this campaign would hit
bottom."

In the final presidential debate on October 22 Carter toned down his sniping
at Ford and spoke of a new spirit in America. In the remaining days on the
campaign Carter trail accentuated a traditional Democratic line. (Patrick Caddell had warned him on October 16 that he was hurting himself with personal
attacks on the President.) At an old-fashioned Democratic rally in Dallas on
October 31, Carter hit his stride, as he went through a medley of campaign
themes. "Ford is a decent man," he said, but he could not provide the bold
leadership the country needed. "It takes a deep dedication to a cause . . . to a
way of life, that has been exemplified in the past by great Presidents who were
Democrats." Then a litany of questions about Ford: "Can you think of a single
program that he's put forward that's been accepted? Can you think of a single
thing?"

Most of Carter's national advertisements at this point emphasized positive
themes he had used in his primary campaign. One advertisement, however,
showed Mondale and Dole on a split screen and asked, "Who would you like
to see a heartbeat away from the Presidency?" In the South, where Caddell's
early October polls had shown Carter threatened with the loss of his most
important base, the tone was more negative. One set of television spots emphasized southern pride and resentment of past ridicule. Another focused on
Ford's "soft" dealings with the Soviet Union, and piggybacked on Ronald Reagan's critique of the Ford-Kissinger detente policy. "My view of detente is that
it has been a one-way street," Carter said. "The Soviet Union knows what they
want in detente, and they have been getting it. And we have been out-traded
in almost every instance."

In the meantime, the President was deep into a negative campaign. In mid-
October Ford traveled around Illinois in a special train, the *Honest Abe,* describing Carter as a man who "will say anything, anywhere to be President."
In the last two weeks of the campaign, commercials based on interviews with
people in the street, were widely used. In one, six Atlantans observed in soft
southern drawls that Jimmy Carter had not been much of a governor. Another
commercial featured a map of Georgia, with an announcer proclaiming that
under Carter: "Government spending increased 58 percent . . . Government
employees up 28 . . . bonded indebtedness up 20." In a more positive television
series former baseball catcher Joe Garagiola, typified as the average American
nice guy, asked Ford questions which he answered with assurance and ease.

At this point the Presidency was both an asset and a liability for the Ford
campaign. In October he raised farm price supports, which doubtless helped in

the farm states. But as president he was also hostage to bad economic news. Just five days before the election, the Commerce Department's index of leading economic indicators fell by .7 percent, the second such drop in two months.

Overall, the campaign had not revolved around high issues or responsible discussions. Instead, it had become a whiney affair where serious questions were drowned out by discussions of whether or not each man was as good as he claimed to be. Although the press contributed to this aspect of the campaign, most journalists blamed the candidates. R. W. Apple complained on October 20, "Neither nominee . . . appears able to decide whether he wants to be a good guy or a rabbit puncher." In a *Chicago Sun-Times* editorial called "The Dirty Duo," Morton Kondracke saw an "increasingly petty, nasty, low-blow campaign, and if voters are turned off by it, it's hard to blame them."

Yet newspapers around the nation made the traditional endorsements. By election day Ford had secured the backing of two-thirds of the dailies, including the *Chicago Tribune,* the *San Francisco Chronicle* and the *Cincinnati Enquirer. The New York Times* and the *Washington Post* endorsed Carter, while the *Wall Street Journal* and the *Los Angeles Times* followed past policies of not endorsing candidates.

The remarkable thing about the campaign was how far Carter had fallen in the course of only three months. From a 33 percent lead over Ford in the Gallup polls in late July, he dropped to 23 percent just before the Republican convention. After the Republican convention, his margin was down to 10 percent. Outside the South he was running even with Ford. Since the beginning of modern polling in 1935, no candidate had experienced such a rapid decline between conventions.

At the start of the fall campaign, Carter bounced back in the Gallup poll to a 15 percent lead. From then on, his lead (with minor fluctuations) gradually evaporated. He held most of the party support he had in early September, but independents moved toward Ford. From a 60 percent peak with the independents in July, Carter was down to 33 percent by mid-October. At that time, Daniel Yankelovich, polling for *Time,* reported that 52 percent of the electorate was "soft" or "undecided"—a figure almost four times that at the same point in 1972.

This decline was partly the result of the breadth of the appeals Carter had made. Unlike his Democratic predecessors, Carter had actively wooed groups no longer a part of the Democratic coalition, with emphasis on conservative themes. One correspondence was apathy in the home base, where strong Democratic voters were puzzled by the unfamiliar slant of his appeals. When Carter responded late in the campaign by making a more traditional pitch for the core Democratic vote, he alienated conservatives who had been attracted by him during the summer.

The unease about Carter—evident in both Caddell's and Teeters polls since the summer— was not just based on a concern about where he stood politically. People were also puzzled by his personality. "There was no way on God's earth," Jody Powell explained later, "that we could shake the fuzziness question in the general election, no matter what Carter did or said." As Hamilton Jordan noted:

the voters may have described Carter as fuzzy "when they were unable to verbalize what they really meant." Perhaps they called him fuzzy "because he was a Southerner," or because of the "weirdo factor."

In all probability this "weirdo" factor was the larger-than-life Carter the media had been projecting in the late spring and early summer of 1976. No man could possess the extraordinary virtues Carter seemed to have had in the summer of 1976. No politician can survive as an outsider and not make deals with other politicians or use traditional methods to hold his organization together. No campaign organization could function as smoothly as the Carter organization seemed to perform in the early spring of 1976. No people live in the perfect harmony that seemed to characterize Plains, Georgia. When Carter began to run as an ordinary Democrat in the fall of 1976, to make mistakes and to show human flaws, the press highlighted these incongruities. But if he was not what he seemed at the beginning, then what was he?

By election day, it was not at all clear who would win. The previous Friday, the Louis Harris poll noted that the soft and undecided vote was going over to Ford. The last Gallup poll before the election showed Carter trailing Ford 46 to 47 percent, with 4 percent undecided. With neither candidate looking particularly strong and issues buried under a cascade of near irrelevancies, many voters stayed home. In the electoral college, Carter won by a narrow margin—297 to 240—the smallest since Woodrow Wilson's victory over Charles Evans Hughes in 1916. (One Washington state elector pledged to Ford cast his vote for Ronald Reagan.) Carter's margin in the popular vote was also slim: 40.8 million votes to Ford's 39.1 million, a margin of only 1.7 million votes. Another 963,505 votes, 1.9 percent, went to all the other minor candidates. Independent candidate Eugene McCarthy received 745,042 votes nationally, and may have cost Carter Iowa, Maine, Oklahoma, and possibly Oregon. After a long legal battle which had gone all the way to the Supreme Court, McCarthy had been kept off the ballot in New York. Had McCarthy remained on the ballot in that state, he might have tipped the election to Ford. Carter won there by 52.2 to 47.8 percent, a margin of only 4.4 percent.

Although more than 81.5 million Americans voted (up 4 million from 1972), the turnout was only 54.4 percent, the lowest since 1948. Regionally Carter won all the South except Virginia and Oklahoma; he took the few northern industrial states he needed to put him over the top—New York, Ohio, and Pennsylvania—as well as Massachusetts, Delaware, Maryland, Rhode Island, Wisconsin, Minnesota, Hawaii, and the District of Columbia. Ford won all the West, most of the Midwest, and Oklahoma, Virginia, New Hampshire, New Jersey, Connecticut, Maine and Vermont.

The Democrats retained their dominance in the Congress—winning the House 292 to 143 (a net gain of one seat) and the Senate 62 to 38 (the same as before). Not since Lyndon Johnson's legislative triumphs after the election of 1964 had a president won such large majorities in both houses. There was no evidence, however, that these Democrats came in on Carter's coattails. In the twelve states which went Democratic in the presidential and senatorial races, Carter led the successful Democrats in only one. Regional and idiosyncratic factors were most important in determining the outcomes. Nine incumbents seeking reelection had been rejected—the greatest number since the Democratic landslide in 1958. Four of the five Democratic incumbents defeated were from the West, and all from states more conservative than they. The four defeated Republican incumbents were from the East and one border state. Incumbency was the most important factor in the success of House candidates. Of the 385 incumbents seeking reelection 366 (95 percent) were reelected. Democrats would end up with 37 governorships, one more than they had before the election. Despite long term trends in the West towards Republican voting in presidential races, the Democrats wound up controlling every statehouse west of the Mississippi except Iowa, Kansas, and Alaska.

Ironically, the outsider Jimmy Carter owed his victory to the traditional party vote. With no compelling personality to attract or repel, no new issues over which to divide, people fell back to traditional cues. As a Gallup poll showed, Carter had secured 82 percent of the voter who identified themselves as Democrats, 85 percent of the nonwhite, 63 percent of union families, 58 percent of the manual labor vote, and 57 percent of the Catholic vote. The black vote roughly equaled the vote for Johnson in 1964. Union families voted for Carter at a rate equal to or better than that for any other candidate since 1952 except Johnson in 1964. Most important, both groups turned out for Carter in the states where he needed them most. Without the disproportionately large vote for Carter by union families, his success in New York, Pennsylvania, and Ohio would have been impossible. Blacks helped push him over the top in the North (New York), the South (Louisiana and Mississippi), and Southwest (Texas).

Carter's ability to hold component groups in the traditional Democratic coalition was partly the result of the voter-registration and election day turnout drives of the Democratic National Committee, a group backed by the Democratic National Committee, called "Wake up Black America," and organized labor. The AFL-CIO, which had endorsed no one in 1972, undertook in 1976 the biggest, the best organized, and most sophisticated campaign in its history to get out the vote. In Pennyslvania, for example, they helped register 500,000 voters, where Carter's margin of victory was 123,073 votes. Overall, three million people were registered—mainly blacks, Latinos, and the poor—in 14 targeted states. Of these new voters, approximately 2.4 million voted Democratic. Total black registration was up 750,000 from 1972; and the black turnout rate was about 70 percent as compared to 58 percent in 1972.

This was not quite the old Roosevelt coalition that Patrick Caddell claimed it to be after the election. In the South, Carter secured 53.7 percent of the vote, larger than any Democrat since Harry Truman in 1948. But Democratic hopes that he had brought the South permanently back into the Democratic fold were premature. Carter's success was nowhere near Truman's (65.6 percent) and Franklin D. Roosevelt's (81.3 percent in 1932, and 74.1 percent in 1944). Moreover, the composition of this vote differed substantially from theirs. Catalyzed by national Democratic efforts to promote the rights of blacks in the South, whites (including the working class) had been moving to the right since the 1960s and voting Republican in presidential elections. Carter did not receive a majority of this white vote. As a consequence of the Voting Rights Act of 1964, the Democratic registration effort in 1976, and Carter's own appeals, considerably more blacks voted in the South than ever before, and they voted overwhelmingly for Carter. Yet Carter's moderation on the issues and his emphasis on traditional values and efficiency in government brought him more Protestant, small-town, over-50, rural, business and professional votes than the Democratic average in recent years. In taking 46 percent of the Protestant vote, for example, he was 10 percentage points higher than the average Democratic candidate for President since 1952.

Despite the importance of party cues for voters at the end, the election did not mark any reversal of the long term decline in the importance of political parties in the selection of American Presidents. Professional campaign managers and their pollsters played key decision-make roles in both political parties, as they had in every presidential campaign since 1952. Their goal was to fashion appeals to capture voters unanchored by party or ideology. Their success depended on their ability to win favorable coverage in a media which had taken over traditional party functions in defining candidates, articulating issues and interpreting outcomes.

Even before the New Hampshire primary in 1976, press coverage influenced judgments about who the viable candidates would be. The disproportionate publicity that the winner of the New Hampshire primaries received marked out front runners. In the Democratic primaries that publicity was so massive that a relative unknown was transformed almost overnight into a household word. After the Pennsylvania primary, only the ninth of thirty, Carter was widely proclaimed as almost unbeatable, and the public tended to agree with the media assessment. In the Republican primaries the process was less important because over 90 percent of the voters knew and had formed strong impressions about each candidate before the campaign. Throughout the entire campaign, the media paid attention to strategic, organizational, and stylistic considerations rather than substantive issues, reversing the pattern found in earlier elections (e.g., in 1940, as reported by Paul Lazarsfeld and others in the *People's Choice*). During the primary campaign, as Thomas Patterson points out in *The Mass Media Election*, only one policy issue received extended coverage, namely, Ronald Reagan's critique of Ford's foreign policy.

During the general election, despite the efforts of both Carter and Ford, no substantive policy issue received extensive coverage—the headlines and evening television news shows featuring instead the mishaps and possible misdeeds of each candidate. Increasingly indifferent to political organizations, voters relied to an extraordinary degree on the mass media for their assessment of candidates during the 1976 primaries, voting only for individuals they recognized and knew something about from media presentations. The issues and events the public remembered were those featured at the top of the news, and policy interpretations, as public reaction to the foreign policy debate particularly showed, were strongly influenced, if not determined, by media commentary.

This account suggests that the media are not equipped to assume the political functions that the parties used to perform. The media's decisions about how to play stories are based mostly on a vague notion of newsworthiness rather than

on political importance. Consequently, trivialities often supplant political substance and, at worst, sensationalism gives professional integrity a back seat. In
the selection process, better candidates may be eliminated and lesser ones elevated because of chance political events, last minute headlines, and a few
thousand votes in the early primaries. Most important, the mass media cannot
and should not aggregate stands on related issues and offer mechanisms for the
implementation of policy, as parties can and ought to do. As the 1976 election
shows, the link between public policy and what the voters do at the polls can
dissolve as the election becomes a series of scattered, uncertain choices made
against a media-colored kaleidoscopic political backdrop.

Inevitably, a winner emerged, but what the election meant to the future of
national policy was by no means clear.

Appendix

Acceptance Speech by Jimmy Carter
New York City, July 15, 1976

In highly populist rhetoric Jimmy Carter accepted the Democratic nomination and pledged to heal the deep wounds inflicted on the American psyche by Vietnam and Watergate. Despite the radical tone and thrust of Carter's speech, his political forces had beaten back many of the more liberal proposals presented to the Democratic Platform Committee earlier in the convention.

My name is Jimmy Carter, and I'm running for President. It's been a long time since I said those words the first time, and now I've come here, after seeing our great country, to accept your nomination.

I accept it in the words of John F. Kennedy: "With a full and grateful heart and with only one obligation—to devote every effort of body, mind and spirit to lead our party back to victory and our nation back to greatness."

It's a pleasure to be with all you Democrats and to see that our Bicentennial celebration and our Bicentennial convention has been one of decorum and order, without any fights or free-for-alls. Among Democrats, that could only happen once every 200 years.

With this kind of a united Democratic Party, we are ready and eager to take on the Republicans, whichever Republican Party they decide to send against us in November.

1976 will not be a year of politics as usual. It can be a year of inspiration and hope. And it will be a year of concern, of quiet and sober reassessment of our nation's character and purpose—a year when voters have already confounded the experts.

And I guarantee you that it will be the year when we give the government of this country back to the people of this country.

There's a new mood in America.

We have been shaken by a tragic war abroad and by scandals and broken promises at home.

Our people are searching for new voices and new ideas and new leaders.

Although government has its limits and cannot solve all our problems, we Americans reject the view that we must be reconciled to failures and mediocrity, or to an inferior quality of life.

For I believe that we can come through this time of trouble stronger than ever. Like troops who've been in combat, we've been tempered in the fire—we've been disciplined and we've been educated. Guided by lasting and simple moral values, we've emerged idealists without illusions, realists who still know the old dreams of justice and liberty—of country and of community.

This year we have had 30 state primaries, more than ever before, making it possible to take our campaign directly to the people of America—to homes and shopping centers, to factory shift lines and colleges, to beauty parlors, and barber shops, to farmers' markets and union halls.

This has been a long and personal campaign—a kind of humbling experience, reminding us that ultimate political influence rests not with the powerbrokers, but with the people. This has been a time for learning and for the exchange of ideas, a time of tough debate on the important issues facing our country. This kind of debate is part of our tradition, and as Democrats we are heirs to a great tradition.

I have never met a Democratic President, but I've always been a Democrat.

Years ago, as a farm boy sitting outdoors with my family on the ground in the middle of the night, gathered close around a battery radio connected to the automobile battery, and listening to the Democratic conventions in far-off cities, I was a long way from the selection process then. I feel much closer to it tonight.

Ours is the party of the man who was nominated by those distant conventions, and who inspired and restored this nation in its darkest hours—Franklin D. Roosevelt.

Ours is the party of a fighting Democrat who showed us that a common man could be an uncommon leader—Harry S Truman.

Ours is the party of a brave young President who called the young in heart, regardless of age, to seek a New Frontier of national greatness—John F. Kennedy.

And ours is also the party of a greathearted Texan, who took office in a tragic hour and who went on to do more than any other President in this century to advance the cause of human rights—Lyndon Johnson.

Now our party was built out of the sweatshops of the old Lower East Side, the dark mills of New Hampshire, the blazing hearths of Illinois, the coal mines of Pennsylvania, the hardscrabble farms of the southern coastal plains and the unlimited frontiers of America.

Ours is a party that welcomed generations of immigrants—the Jews, the Irish, the Italians, the Poles, and all the others—enlisted them in its ranks, and fought the political battles that helped bring them into the American mainstream—and they have shaped the character of our party.

That is our heritage. Our party has not been perfect. We've made mistakes and we've been disillusioned. We've been a wall of leadership and compassion and progress.

Our leaders have fought for every piece of progressive legislation from RFD and REA to Social Security and civil rights. In times of need, the Democrats were there.

But in recent years, our nation has seen a failure of leadership. We've been hurt and we've been disillusioned. We've seen a wall go up that separates us from our own government.

We've lost some precious things that historically have bound our people and our government together.

We feel that moral decay has weakened our country, that it's crippled by a lack of goals and values. And that our public officials have lost faith in us.

We've been a nation adrift too long. We've been without leadership too long. We've had divided and deadlocked government too long. We've been governed by veto too long. We've suffered enough at the hands of a tired and worn-out administration without new ideas, without youth or vitality, without visions, and without the confidence of the American people.

There is a fear that our best years are behind us, but I say to you that our nation's best is still ahead.

Our country has lived through a time of torment. It's now a time for healing.

We want to have faith again!

We want to be proud again!

We *just* want the truth again!

It's time for the people to run the government, and not the other way around.

It's time to honor and strengthen our families and our neighborhoods, and our diverse cultures and customs.

We need a Democratic President and a Congress to work in harmony for a change, with mutual respect for a change, in the open for a change and next year we are going to have that new leadership. You can depend on it.

It's time for America to move and to speak, not with boasting and belligerence, but with a quiet strength—to depend in world affairs not merely on the size of an arsenal but on the nobility of ideas—and to govern at home not by confusion and crisis but with grace and imagination and common sense.

Too many have had to suffer at the hands of a political and economic elite who have shaped decisions and never had to account for mistakes nor to suffer from injustice. When unemployment prevails, they never stand in line looking for a job. When deprivation results from a confused and bewildering welfare system, they never do without food or clothing or a place to sleep. When the public schools are inferior or torn by strife, their children go to exclusive private schools. And when the bureaucracy is bloated and confused, the powerful always manage to discover and occupy niches of special influence and privilege. An unfair tax structure serves their needs. And tight secrecy always seems to prevent reform.

All of us must be careful not to cheat each other.

Too often, unholy, self-perpetuating alliances have been formed between money and politics, and the average citizen has been held at arm's length.

Each time our nation has made a serious mistake, the American people have been excluded from the process. The tragedy of Vietnam and Cambodia, the disgrace of Watergate, and the embarrassment of the CIA revelations could have been avoided if our government had simply reflected the sound judgment and good common sense and the high moral character of the American people.

It's time for us to take a new look at our own government, to strip away the secrecy, to expose the unwarranted pressure of lobbyists, to eliminate waste, to release our civil servants from bureaucratic chaos, to provide tough management and always to remember that in any town or city, the mayor, the governor and the President represent exactly the same constituents.

As a governor, I had to deal each day with the complicated and confused and overlapping and wasteful federal government bureaucracy. As President, I want you to help me evolve an efficient, economical, purposeful and manageable government for our nation. Now I recognize the difficulty, but if I'm elected, it's going to be done, and you can depend on it.

We must strengthen the government closest to the people.

Business, labor, agriculture, education, science education, government should not struggle in isolation from one another, but should be able to strive toward mutual goals and shared opportunities.

We should make major investments in people and not in buildings and weapons. The poor, the aged, the weak, the afflicted must be treated with respect and compassion and with love.

Now I have spoken a lot of times this year about love, but love must be aggressively translated into simple justice.

The test of any government is not how popular it is with the powerful, but how honestly and fairly it deals with those who must depend on it.

It's time for a complete overhaul of our income tax system. I still tell you it's a disgrace to the human race. All my life I have heard promises of tax reform, but it never quite happens. With your help, we are finally going to make it happen and you can depend on it.

Here is something that can really help our country.

It's time for universal voter registration.

It's time for a nationwide, comprehensive health program for all our people.

It's time to guarantee an end to discrimination because of race or sex by full involvement in the decision-making processes of government by those who know what it is to suffer from discrimination, and they'll be in the government if I'm elected.

It's time for the law to be enforced. We cannot educate children, we cannot create harmony among our people, we cannot preserve basic human freedom unless we have an orderly society. Now crime and a lack of justice are especially cruel to those who are least able to protect themselves. Swift arrest and trial, and fair and uniform punishment should be expected by anyone who would break our laws.

It's time for our government leaders to respect the law no less than the humblest citizen, so that we can end once and for all a double standard of justice. I see no reason why big shot crooks should go free and the poor ones go to jail.

A simple and a proper function of government is just to make it easy for us to do good and difficult for us to do wrong.

Now as an engineer, a planner and a businessman, I see clearly the value to our nation of a strong system of free enterprise based on increased productivity and adequate wages. We Democrats believe that competition is better than regulation. And we intend to combine strong safeguards for consumers with minimal intrusion of government in our free economic system.

I believe that anyone who is able to work ought to work—and ought to have a chance to work. We'll never end the inflationary spiral, we'll never have a balanced budget, which I am determined to see, as long as we have eight or nine million Americans out of work who cannot find a job.

Now any system of economics is bankrupt if it sees either value or virtue in unemployment. We simply cannot check inflation by keeping people out of work.

The foremost responsibility of any President above all else is to guarantee the security of our nation—a guarantee of freedom from the threat of successful attack or blackmail and the ability with our allies to maintain peace.

But peace is not the mere absence of war. Peace is action to stamp out international terrorism. Peace is the unceasing effort to preserve human rights. And peace is a combined demonstration of strength and good will. We'll pray for peace and we'll work for peace, until we have removed from all nations for all time the threat of nuclear destruction.

America's birth opened a new chapter in mankind's history. Ours was the first nation to dedicate itself clearly to basic moral and philosophical principles:

That all people are created equal and endowed with inalienable rights to life, liberty and the pursuit of happiness; and that the power of government is derived from the consent of the governed.

This national commitment was a singular act of wisdom and courage, and it brought the best and the bravest from other nations to our shores.

It was a revolutionary development that captured the imagination of mankind.

It created the basis for a unique role for America—that of a pioneer shaping more decent and just relations among people and among societies.

Today, 200 years later, we must address ourselves to that role both in what we do at home and how we act abroad—among people everywhere who have become politically more alert, socially more congested and increasingly impatient with global inequities, and who are now organized as you know, into some 50 different nations.

This calls for nothing less than a sustained architectural effort to shape an international framework of peace within which our own ideals gradually can become a global reality.

Our nation should always derive its character directly from the people and let this be the strength and the image to be presented to the world—the character of the American people.

To our friends and allies I say that what unites us through our common dedication to democracy is much more important than that in which occasionally divides us on economics or politics.

To the nations that seek to lift themselves from poverty, I say that America shares your aspirations and extends its hand to you.

To those nation-states that wish to compete with us, I say that we neither fear competition nor see it as an obstacle to wider cooperation.

And to all people I say that after 200 years America still remains confident and youthful in its commitment to freedom and equality, and we always will be.

During this election year, we candidates will ask you for your votes, and from us will be demanded our vision.

My vision of this nation and its future has been deepened and matured during the 19 months that I have campaigned among you for President.

I've never had more faith in America than I do today.

We have an America that, in Bob Dylan's phrase, is busy being born, not busy dying.

We can have an American government that's turned away from scandal and corruption and official cynicism and is once again as decent and competent as our people.

We can have an America that has reconciled its economic needs with its desire for an environment that we can pass on with pride to the next generation.

We can have an America that provides excellence in education to my child and your child and every child.

We can have an America that encourages and takes pride in our ethnic diversity, our religious diversity, our cultural diversity knowing that out of this pluralistic heritage has come the strength and the vitality and the creativity that made us great and will keep us great.

We can have an American government that does not oppress or spy on its own people, but respects our dignity and our privacy and our right to be let alone.

We can have an America where freedom on the one hand and equality on the other hand are mutually supportive and not in conflict, and where the dreams of our nation's first leaders are fully realized in our own day and age.

And we can have an America which harnesses the idealism of the student, the compassion of the nurse or the social worker, the determination of the farmer, the wisdom of a teacher, the practicality of the business leader, the experience of the senior citizen and the hope of a laborer to build a better life for us all, and we can have it and we are gonna have it.

As I've said many times before, we can have an American President who does not govern with negativism and fear of the future, but with vigor and vision and aggressive leadership—a President who's not isolated from the people, but who feels your pain and shares your dreams, and takes his strength and his wisdom and his courage from you.

I see an America on the move again, united, a diverse and vital and tolerant nation, entering our third century with pride and confidence—an America that lives up to the majesty of our Constitution and the simple decency of our people.

This is the America we want.

This is the America that we will have.

We'll go forward from this convention with some differences of opinion, perhaps, but nevertheless united in a calm determination to make our country large and driving and generous in spirit once again, ready to embark on great national deeds. And once again, as brothers and sisters, our hearts will swell with pride to call ourselves Americans.

Thank you very much.

Acceptance Speech By President Gerald Ford
Kansas City, August 19, 1976

Making no mention of Richard Nixon, although obviously alluding to him, Gerald Ford promised an "open, candid, and forthright Administration" that would help Americans rebuild their "shattered confidence in their highest officials." The President also blamed the country's woes on a Democratic Congress and challenged his opponent, Jimmy Carter, to face-to-face debate.

I am honored by your nomination, and I accept it with pride, with gratitude, and with a total will to win a great victory for the American people. We will wage a winning campaign in every region of this country, from the snowy banks of Minnesota to the sandy plains of Georgia. We concede not a single State. We concede not a single vote.

This evening I am proud to stand before this great convention as the first incumbent President since Dwight D. Eisenhower who can tell the American people America is at peace.

Tonight I can tell you straightaway this Nation is sound, this Nation is secure, this Nation is on the march to full economic recovery and a better quality of life for all Americans.

And I will tell you one more thing: This year the issues are on our side. I am ready, I am eager to go before the American people and debate the real issues face to face with Jimmy Carter. The American people have a right to know first-hand exactly where both of us stand.

I am deeply grateful to those who stood with me in winning the nomination of the party whose cause I have served all of my adult life. I respect the convictions of those who want to change in Washington. I want a change, too. After 22 long years of majority misrule, let's change the United States Congress.

My gratitude tonight reaches far beyond this arena to countless friends whose confidence, hard work, and unselfish support have brought me to this moment. It would be unfair to single out anyone, but may I make an exception for my wonderful family—Mike, Jack, Steve, and Susan and especially my dear wife, Betty.

We Republicans have had some tough competition. We not only preach the virtues of competition, we practice them. But tonight we come together not on a battlefield to conclude a cease-fire, but to join forces on a training field that has conditioned us all for the rugged contest ahead. Let me say this from the bottom of my heart: After the scrimmages of the past few months, it really feels good to have Ron Reagan on the same side of the line.

To strengthen our championship lineup, the convention has wisely chosen one of the ablest Americans as our next Vice President, Senator Bob Dole of Kansas. With his help, with your help, with the help of millions of Americans who cherish peace, who want freedom preserved, prosperity shared, and pride in America, we will win this election. I speak not of a Republican victory, but a victory for the American people.

You at home listening tonight, you are the people who pay the taxes and obey the laws. You are the people who make our system work. Your are the people who make America what it is. It is from your ranks that I come and on your side that I stand.

Something wonderful happened to this country of ours the past 2 years. We all came to realize it on the Fourth of July. Together, out of years of turmoil and tragedy, wars and riots, assassinations and wrongdoing in high places, Americans recaptured the spirit of 1776. We saw again the pioneer vision of our revolutionary founders and our immigrant ancestors. Their vision was of free men and free women enjoying limited government and unlimited opportunity. The mandate I want in 1976 is to make this vision a reality, but it will take the voices and the votes of many more Americans who are not Republicans to make that mandate binding and my mission possible.

I have been called an unelected President, an accidental President. We may even hear that again from the other party, despite the fact that I was welcomed and endorsed by an overwhelming majority of their elected representatives in the Congress who certified my fitness to our highest office. Having become Vice President and President without expecting or seeking either, I have a special feeling toward these high offices. To me, the Presidency and the Vice-Presidency were not prizes to be won, but a duty to be done.

So, tonight it is not the power and the glamour of the Presidency that leads me to ask for another 4 years; it is something every hard-working American will understand—the challenge of a job well begun, but far from finished.

Two years ago, on August 9, 1974, I placed my hand on the Bible, which Betty held, and took the same constitutional oath that was administered to George Washington. I had faith in our people, in our institutions, and in myself. "My fellow Americans," I said, "our long national nightmare is over."

It was an hour in our history that troubled our minds and tore at our hearts. Anger and hatred had risen to dangerous levels, dividing friends and families. The polarization of our political order had aroused unworthy passions of reprisal and revenge. Our governmental system was closer to stalemate than any time since Abraham Lincoln took the same oath of office. Our economy was in the throes of runaway inflation, taking us headlong into the worst recession since Franklin D. Roosevelt took the same oath.

On that dark day I told my fellow countrymen, "I am acutely aware that you have not elected me as your President by your ballots, so I ask you to confirm me as your President with your prayers."

On a marble fireplace in the White House is carved a prayer which John Adams wrote. In concludes, "May none but honest and wise men ever rule under this roof." Since I have resided in that historic house, I have tried to live by that prayer. I faced many tough problems. I probably made some mistakes, but on balance, America and Americans have made an incredible comeback since August 1974. Nobody can honestly say otherwise. And the plain truth is that the great progress we have made at home and abroad was in spite of the majority who run the Congress of the United States.

For 2 years I have stood for all the people against a vote-hungry, free-spending congressional majority on Capitol Hill. Fifty-five times I vetoed extravagant and unwise legislation; 45 times I made those vetoes stick. Those vetoes have saved American taxpayers billions and billions of dollars. I am against the big tax spender and for the little taxpayer.

I called for a permanent tax cut, coupled with spending reductions, to stimulate the economy and relieve hard-pressed, middle-income taxpayers. Your personal exemption must be raised from $750 to $1,000. The other party's platform talks about tax reform, but there is one big problem—their own Congress won't act.

I called for reasonable constitutional restrictions on court-ordered busing of schoolchildren, but the other party's platform concedes that busing should be a last resort. But there is the same problem—their own Congress won't act.

I called for a major overhaul of criminal laws to crack down on crime and illegal drugs. The other party's platform deplores America's $90 billion cost of crime. There is the problem again—their own Congress won't act.

The other party's platform talks about a strong defense. Now, here is the other side of the problem—their own Congress did act. They slashed $50 billion from our national defense needs in the last 10 years.

My friends, Washington is not the problem; their Congress is the problem.

You know, the President of the United States is not a magician who can wave a wand or sign a paper that will instantly end a war, cure a recession, or make bureaucracy disappear. A President has immense powers under the Constitution, but all of them ultimately come from the American people and their mandate to him. That is why, tonight, I turn to the American people and ask not only for your prayers but also for your strength and your support, for your voice, and for your vote.

I come before you with a 2-year record of performance without your mandate. I offer you a 4-year pledge of greater performance with your mandate. As Governor Al Smith used to say, "Let's look at the record."

Two years ago inflation was 12 percent. Sales were off. Plants were shut down. Thousands were being laid off every week. Fear of the future was throttling down our economy and threatening millions of families.

Let's look at the record since August 1974. Inflation has been cut in half. Payrolls are up. Profits are up. Production is up. Purchases are up. Since the recession was turned around, almost 4 million of our fellow Americans have found new jobs or got their old jobs back. This year more men and women have jobs than ever before in the history of the United States. Confidence has returned, and we are in the full surge of sound recovery to steady prosperity.

Two years ago America was mired in withdrawal from Southeast Asia. A decade of Congresses had shortchanged our global defenses and threatened our strategic posture. Mounting tension between Israel and the Arab nations made another war seem inevitable. The whole world watched and wondered where America was going. Did we in our domestic turmoil have the will, the stamina, and the unity to stand up for freedom?

Look at the record since August, 2 years ago. Today America is at peace and seeks peace for all nations. Not a single American is at war anywhere on the face of this Earth tonight.

Our ties with Western Europe and Japan, economic as well as military, were never stronger. Our relations with Eastern Europe, the Soviet Union, and mainland China are firm, vigilant, and forward looking. Policies I have initiated offer sound progress for the peoples of the Pacific, Africa, and Latin America. Israel and Egypt, both trusting the United States, have taken an historic step that promises an eventual just settlement for the whole Middle East.

The world now respects America's policy of peace through strength. The United States is again the confident leader of the free world. Nobody questions our dedication to peace, but nobody doubts our willingness to use our strength when our vital interests are at stake, and we will. I called for an up-to-date, powerful Army, Navy, Air Force, and Marines that will keep America secure for decades. A strong military posture is always the best insurance for peace. But America's strength has never rested on arms alone. It is rooted in our mutual commitment of our citizens and leaders in the highest standards of ethics and morality and in the spiritual renewal which our Nation is undergoing right now.

Two years ago people's confidence in their highest officials, to whom they had overwhelmingly entrusted power, had twice been shattered. Losing faith in the word of their elected leaders, Americans lost some of their own faith in themselves.

Again, let's look at the record since August 1974. From the start my administration has been open, candid, forthright. While my entire public and private life was under searching examination for the Vice-Presidency, I reaffirmed my lifelong conviction that truth is the glue that holds government together—not only government but civilization itself. I have demanded honesty, decency, and personal integrity from everybody in the executive branch of the Government. The House and Senate have the same duty.

The American people will not accept a double standard in the United States Congress. Those who make our laws today must not debase the reputation of our great legislative bodies that have given us such giants as Daniel Webster, Henry Clay, Sam Rayburn, and Robert A. Taft. Whether in the Nation's Capital, the State capital, or city hall, private morality and public trust must go together.

From August of 1974 to August of 1976, the record shows steady progress upward toward prosperity, peace, and public trust. My record is one of progress, not platitudes. My record is one of specifics, not smiles. My record is one of performance, not promises. It is a record I am proud to run on. It is a record the American people—Democrats, Independents, and Republicans alike—will support on November 2.

For the next 4 years I pledge to you that I will hold to the steady course we have begun. But I have no intention of standing on the record alone.

We will continue winning the fight against inflation. We will go on reducing the dead weight and impudence of bureaucracy. We will submit a balanced budget by 1978.

We will improve the quality of life at work, at play, and in our homes and in our neighborhoods. We will not abandon our cities. We will encourage urban programs which assure safety in the streets, create healthy environments, and restore neighborhood pride. We will return control of our children's education to parents and local school authorities.

We will make sure that the party of Lincoln remains the party of equal rights.

We will create a tax structure that is fair for all our citizens, one that preserves the continuity of the family home, the family farm, and the family business.

We will ensure the integrity of the social security system and improve Medicare so that our older citizens can enjoy the health and the happiness that they have earned. There is no reason they should have to go broke just to get well.

We will make sure that this rich Nation does not neglect citizens who are less fortunate, but provides for their needs with compassion and with dignity.

We will reduce the growth and the cost of government and allow individual breadwinners and businesses to keep more of the money that they earn.

We will create a climate in which our economy will provide a meaningful job for everyone who wants to work and a decent standard of life for all Americans. We will ensure that all of our young people have a better chance in life than we had, an education they can use, and a career they can be proud of.

We will carry out a farm policy that assures a fair market price for the farmer, encourages full production, leads to record exports, and eases the hunger within the human family. We will never use the bounty of America's farmer as a pawn in international diplomacy. There will be no embargoes.

We will continue our strong leadership to bring peace, justice, and economic progress where there is turmoil, especially in the Middle East. We will build a safer and saner world through patient negotiations and dependable arms agreements which reduce the danger of conflict and horror of thermonuclear war. While I am President, we will not return to a collision course that could reduce civilization to ashes.

We will build an America where people feel rich in spirit as well as in worldly goods. We will build an America where people feel proud about themselves and about their country.

We will build on performance, not promises; experience, not expediency; real progress instead of mysterious plans to be revealed in some dim and distant future. The American people are wise, wiser than our opponents think. They know who pays for every campaign promise. They are not afraid of the truth. We will tell them the truth.

From start to finish, our campaign will be credible; it will be responsible. We will come out fighting, and we will win. Yes, we have all seen the polls and the pundits who say our party is dead. I have heard that before. So did Harry Truman. I will tell you what I think. the only polls that count are the polls the American people go to on November 2. And right now, I predict that the American people are going to say that night, "Jerry, you have done a good job, keep right on doing it."

As I try in my imagination to look into the homes where families are watching the end of this great convention, I can't tell which faces are Republicans, which are Democrats, and which are Independents. I cannot see their color or their creed. I see only Americans.

I see Americans who love their husbands, their wives, and their children. I see Americans who love their country for what it has been and what it must become. I see Americans who work hard, but who are willing to sacrifice all they have worked for to keep their children and their country free. I see Americans who in their own quiet way pray for peace among nations and peace among themselves. We do love our neighbors, and we do forgive those who have trespassed against us.

I see a new generation that knows what is right and knows itself, a generation determined to preserve its ideals, its environment, our Nation, and the world.

My fellow Americans, I like what I see. I have no fear for the future of this great country. And as we go forward together, I promise you once more what I promised before: to uphold the Constitution, to do what is right as God gives me to see the right, and to do the very best that I can for America.

God helping me, I won't let you down.

Thank you very much.

First Presidential Campaign Debate
Philadelphia, September 23, 1976

Forensic skill was conspicuously absent in the first formal debate between major party presidential candidates since the Nixon-Kennedy encounters of 1960. While Jimmy Carter appeared wooden, nervous, and, to a consensus of media observers, decidedly "unpresidential," Gerald Ford seemed equally ill at ease and had difficulty communicating effectively. Technical difficulties in the broadcast caused a breakdown (which lasted an agonizing 27 minutes) that did little to enhance the composure of either candidate.

THE MODERATOR: I am Edwin Newman, moderator of this first debate of the 1976 Campaign between Gerald R. Ford of Michigan, Republican candidate for President, and Jimmy Carter of Georgia, Democratic candidate for President.

We thank you, President Ford, and we thank you, Governor Carter, for being with us tonight.

There are to be three debates between the Presidential candidates and one between the Vice-Presidential candidates. All are being arranged by the League of Women Voters Education Fund.

Tonight's debate, the first between Presidential candidates in 16 years and the first ever in which an incumbent President has participated, is taking place before an audience in the Walnut Street Theatre in Philadelphia, just 3 blocks from Independence Hall. The television audience may reach 100 million in the United States and many millions overseas.

Tonight's debate focuses on domestic and economic policy. Questions will be put by Frank Reynolds of ABC News, James Gannon of the *Wall Street Journal,* and Elizabeth Drew of the *New Yorker* magazine.

Under the agreed rules the first question will go to Governor Carter. That was decided by the toss of a coin. He will have up to 3 minutes to answer. One followup question will be permitted with up to 2 minutes to reply. President Ford will then have 2 minutes to respond.

The next question will go to President Ford, with the same time arrangements, and questions will continue to be alternated between the candidates. Each man will make a 3-minute statement at the end, Governor Carter to go first.

President Ford and Governor Carter do not have any notes or prepared remarks with them this evening.

Mr. Reynolds, your question for Governor Carter.

MR. REYNOLDS: Mr. President, Governor Carter.

Governor, in an interview with the Associated Press last week, you said you believed these debates would alleviate a lot of concern that some voters have about you. Well, one of those concerns—not an uncommon one about candidates in any year—is that many voters say they don't really know where you stand.

Now, you have made jobs your number one priority, and you have said you are committed to a drastic reduction in unemployment. Can you say now, Governor, in specific terms what your first step would be next January, if you are elected, to achieve that?

MR. CARTER: Yes. First of all it's to recognize the tremendous economic strength of this country and to set the putting back to work of our people as a top priority. This is an effort that ought to be done primarily by strong leadership in the White House, the inspiration of our people, the tapping of business, agriculture, industry, labor, and government at all levels to work on this project. We will never have an end to the inflationary spiral, and we will never have a balanced budget until we get our people back to work.

There are several things that can be done specifically that are not now being done: first of all, to channel research and development funds into areas that will provide large numbers of jobs; secondly, we need to have a commitment in the private sector to cooperate with government in matters like housing. Here, a very small investment of taxpayer's money in the housing field can bring large numbers of extra jobs, in the guarantee of mortgage loans, in the putting forward of 202 programs for housing for older people and so forth, to cut down the roughly 20-percent unemployment that now exists in the construction industry.

Another thing is to deal with our needs in the central cities where the unemployment rate is extremely high—sometimes among minority groups, those who don't speak English or who are black or young people—a 40-percent unemployment. Here, a CCC (Civilian Conservation Corps)-type program would be appropriate, to channel money into the sharing with private sector and also local and State governments to employ young people who are now out of work.

Another very important aspect of our economy would be to increase production in every way possible, to hold down taxes on individuals, and to shift the tax burdens on to those who have avoided paying taxes in the past.

These kinds of specific things, none of which are being done now, would be a great help in reducing unemployment.

There is an additonal factor that needs to be done and covered very succinctly, and that is to make sure that we have a good relationship between management, business on the one hand and labor on the other.

In a lot of places where unemployment is very high, we might channel specific, targeted job opportunities by paying part of the salary of unemployed people and also sharing with local governments the payments of salaries, which would let us cut down the unemployment rate much lower before we hit the inflationary level.

But I believe that by the end of the first 4 years of the next term, we could have the unemployment rate down to 3 percent—adult unemployment—which is about 4 to 4 1/2 percent overall, a controlled inflation rate, and have a balanced growth of about 4 to 6 percent, around 5 percent, which would give us a balanced budget.

MR. REYNOLDS: Governor, in the event you are successful and you do achieve a drastic drop in unemployment, that is likely to create additional pressure on prices. How willing are you to consider an incomes policy; in other words, wage and price controls?

MR. CARTER: Well, we now have such a low utilization of our productive capacity, about 73 percent—I think it's about the lowest since the Great Depression years—and such a high unemployment rate now—7.9 percent—that we have a long way to go in getting people to work before we have the inflationary pressures. And I think this would be easy to accomplish, to get jobs now without having the strong inflationary pressures that would be necessary.

I would not favor the payment of a given fixed income to people unless they are not able to work. But with tax incentives for the low-income groups, we could build up their income levels above the poverty level and not make welfare more profitable than work.

THE MODERATOR: Mr. President, your response?

MR. FORD: I don't believe that Mr. Carter has been any more specific in this case than he has been on many other instances. I notice particularly that he didn't endorse the Humphrey-Hawkins bill, which he has on occasions and which is included as a part of the Democratic platform. That legislation allegedly would help our unemployment, but we all know that it would have controlled our economy. It would have added $10 to $30 billion each year in additional expenditures by the Federal government. It would have called for export controls on agricultural products.

In my judgment the best way to get jobs is to expand the private sector, where five out of six jobs today exist in our economy. We can do that by reducing Federal taxes, as I proposed about a year ago when I called for a tax reduction of $28 billion, three-quarters of it to go to private taxpayers and one-quarter to the business sector. We could add to jobs in the major metropolitan areas by a proposal that I recommended that would give tax incentives to business to move into the inner city and to expand or to build new plants so they would take a plant or expand a plant where people are and people are currently unemployed.

We could also help our youth with some of the proposals that would give to young people an opportunity to work and learn at the same time, just like we give money to young people who are going to college.

Those are the kind of specifics that I think we have to discuss on these debates, and these are the kind of programs that I will talk about on my time.

THE MODERATOR: Mr. Gannon, your question to President Ford.

MR. GANNON: Mr. President, I would like to continue for a moment on this question of taxes which you have just raised. You have said that you favor more tax cuts for middle-income Americans, even those earning up to $30,000 a year. That presumably would cost the Treasury quite a bit of money in lost revenue.

In view of the very large budget deficits that you have accumulated and that are still in prospect, how is it possible to promise further tax cuts and to reach your goal of balancing the budget?

MR. FORD: At the time, Mr. Gannon, that I made the recommendation for a $28 billion tax cut—three-quarters of it to go to individual taxpayers and 25 percent to American business—I said at the same time that we had to hold the lid on federal spending; that for every dollar of a tax reduction, we had to have an equal reduction in Federal expenditures—a one-for-one proposition. And I recommended that to the Congress with a budget ceiling of $395 billion, and that would have permitted us to have a $28 billion tax reduction.

In my tax reduction program for middle-income taxpayers, I recommended that the Congress increase personal exemptions from $750 per person to $1,000 per person. That would mean, of course, that for a family of four that they could spend for their own purposes, money that the Government wouldn't have to spend. But if we keep the lid on Federal spending, which I think we can with the help of the Congress, we can justify fully a $28 billion tax reduction.

In the budget that I submitted to the Congress in January of this year, I recommended a 50-percent cutback in the rate of growth of Federal spending. For the last 10 years the budget of the United States has grown from about 11 percent per year. We can't afford that kind of growth in Federal spending. And in the budget that I recommended, we cut it in half—a growth rate of 5 to 5 1/2 percent. With that kind of limitation on Federal spending, we can fully justify the tax reductions that I have proposed. And it seems to me, with the stimulant of more money in the hands of the taxpayers and with more money in the hands of business to expand, to modernize, to provide more jobs, our economy will be stimulated so that we will get more revenue, and we will have a more prosperous economy.

MR. GANNON: Mr. President, to follow up a moment, the Congress has passed a tax bill which is before you now which did not meet exactly the sort of outline that you requested. What is your intention on that bill since it doesn't meet your requirements? Do you plan to sign that bill?

MR. FORD: That tax bill does not entirely meet the criteria that I established. I think the Congress should have added another $10 billion reduction in personal income taxes, including the increase of personal exemptions from $750 to $1,000. And Congress could have done that if the budget committees of the Congress and the Congress as a whole had not increased the spending that I recommended in the budget. I am sure you know that in the resolutions passed by the Congress, they have added about $17 billion in more spending by the Congress over the budget that I recommended. So, I would prefer in that tax bill to have an additional tax cut and a further limitation on Federal spending.

Now, this tax bill that hasn't reached the White House yet—but is expected in a day or two—it's about 1,500 pages. It has some good provisions in it; it has left out some that I have recommended, unfortunately. On the other hand, when you have a bill of that magnitude, with those many provisions, a President has to sit and decide if there is more good than bad. And from the analysis that I have made so far, it seems to me that the tax bill does justify my signature and my approval.

THE MODERATOR: Governor Carter, your response.

MR. CARTER: Well, Mr. Ford is changing considerably his previous philosophy. The present tax structure is a disgrace to this country. It's just a welfare program for the rich. As a matter of fact, 25 percent of the total tax deductions go for only 1 percent of the richest people in this country, and over 50 percent of the tax credits go for the 14 percent of the richest people in this country.

When Mr. Ford first became President in August of 1974, the first thing he did in October was to ask for a $4.7 billion increase in taxes on our people in the midst of the heaviest recession since the Great Depression of the 1940's. In January of 1975, he asked for a tax change, a $5.6 billion increase on low- and middle-income private individuals, a $6 1/2 billion decrease on the corporations and the special interests. In December of 1975, he vetoed the roughly $18 to $20 billion tax reduction bill that had passed by the Congress. And then he came back later on in January of this year, and he did advocate a $10 billion tax reduction, but it would be offset by a $6 billion increase this coming January in deductions for social security payments and for unemployment compensation.

The whole philosophy of the Republican Party, including my opponent, has been to pile on taxes on low-income people, to take them off on the corporations. As a matter of fact, since the late sixties when Mr. Nixon took office, we've had a reduction in the percentage of taxes paid by corporations from 30 percent down to about 20 percent. We've had an increase in taxes paid by individuals, payroll taxes, from 14 percent up to 20 percent. This is what the Republicans have done to us. This is why tax reform is so important.

THE MODERATOR: Mrs. Drew, your question to Governor Carter.

Ms. DREW: Governor Carter, you've proposed a number of new or enlarged programs, including jobs and health, welfare reform, child care, aid to education, aid to cities, changes in social security and housing subsidies. You've also said that you want to balance the budget by the end of your first term. Now you haven't put a price tag on those programs, but even if we priced them conservatively, and we count for full employment by the end of your first term, and we count for the economic growth that would occur during that period, there still isn't enough money to pay for those programs and balance the budget by any estimates that I've been able to see.

So, in that case, what would give?

MR. CARTER: Well, as a matter of fact, there is. If we assume a rate of growth of our economy equivalent to what it was during President Johnson and President Kennedy, even before the Vietnamese war, and if we assume that, at the end of the 4-year period we can cut our unemployment rate down to 4 to 4 1/2 percent. Under those circumstances, even assuming no elimination of unnecessary programs and assuming an increase in the allotment of money to finance programs increasing as the inflation rate does, my economic projects, I think confirmed by the House and the Senate committees, have been with a $60 billion extra amount of money that can be spent in fiscal year '81—which would be the last year of this next term—within that $60 billion increase, there would be fit the programs that I promised the American people. I might say, too, that if we see that these goals cannot be reached—and I believe they are reasonable goals—then I would cut back on the rate of implementation of new programs in order to accommodate a balanced budget by fiscal year '81, which is the last year of the next term.

I believe that we ought to have a balanced budget during normal economic circumstances. And these projections have been very carefully made. I stand behind them. And if they should be in error slightly on the down side, then I will phase in the programs that we've advocated more slowly.

Ms. DREW: Governor, according to the budget committees of the Congress that you referred to, if we get to full employment, what they project at a 4-percent unemployment and, as you say, even allowing for the inflation in the programs, there would not be anything more than a surplus of $5 billion by 1981. Conservative estimates of your programs would be that they'd be about $85 to $100 billion. So, how do you say that you are going to be able to do these things and balance the budget?

MR. CARTER: Well, the assumption that you have described that's different is in the rate of growth of our economy.

Ms. DREW: No, they took that into account in those figures.

MR. CARTER: I believe that it's accurate to say that the committees to whom you refer, with the employment rate that you state and with the 5 to 5 1/2 percent growth rate in our economy, that the projections would be a $60 billion increase in the amount of money that we have to spend in 1981 compared to now.

And in that framework would be fit any improvements in the programs. Now, this does not include any extra control over unnecessary spending, the weeding out of obsolete or obsolescent programs. We will have a safety version built in with complete reorganization of the executive branch of Government, which I am pledged to do.

The present bureaucratic structure of the Federal government is a mess. And if I am elected President, that's going to be a top priority of mine—to completely revise the structure of the Federal Government to make it economical, efficient, purposeful, and manageable for a change. And also, I am going to institute zero-base budgeting, which I used 4 years in Georgia, which assesses every program every year and eliminates those programs that are obsolete or obsolescent.

But with these projections we will have a balanced budget by fiscal year 1981 if I am elected President, keep my promises to the American people. And it's just predicated on very modest, but I think accurate, projections of employment increases and a growth in our national economy equal to what was experienced under Kennedy, Johnson, before the Vietnam war.

THE MODERATOR: President Ford.

MR. FORD: If it is true that there will be a $60 billion surplus by fiscal year 1981, rather than spend that money for all the new programs that Governor Carter recommends and endorses and which are included in the Democratic platform, I think the American taxpayer ought to get an additional tax break, a tax reduction of that magnitude. I feel that the taxpayers are the ones that need the relief. I don't think we should add additional programs of the magnitude that Governor Carter talks about.

It seems to me that our tax structure today has rates that are too high. But I am very glad to point out has since 1969, during a Republican administration, we have had 10 million people taken off of the tax rolls at the lower end of the taxpayer area. And at the same time, assuming that I sign the tax bill that was mentioned by Mr. Gannon, we will, in the last two tax bills, have increased the minimum tax on all wealthy taxpayers.

And I believe that by eliminating 10 million taxpayers in the last 8 years and by putting a heavier tax burden on those in the higher tax brackets, plus the other actions that have been taken, we can give taxpayers adequate tax relief.

Now, it seems to me that as we look at the recommendations of the budget committees and our own projections, there isn't going to be any $60 billion dividend. I've heard of those dividends in the past. It always happens. We expected one at the time of the Vietnam war, but it was used up before we ever ended the war, and taxpayers never got the adequate relief they deserved.

THE MODERATOR: Mr. Reynolds

MR. REYNOLDS: Mr. President, when you came into office, you spoke very eloquently of the need for a time for healing. And very early in your administration you went out to Chicago and you announced, you proposed a program of case-by-case pardons for draft resisters to restore them to full citizenship. Some 14,000 young men took advantage of your offer, but another 90,000 did not. In granting the pardon to former President Nixon, sir, part of your rationale was to put Watergate behind us, to, if I may quote you again, truly end "our long national nightmare."

Why does not the same rationale apply now, today, in our Bicentennial Year to the young men who resisted in Vietnam and many of them still in exile abroad?

MR. FORD: The amnesty program that I recommended in Chicago in September of 1974 would give to all draft evaders and military deserters the opportunity to earn their good record back. About 14 to 15,000 did take advantage of that program. We gave them ample time. I am against an across-the-board pardon of draft evaders or military deserters.

Now, in the case of Mr. Nixon, the reason the pardon was given was that when I took office this country was in a very, very divided condition. There was hatred; there was divisiveness; people had lost faith in their government in many, many respects. Mr. Nixon resigned, and I became President. It seemed to me that if I was to adequately and effectively handle the problems of high inflation, a growing recession, the involvement of the United States still in Vietnam, that I had to give 100 percent of my time to those two major problems.

Mr. Nixon resigned; that is disgrace—the first President out of 38 that ever resigned from public office under pressure. So, when you look at the penalty that he paid, and when you analyze the requirements that I had to spend all of my time working on the economy, which was in trouble, that I inherited, working on our problems in Southeast Asia, which were still plaguing us, it seemed to me that Mr. Nixon had been penalized enough by his resignation in disgrace. And the need and necessity for me to concentrate on the problems of the country fully justified the action that I took.

MR. REYNOLDS: I take it, then, sir, that you do not believe that you are going to reconsider and think about those 90,000 who are still abroad? Have they not been penalized enough? Many of them have been there for years.

MR. FORD: Well, Mr. Carter has indicated that he would give a blanket pardon to all draft evaders. I do not agree with that point of view. I gave in September of 1974 an opportunity for all draft evaders, all deserters, to come in voluntarily, clear their records by earning an opportunity to restore their good citizenship. I think we gave them a good opportunity. I don't think we should go any further.

THE MODERATOR: Governor Carter.

MR. CARTER: Well, I think it's very difficult for President Ford to explain the difference between the pardon of President Nixon and his attitude toward those who violated the draft laws. As a matter of fact now, I don't advocate amnesty; I advocate pardon. There is a difference, in my opinion, and in accordance with the ruling of the Supreme Court and in accordance with the definition in the dictionary.

Amnesty means that what you did was right. Pardon means that what you did, whether it's right or wrong, you are forgiven for it. And I do advocate a pardon for draft evaders. I think it's accurate to say that 2 years ago, when Mr. Ford put in this amnesty, that three times as many deserters were excused as were the ones who evaded the draft.

But I think that now is the time to heal our country after the Vietnam war. And I think that what the people are concerned about is not the pardon or the amnesty of those who evaded the draft, but whether or not our crime system is fair.

We have got a sharp distinction drawn between white collar crime. The big-shots who are rich, who are influential, very seldom go to jail. Those who are poor and who have no influence quite often are the ones who are punished. And the whole subject of crime is one that concerns our people very much. And I believe that the fairness of it is what is the major problem that addresses our leader, and this is something that hasn't been addressed adequately by this administration.

But I hope to have a complete responsibility on my shoulders to help bring about a fair criminal justice system and also to bring about an end to the divisiveness that has occurred in our country as a result of the Vietnam war.

THE MODERATOR: Mr. Gannon.

MR. GANNON: Governor Carter, you have promised a sweeping overhaul of the Federal Government including a reduction in the number of Government agencies you say would go down to about 200 from some 1,900. That sounds indeed like a very deep cut in the Federal Government. But isn't it a fact that you are not really talking about fewer Federal employees or less Government spending, but rather that you are talking about reshaping the Federal Government, not making it smaller?

MR. CARTER: Well, I've been through this before, Mr. Gannon, as the Governor of Georgia. When I took over we had a bureaucratic mess like we have in Washington now. And we had 300 agencies, departments, bureaus, commissions—some fully budgeted, some not—but all having responsibility to carry out that was in conflict. And we cut those 300 agencies and so forth down substantially; we eliminated 278 of them. We set up a simple structure of government that could be administered fairly, and it was a tremendous success. It hasn't been undone since I was there.

It resulted also in an ability to reshape our court system, our prison system, our education system, our mental health programs, and a clear assignment of responsibility and authority, and also to have our people once again understand and control our Government.

I intend to do the same thing if I am elected President. When I get to Washington, coming in as an outsider, one of the major responsibilities that I will have on my shoulder is a complete reorganization of the executive branch of Government.

We now have a greatly expanded White House staff. When Mr. Nixon went in office, for instance, we had $3 1/2 million spent on the White House and its staff. That has escalated now to $16 1/2 million in the last Republican administration. This needs to be changed. We need to put the responsibilities back on the Cabinet members. We also need to have a great reduction in agencies and programs. For instance, we now have in the health area 302 different programs administered by 11 major departments and agencies. Sixty other advisory commissions are responsible for this. Medicaid is in one agency; Medicare is in a different one; the check on the quality of health care is in a different one. None of them are responsible for health care itself. This makes it almost impossible for us to have a good health program.

We have just advocated this past week a consolidation of the responsibilities for energy. Our country now has no comprehensive energy program or policy. We have 20 different agencies in the Federal Government responsible for the production, the regulation, the information about energy, the conservation of energy spread all over Government. This is a gross waste of money. So, tough, competent management of Government, giving us a simple, efficient, purposeful, and manageable Government will be a great step forward. And if I am elected—and I intend to be—then it's going to be done.

MR. GANNON: Well, I'd like to press my question on the number of Federal employees—whether you would really plan to reduce the overall number or merely put them in different departments and relabel them? In your energy plan, you consolidate a number of agencies into one, or you would, but does that really change the overall?

MR. CARTER: I can't say for sure that we would have fewer Federal employees when I go out of office than when I come in. It took me about 3 years to completely reorganize the Georgia government. The last year I was in office our budget was actually less than it was a year before, which showed a great improvement.

Also, we had a 2-percent increase in the number of employees the last year, but it was a tremendous shift from administrative jobs into the delivery of services. For instance, we completely revised our prison system. We established 84 new mental health treatment centers, and we shifted people out of administrative jobs into the field to deliver better services. The same thing will be done at the Federal Government level.

I accomplished this with substantial reductions in employees in some departments. For instance, in the Transportation Department we cut back about 25 percent of the total number of employees. In giving our people better mental health care, we increased the number of employees. But the efficiency of it, the simplicity of it, the ability of people to understand their own government and control it was a substantial benefit derived from complete reorganization.

We have got to do this at the Federal Government level. If we don't, the bureaucratic mess is going to continue. There is no way for our people now to understand what their Government is; there is no way to get the answer to a question. When you come to Washington to try to—as a Governor—to try to begin a new program for your people, like the treatment of drug addicts, I found there were 13 different Federal agencies that I had to go to to manage the drug treatment program. In the Georgia government we only had one agency responsible for drug treatment.

This is the kind of change that would be made. And it would be of tremendous benefit in long-range planning, in tight budgeting, saving the taxpayers' money, making the Government more efficient, cutting down on bureaucratic waste, having a clear delineation of authority and responsibility of employees, and giving our people a better chance to understand and control their Government.

THE MODERATOR: President Ford.

MR. FORD: I think the record should show, Mr. Newman, that the Bureau of Census—we checked it just yesterday—indicates that in the 4 years that Governor Carter was Governor of the State of Georgia, expenditures by the government went up over 50 percent. Employees of the government in Georgia during his term of office went up over 25 percent. And the figures also show that the bonded indebtedness of the State of Georgia during his Governorship went up over 20 percent.

And there was some very interesting testimony given by Governor Carter's successor, Governor Busbee, before a Senate committee a few months ago, on how he found the Medicaid program when he came into office following Governor Carter. He testified, and these are his words, the present Governor of Georgia, he says he found the Medicaid program in Georgia in shambles.

Now, let me talk about what we've done in the White House as far as Federal employees are concerned. The first order that I issued after I became President was to cut or eliminate the prospective 40,000 increase in Federal employees that had been scheduled by my predecessor. And in the term that I have been President—some 2 years—we have reduced Federal employment by 11,000.

In the White House staff itself, when I became President we had roughly 540 employees. We now have about 485 employees. So, we've made a rather significant reduction in the number of employees on the White House staff working for the President.

So, I think our record of cutting back employees, plus the failure on the part of the Governor's program to actually save employment in Georgia, shows which is the better plan.

THE MODERATOR: Mrs. Drew.

MS. DREW: Mr. President, at Vail, after the Republican convention, you announced that you would now emphasize five new areas. Among those were jobs and housing and health, improved recreational facilities for Americans, and you also added crime. You also mentioned education.

For 2 years you've been telling us that we couldn't do very much in these areas because we couldn't afford it, and in fact, we do have a $50 billion deficit now. In rebuttal to Governor Carter a little bit earlier, you said that if there were to be any surplus in the next few years, you thought it should be turned back to the people in the form of tax relief. So, how are you going to pay for any new initiatives in these areas you announced at Vail you were going to now stress?

MR. FORD: Well, in the last 2 years, as I indicated before, we had a very tough time. We were faced with heavy inflation—over 12 percent; we were faced with substantial unemployment. But in the last 24 months we've turned the economy around, and we've brought inflation down to under 6 percent. And we have added employment of about 4 million in the last 17 months to the point where we have 88 million people working in America today, the most in the history of the country. The net result is we are going to have some improvement in our receipts, and I think we will have some decrease in our disbursements. We expect to have a lower deficit in fiscal year 1978.

We feel that with this improvement in the economy, we feel with more receipts and fewer disbursements, we can, in a moderate way, increase, as I recommended, over the next 10 years a new parks program that would cost a billion and a half dollars, doubling our national park system.

We have recommended that in the housing program we can reduce down payments and moderate monthly payments. But that doesn't cost any more as far as the Federal Treasury is concerned.

We believe that we can do a better job in the area of crime, but that requires tougher sentencing—mandatory, certain prison sentences for those who violate our criminal laws. We believe that you can revise the Federal Criminal Code, which has not been revised in a good many years. That doesn't cost any more money. We believe that you can do something more effectively with a moderate increase in money in the drug abuse program.

We feel that in education we can have a slight increase, not a major increase. It's my understanding that Governor Carter has indicated that he approves of a $30 billion expenditure by the Federal Government, as far as education is concerned. At the present time we are spending roughly $3,500 million. I don't know where that money would come from.

But, as we look at the quality of life programs—jobs, health, education, crime, recreation—we feel that as we move forward with a healthier economy, we can absorb the small, necessary costs that will be required.

MS. DREW: But, sir, in the next few years would you try to reduce the deficit, would you spend money for these programs that you have just outlined, or would you, as you said earlier, return whatever surplus you got to the people in the form of tax relief?

MR. FORD: We feel that with the programs that I have recommended, the additional $10 billion tax cut, with the moderate increases in the quality of life area, we can still have a balanced budget, which I will submit to the Congress in January of 1978. We won't wait 1 year or 2 years longer, as Governor Carter indicates.

As the economy improves, and it is improving—our gross national product this year will average about 6-percent increase over last year—we will have a lower rate of inflation for the calendar year this year, something slightly under 6 percent; employment will be up; revenues will be up. We will keep the lid on some of these programs that we can hold down, as we have a little extra money to spend for those quality of life programs, which I think are needed and necessary.

Now, I cannot and would not endorse the kind of programs that Governor Carter recommends. He endorses the Democratic platform which, as I read it, calls for approximately 60 additional programs. We estimate that those programs would add $100 billion minimum and probably $200 billion maximum each year to the Federal budget. Those programs you cannot afford and give tax relief.

We feel that you can hold the line and restrain Federal spending, give a tax reduction, and still have a balanced budget by 1978.

THE MODERATOR: Governor Carter.

MR. CARTER: Well, Mr. Ford takes the same attitude that the Republicans always take. In the last 3 months before an election, they are always for the programs that they fight the other 3 1/2 years. I remember when Herbert Hoover was against jobs for people. I remember when Alf Landon was against social security. And later President Nixon—16 years ago—was telling the public that John Kennedy's proposals would bankrupt the country and would double the cost.

The best thing to do is to look at the record of Mr. Ford's administration and Mr. Nixon's before his.

We had last year a $65 billion deficit, the largest deficit in the history of our country, more of a deficit spending than we had in the entire 8-year period under President Johnson and President Kennedy. We've got 500,000 more Americans out of jobs today than were out of work 3 months ago. And since Mr. Ford has been in office, in 2 years we've had a 50-percent increase in unemployment, from 5 million people out of work to 2 1/2 million more people out of work, or a total of 7 1/2 million. We've also got a comparison between himself and Mr. Nixon. He's got four times the size of the deficits that Mr. Nixon even had himself.

This talking about more people at work is distorted because with the 14-percent increase in the cost of living in the last 2 years, it means that women and young people have had to go to work when they didn't want to because their fathers couldn't make enough to pay the increased cost of food and housing and clothing.

We have, in this last 2 years alone, $120 billion total deficits under President Ford, and at the same time we've had in the last 8 years a doubling in the number of bankruptcies for small business. We've had a negative growth in our national economy, measured in real dollars. The take-home pay of a worker in this country is actually less now than it was in 1968, measured in real dollars. This is the kind of record that is there, and talk about the future and a drastic change of conversion on the part of Mr. Ford at the last minute is one that just doesn't go.

THE MODERATOR: Mr. Reynolds.

MR. REYNOLDS: Governor Carter, I'd like to turn to what we used to call the energy crisis.

Yesterday a British Government commission on air pollution, but one headed by a nuclear physicist, recommended that any further expansion of nuclear energy be delayed in Britain as long as possible. Now, this is a subject that is quite controversial among our own people, and there seems to be a clear difference between you and the President on the use of nuclear powerplants, which you say you would use as a last priority. Why sir? Are they unsafe?

MR. CARTER: Well, among my other experiences in the past I've been a nuclear engineer, and I did graduate work in this field. I think I know the capabilities and limitations of atomic power.

But the energy policy of our Nation is one that has not yet been established under this administration. I think almost every other developed nation in the world has an energy policy except us.

We have seen the Federal Energy Agency [Administration] established, for instance, in the crisis of 1973. It was supposed to be a temporary agency; now it's permanent. It's enormous; it's growing every day. And I think the *Wall Street Journal* reported not too long ago they have 112 public relations experts working for the Federal Energy Agency [Administration] to try to justify to the American people its own existence.

We've got to have a firm way to handle the energy question. The reorganization proposal that I've put forward is one first step. In addition to that, we need to have a realization that we've got about 35 years worth of oil left in the whole world. We are going to run out of oil. When Mr. Nixon made his famous speech on operation independence, we were importing about 35 percent of our oil. Now we've increased that amount 25 percent. We now import about 44 percent of our oil.

We need a shift from oil to coal. We need to concentrate our research and development effort on coalburning and extraction that's safe for miners, that also is clean burning. We need to shift very strongly toward solar energy and have strict conservation measures and then, as a last resort only, continue to use atomic power.

I would certainly not cut out atomic power altogether. We can't afford to give up that opportunity until later. But to the extent that we continue to use atomic power, I would be responsible as President to make sure that the safety precautions were inititated and maintained. For instance, some that have been forgotten: We need to have the reactor core below ground level, the entire powerplant that uses atomic power tightly sealed, and a heavy vacuum maintained. There ought to be a standardized design. There ought to be a full-time atomic energy specialist, independent of the power company, in the control room full-time, 24 hours a day, to shut down a plant if an abnormality develops. These kinds of procedures, along with evacuation procedures, adequate insurance, ought to be initiated.

So, shift from oil to coal; emphasize research and development on coal use and also on solar power; strict conservation measures—not yield every time the special interest groups put pressure on the President, like this administration has done; and use atomic energy only as a last resort with the strictest possible safety precautions. That's the best overall energy policy in the brief time we have to discuss it.

MR. REYNOLDS: Well, Governor, on the same subject, would you require mandatory conservation efforts to try to conserve fuel?

MR. CARTER: Yes, I would. Some of the things that can be done about this is a change in the rate structure of electric power companies. We now encourage people to waste electricity by giving the lowest rates to the biggest users. We don't do anything to cut down on peak load requirements. We don't have an adequate requirement for the insulation of homes, for the efficiency of automobiles. And whenever the automobile manufacturers come forward and say they can't meet the limits that the Congress has put forward, this Republican administration has delayed the implementation dates.

In addition to that, we ought to have a shift to the use of coal, particularly in the Appalachian regions where the coal is located—a lot of very high-quality, low-carbon coal—I mean low-sulfur coal is there—it's where our employment is needed. This would help a great deal.

So, mandatory conservation measures, yes. Encouragement by the President for people to voluntarily conserve, yes. And also the private sector ought to be encouraged to bring forward to the public the benefits from efficiency. One bank in Washington, for instance, gives lower interest loans for people who adequately insulate their homes or who buy efficient automobiles. And some major manufacturing companies, like Dow Chemical, have, through very effective efficiency mechanisms, cut down the use of energy by as much as 40 percent with the same out-product.

These kind of things ought to be done; they ought to be encouraged and supported and even required by the Government, yes.

THE MODERATOR: President Ford.

MR. FORD: Governor Carter skims over a very serious and a very broad subject. In January of 1975, I submitted to the Congress and to the American people the first comprehensive energy program recommended by any President. It called for an increase in the production of energy in the United States. It called for conservation measures so that we would save the energy that we have.

If you are going to increase domestic oil and gas production—and we have to—you have to give to those producers an opportunity to develop their land or their wells. I recommended to the Congress that we should increase coal production in this country from 600 million tons a year to 1,200 million tons by 1985. In order to do that, we have to improve our extraction of coal from the ground; we have to improve our utilization of coal, make it more efficient, make it cleaner.

In addition, we have to expand our research and development. In my program for energy independence, we have increased, for example, solar energy research from about $84 million a year to about $120 million a year. We are going as fast as the experts say we should. In nuclear power we have increased the research and development under the Energy Research and Development Agency [Administration] very substantially to ensure that our nuclear power-plants are safer, that they are more efficient, and that we have adequate safe-guards.

I think you have to have greater oil and gas production, more coal production, more nuclear production, and in addition, you have to have energy conservation.

THE MODERATOR: Mr. Gannon.

MR. GANNON: Mr. President, I'd like to return for a moment to this problem of unemployment. You have vetoed or threatened to veto a number of jobs bills passed or in development in the Democratic-controlled Congress. Yet, at the same time, the Government is paying out, I think it is, $17 billion, perhaps $20 billion, a year in unemployment compensation caused by the high unem-ployment. Why do you think it is better to pay out unemployment compensation to idle people than to put them to work in public service jobs?

MR. FORD: The bills that I've vetoed, the one for an additional $6 billion was not a bill that would have solved our unemployment problems. Even the pro-ponents of it admitted that no more than 400,000 jobs would be made available. Our analysis indicates that something in the magnitude of about 150 to 200,000 jobs would be made available. Each one of those jobs would have cost the taxpayer $25,000. In addition, the jobs would not be available right now; they would not have materialized for about 9 to 18 months.

The immediate problem we have is to stimulate our economy now so that we can get rid of unemployment. What we have done is to hold the lid on spending in an effort to reduce the rate of inflation. And we have proven, I think very conclusively, that you can reduce the rate of inflation and increase jobs.

For example, as I have said, we have added some 4 million jobs in the last 17 months. We have now employed 88 million people in America—the largest number in the history of the United States. We've added 500,000 jobs in the last 2 months.

Inflation is the quickest way to destroy jobs. And by holding the lid on Federal spending, we have been able to do a good job, an affirmative job in inflation and, as a result, have added to the jobs in this country.

I think it's also appropriate to point out that through our tax policies we have stimulated added employment throughout the country—the investment tax credit, the tax incentives for expansion and modernization of our industrial capacity. It's my opinion that the private sector, where five out of six jobs are, where you have permanent jobs with the opportunity for advancement, is a better place than make-work jobs under the program recommended by the Congress.

MR. GANNON: Just to follow up, Mr. President, the Congress has just passed a $3.7 billion appropriation bill which would provide money for the public works jobs program that you earlier tried to kill by your veto of the authorization legislation.

In light of the fact that unemployment again is rising or has in the past 3 months, I wonder if you have rethought that question at all, whether you would consider allowing this program to be funded, or will you veto that money bill?

MR. FORD: Well, this bill has not yet come down to the Oval Office so I am not in a position to make any judgment on it tonight. But this is an extra $4 billion that would add to the deficit, which would add to the inflationary pressures, which would help to destroy jobs in the private sector, not make jobs where the jobs really are. These make-work, temporary jobs, dead end as they are, are not the kind of jobs that we want for our people.

I think it's interesting to point out that in the 2 years that I've been President, I've vetoed 56 bills. Congress has sustained 42 vetoes. As a result we have saved over $9 billion in Federal expenditures. And the Congress—by overriding the bills that I did veto—the Congress has added some $13 billion to the Federal expenditures and to the Federal deficit.

Now, Governor Carter complains about the deficits that this administration has had, and yet he condemns the vetoes that I have made that have saved the taxpayer $9 billion and could have saved an additional $13 billion. Now, he can't have it both ways. And, therefore, it seems to me that we should hold the lid as we have to the best of our ability so we can stimulate the private economy and get the jobs where the jobs are—five out of six—in this economy.

THE MODERATOR: Governor Carter.

MR. CARTER: Well, Mr. Ford doesn't seem to put into perspective the fact that when 500,000 more people are out of work then there were 3 months ago, where we have 2 1/2 million more people out of work than were when he took office, that this touches human beings.

I was in a city in Pennsylvania not too long ago near here, and there were about 4,000 or 5,000 people in the audience—it was on a train trip—and I said, "How many adults here are out of work?" About a thousand raised their hands.

Mr. Ford actually has fewer people now in the private sector in nonfarm jobs than when he took office, and still he talks about a success; 7.9 percent unemployment is a terrible tragedy in this country.

He says he has learned how to match unemployment with inflation. That's right. We've got the highest inflation we've had in 25 years right now—except under this administration—and that was 50 years ago—and we've got the highest unemployment we've had under Mr. Ford's administration since the Great Depression. This affects human beings. And his insensitivity in providing those people a chance to work has made this a welfare administration and not a work administration.

He hasn't saved $9 billion with his vetoes. It has only been a net saving of $4 billion. And the cost in unemployment compensation, welfare compensation, and lost revenues has increased $23 billion in the last 2 years. This is a typical attitude that really causes havoc in people's lives. And then it's covered over by saying that our country has naturally got a 6-percent unemployment rate or 7-percent unemployment rate and a 6-percent inflation. It's a travesty. It shows a lack of leadership. And we've never had a President since the War Between the States that vetoed more bills. Mr. Ford has vetoed four times as many bills as Mr. Nixon, per year, and 11 of them have been overridden. One of his bills that was overriden—he only got one vote in the Senate and seven votes in the House from Republicans. So, this shows a breakdown in leadership.

THE MODERATOR: Governor Carter, under the rules I must stop you.

Ms. DREW: Governor Carter, I'd like to come back to the subject of taxes. You have said that you want to cut taxes for the middle- and lower-income groups.

MR. CARTER: Right.

Ms. DREW: But unless you are willing to do such things as reduce the itemized deductions for charitable contributions or home mortgage payments or interest or taxes or capital gains, you can't really raise sufficient revenue to provide an overall tax cut of any size. So, how are you going to provide that tax relief that you are talking about?

MR. CARTER: Now we have such a grossly unbalanced tax system, as I said earlier, that it is a disgrace. Of all the tax benefits now, 25 percent of them go to the 1 percent of the richest people in this country. Over 50 percent—53 to be exact—percent of the tax benefits go to the 14 percent richest people in this country.

We've had a 50-percent increase in payroll deductions since Mr. Nixon went in office 8 years ago. Mr. Ford has advocated, since he has been in office, over $5 billion in reductions for corporations, special interest groups, and the very, very wealthy, who derive their income not from labor, but from investments.

That has got to be changed. A few things that can be done: We have now a deferral system so that the multinational corporations, who invest overseas, if they make $1 million in profits overseas, they don't have to pay any of their taxes unless they bring their money back into this country. Where they don't pay their taxes, the average American pays their taxes for them. Not only that but it robs this country of jobs because instead of coming back with that million dollars and creating a shoe factory, say, in New Hampshire or Vermont, if the company takes the money down to Italy and builds a shoe factory, they don't have to pay any taxes on the money.

Another thing is a system called DISC [Domestic International Sales Corporation], which was originally designed and proposed by Mr. Nixon, to encourage exports. This permits a company to create a dummy corporation to export their products and then not to pay the full amount of taxes on them. This costs our Government about $1.4 billion a year, and when those rich corporations don't pay that tax, the average American taxpayer pays it for them.

Another one that is very important is the business deductions. Jet airplanes, first-class travel, the $50 martini lunch—the average working person can't take advantage of that, but the wealthier people can.

Another system is where a dentist can invest money in, say, raising cattle and can put in $100,000 of his own money, borrow $900,000—$900,000, that makes a million—and mark off a great amount of loss through that procedure. There was one example, for instance, where somebody produced pornographic movies. They put in $30,000 of their money and got $120,000 in tax savings.

These special kinds of programs have robbed the average taxpayer and have benefited those who are powerful and who can employ lobbyists and who can have their C.P.A.'s and their lawyers to help them benefit from the roughly

8,000 pages of the tax code. The average American person can't do it. You can't hire a lobbyist out of unemployment compensation checks.

Ms. Drew: Governor, to follow up on your answer, in order for any kind of tax relief to really be felt by the middle- and lower-income people, according to congressional committees on this, you need about $10 billion. Now, you listed some things. The deferral on foreign income is estimated it would save about $500 million. DISC, you said, was $1.4 billion. The estimate of the outside, if you eliminated all tax shelters, is $5 billion.

So, where else would you raise the revenue to provide this tax relief? Would you, in fact, do away with all business deductions, and what other kinds of preferences would you do away with?

Mr. Carter: No, I wouldn't do away with all business deductions. I think that would be a very serious mistake. But if you could just do away with the ones that are unfair, you could lower taxes for everyone. I would never do anything that would increase the taxes for those who work for a living or who are presently required to list all their income.

What I want to do is not to raise taxes, but to eliminate loopholes. And this is the point of my first statistic that I gave you, that the present tax benefits that have carved out over a long period of years—50 years—by sharp tax lawyers and by lobbyists, have benefited just the rich. These programs that I described to you earlier—the tax deferrals for overseas, the DISC, and the tax shelters— they only apply to people in the $50,000-a-year bracket or up. And I think this is the best way to approach it, is to make sure that everybody pays taxes on the income that they earn and make sure that you take whatever savings there is from the higher income levels and give it to the lower- and middle-income families.

The Moderator: President Ford.

Mr. Ford: Governor Carter's answer tonight does not coincide with the answer that he gave in an interview to the Associated Press a week or so ago. In that interview Governor Carter indicated that he would raise the taxes on those in the medium- or middle-income brackets or higher. Now, if you take the medium- or middle-income taxpayer—that's about $14,000 per person— Governor Carter has indicated, publicly, in an interview, that he would increase the taxes on about 50 percent of the working people of this country.

I think the way to get tax equity in this country is to give tax relief to the middle-income people who have an income from roughly $8,000 up to $25 or $30,000. They have been shortchanged as we have taken 10 million taxpayers off the tax rolls in the last 8 years and as we have added to the minimum tax provision to make all people pay more taxes.

I believe in tax equity for the middle-income taxpayer—increasing the personal exemption. Mr. Carter wants to increase taxes for roughly half of the taxpayers of this country.

Now, the Governor has also played a little fast and loose with the facts about vetoes. The records show that President Roosevelt vetoed on an average of 55 bills a year. President Truman vetoed on the average, while he was President, about 38 bills a year. I understand that Governor Carter, when he was Governor of Georgia, vetoed between 35 and 40 bills a year. My average in 2 years is 26, but in the process of that, we have saved $9 billion.

And one final comment. Governor Carter talks about the tax bills and all of the inequities that exist in the present law. I must remind him the Democrats have controlled the Congress for the last 22 years, and they wrote all the tax bills.

THE MODERATOR: Mr. Reynolds.

MR. REYNOLDS: I suspect that we could continue on this tax argument for some time, but I'd like to move on to another area.

Mr. President, everybody seems to be running against Washington this year, and I'd like to raise two coincidental events, then ask you whether you think perhaps this may have a bearing on the attitude throughout the country.

The House Ethics Committee has just now ended its investigation of Daniel Schorr, after several months and many thousands of dollars, trying to find out how he obtained and caused to be published a report of the Congress that probably is the property of the American people. At the same time the Senate Select Committee on Standards and Conduct has voted not really to begin an investigation of a United States Senator because of allegations against him that he may have been receiving corporate funds illegally over a period of years.

Do you suppose, sir, that events like this contribute to the feeling in the country that maybe there is something wrong in Washington, and I don't mean just in the executive branch, but throughout the whole Government?

MR. FORD: There is a considerable anti-Washington feeling throughout the country but I think the feeling is misplaced. In the 2 years we have restored integrity in the White House and we have set high standards in the executive branch of the Government.

The anti-Washington feeling, in my opinion, ought to be focused on the Congress of the United States. For example, this Congress very shortly will spend a billion dollars a year for its housekeeping, its salaries, its expenses, and the like. The next Congress will probably be the first billion dollar Congress in the history of the United States. I don't think the American people are getting their money's worth from the majority party that runs this Congress.

We, in addition, see that in the last 4 years the number of employees hired by the Congress has gone up substantially, much more than the gross national product, much more than any other increase throughout our society. Congress is hiring people by the droves, and the cost, as a result, has gone up.

And I don't see any improvement in the performance of the Congress under the present leadership. So, it seems to me, instead of the anti-Washington feeling being aimed at everybody in Washington, it seems to me that the focus should be where the problem is, which is the Congress of the United States, and particularly the majority in the Congress.

They spend too much money on themselves. They have too many employees. There is some question about their morality. It seems to me that in this election the focus should not be on the executive branch, but the correction should come as the voters for their Members of the House of Representatives or for their United States Senator. That's where the problem is. And I hope there will be some corrective action taken, so we can get some new leadership in the Congress of the United States.

MR. REYNOLDS: Mr. President, if I may follow up, I think you have made it plain that you take a dim view of the majority in the Congress. Isn't it quite likely, sir, that you will have a Democratic Congress in the next session if you are elected President, and hasn't the country a right to ask whether you can get along with that Congress or whether we will have continued confrontation?

MR. FORD: Well, it seems to me that we have a chance, the Republicans, to get a majority in the House of Representatives. We will make some gains in the United States Senate. So there will be different ratios in the House as well as in the Senate, and as President I will be able to work with that Congress.

But let me take the other side of the coin, if I might. Supposing we had had a Democratic Congress for the last 2 years and we had had Governor Carter as President. He has, in effect, said that he would agree with all of—he would disapprove of the vetoes that I have made and would have added significantly to expenditures and the deficit in the Federal Government. I think it would be contrary to one of the basic concepts in our system of government, a system of checks and balances.

We have a Democratic Congress today, and fortunately, we've had a Republican President to check their excesses with my vetoes. If we have a Democratic Congress next year and a President who wants to spend an additional $100 billion a year or maybe $200 billion a year, with more programs, we will have, in my judgment, greater deficits with more spending, more dangers of inflation.

I think the American people want a Republican President to check on any excesses that come out of the next Congress if it is a Democratic Congress.

THE MODERATOR: Governor Carter.

MR. CARTER: Well, it's not a matter of Republican and Democrat; it's a matter of leadership or no leadership. President Eisenhower worked with a Democratic Congress very well. Even President Nixon, because he was a strong leader, at least, worked with a Democratic Congress very well.

Mr. Ford has vetoed, as I said earlier, four times as many bills per year as Mr. Nixon. Mr. Ford quite often puts forward a program just as a public relations stunt and never tries to put it through the Congress by working with the Congress. I think under President Nixon and Eisenhower—they passed about 60 to 75 percent of their legislation. This year Mr. Ford will not pass more than 26 percent of all the legislative proposals he puts forward.

This is government by stalemate. And we've seen almost a complete breakdown in the proper relationship between the President, who represents this country, and the Congress, who, collectively, also represent this country.

We've had Republican Presidents before who have tried to run against a Democratic Congress. And I don't think it's—the Congress is Mr. Ford's opponent. But if he insists that I be responsible for the Democratic Congress, of which I have not been a part, then I think it's only fair that he be responsible for the Nixon administration in its entirety, of which he was a part. That, I think, is a good balance.

But the point is that a President ought to lead this country. Mr. Ford, so far as I know, except for avoiding another Watergate, has not accomplished one single major program for his country. And there has been a constant squabbling between the President and the Congress, and that's not the way this country ought to be run.

I might go back to one other thing. Mr. Ford has misquoted an AP news story that was in error to begin with. That story reported several times that I would lower taxes for lower and middle-income families, and that correction was delivered to the White House. And I am sure that the President knows about this correction, but he still insists on repeating an erroneous statement.

THE MODERATOR: President Ford, Governor Carter, we no longer have enough time for two complete sequences of questions. We have only about 6 minutes left for questions and answers. For that reason we will drop the follow-up questions at this point, but each candidate will still be able to respond to the other's answers.

To the extent that you can, gentlemen, please keep your remarks brief.

MR. GANNON: Governor Carter, one important part of the Government's economic policy apparatus we haven't talked about is the Federal Reserve Board. I would like to ask you something about what you have said, and that is that you believe that a President ought to have a Chairman of the Federal Reserve Board whose views are compatible with his own.

Based on the record of the last few years, would you say your views are compatible with those of Chairman Arthur Burns, and if not, would you seek his resignation if you are elected?

MR. CARTER: What I have said is that the President ought to have a chance to appoint the Chairman of the Federal Reserve Board to have a coterminus term; in other words, both of them serve the same 4 years.

The Congress can modify the supply of money by modifying the income tax laws. The President can modify the economic structure of the country by public statements and general attitudes and the budget that he proposes. The Federal Reserve has an independent status that ought to be preserved.

I think that Mr. Burns did take a typical erroneous Republican attitude in the 1973 year when inflation was so high. He assumed that the inflation rate was because of excessive demand and, therefore, put into effect tight constraint on the economy, very high interest rates—which is typical, also, of a Republican administration—tried to increase the tax payments by individuals, cut the tax payments by corporations. I would have done it opposite. I think the problem should have been addressed by increasing productivity, by having put people back to work so they could purchase more goods, lower income taxes on individuals, perhaps raise them if necessary on corporations in comparison. But Mr. Burns in that respect made a very serious mistake.

I would not want to destroy the independence of the Federal Reserve Board. But I do think we ought to have a cohesive economic policy with at least the Chairman of the Federal Reserve Board and the President's terms being the same and letting the Congress of course be the third entity with independence, subject only to the President's veto.

THE MODERATOR: President Ford, your response.

MR. FORD: The Chairman of the Federal Reserve Board should be independent. Fortunately, he has been during Democratic as well as Republican administrations. As a result, in the last 2 years we have had a responsible monetary policy.

The Federal Reserve Board indicated that the supply of money would be held between 4 to 4 1/2 and 7 and 7 1/2. They have done a good job in integrating the money supply with the fiscal policy of the executive and legislative branches of the Government.

It would be catastrophic if the Chairman of the Federal Reserve Board became the tool of the political party that was in power. It's important for our future economic security that that job be nonpolitical and separate from the executive and the legislative branches.

THE MODERATOR: Mrs. Drew.

MS. DREW: Mr. President, the real problem with the FBI—in fact, all of the intelligence agencies—is there are no real laws governing them. Such laws as there are tend to be vague and open-ended. Now, you have issued some Executive orders, but we have learned that leaving these agencies to executive discretion and direction can get them and in fact the country in a great deal of trouble. One President may be a decent man, the next one might not be.

So, what do you think about trying to write in some more protection by getting some laws governing these agencies?

MR. FORD: You are familiar, of course, with the fact that I am the first President in 30 years who has reorganized the intelligence agencies in the Federal Government—the CIA, the Defense Intelligence Agency, the National Security Agency, and the others. We've done that by Executive order. And I think we've tightened it up; we've straightened out their problems that developed over the last few years. It doesn't seem to me that it's needed or necessary to have legislation in this particular regard.

I have recommended to the Congress, however—I'm sure you are familiar with this—legislation that would make it very proper and in the right way that the Attorney General could go in and get the right for wiretapping under security cases. This was an effort that was made by the Attorney General and myself working with the Congress. But even in this area where I think new legislation would be justified, the Congress has not responded.

So, I feel in that case as well as in the reorganization of the intelligence agencies—as I've done—we have to do it by Executive order. And I'm glad that we have a good Director in George Bush; we have good Executive orders. And the CIA and the DIA and NSA are now doing a good job under proper supervision.

THE MODERATOR: Governor Carter.

MR. CARTER: Well, one of the very serious things that's happened in our Government in recent years and has continued up until now is a breakdown in the trust among our people in the—

[At this point, there was an audio failure which caused a delay in the debate until 11:18 p.m.]

THE MODERATOR: Ladies and gentlemen, probably it is not necessary for me to say that we had a technical failure during the debates. It was not a failure in the debate; it was failure in the broadcasting of the debate. It occurred 27 minutes ago. The fault has been dealt with, and we want to thank President Ford and Governor Carter for being so patient and understanding while this delay went on.

We very much regret the technical failure that lost the sound as it was leaving the theatre. It occurred during Governor Carter's response to what would have been and what was the last question put to the candidates. That question went to President Ford. It dealt with the control of Government intelligence agencies. Governor Carter was making his response and had very nearly finished it. He will conclude that response now, after which President Ford and Governor Carter will make their closing statements.

MR. CARTER: There has been too much Government secrecy and not enough respect for the personal privacy of American citizens.

THE MODERATOR: It is now time for the closing statements which are to be up to 4 minutes long.

Governor Carter, by the same toss of the coin that directed the first question to you, you are to go first now.

MR. CARTER: Well, tonight, we've had a chance to talk a lot about the past, but I think it is time to talk about the future. Our Nation in the last 8 years has been divided as never before. It's a time for unity. It is time to draw ourselves together, to have a President and a Congress that can work together with mutual respect for a change, cooperating for a change, in the open for a change, so the people can understand their own Government. It is time for Government, industry and labor, manufacturing, agriculture, education, other entities in our society to cooperate. And it's a time for Government to understand and to cooperate with our people.

For a long time our American citizens have been excluded, sometimes misled, sometimes have been lied to. This is not compatible with the purpose of our Nation. I believe in our country. It needs to be competent, the Government needs to be well managed, efficient, economical. We need to have a Government that's sensitive to our people's needs, to those who are poor, who don't have adequate health care, who have been cheated too long by our tax programs, who've been out of jobs, whose families have been torn apart. We need to restore the faith and the trust of the American people in their own Government.

In addition to that, we've suffered because we haven't had leadership in this administration. We have got a Government of stalemate. We've lost the vis of what our country can and ought to be. This is not the America tha known in the past. It's not the America that we have to have in the

I don't claim to know all the answers, but I've got confidence in Our economic strength is still there. Our system of governme Vietnam, Cambodia, CIA, Watergate, is still the best system of

Earth. And the greatest resource of all are the 215 million Americans who still have within us the strength, the character, the intelligence, the experience, the patriotism, the idealism, the compassion, the sense of brotherhood on which we can rely in the future to restore the greatness to our country.

We ought not to be excluded from our Government anymore. We need a President that can go in who derives his strength from the people. I owe the special interests nothing. I owe everything to you, the people of this country. And I believe that we can bind our wounds. I believe that we can work together. And I believe that if we can tap the tremendous untapped reservoir of innate strength in this country, that we can once again have a Government as good as our people and let the world know what we still know and hope for—that we still live in the greatest and strongest and the best country on Earth.

THE MODERATOR: President Ford.

MR. FORD: On November 2 all of you will make a very, very important decision. One of the major issues in this campaign is trust. A President should never promise more than he can deliver, and a President should always deliver everything that he has promised. A President can't be all things to all people. A President should be the same thing to all people.

Another issue in this campaign: Governor Carter has endorsed the Democratic platform, which calls for more spending, bigger deficits, more inflation, or more taxes. Governor Carter has embraced the record of the present Congress, dominated by his political party. It calls for more of the same. Governor Carter in his acceptance speech called for more and more programs, which means more and more Government. I think the real issue in this campaign—and that which you must decide on November 2—is whether you should vote for his promises or my performance in 2 years in the White House.

On the Fourth of July, we had a wonderful 200th birthday for our great country. It was a superb occasion. It was a glorious day.

In the first century of our Nation's history, our forefathers gave us the finest form of government in the history of mankind. In the second century of our Nation's history, our forefathers developed the most productive industrial nation in the history of the globe. Our third century should be the century of individual freedom for all our 215 million Americans today and all that join us.

In the last few years government has gotten bigger and bigger; industry has gotten larger and larger; labor unions have gotten bigger and bigger; and our children have been the victims of mass education.

We must make this next century the century of the individual. We should never forget that a government big enough to give us everything we want is a government big enough to take from us everything we have.

The individual worker in the plants throughout the United States should not ... small cog in a big machine. The member of a labor union must have his ...rengthened and broadened, and our children in their education should ...pportunity to improve themselves based on their talents and their

...and father, during the Depression, worked very hard to give me ...to do better in our great country. Your mothers and fathers did the same thing for you and others. Betty and I have worked very hard to give our children a brighter future in the United States, our beloved country. You and others in this great country have worked hard and done a great deal to give your children and your grandchildren the blessings of a better America. I believe we can all work together to make the individuals in the future have more, and all of us working together can build a better America.

THE MODERATOR: Thank you, President Ford. Thank you, Governor Carter. Our thanks also to the questioners and to the audience in this theatre. We much regret the technical failure that caused a 28-minute delay in the broadcast of the debate. We believe, however, that everyone will agree that it did not detract from the effectiveness of the debate or from its fairness.

The next Presidential debate is to take place on Wednesday, October 6, in San Francisco, at 9:30 p.m., eastern daylight time. The topics are to be foreign and defense issues. As with all three debates between the Presidential candidates and the one between the Vice-Presidential candidates, it is being arranged by the League of Women Voters Education Fund in the hope of promoting a wider and better informed participation by the American people in the election in November.

Now, from the Walnut Street Theatre in Philadelphia, good night.

Second Presidential Campaign Debate
San Francisco, October 6, 1976

While explaining his view on foreign policy during his second debate with Jimmy Carter, President Gerald Ford hurt his chances for election when he inexplicably blurted out that "there is no Soviet domination of Eastern Europe." This obvious misstatement only added to the increasingly comic reputation of a man once ungenerously characterized by Lyndon Johnson as not having the intellectual capacity to "walk and chew gum at the same time." Ford's penchant for innocuous, but self-damaging, blunders had typified his brief presidency.

THE MODERATOR: Good evening. I am Pauline Frederick of NPR [National Public Radio], moderator of the second of the historic debates of the 1976 campaign between Gerald R. Ford of Michigan, Republican candidate for President, and Jimmy Carter of Georgia, Democratic candidate for President.

Thank you, President Ford, and thank you, Governor Carter, for being with us tonight.

The debates take place before an audience in the Palace of Fine Arts Theatre in San Francisco. An estimated 100 million Americans are watching on television as well. San Francisco was the site of the signing of the United Nations Charter 31 years ago. Thus, it is an appropriate place to hold this debate, the subject of which is foreign and defense issues.

The questioners tonight are Max Frankel, associate editor of the New York Times, Henry L. Trewhitt, diplomatic correspondent of the Baltimore Sun, and Richard Valeriani, diplomatic correspondent of NBC News.

The ground rules tonight are basically the same as they were for the first debate 2 weeks ago. The questions will be alternated between candidates. By the toss of a coin, Governor Carter will take the first question.

Each question sequence will be as follows: The question will be asked, and the candidate will have up to 3 minutes to answer. His opponent will have up to 2 minutes to respond. And prior to the response, the questioner may ask a followup question to clarify the candidate's answer, when necessary, with up to 2 minutes to reply. Each candidate will have 3 minutes for a closing statement at the end.

President Ford and Governor Carter do not have notes or prepared remarks with them this evening, but they may take notes during the debate and refer to them.

Mr. Frankel, you have the first question for Governor Carter.

MR. FRANKEL: Governor, since the Democrats last ran our foreign policy, including many of the men who are advising you, the country has been relieved of the Vietnam agony and the military draft; we've started arms control negotiations with the Russians; we've opened relations with China; we've arranged

146

the disengagement in the Middle East; we've regained influence with the Arabs without deserting Israel. Now, maybe, we've even begun a process of peaceful change in Africa.

Now, you've objected in this campaign to the style with which much of this was done, and you've mentioned some other things that you think ought to have been done. But do you really have a quarrel with this Republican record? Would you not have done any of those things?

MR. CARTER: Well, I think this Republican administration has been almost all style and spectacular and not substance. We've got a chance tonight to talk about, first of all, leadership, the character of our country, and a vision of the future. In every one of these instances, the Ford administration has failed. And I hope tonight that I and Mr. Ford will have a chance to discuss the reason for those failures.

Our country is not strong any more; we're not respected any more. We can only be strong overseas if we're strong at home, and when I become President, we'll not only be strong in those areas but also in defense—a defense capability second to none.

We've lost, in our foreign policy, the character of the American people. We've ignored or excluded the American people and the Congress from participation in the shaping of our foreign policy. It's been one of secrecy and exclusion.

In addition to that, we've had a chance to become now, contrary to our longstanding beliefs and principles, the arms merchant of the whole world. We've tried to buy success from our enemies, and at the same time we've excluded from the process the normal friendship of our allies.

In addition to that, we've become fearful to compete with the Soviet Union on an equal basis. We talk about détente. The Soviet Union knows what they want in détente, and they've been getting it. We have not known what we've wanted, and we've been out-traded in almost every instance.

The other point I want to make is about our defense. We've got to be a nation blessed with the defense capability that's efficient, tough, capable, well organized, narrowly focused fighting capability. The ability to fight if necessary is the best way to avoid the chance for or the requirement to fight.

And the last point I want to make is this: Mr. Ford, Mr. Kissinger have continued on with the policies and failures of Richard Nixon. Even the Republican platform has criticized the lack of leadership in Mr. Ford, and they've criticized the foreign policy of this administration. This is one instance where I agree with the Republican platform.

I might say this in closing, and that is, that as far as foreign policy goes, Mr. Kissinger has been the President of this country. Mr. Ford has shown an absence of leadership and an absence of a grasp of what this country is and what it ought to be. That's got to be changed, and that is one of the major issues in this campaign of 1976.

THE MODERATOR: President Ford, would you like to respond?

MR. FORD: Governor Carter again is talking in broad generalities. Let me take just one question that he raises—the military strength and capability of the United States. Governor Carter, in November of 1975, indicated that he wanted to cut the defense budget by $15 billion. A few months later he said he wanted to cut the defense budget by $8 billion or $9 billion. And more recently he talks about cutting the defense budget by $5 billion to $7 billion. There is no way you can be strong militarily and have those kinds of reductions in our military appropriations.

Now let me just tell you a little story. About late October of 1975, I asked the then Secretary of Defense, Mr. Schlesinger, to tell me what had to be done if we were going to reduce the defense budget by $3 to $5 billion. A few days later Mr. Schlesinger came back and said if we cut the defense budget by $3 to $5 billion, we will have to cut military personnel by 250,000, civilian personnel by 100,000, jobs in America by 100,000. We would have to stretch out our aircraft procurement. We would have to reduce our naval construction program. We would have to reduce the research and development for the Army, the Navy, the Air Force, and Marines by 8 percent. We would have to close 20 military bases in the United States immediately. That's the kind of a defense program that Mr. Carter wants.

Let me tell you this straight from the shoulder: You don't negotiate with Mr. Brezhnev from weakness. And the kind of a defense program that Mr. Carter wants will mean a weaker defense and a poorer negotiating position.

THE MODERATOR: Mr. Trewhitt, a question for President Ford.

MR. TREWHITT: Mr. President, my question really is the other side of the coin from Mr. Frankel's. For a generation the United States has had a foreign policy based on containment of communism; yet we have lost the first war in Vietnam, we lost a shoving match in Angola, Communists threaten to come to power by peaceful means in Italy, and relations generally have cooled with the Soviet Union in the last few months. So, let me ask you, first, what do you do about such cases as Italy, and, secondly, does this general drift mean that we're moving back toward something like an old cold war relationship with the Soviet Union?

MR. FORD: I don't believe we should move to a cold war relationship. I think it's in the best interest of the United States and the world as a whole that the United States negotiate rather than go back to the cold war relationship with the Soviet Union.

I don't look at the picture as bleakly as you have indicated in your question, Mr. Trewhitt. I believe that the United States has had many successes in recent years and recent months as far as the Communist movement is concerned. We have been successful in Portugal where, a year ago, it looked like there was a very great possibility that the Communists would take over in Portugal. It didn't happen. We have a democracy in Portugal today.

A few months ago—or I should say maybe 2 years ago—the Soviet Union looked like they had continued strength in the Middle East. Today, according to Prime Minister Rabin, the Soviet Union is weaker in the Middle East than they have been in many, many years. The facts are the Soviet Union relationship with Egypt is at a low level; the Soviet Union relationship with Syria is at a very low point. The United States today, according to Prime Minister Rabin of Israel, is at a peak in its influence and power in the Middle East.

But let's turn for a minute to the southern African operations that are now going on. The United States of America took the initiative in southern Africa.

We wanted to end the bloodshed in southern Africa. We wanted to have the right of self-determination in southern Africa. We wanted to have majority rule with the full protection of the rights of the minority. We wanted to preserve human dignity in southern Africa. We have taken initiative, and in southern Africa today the United States is trusted by the black frontline nations and black Africa. The United States is trusted by the other elements in southern Africa.

The United States foreign policy under this administration has been one of progress and success. And I believe that instead of talking about Soviet progress, we can talk about American successes.

And may I make an observation—part of the question you asked, Mr. Trewhitt—I don't believe that it's in the best interests of the United States and the NATO nations to have a Communist government in NATO. Mr. Carter has indicated he would look with sympathy to a Communist government in NATO. I think that would destroy the integrity and the strength of NATO, and I am totally opposed to it.

Mr. CARTER: Well, Mr. Ford, unfortunately, has just made a statement that's not true. I have never advocated a Communist government for Italy; that would, obviously, be a ridiculous thing for anyone to do who wanted to be President of the country. I think that this is an instance for deliberate distortion, and this has occurred also in the question about defense. As a matter of fact, I've never advocated any cut of $15 billion in our defense budget. As a matter of fact, Mr. Ford has made a political football out of the defense budget.

About a year ago, he cut the Pentagon budget $6.8 billion. After he fired James Schlesinger the political heat got so great that he added back about $3 billion. When Ronald Reagan won the Texas primary election, Mr. Ford added back another $1 1/2 billion. Immediately before the Kansas City convention he added another $1.8 billion in the defense budget. And his own Office of Management and Budget testified that he had a $3 billion cut insurance added to the defense budget under the pressure from the Pentagon. Obviously, this is another indication of trying to use the defense budget for political purposes, which he's trying to do tonight.

Now, we went into South Africa late, after Great Britain, Rhodesia, the black nations had been trying to solve this problem for many, many years. We didn't go in until right before the election, similar to what was taking place in 1972, when Mr. Kissinger announced peace is at hand just before the election at that time.

And we have weakened our position in NATO, because the other countries in Europe supported the democratic forces in Portugal long before we did. We stuck to the Portugal dictatorships much longer than other democracies did in this world.

THE MODERATOR: Mr. Valeriani, a question for Governor Carter.

MR. VALERIANI: Governor Carter, much of what the United States does abroad is done in the name of the national interest. What is your concept of the national interest? What should the role of the United States in the world be? And in that connection, considering your limited experience in foreign affairs and the fact that you take some pride in being a Washington outsider, don't you think it would be appropriate for you to tell the American voters, before the election, the people that you would like to have in key position such as Secretary of State, Secretary of Defense, national security affairs adviser at the White House?

Mr. CARTER: Well, I'm not going to name my Cabinet before I get elected; I've got a little ways to go before I start doing that. But I have adequate background, I believe. I am a graduate of the U.S. Naval Academy, the first military graduate since Eisenhower. I've served as Governor of Georgia and have traveled extensively in foreign countries—in South America, Central America, Europe, the Middle East, and in Japan.

I've traveled the last 21 months among people of this country. I've talked to them, and I've listened. And I've seen at firsthand, in a very vivid way, the deep hurt that's come to this country in the aftermath of Vietnam and Cambodia and Chile and Pakistan and Angola and Watergate, CIA revelations.

What we were formerly so proud of—the strength of our country, its moral integrity, the representation in foreign affairs of what our people are, what our Constitution stands for—has been gone. And in the secrecy that has surrounded our foreign policy in the last few years, the American people and the Congress have been excluded.

I believe I know what this country ought to be. I've been one who's loved my Nation, as many Americans do. And I believe that there is no limit placed on what we can be in the future if we can harness the tremendous resources— militarily, economically—and the stature of our people, the meaning of our Constitution in the future.

Every time we've made a serious mistake in foreign affairs, it's been because the American people have been excluded from the process. If we can just tap the intelligence and ability, the sound commonsense, and the good judgment of the American people, we can once again have a foreign policy to make us proud instead of ashamed. And I'm not going to exclude the American people from that process in the future, as Mr. Ford and Kissinger have done.

This is what it takes to have a sound foreign policy: strong at home, strong defense, permanent commitments, not betray the principles of our country, and involve the American people and the Congress in the shaping of our foreign policy.

Every time Mr. Ford speaks from a position of secrecy—in negotiations and secret treaties that have been pursued and achieved, in supporting dictatorships, in ignoring human rights—we are weak and the rest of the world knows it.

So these are the ways that we can restore the strength of our country. And they don't require long experience in foreign policy—nobody has that except a President who served a long time or a Secretary of State. But my background, my experience, my knowledge of the people of this country, my commitment to our principles that don't change—those are the best bases to correct the horrible mistakes of this administration and restore our own country to a position of leadership in the world.

Mr. VALERIANI: How specifically, Governor, are you going to bring the American people into the decisionmaking process in foreign policy? What does that mean?

Mr. CARTER: First of all, I would quit conducting the decisionmaking process in secret, as has been a characteristic of Mr. Kissinger and Mr. Ford. In many instances we've made agreements, like in Vietnam, that have been revealed later on to our embarrassment.

Recently, Ian Smith, the President of Rhodesia, announced that he had unequivocal commitments from Mr. Kissinger that he could not reveal. The American people don't know what those commitments are. We've seen in the past a destruction of elected governments, like in Chile, and the strong support of military dictatorship there. These kinds of things have hurt us very much.

I would restore the concept of the fireside chat, which was an integral part of the administration of Franklin Roosevelt. And I would also restore the involvement of the Congress. When Harry Truman was President, he was not afraid to have a strong Secretary of Defense—Dean Acheson, George Marshall were strong Secretaries of State—excuse me, State. But he also made sure that there was a bipartisan support. The Members of Congress, Arthur Vandenburg, Walter George, were part of the process. And before our Nation made a secret agreement and before we made a bluffing statement, we were sure that we had the backing not only of the President and the Secretary of State but also of the Congress and the people. This is the responsibility of the President, and I think it's very damaging to our country for Mr. Ford to have turned over this responsibility to the Secretary of State.

THE MODERATOR: President Ford, do you have a response?

Mr. FORD: Governor Carter again contradicts himself. He complains about secrecy, and yet he is quoted as saying that in the attempt to find a solution in the Middle East, that he would hold unpublicized meetings with the Soviet Union—I presume for the purpose of imposing a settlement on Israel and the Arab nations.

But let me talk just a minute about what we've done to avoid secrecy in the Ford administration. After the United States took the initiative in working with Israel and with Egypt and achieving the Sinai II agreement—and I am proud to say that not a single Egyptian or Israeli soldier has lost his life since the signing of the Sinai agreement—but at the time that I submitted the Sinai agreement to the Congress of the United States, I submitted every single document that was applicable to the Sinai II agreement. It was the most complete documentation by any President of any agreement signed by a President on behalf of the United States.

Now, as far as meeting with the Congress is concerned, during the 24 months that I've been the President of the United States, I have averaged better than one meeting a month with responsible groups or committees of the Congress, both House and Senate.

The Secretary of State has appeared, in the several years that he's been the Secretary, before 80 different committee hearings in the House and in the Senate. The Secretary of State has made better than 50 speeches all over the United States explaining American foreign policy. I have made, myself, at least 10 speeches in various parts of the country, where I have discussed with the American people defense and foreign policy.

THE MODERATOR: Mr. Frankel, a question for President Ford.

MR. FRANKEL: Mr. President, I'd like to explore a little more deeply our relationship with the Russians. They used to brag, back in Krushchev's day, that because of their greater patience and because of our greed for business deals, that they would sooner or later get the better of us. Is it possible that, despite some setbacks in the Middle East, they've proved their point? Our allies in France and Italy are now flirting with communism; we've recognized a permanent Communist regime in East Germany; we virtually signed, in Helsinki, an agreement that the Russians have dominance in Eastern Europe; we bailed out Soviet agriculture with our huge grain sales, we've given them large loans, access to our best technology, and if the Senate hadn't interfered with the Jackson Amendment, maybe you would have given them even larger loans. Is that what you call a two-way street of traffic in Europe?

MR. FORD: I believe that we have negotiated with the Soviet Union since I've been President from a position of strength. And let me cite several examples.

Shortly after I became President, in December of 1974, I met with General Secretary Brezhnev in Vladivostok. And we agreed to a mutual cap on the ballistic missile launchers at a ceiling of 2,400, which means that the Soviet Union, if that becomes a permanent agreement, will have to make a reduction in their launchers that they now have or plan to have. I negotiated at Vladivostok with Mr. Brezhnev a limitation of the MIRVing of the ballistic missiles at a figure of 1,320, which is the first time that any President has achieved a cap either on launchers or on MIRV's.

It seems to me that we can go from there to the grain sales. The grain sales have been a benefit to American agriculture. We have achieved a 5 3/4-year sale of a minimum of 6 million metric tons, which means that they have already bought about 4 million metric tons this year and are bound to buy another 2 million metric tons, to take the grain and corn and wheat that the American farmers have produced in order to have full production. And these grain sales to the Soviet Union have helped us tremendously in meeting the cost of the additional oil and the oil that we have bought from overseas.

If we turn to Helsinki—I am glad you raised it, Mr. Frankel—in the case of Helsinki, 35 nations signed an agreement, including the Secretary of State for the Vatican. I can't under any circumstances believe that His Holiness the Pope would agree, by signing that agreement, that the 35 nations have turned over to the Warsaw Pact nations the domination of Eastern Europe. It just isn't true. And if Mr. Carter alleges that His Holiness, by signing that, has done it, he is totally inaccurate.

Now, what has been accomplished by the Helsinki agreement? Number one, we have an agreement where they notify us and we notify them of any military maneuvers that are to be undertaken. They have done it in both cases where they've done so. There is no Soviet domination of Eastern Europe, and there never will be under a Ford administration.

MR. FRANKEL: I'm sorry, could I just follow—did I understand you to say, sir, that the Russians are not using Eastern Europe as their own sphere of influence and occupying most of the countries there and making sure with their troops that it's a Communist zone, whereas on our side of the line the Italians and the French are still flirting with the possiblity of communism?

MR. FORD: I don't believe, Mr. Frankel, that the Yugoslavians consider themselves dominated by the Soviet Union. I don't believe that the Romanians consider themselves dominated by the Soviet Union. I don't believe that the Poles consider themselves dominated by the Soviet Union. Each of those countries is independent, autonomous; it has its own territorial integrity. And the United States does not concede that those countries are under the domination of the Soviet Union. As a matter of fact, I visited Poland, Yugoslavia, and Romania, to make certain that the people of those countries understood that the President of the United States and the people of the United States are dedicated to their independence, their autonomy, and their freedom.

THE MODERATOR: Governor Carter, have you a response?

MR. CARTER: Well, in the first place, I am not criticizing His Holiness the Pope. I was talking about Mr. Ford.

The fact is that secrecy has surrounded the decisions made by the Ford administration. In the case of the Helsinki agreement, it may have been a good agreement at the beginning, but we have failed to enforce the so-called Basket 3 part, which ensures the right of people to migrate, to join their families, to be free to speak out. The Soviet Union is still jamming Radio Free Europe. Radio Free Europe is being jammed.

We've also seen a very serious problem with the so-called Sonnenfeldt document which, apparently, Mr. Ford has just endorsed, which said that there is an organic linkage between the Eastern European countries and the Soviet Union. And I would like to see Mr. Ford convince the Polish Americans and the Czech Americans and the Hungarian Americans in this country that those countries don't live under the domination and supervision of the Soviet Union behind the Iron Curtain.

We also have seen Mr. Ford exclude himself from access to the public. He hasn't had a tough, cross-examination-type press conference in over 30 days. One press conference he had without sound.

He's also shown a weakness in yielding to pressure. The Soviet Union, for instance, put pressure on Mr. Ford, and he refused to see a symbol of human freedom recognized around the world—Alexander Solzhenitsyn.

The Arabs have put pressure on Mr. Ford, and he's yielded, and he has permitted a boycott by the Arab countries of American businesses who trade with Israel, who have American Jews owning or taking part in the management of Americna companies. His own Secretary of Commerce had to be subpenaed by the Congress to reveal the names of businesses who were subject to this boycott. They didn't volunteer the information; he had to be subpenaed.

And the last thing I'd like to say is this: This grain deal with the Soviet Union in '72 was terrible, and Mr. Ford made up for it with three embargoes—one against our own ally in Japan. That's not the way to run our foreign policy, including international trade.

THE MODERATOR: Mr. Trewhitt, a question for Governor Carter.

MR. TREWHITT: Governor, I'd like to pick up on that point, actually, and on your appeal for a greater measure of American idealism in foreign affairs. Foreign affairs come home to the American public pretty much in such issues as oil embargoes and grain sales, that sort of thing. Would you be willing to risk an oil embargo in order to promote human rights in Iran, Saudi Arabia— withhold arms from Saudi Arabia for the same purpose? As a matter of fact, I think you have perhaps answered this final part, but would you withhold grain from the Soviet Union in order to promote civil rights in the Soviet Union?

MR. CARTER: I would never single out food as a trade embargo item. If I ever decided to impose an embargo because of a crisis in international relationships, it would include all shipments of all equipment. For instance, if the Arab countries ever again declare an embargo against our Nation on oil, I would consider that not a military but an economic declaration of war. And I would respond instantly and in kind. I would not ship that Arab country anything—no weapons, no spare parts for weapons, no oil-drilling rigs, no oil pipe, no nothing. I wouldn't single out just food.

Another thing I'd like to say is this: In our international trade, as I said in my opening statement, we have become the arms merchant of the world. When this Republican administration came into office, we were shipping about $1 billion worth of arms overseas; now $10 to $12 billion worth of arms overseas to countries that quite often use these weapons to fight each other.

The shift in emphasis has been very disturbing to me, speaking about the Middle East. Under the last Democratic administration 60 percent of all weapons that went into the Middle East were for Israel. Nowadays—75 percent were for Israel before—now 60 percent go to the Arab countries, and this does not include Iran. If you include Iran, our present shipment of weapons to the Middle East— only 20 percent goes to Israel. This is a deviation from idealism; it's a deviation from a commitment to our major ally in the Middle East, which is Israel; it's yielding to economic pressure on the part of the Arabs on the oil issue; and it's also a tremendous indication that under the Ford administration, we have not addressed the energy policy adequately.

We still have no comprehensive energy policy in this country, and it's an overall sign of weakness. When we are weak at home economically—high unemployment, high inflation, a confused Government, a wasteful Defense Establishment—this encourages the kind of pressure that's been put on us successfully. It would have been inconceivable 10, 15 years ago for us to be brought to our knees with an Arab oil embargo. But it was done 3 years ago and they're still putting pressure on us from the Arab countries to our discredit around the world.

These are the weaknesses that I see, and I believe it's not just a matter of idealism. It's a matter of being tough. It's a matter of being strong. It's a matter of being consistent. Our priorities ought to be, first of all, to meet our own military needs; secondly, to meet the needs of our allies and friends, and only then should we ship military equipment to foreign countries. As a matter of fact, Iran is going to get 80 F–14's before we even meet our own Air Force orders for F–14's, and the shipment of Spruance Class Destroyers to Iran are much more highly sophisticated than the Spruance Class Destroyers that are presently being delivered to our own Navy. This is ridiculous, and it ought to be changed.

MR. TREWHITT: Governor, let me pursue that, if I may. If I understand you correctly, you would, in fact, to use my examples, withhold arms from Iran and Saudi Arabia even if the risk was an oil embargo and if they should be securing those arms from somewhere else. And then, if the embargo came, then you would respond in kind. Do I have it correctly?

MR. CARTER: If—Iran is not an Arab country, as you know, it's a Moslem country. But if Saudi Arabia should declare an oil embargo against us, then I would consider that an economic declaration of war. And I would make sure that the Saudis understood this ahead of time, so there would be no doubt in their mind. I think under those circumstances, they would refrain from pushing us to our knees as they did in 1973 with the previous oil embargo.

THE MODERATOR: President Ford.

MR. FORD: Governor Carter apparently doesn't realize that since I've been President, we have sold to the Israelis over $4 billion in military hardware. We have made available to the Israelis over 45 percent of the total economic and military aid since the establishment of Israel 27 years ago. So, the Ford administration has done a good job in helping our good ally, Israel, and we're dedicated to the survival and security of Israel.

I believe that Governor Carter doesn't realize the need and necessity for arms sales to Iran. He indicates he would not make those. Iran is bordered very extensively by the Soviet Union. Iran has Iraq as one of its neighbors. The Soviet Union and the Communist-dominated government of Iraq are neighbors of Iran, and Iran is an ally of the United States. It's my strong feeling that we ought to sell arms to Iran for its own national security and as an ally, a strong ally of the United States.

The history of our relationship with Iran goes back to the days of President Truman, when he decided that it was vitally necessary for our own security, as well as that of Iran, that we should help that country. And Iran has been a good ally. In 1973 when there was an oil embargo, Iran did not participate; Iran continued to sell oil to the United States. I believe that it's in our interest and in the interest of Israel and Iran and Saudi Arabia for the United States to sell arms to those countries. It's for their security as well as ours.

THE MODERATOR: Mr. Valeriani, a question for President Ford.

MR. VALERIANI: Mr. President, the policy of your administration is to normalize relations with mainland China. That means establishing, at some point, full diplomatic relations and, obviously, doing something about the mutual defense treaty with Taiwan. If you are elected, will you move to establish full diplomatic relations with Peking, and will you abrogate the mutual defense treaty with Taiwan? And, as a corollary, would you provide mainland China with military equipment if the Chinese were to ask for it?

MR. FORD: Our relationship with the People's Republic of China is based upon the Shanghai communique of 1972. That communique calls for the normalization of relations between the United States and the People's Republic. It doesn't set a time schedule; it doesn't make a determination as to how that relationship should be achieved in relationship to our current diplomatic recognition and obligations to the Taiwanese Government. The Shanghai communique does say that the differences between the People's Republic on the one hand and Taiwan on the other shall be settled by peaceful means.

The net result is this administration—and during my time as the President for the next 4 years—we will continue to move for normalization of relations in the traditional sense. And we will insist that the disputes between Taiwan and the People's Republic be settled peacefully, as was agreed in the Shanghai communique of 1972.

The Ford administration will not let down, will not eliminate or forget our obligation to the people of Taiwan. We feel that there must be a continued obligation to the people, the some 19 or 20 million in Taiwan, and as we move during the next 4 years, those will be the policies of this administration.

MR. VALERIANI: Sir, the military equipment for the mainland Chinese?

MR. FORD: There is no policy of this Government to give to the People's Republic, or to sell to the People's Republic of China, military equipment. I do not believe that we, the United States, should sell, give, or otherwise transfer military hardware to the People's Republic of China or any other Communist nations, such as the Soviet Union and the like.

THE MODERATOR: Governor Carter.

MR. CARTER. I'd like to go back just one moment to the previous question, where Mr. Ford, I think, confused the issue by trying to say that we're shipping Israel 40 percent of our aid. As matter of fact, during this current year, we are shipping Iran—or have contracted to ship to Iran—about $7 1/2 billion worth of arms and also to Saudi Arabia about $7 1/2 billion of worth of arms.

Also, in 1975 we almost brought Israel to their knees after the Yom Kippur war by the so-called reassessment of our relationship to Israel. We, in effect, tried to make Israel the scapegoat for the problems in the Middle East. And this weakened our relationship with Israel a great deal and put a cloud on the total commitment that our people feel toward the Israelis. There ought to be a clear, unequivocal commitment without change to Israel.

In the Far East I think we need to continue to be strong, and I would certainly pursue the normalization of relationships with the People's Republic of China. We opened up a great opportunity in 1972—which has pretty well been frittered away under Mr. Ford—that ought to be a constant inclination toward friendship. But I would never let that friendship with the People's Republic of China stand in the way of the preservation of the independence and freedom of the people of Taiwan.

THE MODERATOR: Mr. Frankel, a question for Governor Carter.

MR. FRANKEL: Governor, we always seem, in our elections, and maybe in between, too, to argue about who can be tougher in the world. Give or take a few billion dollars, give or take one weapons systems, our leading politicians, and I think you two gentlemen, seem to settle roughly on the same strategy in the world at roughly the same Pentagon budget cost.

How bad do things have to get in our economy, or how much backwardness and hunger would it take in the world to persuade you that our national security and our survival required very drastic cutbacks in arms spending and dramatic new efforts in other directions?

MR. CARTER: Well, always in the past we have had an ability to have a strong defense and also to have a strong domestic economy and also to be strong in our reputation and influence within the community of nations. These characteristics of our country have been endangered under Mr. Ford. We are no longer respected. In a showdown vote in the United Nations or in any other international council we are lucky to get 20 percent of the other nations to vote with us. Our allies feel that we've neglected them. The so-called Nixon shocks against Japan have weakened our relationships there. Under this administration we have also had an inclination to keep separate the European countries, thinking that if they are separate, then we can dominate them and proceed with our secret Lone Ranger-type diplomatic efforts.

I would also like to point out that we in this country have let our economy go down the drain—the worst inflation since the Great Depression, the highest unemployment of any developed nation of the world. We have a higher unemployment rate in this country than Great Britain, than West Germany; our unemployment rate is twice as high as it is in Italy; it's three or four times as high as it is in Japan. And that terrible circumstance in this country is exported overseas. We comprise about 30 percent of the world's economic trade power influence. And when we are weak at home, weaker than all our allies, that weakness weakens the whole free world. So, strong economy is very important.

Another thing that we need to do is to reestablish the good relationships that we ought to have between the United States and our natural allies and friends—they have felt neglected. And using that base of strength, and using the idealism, the honesty, the predictability, the commitment, the integrity of our own country—that's where our strength lies. And that would permit us to deal with the developing nations in a position of strength.

Under this administration, we've had a continuation of a so-called "balance of power politics" where everything is looked on as a struggle between us on the one side and the Soviet Union on the other. Our allies, the smaller countries, get trampled in the rush.

What we need is to try to seek individualized, bilateral relationships with countries regardless of their size and to establish world order politics, which means we want to preserve peace through strength. We also want to revert back to the stature and the respect that our country had in previous administrations. Now, I can't say when this can come, but I can guarantee it will not come if Gerald Ford is reelected and this present policy is continued. It will come if I am elected.

MR. FRANKEL: If I hear you right, sir, you are saying guns and butter both, but President Johnson also had trouble keeping up both Vietnam and his domestic programs. I was really asking, when do the needs of the cities and our own needs and those of other backward and even more needy countries and societies around the world take precedence over some of our military spending? Ever?

MR. CARTER: Let me say very quickly that under President Johnson, in spite of the massive investment in the Vietnam war, he turned over a balanced budget to Mr. Nixon. The unemployment rate was less than 4 percent. The inflation rate under Kennedy and Johnson was about 2 percent—one-third what it is under this administration. So, we did have at that time, with good management, the ability to do both. I don't think anybody can say that Johnson and Kennedy neglected the poor and the destitute people in this country or around the world.

But I can say this: The number one responsibility of any President, above all else, is to guarantee the security of our Nation, an ability to be free of the threat of attack or blackmail and to carry out our obligations to our allies and friends and to carry out a legitimate foreign policy. they must go hand in hand. But the security of this Nation has got to come first.

THE MODERATOR: President Ford.

MR. FORD: Let me say very categorically, you cannot maintain the security and the strength of the United States with the kind of defense budget cuts that Governor Carter has indicated. In 1975 he wanted to cut the budget $15 billion. He is now down to a figure of $5 billion to $7 billion. Reductions of that kind will not permit the United States to be strong enough to deter agression and maintain the peace.

Governor Carter apparently does not know the facts. As soon as I became President, I initiated meetings with the NATO heads of state and met with them in Brussels to discuss how we could improve the defense relationship in Western Europe. In November of 1975, I met with the leaders of the five industrial nations in France for the purpose of seeing what we could do, acting together, to meet the problems of the coming recession. In Puerto Rico this year, I met with six of the leading industrial nations' heads of state to meet the problems of inflation so we would be able to solve it before it got out of hand.

I have met with the heads of government, bilaterally as well as multilaterally. Our relations with Japan have never been better. I was the first United States President to visit Japan. And we had the Emperor of Japan here this past year. And the net result is Japan and the United States are working more closely together now than at any time in the history of our relationship. You can go around the world—and let me take Israel, for example. Just recently, President (Prime Minister) Rabin said that our relations were never better.

THE MODERATOR: Mr. Trewhitt, a question for President Ford.

MR. TREWHITT: Mr. President, you referred earlier to your meeting with Mr. Brezhnev at Vladivostok in 1974. You agreed on that occasion to try to achieve another strategic arms limitation—SALT—agreement within the year. Nothing happened in 1975 or not very much publicly, at least, and those talks are still dragging, and things got quieter as the current season approached. Is there a bit of politics involved there, perhaps on both sides? Or, perhaps more important, are interim weapons developments—and I am thinking of such things as the cruise missile and the Soviet SS—20 intermediate range rocket—making SALT irrelevant, bypassing the SALT I negotiations?

MR. FORD: First, we have to understand that SALT expires October 3, 1977. Mr. Brezhnev and I met in Vladivostok in December of 1974 for the purpose of trying to take the initial steps so we could have a SALT II agreement that would go to 1985. As I indicated earlier, we did agree on a 2,400 limitation on launchers of ballistic missiles. That would mean a cutback in the Soviet program. It would not interfere with our own program. At the same time we put a limitation of 1,320 on MIRV's.

Our technicians have been working since that time in Geneva trying to put into technical language an agreement that can be verified by both parties. In the meantime there has developed the problem of the Soviet Backfire, their high performance aircraft, which they say is not a long-range aircraft and which some of our people say is an intercontinental aircraft. In the iterim there has been the development on our part primarily, the cruise missiles—cruise missiles that could be launched from land-based mobile installations; cruise missiles that could be launched from high performance aircraft like the B–52's or the B–1's which I hope we proceed with; cruise missiles which could be launched from either surface or submarine naval vessels. Those gray area weapons systems are creating some problems in the agreement for a SALT II negotiation.

But I can say that I am dedicated to proceeding. And I met just last week with the Foreign Minister of the Soviet Union, and he indicated to me that the Soviet Union was interested in narrowing the differences and making a realistic and a sound compromise.

I hope and trust in the best interests of both countries and in the best interests of all peoples throughout this globe that the Soviet Union and the United States can make a mutually beneficial agreement because, if we do not and SALT I expires on October 3, 1977, you will unleash again an all-out nuclear arms race with the potential of a nuclear holocaust of unbelievable dimension. So, it is the obligation of the President to do just that, and I intend to do so.

MR. TREWHITT: Mr. President, let me follow that up. I'll submit that the cruise missile adds a whole new dimension to the arms competition, and then cite a statement by your office to the arms control association a few days ago in which you said that the cruise missile might eventually be included in a comprehensive arms limitation agreement, but that in the meantime it was an essential part of the American strategic arsenal. Now, may I assume from that that you are tending to exclude the cruise missile from the next SALT agreement, or is it still negotiable in that context?

MR. FORD: I believe that the cruise missiles which we are now developing in research and development across the spectrum—from air, from the sea, or from the land—can be included within a SALT II agreement. They are a new weapons system that has a great potential, both conventional and nuclear armed. At the same time we have to make certain that the Soviet Union's Backfire, which they claim is not an intercontinental aircraft and which some of our people contend is, must also be included if we are to get the kind of agreement which is in the best interest of both countries.

And I really believe that it's far better for us and for the Soviet Union and, more importantly, for the people around the world that these two super powers find an answer for a SALT II agreement before October 3, 1977. I think good will on both parts, hard bargaining by both parties, and a reasonable compromise will be in the best interests of all parties.

THE MODERATOR: Governor Carter.

MR. CARTER: Well, Mr. Ford acts like he is running for President for the first time. He has been in office 2 years, and there has been absolutely no progress made toward a new SALT agreement. He has learned the date of the expiration of SALT I, apparently.

We have seen in this world a development of a tremendous threat to us. As a nuclear engineer myself, I know the limitations and capabilities of atomic power. I also know that as far as the human beings on this Earth are concerned, that the nonproliferation of atomic weapons is number one. Only in the last few days, with the election approaching, has Mr. Ford taken any interest in a nonproliferation movement.

I advocated last May, in a speech at the United Nations, that we move immediately as a nation to declare a complete moratorium on the testing of all nuclear devices, both weapons and peaceful devices, that we not ship any more atomic fuel to a country that refuses to comply with strict controls over the waste which can be reprocessed into explosives. I've also advocated that we stop the sale by Germany and France of reprocessing plants to Pakistan and Brazil. Mr. Ford hasn't moved on this. We also need to provide an adequate supply of enriched uranium. Mr. Ford again, under pressure from the atomic energy lobby, has insisted that this reprocessing or rather reenrichment be done by private industry and not by the existing government plants.

This kind of confusion and absence of leadership has let us drift now for 2 years with the constantly increasing threat of atomic weapons throughout the world. We now have five nations that have atomic bombs that we know about. If we continue under Mr. Ford's policy, by 1985 or '90 we will have 20 nations that have the capability of exploding atomic weapons. This has got to be stopped. That is one of the major challenges and major undertakings that I will assume as the next President.

THE MODERATOR: Mr. Valeriani, a question for Governor Carter.

MR. VALERIANI: Governor Carter, earlier tonight you said America is not strong anymore, America is not respected anymore. And I feel I must ask you, do you really believe that the United States is not the strongest country in the world? Do you really believe that the United States is not the most respected country in the world, or is that just campaign rhetoric?

MR. CARTER: No, it's not just campaign rhetoric. I think that militarily we are as strong as any nation on Earth. I think we've got to stay that way and continue to increase our capabilities to meet any potential threat. But as far as strength derived from commitment to principles; as far as strength derived from the unity within our country; as far as strength derived from the people, the Congress, the Secretary of State, the President, sharing in the evolution and carrying out of a foreign policy; as far as strength derived from the respect of our own allies and friends, their assurance that we will be staunch in our commitment, that we will not deviate, and we will give them adequate attention; as far as strength derived from doing what is right, caring for the poor, providing food, becoming the breadbasket of the world instead of the arms merchant of the world—in those respects we are not strong. Also, we will never be strong again overseas unless we are strong at home. And with our economy in such terrible disarray, and getting worse by the month—we have got 500,000 more Americans unemployed today than we had 3 months ago; we have got 2 1/2 million more Americans out of work now than we had when Mr. Ford took office—this kind of deterioration in our economic strength is bound to weaken us around the world.

And we not only have problems at home but we export those problems overseas. So, as far as the respect of our own people toward our own Government, as far as participation in the shaping of concepts and commitments, as far as a trust of our country among the nations of the world, as far as dependence of our country in meeting the needs and obligations that we've expressed to our allies, as far as the respect of our country, even among our potential adversaries, we are weak. Potentially, we are strong. Under this administration that strength has not been realized.

THE MODERATOR: President Ford.

MR. FORD: Governor Carter brags about the unemployment during Democratic administrations and condemns the unemployment at the present time. I must remind him that we are at peace, and during the period that he brags about unemployment being low, the United States was at war.

Now let me correct one other comment that Governor Carter has made. I have recommended to the Congress that we develop the uranium enrichment plant at Portsmouth, Ohio, which is a publicly owned U.S. Government facility, and have indicated that the private program which would follow on in Alabama is one that may or may not be constructed, but I committed to the one at Portsmouth, Ohio.

The Governor also talks about morality in foreign policy. The foreign policy of the United States meets the highest standards of morality. What is more moral than peace? And the United States is at peace today. What is more moral in foreign policy than for the administration to take the lead in the World Food Conference in Rome in 1974, when the United States committed 6 million metric tons of food, over 60 percent of the food committed for the disadvantaged and underdeveloped nations of the world? The Ford administration wants to eradicate hunger and disease in our underdeveloped countries throughout the world. What is more moral than for the United States under the Ford administration to take the lead in southern Africa, in the Middle East? Those are initiatives in foreign policy which are of the highest moral standards. And that is indicative of the foreign policy of this country.

THE MODERATOR: Mr. Frankel, a question for President Ford.

MR FRANKEL: Mr. President, can we stick with morality? For a lot of people it seems to cover a bunch of sins.

Mr. Nixon and Mr. Kissinger used to tell us that instead of morality we had to worry in the world about living with and letting live all kinds of governments that we really didn't like—North and South Korean dictators, Chilean fascists, Chinese Communists, Iranian emperors, and so on. The said the only way to get by in a wicked world was to treat others on the basis of how they treated us and not how they treated their own people.

But more recently we seem to have taken a different tack. We seem to have decided that it is part of our business to tell the Rhodesians, for instance, that the way they are treating their own black people is wrong and they've got to change their government. And we put pressure on them. We were rather liberal in our advice to the Italians as to how to vote.

Is this a new Ford foreign policy in the making? Can we expect that you are now going to turn to South Africa and force them to change their government, to intervene in similar ways to end the bloodshed, as you called it, say in Chile or Chilean prisons, and to throw our weight around for the values that we hold dear in the world?

MR. FORD: I believe that our foreign policy must express the highest standards of morality, and the initiatives that we took in southern Africa are the best examples of what this administration is doing and will continue to do in the next 4 years.

If the United States had not moved when we did in southern Africa, there is no doubt there would have been an acceleration of bloodshed in that tragic part of the world. If we had not taken our initiative, it's very, very possible that the Government of Rhodesia would have been overrun and that the Soviet Union and the Cubans would have dominated southern Africa.

So, the United States, seeking to preserve the principle of self-determination, to eliminate that possibility of bloodshed, to protect the rights of the minority as we insisted upon the rights of the majority, I believe followed the good conscience of the American people in foreign policy, and I believe that we have used our skill. Secretary of State Kissinger has done a superb job in working with the black African nations, the so-called frontline nations. He has done a superb job in getting the Prime Minister of South Africa, Mr. Vorster, to agree that the time had come for a solution to the problem of Rhodesia. Secretary Kissinger, in his meeting with Prime Minister Smith of Rhodesia, was able to convince him that it was in the best interests of whites as well as blacks in Rhodesia to find an answer for a transitional government and then a majority government.

This is a perfect example of the kind of leadership that the United States, under this administration, has taken. And I can assure you that this administration will follow that high moral principle in our future efforts in foreign policy, including our efforts in the Middle East, where it is vitally important because the Middle East is the crossroads of the world. There have been more disputes, and it's an area where there is more volatility than any other place in the world. But because Arab nations and the Israelis trust the United States, we were able to take the lead in the Sinai II agreement.

And I can assure you that the United States will have the leadership role in moving toward a comprehensive settlement of the Middle Eastern problems— I hope and trust as soon as possible—and we will do it with the highest moral principles.

MR. FRANKEL: Mr. President, just clarify one point. There are lots of majorities in the world that feel they are being pushed around by minority governments. And are you saying they can now expect to look to us for not just good cheer but throwing our weight on their side in South Africa or on Taiwan or in Chile, to help change their governments as in Rhodesia?

MR. FORD: I would hope that as we move to one area of the world from another—and the United States must not spread itself too thinly; that was one of the problems that helped to create the circumstances in Vietnam—but as we as a nation find that we are asked by the various parties, either one nation against another or individuals within a nation, that the United States will take the leadership and try to resolve the differences.

Let me take South Korea as an example. I have personally told President Park that the United States does not condone the kind of repressive measures that he has taken in the country. But I think in all fairness and equity, we have to recognize the problem that South Korea has. On the north they have North Korea with 500,000 well-trained, well-equipped troops. They are supported by the People's Republic of China. They are supported by the Soviet Union. South Korea faces a very delicate situation. Now, the United States in this case, this administration has recommended a year ago—and we have reiterated it again this year—that the United States, South Korea, North Korea, and the People's Republic of China sit down at a conference table to resolve the problems of the Korean peninsula. This is a leadership role that the United States, under this administration, is carrying out. And if we do it—and I think the opportunities and the possibilities are getting better—we will have solved many of the internal domestic problems that exist in South Korea at the present time.

THE MODERATOR: Governor Carter?

MR. CARTER: I noticed that Mr. Ford didn't comment on the prisons in Chile. This is a typical example, maybe of many others, where this administration overthrew an elected government and helped to establish a military dictatorship. This has not been an ancient history story. Last year, under Mr. Ford, of all the Food for Peace that went to South America, 85 percent went to the military dictatorship in Chile.

Another point I want to make is this: He says we have to move from one area of the world to another. That is one of the problems with this administration's so-called shuttle diplomacy. While the Secretary of State is in one country, there are almost 150 others that are wondering what we are going to do next, what will be the next secret agreement. We don't have a comprehensive, understandable foreign policy that deals with world problems or even regional problems.

Another thing that concerned me was what Mr. Ford said about unemployment, that insinuating that under Johnson and Kennedy that unemployment could only be held down when this country is at war. Karl Marx said that the free enterprise system in a democracy can only continue to exist when they are at war or preparing for war. Karl Marx was the grandfather of communism. I don't agree with that statement; I hope Mr. Ford doesn't either.

He has put pressure on the Congress—and I don't believe Mr. Ford would even deny this—to hold up on nonproliferation legislation until the Congress agreed for an $8 billion program for private industry to start producing enriched uranium.

And the last thing I want to make is this: He talks about peace, and I am thankful for peace. We were peaceful when Mr. Ford went into office, but he and Mr. Kissinger and others tried to start a new Vietnam in Angola. And it was only the outcry of the American people and the Congress when this secret deal was discovered that prevented our renewed involvement in the conflagration which was taking place there.

THE MODERATOR: Gentlemen, I am sorry to say we do not have time enough for two complete sequences of questions. We now have only 12 minutes left. Therefore, I would like to ask for shorter questions and shorter answers. And we also will drop the followup question. Each candidate may still respond, of course, to the other's answer.

Mr. Trewhitt, a question for Governor Carter.

MR. TREWHITT: Governor Carter, before this event the most communication I received concerned Panama. Would you, as President, be prepared to sign a treaty which at a fixed date yielded administrative and economic control of the Canal Zone and shared defense which, as I understand it, is the position the United States took in 1974?

MR. CARTER: Well, here again, the Panamanian question is one that has been confused by Mr. Ford. He had directed his diplomatic representative to yield to the Panamanians full sovereignty over the Panama Canal Zone at the end of a certain period of time. When Mr. Reagan raised this question in Florida, Mr. Ford not only disavowed his instructions but he also even dropped, parenthetically, the use of the word "détente."

I would never give up complete control or practical control of the Panama Canal Zone, but I would continue to negotiate with the Panamanians. When the original treaty was signed back in the early 1900's, when Theodore Roosevelt was President, Panama retained sovereignty over the Panama Canal Zone. We retained control as though we had sovereignty.

Now, I would be willing to go ahead with negotiations. I believe that we could share more fully responsibilities for the Panama Canal Zone with Panama. I would be willing to continue to raise the payment for shipment of goods through the Panama Canal Zone. I might even by willing to reduce to some degree our military emplacements in the Panama Canal Zone, but I would not relinquish practical control of the Panama Canal Zone any time in the foreseeable future.

THE MODERATOR: President Ford.

MR. FORD: The United States must and will maintain complete access to the Panama Canal. The United States must maintain a defense capability of the Panama Canal, and the United States will maintain our national security interests in the Panama Canal.

The negotiations for the Panama Canal started under President Johnson and have continued up to the present time. I believe those negotiations should continue. But there are certain guidelines that must be followed, and I've just defined them.

Let me take just a minute to comment on something that Governor Carter said on nonproliferation. In May of 1975, I called for a conference of nuclear suppliers. That conference has met six times. In May of this year, Governor Carter took the first initiative, approximately 12 months after I had taken my initiative a year ago.

THE MODERATOR: Mr. Valeriani, a question for President Ford.

MR. VALERIANI: Mr. President, the Government [General] Accounting Office has just put out a report suggesting that you shot from the hip in the *Mayaguez* rescue mission and that you ignored diplomatic messages saying that a peaceful solution was in prospect. Why didn't you do more diplomatically at that time? And a related question: Did the White House try to prevent the release of that report?

MR. FORD: The White House did not prevent the release of that report. On July 12 of this year, we gave full permission for the release of the report. I was very disappointed in the fact that the GAO released that report because I think it interjected political, partisan politics at the present time.

But let me comment on the report. Somebody who sits in Washington, D.C., 18 months after the *Mayaguez* incident can be a very good grandstand quarterback. And let me make another observation. This morning I got a call from the skipper of the *Mayaguez*. He was furious, because he told me that it was the action of me, President Ford, that saved the lives of the crew of the *Mayaguez*. And I can assure you that if we had not taken the strong and forceful action that we did, we would have been criticized very, very severely for sitting back and not moving.

Captain Miller is thankful, the crew is thankful. We did the right thing. It seems to me that those who sit in Washington 18 months after the incident are not the best judges of the decisionmaking process that had to be made by the National Security Council and by myself at the time the incident was developing in the Pacific.

Let me assure you that we made every possible overture to the People's Republic of China and, through them, to the Cambodian Government; we made diplomatic protest to the Cambodian Government through the United Nations. Every possible diplomatic means was utilized. But at the same time I had a responsibility, and so did the National Security Council, to meet the problem at hand, and we handled it responsibly. And I think Captain Miller's testimony to that effect is the best evidence.

THE MODERATOR: Governor Carter.

MR. CARTER: Well, I am reluctant to comment on the recent report. I haven't read it. I think the American people have only one requirement—that the facts about *Mayaguez* be given to them accurately and completely.

Mr. Ford has been there for 18 months. He had the facts that were released today immediately after the *Mayaguez* incident. I understand that the report today is accurate. Mr. Ford has said, I believe, that it was accurate and that the White House made no attempt to block the issuing of that report. I don't know if that is exactly accurate or not.

I understand that both the Department of State and the Defense Department have approved the accuracy of today's report, or yesterday's report, and also the National Security Agency. I don't know what was right or what was wrong or what was done. The only thing I believe is that whatever the knowledge was that Mr. Ford had should have been given to the American people 18 months ago, immediately after the *Mayaguez* incident occurred.

This is what the American people want. When something happens that endangers our security, or when something happens that threatens our stature in the world, or when American people are endangered by the actions of a foreign country, just 40 sailors on the *Mayaguez,* we obviously have to move agressively and quickly to rescue them. But then, after the immediate action is taken, I believe the President has an obligation to tell the American people the truth and not wait 18 months later for the report to be issued.

THE MODERATOR: Gentlemen, at this time we have time for only two very short questions. Mr. Frankel, a question for Governor Carter.

MR. FRANKEL: Governor Carter, if the price of gaining influence among the Arabs is closing our eyes a little bit to the boycott against Israel, how would you handle that?

MR. CARTER: I believe that the boycott of American businesses by the Arab countries, because those businesses trade with Israel or because they have American Jews who are owners or directors in the company, is an absolute disgrace. This is the first time that I remember in the history of our country when we've let a foreign country circumvent or change our Bill of Rights. I will do everything I can as President to stop the boycott of American businesses by the Arab countries.

It's not a matter of diplomacy or trade with me; it's a matter of morality. And I don't believe that the Arab countries will pursue it when we have a strong President who will protect the integrity of our country, the commitment of our Constitution and Bill of Rights, and protect people in this country who happen to be Jews—it may later be Catholics, it may later be Baptists—who are threatened by some foreign country. But we ought to stand staunch. And I think it is a disgrace that so far Mr. Ford's administration has blocked the passage of legislation that would have revealed by law every instance of the boycott, and it would have prevented the boycott from continuing.

THE MODERATOR: President Ford?

MR. FORD: Again. Governor Carter is inaccurate. The Arab boycott action was first taken in 1952. And in November of 1975, I was the first President to order the executive branch to take action—affirmative action through the Department of Commerce and other Cabinet Departments—to make certain that no American businessman or business organization should discriminate against Jews because of an Arab boycott.

And I might add that my administration—and I am very proud of it—is the first administration that has taken an antitrust action against companies in this country that have allegedly cooperated with the Arab boycott. Just on Monday of this week, I signed a tax bill that included an amendment that would prevent companies in the United States from taking a tax deduction if they have, in any way whatsoever, cooperated with the Arab boycott.

And last week, when we were trying to get the Export Administration Act through the Congress—necessary legislation—my administration went to Capitol Hill and tried to convince the House and the Senate that we should have an amendment on the legislation which would take strong and effective action against those who participate or cooperate with the Arab boycott.

One other point: Because the Congress failed to act I am going to announce tomorrow that the Department of Commerce will disclose those companies that have participated in the Arab boycott. This is something that we can do. The Congress failed to do it, and we intend to do it.

THE MODERATOR: Mr. Trewhitt, a very brief question for President Ford.

MR. TREWHITT: Mr. President, if you get the accounting of missing in action you want from North Vietnam—or from Vietnam, I am sorry, now—would you then be prepared to reopen negotiations for restoration of relations with that country?

MR. FORD: Let me restate our policy. As long as Vietnam, North Vietnam, does not give us a full and complete accounting of our missing in action, I will never go along with the admission of Vietnam to the United Nations. If they do give us a bona fide, complete accounting of the 800 MIA's, then I believe that the United States should begin negotiations for the admission of Vietnam to the United Nations, but not until they have given us the full accounting of our MIA's.

THE MODERATOR: Governor Carter?

MR. CARTER: One of the most embarassing failures of the Ford administration, and one that touches specifically on human rights, is his refusal to appoint a Presidential commission to go to Vietnam, to go to Laos, to go to Cambodia and try to trade for the release of information about those who are missing in action in those wars. This is what the families of MIA's want. So far, Mr. Ford has not done it. We have had several fragmentary efforts by Members of the Congress and by private citizens.

Several months ago the Vietnam Government said we are ready to sit down and negotiate for release of information on MIA's. So far, Mr. Ford has not responded.

I also would never formalize relationships with Vietnam nor permit them to join the United Nations until they have taken this action. But that is not enough. We need to have an active and aggressive action on the part of the President, the leader of this country, to seek out every possible way to get that information which has kept the MIA families in despair and doubt, and Mr. Ford has just not done it.

THE MODERATOR: Thank you, Governor Carter.

That completes the questioning for this evening. Each candidate now has up to 3 minutes for a closing statement. It was determined by the toss of a coin that Governor Carter would take the first question, and he now goes first with his closing remarks.

Governor Carter.

MR. CARTER: The purpose of this debate and the outcome of the election will determine three basic things—leadership, upholding the principles of our country, and proper priorities and commitments for the future.

This election will also determine what kind of world we leave our children. Will it be a nightmare world, threatened with the proliferation of atomic bombs, not just in five major countries, but dozens of smaller countries that have been permitted to develop atomic weapons because of a failure of our top leadership to stop proliferation? Will we have a world of hunger and hatred, and will we be living in an armed camp, stripped of our friendships and allies, hiding behind a tight defense that has been drawn in around us because we are fearful of the outside world? Will we have a government of secrecy that excludes the American people from participation in making basic decisions and therefore covers up mistakes and makes it possible for our Government—our Government—to depart from the principles of our Constitution and Bill of Rights? Or will we have a world of peace with the threat of atomic weapons eliminated, with full trade, with our people at work, inflation controlled, openness in government, our people proud once again; Congress, citizens, President, Secretary of State, working in harmony and unity toward a common future, a world where people have enough to eat, and a world where we care about those who don't? Can we become a breadbasket of the world, instead of the arms merchant of the world? I believe we can and we ought to.

Now, we have been hurt in recent years in this country, in the aftermath of Vietnam, Cambodia, Chile, Pakistan, Angola, Watergate, CIA. We have been hurt. Our people feel that we have lost something precious. That's not necessary. I want to see our Nation return to a posture and an image and a standard to make us proud once again. I remember the world of NATO and the world of point four and the world of the Marshall plan and a world of the Peace Corps. Why can't we have that once again?

We ought to be a beacon for nations who search for peace and who search for freedom, who search for individual liberty, who search for basic human rights. We haven't been lately. We can be once again.

We will never have that world leadership until we are strong at home, and we can have that strength if we return to the basic principles. It ought not to be a strength of bombast and threats. It ought to be a quiet strength based on the integrity of our people, the vision of the Constitution, and an innate strong will and purpose that God has given us in the greatest nation on Earth, the United States.

THE MODERATOR: President Ford.

MR. FORD: As we have seen tonight, foreign policy and defense policy are difficult and complex issues. We can debate methods; we can debate one decision or another. But there are two things which cannot be debated—experience and results.

In the last 2 years I have made policy decisions involving long-range difficulties and policies and made day-to-day judgments, not only as President of the United States but as the leader of the free world.

What is the result of the leadership? America is strong, America is free, America is respected. Not a single young American today is fighting or dying on any foreign battlefield. America is at peace, with freedom.

Thank you, and good night.

THE MODERATOR: Thank you, President Ford. Thank you, Governor Carter. I also want to thank our questioners and the audience here this evening.

The third and final debate between President Ford and Governor Carter will take place on October the 22d at 9:30 p.m. eastern daylight time, on the campus of the College of William and Mary in Williamsburg, Virginia. The subject matter will cover all issues.

These debates are sponsored by the League of Women Voters Education Fund to help voters become better informed on the issues and to generate greater voter turnout in the November election.

Now from the Palace of Fine Arts Theatre in San Francisco, good night.

Third Presidential Campaign Debate
Williamsburg, October 22, 1976

In the final televised debate, Carter toned down his attacks on Ford and spoke of a new spirit in America. For his part, Ford emphasized a new respect for the Presidency and an economic upturn inspired by his policies.

THE MODERATOR: Good evening, I am Barbara Walters, moderator of the last of the debates of 1976 between Gerald R. Ford, Republican candidate for President, and Jimmy Carter, Democratic candidate for President.

Welcome, President Ford, welcome, Governor Carter, and thank you for joining us this evening.

This debate takes place before an audience in Phi Beta Kappa Memorial Hall on the campus of the College of William and Mary in historic Williamsburg, Virginia. It is particularly appropriate in this Bicentennial Year that we meet on these grounds to hear this debate. Two hundred years ago, five William and Mary students met at nearby Raleigh Tavern to form Phi Beta Kappa, a fraternity designed, they wrote, "to search out and dispel the clouds of falsehood by debating without reserve the issues of the day."

In that spirit of debate—"without reserve," "to dispel the clouds of falsehood"—gentlemen, let us proceed.

The subject matter of this debate is open, covering all issues and topics. Our questioners tonight are Joseph Kraft, syndicated columnist, Robert Maynard, editorial writer for the Washington Post, and Jack Nelson, Washington bureau chief of the *Los Angeles Times*.

The ground rules tonight are as follows: Questioners will alternate questions between the candidates. The candidate has up to 2 1/2 minutes to answer the question. The other candidate then has up to 2 minutes to respond. If necessary, a questioner may ask a followup question for further clarification, and in that case the candidate has up to 2 minutes to respond. As was initially agreed to by both candidates, the answers should be responsive to the particular questions. Finally, each candidate has up to 3 minutes for a closing statement.

President Ford and Governor Carter do not have prepared notes or comments with them this evening, but they may make notes and refer to them during the debate.

It has been determined that President Ford would take the first question in this last debate, and, Mr. Kraft, you have that first question for President Ford.

MR. KRAFT: Mr. President, I assume that the Americans all know that these are difficult times and that there is no pie in the sky and that they don't expect something for nothing. So I'd like to ask you, as a first question, as you look ahead in the next 4 years, what sacrifices are you going to call on the American people to make? What price are you going to ask them to pay to realize your objectives?

Let me add, Governor Carter, that if you felt that it was appropriate to answer that question in your comments, as to what price it would be appropriate for the American people to pay for a Carter administration, I think that would be proper, too.

Mr. President?

MR. FORD: Mr. Kraft, I believe that the American people in the next 4 years, under a Ford administration, will be called upon to make those necessary sacrifices to preserve the peace—which we have—which means, of course, that we will have to maintain an adequate military capability; which means, of course, that we will have to add, I think, a few billion dollars to our defense appropriations to make certain that we have adequate strategic forces, adequate conventional forces.

I think the American people will be called upon to be in the forefront in giving leadership to the solution of those problems that must be solved in the Middle East, in Southern Africa, and any problems that might arise in the Pacific.

The American people will be called upon to tighten their belts a bit in meeting some of the problems that we face domestically. I don't think that America can go on a big spending spree with a whole lot of new programs that would add significantly to the Federal budget.

I believe that the American people, if given the leadership that I would expect to give, would be willing to give this thrust to preserve the peace and the necessary restraint at home to hold the lid on spending so that we could, I think, have a long overdue and totally justified tax decrease for the middle-income people. And then—with the economy that would be generated from a restraint on spending and a tax reduction primarily for the middle-income people—then I think the American people would be willing to make those sacrifices for peace and prosperity in the next 4 years.

MR. KRAFT: Could I be a little more specific, Mr. President?

MR. FORD: Sure, sure.

MR. KRAFT: Doesn't your policy really imply that we are going to have to have a pretty high rate of unemployment over a fairly long time, that growth is going to be fairly slow, and that we are not going to be able to do very much in the next 4 or 5 years to meet the basic agenda of our national needs in the cities, in health, in transit, and a whole lot of other things like that?

MR. FORD: Not at all.

MR. KRAFT: Aren't those real costs?

MR. FORD: No, Mr. Kraft. We're spending very significant amounts of money now, some $200 billion a year, almost 50 percent of our total Federal expenditure by the Federal Government at the present time, for human needs. Now, we will probably have to increase that to some extent, but we don't have to have growth in spending that will blow the lid off and add to the problems of inflation. I believe we can meet the problems within the cities of this country and still give a tax reduction. I proposed, as you know, a reduction to increase the personal exemption from $750 to $1,000, with the fiscal program that I have. And if you look at the projections, it shows that we will reduce unemployment, that we will continue to win the battle against inflation, and at the same time, give the kind of quality of life that I believe is possible in America: a job, a home for all those that will work and save for it, safety in the streets, health care that is affordable. These things can be done if we have the right vision and the right restraint and the right leadership.

THE MODERATOR: Thank you. Governor Carter, your response, please.

MR. CARTER: Well, I might say first of all, that I think in case of a Carter administration, the sacrifices would be much less. Mr. Ford's own environmental agency has projected a 10 percent unemployment rate by 1978 if he is President. The American people are ready to make sacrifices if they are part of the process, if they know that they will be helping to make decisions and won't be excluded from being an involved party to the national purpose.

The major effort that we must put forward is to put our people back to work. And I think that this is one example where a lot of people have selfish, grasping ideas now. I remember in 1973, in the depth of the energy crisis, when President Nixon called on the American people to make a sacrifice to cut down on the waste of gasoline, to cut down on the speed of automobiles. It was a tremendous surge of patriotism. "I want to make a sacrifice for my country."

I think we could call together—with strong leadership in the White House—business, industry, and labor, and say, let's have voluntary price restraints, let's lay down some guidelines so we don't have continuing inflation.

We could also have an end to the extremes. We now have one extreme, for instance, of some welfare recipients who, by taking advantage of the welfare laws, the housing laws, the Medicaid laws, and the food stamp laws, make over $10,000 a year, and they don't have to pay any taxes on it. At the other extreme just 1 percent of the richest people in our country derive 25 percent of all the tax benefits. So both those extremes grasp for advantage, and the person who has to pay that expense is the middle-income family who is still working for a living. And they have to pay for the rich who have the privilege and for the poor who are not working.

But I think that a balanced approach, with everybody being part of it, and striving for unselfishness could help, as it did in 1973, to let people sacrifice for their own country. I know I'm ready for it; I think American people are, too.

THE MODERATOR: Thank you. Mr. Maynard, your question to Governor Carter.

MR. MAYNARD: Governor, by all indications, the voters are so turned off by this election campaign so far that only half intend to vote. One major reason for this apathetic electorate appears to be the low level at which this campaign has been conducted. It has digressed frequently from important issues into allegations of blunders and brainwashing and fixations on lust in Playboy. What responsibility do you accept for the low level of the campaign for the Nation's highest office?

MR. CARTER: I think the major reason for a decrease in participation that we've experienced ever since 1960 has been the deep discouragement of the American people about the performance of public officials. When you've got 7 1/2, 8 million people out of work, when you've got inflation as you had during the last 8-year Democratic administration, when you have the highest deficits in history, when you have it becoming increasingly difficult for a family to put a child through college or to own a home, there is a natural inclination to be turned off. Also, in the aftermath of Vietnam and Cambodia and Watergate and the CIA revelations, people have felt that they've been betrayed by public officials.

I have to admit that in the heat of the campaign—I've been in 30 primaries during the springtime; I've been campaigning for 22 months—I've made some mistakes. And I think this is part of just being a human being. I have to say that my campaign has been an open one. The Playboy thing has been of very great concern to me. I don't know how to deal with it exactly. I agreed to give the interview to Playboy. Other people have done it who are notable—Governor Jerry Brown, Walter Cronkite, Albert Schweitzer, Mr. Ford's own Secretary of Treasury, Mr. Simon, William Buckley, many other people. But they weren't running for President. And in retrospect, from hindsight, I would not have given that interview had I to do it over again. If I should ever decide in the future to discuss my deep Christian beliefs and condemnation and sinfulness, I would use another forum besides Playboy.

But I can say this: I'm doing the best I can to get away from that. And during the next 10 days, the American people will not see the Carter campaign running television advertisements or newspaper advertisements based on a personal attack on President Ford's character. I believe that the opposite is true with President Ford's campaign. And I hope that we can leave those issues, in the next 10 days, about personalities and mistakes of the past—we've both made some mistakes—and talk about unemployment, inflation, housing, education, taxation, government organization, stripping away of secrecy, and the things that are crucial to the American people.

I regret the things in my own long campaign that have been mistaken, but I'm trying to do away with those the last 10 days.

THE MODERATOR: Thank you, Governor Carter, President Ford, your response?

MR. FORD: I believe that the American people have been turned off in this election, Mr. Maynard, for a variety of reasons. We have seen on Capitol Hill, in the Congress, a great many allegations of wrongdoing, of alleged immorality. Those are very disturbing to the American people. They wonder how an elected representative can serve them and participate in such activities, serving in the Congress of the United States. Yes, and I'm certain many, many Americans were turned off by the revelations of Watergate, a very, very bad period of time in American political history. Yes, and thousands, maybe millions of Americans were turned off because of the problems that came out of our involvement in Vietnam.

But on the other hand, I found on July 4 of this year a new spirit born in America. We were celebrating our Bicentennial. And I find that there is a movement—as I traveled the country—of greater interest in this campaign. Now, like any hard-working person seeking public office, in the campaign, inevitably, sometimes you will use rather graphic language. And I am guilty of that just like, I think, most others in the political arena. But I do make a pledge that in the next 10 days when we are asking the American people to make one of the most important decisions in their lifetime, because I think this election is one of the most vital in the history of America, that we do together what we can to stimulate voter participation.

THE MODERATOR: Thank you, President Ford.

Mr. Nelson, your question to President Ford.

MR. NELSON: Mr. President, you mentioned Watergate, and you became President because of Watergate, so don't you owe the American people a special obligation to explain in detail your role of limiting one of the original investigations of a Watergate—that was the one by the House Banking Committee? And I know you've answered questions on this before, but there are questions that still remain, and I think people want to know what your role was.

Will you name the persons you talked to in connection with that investigation, and since you say you have no recollection of talking to anyone for the White House, would you be willing to open for examination the White House tapes of conversations during that period?

MR. FORD: Mr. Nelson, I testified before two committees, House and Senate, on precisely the questions that you have asked. And the testimony, under oath, was to the effect that I did not talk to Mr. Nixon, to Mr. Haldeman, to Mr. Ehrlichman, or to any of the people at the White House. I said I had no recollection whatsoever of talking with any of the White House legislative liaison people.

I indicated under oath that the initiative that I took was at the request of the ranking members of the House Banking and Currency Committee on the Republican side, which was a legitimate request and a proper response by me.

Now, that was gone into by two congressional committees, and following that investigation both committees overwhelmingly approved me, and both the House and the Senate did likewise.

Now, in the meantime the Special Prosecutor—within the last few days after an investigation himself—said there was no reason for him to get involved, because he found nothing that would justify it. And then, just a day or two ago, the Attorney General of the United States made a further investigation and came to precisely the same conclusion.

Now, after all of those investigations by objective, responsible people, I think the matter is closed once and for all. But to add one other feature: I don't control any of the tapes. Those tapes are in the jurisdiction of the courts, and I have no right to say yes or no. But all the committees, the Attorney General, the Special Prosecutor—all of them have given me a clean bill of health. I think the matter is settled once and for all.

MR. NELSON: Well, Mr. President, if I do say so, though, the question is that I think you still have not gone into details about what your role in it was. And I don't think there was any question about whether or not there was a criminal prosecution, but whether you have told the American people your entire involvement in it and whether you would be willing—even though you don't control the tapes—whether you would be willing to ask that the tapes be released for examination?

MR. FORD: That's for the proper authorities who have control over those tapes to make that decision. I have given every bit of evidence, answered every question that's been asked me by any Senator or any Member of the House, plus the fact that the Special Prosecutor, on his own initiation, and the Attorney General, on his initiation—the highest law enforcement official in this country— all of them have given me a clean bill of health. And I've told everything I know about it. I think the matter is settled once and for all.

THE MODERATOR: Governor Carter, your response.

MR. CARTER: I don't have any response.

THE MODERATOR: Thank you.

Then we will have the next question from Mr. Kraft to Governor Carter.

MR. KRAFT: Governor Carter, the next big crisis spot in the world may be Yugoslavia. President Tito is old and sick, and there are divisions in his country. It's pretty certain that the Russians are going to do everything they possibly can after Tito dies to force Yugoslavia back into the Soviet camp.

But last Saturday, you said—and this is a quote—"I would not go to war in Yugoslavia even if the Soviet Union sent in troops." Doesn't that statement practically invite the Russians to intervene in Yugoslavia? Doesn't it discourage Yugoslavs who might be tempted to resist? And wouldn't it have been wiser on your part to say nothing and to keep the Russians in the dark, as President Ford did and as, I think, every President has done since President Truman?

MR. CARTER: In the last 2 weeks I've had a chance to talk to two men who have visited the Soviet Union, Yugoslavia, and China. One is Governor Averell Harriman, who visited the Soviet Union and Yugoslavia, and the other one is James Schlesinger, whom I think you accompanied to China. I got a complete report back from those countries from these two distinguished gentlemen.

Mr. Harriman talked to the leaders in Yugoslavia, and I think it's accurate to say that there is no prospect, in their opinion, of the Soviet Union invading Yugoslavia should Mr. Tito pass away. The present leadership there is fairly uniform in their purpose. I think it's a close-knit group, and I think it would be unwise for us to say that we will go to war in Yugoslavia if the Soviets should invade, which I think would be an extremely unlikely thing.

I have maintained from the very beginning of my campaign—and this was a standard answer that I made in response to the Yugoslavian question—that I would never go to war, become militarily involved in the internal affairs of another country, unless our own security was directly threatened. And I don't believe that our security would be directly threatened if the Soviet Union went into Yugoslavia. I don't believe it will happen. I certainly hope it won't. I would take the strongest possible measures short of actual military action there by our own troops, but I doubt that that would be an eventuality.

MR. KRAFT: One quick followup. Did you clear the response you made with Secretary Schlesinger and Governor Harriman?

MR. CARTER: No, I did not.

THE MODERATOR: President Ford, your response.

MR. FORD: Well, I firmly believe, Mr. Kraft, that it's unwise for a President to signal in advance what options he might exercise if any international problem arose.

I think we all recall with some sadness that at the period of the late 1940's, early 1950's, there were some indications that the United States would not include South Korea in an area of defense. There are some who allege—I can't prove it true or untrue—that such a statement, in effect, invited the North Koreans to invade South Korea. It's a fact they did.

But no President of the Untied States, in my opinion, should signal in advance to a prospective enemy what his decision might be or what option he might exercise. It's far better for a person sitting in the White House, who has a number of options, to make certain that the other side, so to speak, doesn't know precisely what you're going to do. And therefore, that was the reason that I would not identify any particular course of action when I responded to a question a week or so ago.

THE MODERATOR: Thank you.

Mr. Maynard, your question to President Ford, please.

MR. MAYNARD: Sir, this question concerns your administrative performance as President. The other day, General George Brown, the Chairman of the Joint Chiefs of Staff, delivered his views on several sensitive subjects, among them Great Britain, one of this country's oldest allies. He said, and I quote him now, "Great Britain—it's a pathetic thing, it just makes you cry. They are no longer a world power. All they have are generals, admirals, and bands." Since General Brown's comments have caused this country embarrassment in the past, why is he still this Nation's leading military officer?

MR. FORD: I have indicated to General Brown that the words that he used in that interview, in that particular case, and in several others were very ill-advised. And General Brown has indicated his apology, his regrets, and I think that will, in this situation, settle the matter.

It is tragic that the full transcript of that interview was not released, and that there were excerpts, some of the excerpts, taken out of context—not this one, however—that you bring up.

General Brown has an exemplary record of military performance. He served this Nation with great, great skill and courage and bravery for 35 years. And I think it's the consensus of people who are knowledgeable in the military field that he is probably the outstanding military leader and strategist that we have in America today.

Now, he did use ill-advised words. But I think in the fact that he apologized, that he was reprimanded, does permit him to stay on and continue that kind of leadership that we so badly need as we enter into negotiations under the SALT II agreement, or if we have operations that might be developing in the Middle East or in southern Africa or in the Pacific—we need a man with that experience, that knowledge, that know-how. And I think in light of the fact that he has apologized, would not have justified my asking for his resignation.

THE MODERATOR: Thank you.

Governor Carter, your response.

MR. CARTER: Well, just briefly, I think this is the second time that General Brown has made a statement for which we did have to apologize —and I know that everybody makes mistakes. I think the first one was related to the unwarranted influence of American Jews on the media and in the Congress. This one concerned Great Britain. I think he said Israel was a military burden on us and that Iran hoped to reestablish the Persian Empire.

I am not sure that I remembered earlier that President Ford had expressed his concern about the statement or apologized for it. This is something, though, that I think is indicative of a need among the American people to know how the Commander in Chief, the President, feels. And I think the only criticism that I would have of Mr. Ford is that immediately when the statement was revealed, perhaps a statement from the President would have been a clarifying and a very beneficial thing.

THE MODERATOR: Mr. Nelson, your question now to Governor Carter.

MR. NELSON: Governor, despite the fact that you've been running for President a long time now, many Americans still seem to be uneasy about you. They don't feel that they know you or the people around you. And one problem seems to be that you haven't reached out to bring people with broad background or national experience into your campaign or your Presidential plans. Most of the people around you on a day-to-day basis are the people you've know in Georgia. Many of them are young and relatively inexperienced in national affairs. Doesn't this raise a serious question as to whether you would bring into a Carter administration people with the necessary background to run the Federal Government?

MR. CARTER: I don't believe it does. I began campaigning 22 months ago. At that time nobody thought I had a chance to win. Very few people knew who I was. I came from a tiny town, as your know—Plains—and didn't hold public office, didn't have very much money. And my first organization was just four or five people plus my wife and my children, and my three sons and their wives.

And we won the nomination by going out into the streets, barbershops, beauty parlors, restaurants, stores, in factory shift lines, also in farmers' markets and livestock sale barns, and we talked a lot and we listened a lot, and we learned from the American people. We built up an awareness among the voters of this country, particularly those in whose primaries I entered—30 of them, nobody has ever done that before—about who I was and what I stood for.

Now we have a very wide-ranging group of advisers who help me prepare for these debates and who teach me about international economics and foreign affairs, defense matters, health, education, welfare, government reorganization—I'd say several hundred of them, and they are very fine and very highly qualified.

The one major decision that I have made since acquiring the nomination—and I share this with President Ford—is the choice of the Vice President. I think this would be indicative of the kind of leaders that I would choose to help me if I am elected.

I chose Senator Walter Mondale. And the only criterion that I have put forward in my own mind was, who among the several million people in this country would be the best person qualified to be President if something should happen to me and to join me in being Vice President if I should serve out my term? And I'm convinced now, more than I was when I got the nomination, that Walter Mondale was the right choice. And I believe this is a good indication of the kind of people that I would choose in the future.

Mr. Ford has had that same choice to make. I don't want to say anything critical of Senator Dole, but I have never heard Mr. Ford say that that was his primary consideration—who is the best person I could choose in this country to be President of the United States.

I feel completely at ease knowing that some day Senator Mondale might very well be President. In the last five Vice-Presidential nominees, incumbents, three of them have become President. But I think this is indicative of what I would do.

THE MODERATOR: President Ford, your response please.

MR. FORD: The Governor may not have heard my established criteria for the selection of a Vice President, but it was a well-established criteria that the person I selected would be fully qualified to be President of the United States. And Senator Bob Dole is so qualified—16 years in the House of Representatives and in the Senate, very high responsibilities on important committees.

I don't mean to be critical of Senator Mondale, but I was very, very surprised when I read that Senator Mondale made a very derogatory, very personal comment about General Brown after the news story that broke about General Brown. If my recollection is correct, he indicated that General Brown was not qualified to be a sewer commissioner. I don't think that's a proper way to describe a Chairman of the Joint Chiefs of Staff who has fought for this country for 35 years. And I'm sure the Governor would agree with me on that. I think Senator Dole would show more good judgment and discretion than to so describe a heroic and brave and very outstanding leader of the military.

So, I think our selection of Bob Dole as Vice President is based on merit. And if he should ever become the President of the United States, with his vast experience as a Member of the House and a Member of the Senate, as well as a Vice President, I think he would do an outstanding job as President of the United States.

THE MODERATOR: Mr. Kraft, your question to President Ford.

MR. KRAFT: Mr. President, let me assure you and maybe some of the viewing audience that being on this panel hasn't been, as it may seem, all torture and agony. One of the heartening things is that I and my colleagues have received literally hundreds and maybe even thousands of suggested questions from ordinary citizens all across the country who want answers.

MR. FORD: That's a tribute to their interest in this election.

MR. KRAFT: I will give you that. But let me go on, because one main subject on the minds of all of them has been the environment, particularly curious about your record. People really want to know why you vetoed the strip mining bill. They want to know why you worked against strong controls on auto emissions. They want to know why you aren't doing anything about pollution of the Atlantic Ocean. They want to know why a bipartisan organization such as the National League of Conservation Voters says that when it comes to environmental issues, you are—and I am quoting—"hopeless."

MR. FORD: First, let me set the record straight. I vetoed the strip mining bill, Mr. Kraft, because it was the overwhelming concensus of knowledgeable people that the strip mining bill would have meant the loss of literally thousands of jobs, something around 140,000 jobs. Number two, that strip mining bill would have severely set back our need for more coal, and Governor Carter has said repeatedly that coal is the resource that we need to use more in the effort to become independent of the Arab oil supplies. So, I vetoed it because of a loss of jobs and because it would have interfered with our energy independence program.

The auto emissions—it was agreed by Leonard Woodcock, the head of the UAW, and by the heads of all of the automobile industry—we had labor and management together saying that those auto emission standards had to be modified.

But let's talk about what the Ford administration has done in the field of environment. I have increased, as President, by over 60 percent, the funding for water treatment plants in the United States, the Federal contribution. I have fully funded the land and water conservation program; in fact, have recommended, and the Congress approved, a substantially increased land and water conservation program.

I have added in the current year budget, the funds for the National Park Service. For example, we proposed about $12 million to add between 400 and 500 more employees for the National Park Service.

And a month or so ago, I did likewise say over the next 10 years we should expand—double—the national parks, the wilderness areas, the scenic river areas. And then, of course, the final thing is that I have signed and approved of more scenic rivers, more wilderness areas since I've been President than any other President in the history of the United States.

THE MODERATOR: Governor Carter.

MR. CARTER: Well, I might say I think the League of Conservation Voters is absolutely right. This administration's record of environment is very bad.

I think it's accurate to say that the strip mining law, which was passed twice by the Congress and only lacked two votes, I believe, of being overriden, would have been good for the country. The claim that it would have put 140,000 miners out of work is hard to believe when at the time Mr. Ford vetoed it, the United Mine Workers was supporting the bill. And I don't think they would have supported the bill had they known that they would lose 140,000 jobs.

There has been a consistent policy on the part of this administration to lower or to delay enforcement of air pollution standards and water pollution standards. And under both Presidents Nixon and Ford, moneys have been impounded that would have gone to cities and others to control water pollution.

We have no energy policy. We, I think, are the only developed nation in the world that has no comprehensive energy policy to permit us to plan, in an orderly way, how to shift from increasing the scarce energy forms—oil—and have research and development concentrated on the increased use of coal, which I strongly favor—the research and development to be used primarily to make the coal burning be clean.

We need a heritage trust program, similar to the one we had in Georgia, to set aside additional lands that have geological and archeological importance, natural areas for enjoyment. The lands that Mr. Ford brags about having approved are in Alaska, and they are enormous in size, but as far as the accessibility of them by the American people, is very far in the future.

We have taken no strong position in the control of pollution of our oceans. And I would say the worst threat to the environment of all is nuclear proliferation. And this administration, having been in office now for 2 years or more, has still not taken a strong and bold action to stop the proliferation of nuclear waste around the world, particularly plutonium.

Those are some brief remarks about the failures of this administration. I would do the opposite in every respect.

THE MODERATOR: Mr. Maynard to Governor Carter.

MR. MAYNARD: Governor, Federal policy in this country since World War II has tended to favor the development of suburbs at the great expense of central cities. Does not the Federal Government now have an affirmative obligation to revitalize the American city? We have heard little in this campaign suggesting that you have an urban reconstruction program. Could you please outline your urban intentions for us tonight?

MR. CARTER: Yes, I would be glad to. In the first place, as is the case with the environmental policy and energy policy that I just described, and the policy for nonproliferation of nuclear waste, this administration has no urban policy. It's impossible for mayors or Governors to cooperate with the President, because they can't anticipate what is going to happen next.

A mayor of a city like New York, for example, needs to know 18 months or 2 years ahead of time what responsibility the city will have in administration and in financing, in things like housing, pollution control, crime control, education, welfare and health. This has not been done, unfortunately. I remember the headline in the Daily News that said, "Ford to New York—Drop Dead."

I think it's very important that our cities know that they have a partner in the Federal Government. Quite often, Congress has passed laws in the past designed to help people with the ownership of homes and with the control of crime and with adequate health care and better education programs and so forth. Those programs were designed to help those who need it most, and quite often this has been in the very poor people and neighborhoods in the downtown urban centers. Because of the greatly advantaged persons who live in the suburbs—better education, better organization, more articulate, more aware of what the laws are—quite often this money has been channeled out of the downtown centers where it's needed.

Also, I favor all revenue sharing money being used for local governments and also to remove the prohibitions in the use of revenue sharing money, so that it can be used to improve education and health care. We have now, for instance, only 7 percent of the total education costs being financed by the Federal Government. When the Nixon-Ford adminstration started, this was 10 percent. That's a 30-percent reduction in the portion that the Federal Government contributes to education in just 8 years and, as you know, the education costs have gone up tremendously.

The last point is that the major thrust has got to be to put people back to work. We've got an extraordinarily high unemployment rate among downtown, urban ghetto areas; particularly among the very poor and particularly among minority groups, sometimes 50 or 60 percent.

And the concentration of employment opportunities in those areas would help greatly not only to reestablish the tax base, but also to help reduce the extraordinary welfare costs. One of the major responsibilities on the shoulders of New York City is to finance welfare. And I favor the shifting of the welfare cost away from the local governments altogether and, over a longer period of time, let the Federal Government begin to absorb part of it that is now paid by the State government. Those things would help a great deal with the cities, but we still have a very serious problem there.

THE MODERATOR: President Ford.

MR. FORD: Let me speak out very strongly. The Ford administration does have a very comprehensive program to help our major metropolitan areas. I fought for, and the Congress finally went along with, a general revenue sharing program whereby cities and States—the cities, two-thirds, and the States, one-third—get over $6 billion a year, in cash, with which they can provide many, many services, whatever they really want.

In addition, we in the Federal Government make available to cities about $3,300 million in what we call community developments. In addition, as a result of my pressure on the Congress, we got a major mass transit program over a 4-year period—$11,800 million. We have a good housing program that will result in cutting the downpayments by 50 percent and having mortgage payments lower at the beginning of any mortgage period. We are expanding our homestead housing program.

The net result is, we think, under Carla Hills, who is the Chairman of my Urban Development and Neighborhood Revitalization program, we will really do a first-class job in helping the communities throughout the country. As a matter of fact, that committee, under Secretary Hills, released about a 75-page report with specific recommendations, so we can do a better job in the weeks ahead.

And in addition, the tax program of the Ford administration, which provides an incentive for industry to move into our major metropolitan areas, into the inner cities, will bring jobs where people are and help to revitalize those cities as they can be.

THE MODERATOR: Mr. Nelson, your question next to President Ford.

MR. NELSON: Mr. President, your campaign has run ads in black newspapers saying that "for black Americans, President Ford is quietly getting the job done." Yet, study after study has shown little progress in desegregation and, in fact, actual increases in segregated schools and housing in the Northeast.

MR. FORD: Well, let me say at the outset, I am very proud of the record of this administration. In the Cabinet I have one of the outstanding, I think, administrators as the Secretary of Transportation—Bill Coleman. You are familiar, I am sure, with the recognition given in the Air Force to General James. And there was just approved a three-star admiral, the first in the history of the United States Navy. So, we are giving full recognition to individuals, of quality in the Ford administration in positions of great responsibility.

In addition, the Department of Justice is fully enforcing, and enforcing effectively, the Voting Rights Act—the legislation that involves jobs, housing for minorities, not only blacks but all others.

The Department of HUD is enforcing the new legislation that takes care of redlining. What we are doing is saying that there are opportunities—business opportunities, educational opportunities, responsibilities—where people with talent—blacks or any other minority—can fully qualify.

The office of minority business in the Department of Commerce has made available more money in trying to help black businessmen, or other minority businessmen, than any other administration since the office was established.

The office of small business, under Mr. Kobelinski, has a very massive program trying to help the black community. The individual who wants to start a business or expand his business as a black businessman is able to borrow either directly or with guaranteed loans.

I believe on the record that this administration has been responsive and we have carried out the law to the letter, and I am proud of the record.

THE MODERATOR: Governor Carter, your response, please.

MR. CARTER: The description just made of this administration's record is hard to recognize. I think it is accurate to say that Mr. Ford voted against the voting rights acts and against the civil rights acts in their debative stage. I think once it was assured they were going to pass, he finally voted for it.

This country changed drastically in 1969 when the terms of John Kennedy and Lyndon Johnson were over, and Richard Nixon and Gerald Ford became the Presidents. There was a time when there was hope for those who were poor and downtrodden and who were elderly or who were ill or who were in minority groups. That time has been gone.

I think the greatest thing that ever happened to the South was the passage of the civil rights acts and the opening up of opportunities to black people, to have a chance to vote, to hold a job, to buy a house, to go to school, and to participate in public affairs. It not only liberated black people but it also liberated the whites.

We have seen in many instances in recent years a minority affairs section of a small loan administration, Small Business Administration, lend a black entrepreneur just enough money to get started, and then to go bankrupt. The bankruptcies have gone up an extraordinary degree.

The FHA [Federal Housing Administration], which used to be a very responsible agency that everyone looked to to help own a home, lost $600 million last year. There have been over 1,300 indictments in HUD, over 800 convictions relating just to home loans. And now the Federal Government has become the world's greatest slum landlord.

We've got a 30-percent or 40-percent unemployment rate among minority young people. And there has been no concerted effort given to the needs of those who are both poor and black, or poor and who speak a foreign language. And that's where there has been a great generation of despair and ill-health and lack of education and lack of purposefulness and a lack of hope for the future.

But it doesn't take just a quiet, dormant, minimum enforcement of the law. It requires an aggressive searching out and reaching out to help people who especially need it. And that's been lacking in the last 8 years.

THE MODERATOR: Mr. Kraft, to Governor Carter.

MR. KRAFT: Governor Carter, in the nearly 200-year history of the Constitution, there have been only, I think it is, 25 amendments, most of them on issues of the very broadest principle. Now we have proposed amendments in many highly specialized causes like gun control, school busing, balanced budget, school prayer, abortion, things like that. Do you think it's appropriate to the dignity of the Constitution to tack on amendments in a wholesale fashion, and which of the ones I listed—that is, balanced budget, school busing, school prayer, abortion, gun control—which of those would you really work hard to support if you were President?

MR. CARTER: I would not work hard to support any of those. We have always had, I think, a lot of constitutional amendments proposed but the passage of them has been fairly slow and few and far between. In the 200-year history, there has been a very cautious approach to this. Quite often we have a transient problem. I am strongly against abortion. I think abortion is wrong. I don't think the Government ought to do anything to encourage abortion, but I don't favor a constitutional amendment on the subject. But short of constitutional amendment, and within the confines of a Supreme Court ruling. I will do everything I can to minimize the need for abortions with better sex education, family planning, with better adoptive procedures. I personally don't believe that the Federal Government ought to finance abortions, but I draw the line and don't support a constitutional amendment. However, I honor the right of people to seek the constitutional amendments on school busing, on prayer in the schools, and on abortion, but among those you named, I won't actively work for the passage of any of them.

THE MODERATOR: President Ford, your response, please.

MR. FORD: I support the Republican platform which calls for a constitutional amendment that would outlaw abortions. I favor the particular constitutional amendment that would turn over to the States the individual right of the voters in those States the chance to make a decision by public referendum. I call that the peoples' amendment. I think if you really believe that the people of a State ought to make a decision on a matter of this kind, that we ought to have a Federal constitutional amendment that would permit each one of the 50 states to make the choice.

I think this is a reasonable and proper way to proceed. I believe also that there is some merit to an amendment that Senator Everett Dirksen proposed very frequently, an amendment that would change the Court decision as far as voluntary prayer in public schools. It seems to me that there should be an opportunity, as long as it's voluntary, as long as there is no compulsion whatsoever, that an individual ought to have that right.

So, in those two cases I think such a constitutional amendment would be proper. And I really don't think in either case they are trivial matters. I think they are matters of very deep conviction as far as many, many people in this country believe, and therefore they shouldn't be treated lightly, but they are matters that are important. And in those two cases I would favor them.

THE MODERATOR: Mr. Maynard, to President Ford.

MR. MAYNARD: Mr. President, twice you have been the intended victim of would-be assassins using handguns, yet you remain a steadfast opponent of substantive handgun control. There are now some 40 million handguns in this country, going up at the rate of 2.5 million a year, and tragically those handguns are frequently purchased for self-protection and wind up being used against a relative or a friend. In light of that, why do you remain so adamant in your opposition to substantive gun control in this country?

MR. FORD: Mr. Maynard, the record of gun control, whether it's in one city or another or in some States does not show that the registration of a gun, handgun, or the registration of the gun owner has in any way whatsoever decreased the crime rate or the use of that gun in the committing of a crime. The record just doesn't prove that such legislation or action by a local city council is effective.

What we have to do—and this is the crux of the matter—is to make it very very difficult for a person who uses a gun in the commission of a crime to stay out of jail. If we make the use of a gun in the commission of a crime a serious criminal offense and that person is prosecuted, then in my opinion we are going after the person who uses the gun for the wrong reason. I don't believe in the registration of handguns or the registration of the handgun owner. That has not proven to be effective. And, therefore, I think the better way is to go after the criminal, the individual who commits a crime in the posession of a gun and uses that gun for a part of his criminal activity.

Those are the people who ought to be in jail. And the only way to do it is to pass strong legislation so that once apprehended, indicted, convicted, they will be in jail and off the streets and not using guns in the commission of a crime.

MR. MAYNARD: But, Mr. President, don't you think that the proliferation of the availability of handguns contributes to the possibility of those crimes being committed? And there is a second part to my followup. Very quickly, there are, as you know and as you've said, jurisdictions around the country with strong gun control laws. The police officials in those cities contend that if there were a national law to prevent other jurisdictions from providing the weapons that then come into places like New York, that they might have a better handle on the problem. Have you considered that in your analysis of the handgun proliferation problem?

MR. FORD: Yes, I have, and the individuals with whom I have consulted have not convinced me that a national registration of handguns or handgun owners will solve the problem you are talking about. The person who wants to use a gun for an illegal purpose can get it whether it's registered or outlawed—they will be obtained—and they are the people who ought to go behind bars. You should not, in the process, penalize the legitimate handgun owner. And when you go through the process of registration, you, in effect, are penalizing that individual who uses his gun for a very legitimate purpose.

THE MODERATOR: Governor Carter.

MR. CARTER: I think it's accurate to say that Mr. Ford's position on gun control has changed. Earlier, Mr. Levi, his Attorney General, put forward a gun control proposal which Mr. Ford later, I believe, espoused that called for the prohibition against the sale of the so-called "Saturday night specials." It would have put very strict control over who owned a handgun.

I have been a hunter all my life and happen to own both shotguns, rifles, and a handgun. And the only purpose that I would see in registering handguns and not long guns of any kind would be to prohibit the ownership of those guns by those who have used them in the commission of a crime or who have been proven to be mentally incompetent to own a gun. I believe that limited approach to the question would be advisable, and I think adequate, but that's as far as I would go with it.

THE MODERATOR: Mr. Nelson, to Governor Carter.

MR. NELSON: Governor, you've said the Supreme Court today is, as you put it, moving back in the proper direction in rulings that have limited the rights of criminal defendants, and you've compared the present Supreme Court under Chief Justice Burger very favorable with the more liberal Court that we had under Chief Justice Warren. So, exactly what are you getting at, and can you elaborate on the kind of Court you think this country should have? And can you tell us the kind of qualifications and philosophy you would look for as President in making Supreme Court appointments?

MR. CARTER: While I was Governor of Georgia, although I am not a lawyer, we had complete reform of the Georgia court system. We streamlined the structure of the courts, put in administrative offices, put a unified court system in, and required that all severe sentences be reviewed for uniformity; and, in addition to that, put forward a proposal that was adopted and used throughout my own term of office—selection of all judges and district attorneys, prosecuting attorneys, on the basis of merit.

Every time I had a vacancy on the Georgia Supreme Court—and I filled five of those vacancies out of seven total, and about half of the Court of Appeals judges, about 35 percent of the trial judges—I was given from an objective panel the five most highly qualified persons in Georgia, and from those five I always chose the first or second one. So, merit selection of judges is the most important single criterion. And I would institute the same kind of procedure as President, not only in judicial appointments but also in diplomatic appointments.

Secondly, I think that the Burger Court has fairly well confirmed the major and most far-reaching and most controversial decisions of the Warren Court. Civil rights has been confirmed by the Burger Court. It hasn't been reversed.

And I don't think there is any inclination to reverse those basic decisions—of the one man-one vote rule, which is a very important one that struck down the unwarranted influence in the legislature of sparsely populated areas of the States. The right of indigent or very poor accused persons to legal counsel—I think the Burger Court has confirmed that basic and very controversial decision of the Warren Court. Also, the protection of an arrested person against unwarranted persecution in trying to get a false confession.

But now, I think there have been a couple of instances where the Burger Court has made technical rulings where an obviously guilty person was later found to be guilty. And I think that in that case some of the more liberal members of the so-called Warren Court agreed with those decisions.

But the only thing that I have pointed out was what I've just said, and that there was a need to clarify the technicalities so that you couldn't be forced to release a person who is obviously guilty just because of a small technicality in the law. And that's a reversal of position by the Burger Court with which I do agree.

MR. NELSON: Governor, I don't believe you answered my question, though, about the kinds of people you would be looking for if you were making appointments to the Supreme Court as President.

MR. CARTER: Okay, I thought I answered it by saying that it would be on the basis of merit. Once the search and analysis procedure had been completed, and once I am given a list of the 5 or 7 or 10 best qualified persons in the country, I would make a selection from among those persons. If the list was in my opinion fairly uniform, if there was no outstanding person, then I would undoubtedly choose someone who would most accurately reflect my own basic political philosophy, as best as I could determine it, which would be to continue the progress that has been made under the last two Courts—the Warren Court and the Burger Court.

I would also like to completely revise our criminal justice system to do some of the things at the Federal level and court reform that I just described, as has been done in Georgia and other States. And I would like to appoint people who would be interested in helping with that. I know Chief Justice Burger is. He hasn't had help yet from the administration and from the Congress to carry this out.

The emphasis, I think, of the court system should be to interpret the Constitution and the laws equally between property protection and personal protection. But when there is a very narrow decision—which quite often is one that reaches the Supreme Court—I think the choice should be with human rights, and that would be another factor that I would follow.

THE MODERATOR: President Ford.

MR. FORD: I think the answer as to the kind of person that I would select is obvious. I had one opportunity to nominate an individual to the Supreme Court, and I selected the Circuit Court of Appeals judge from Illinois, John Paul Stevens. I selected him because of this outstanding record as a Circuit Court of Appeals judge. And I was very pleased that an overwhelmingly Democratic United States Senate, after going into his background, came to the conclusion that he was fit and should serve, and the vote in his behalf was overwhelming.

So, I would say somebody in the format of Justice Stevens would be the kind of an individual that I would select in the future, as I did him in the past.

I believe, however, a comment ought to be made about the direction of the Burger Court vis-a-vis the Court that preceded it. It seems to me that the *Miranda* case was a case that really made it very, very difficult for the police, the law enforcement people in this country, to do what they could to make certain that the victim of a crime was protected and that those that commit crimes were properly handled and sent to jail. The *Miranda* case, the Burger Court is gradually changing. And I am pleased to see that there are some steps being made by the Burger Court to modify the so-called *Miranda* decision.

I might make a correction of what Governor Carter said, speaking of gun control. Yes, it is true, I believe that the sale of Saturday night specials should be cut out, but he wants the registration of handguns.

THE MODERATOR: Mr. Kraft.

MR. KRAFT: Mr. President, the country is now in something that your advisers call an economic pause. I think to most Americans that sounds like an antiseptic term for low growth, unemployment, standstill at a high, high level, decline in take-home pay, lower factory earnings, more layoffs. Isn't that really a rotten record, and doesn't your administration bear most of the blame for it?

MR. FORD: Well, Mr. Kraft, I violently disagree with your assessment, and I don't think the record justifies the conclusion that you come to. Let me talk about the economic announcements that were made just this past week.

Yes, it was announced that the GNP real growth in the third quarter was at 4 percent. But do you realize that over the last 10 years that's a higher figure than the average growth during the 10-year period. Now, it's lower than the 9.2-percent growth in the first quarter and it's lower than the 5-percent growth in the second quarter. But, every economist—liberal, conservative—that I am familiar with, recognizes that in the fourth quarter of this year and in the first quarter of next year that we will have an increase in real GNP.

But now let's talk about the pluses that came out this week. We had an 18-percent increase in housing starts. We had a substantial increase in new permits for housing. As a matter of fact, based on the announcement this week, there will be at an annual rate, 1 million 800-some thousand new houses built, which is a tremendous increase over last year and a substantial increase over the earlier part of this year.

Now, in addition, we had some very good news in the reduction in the rate of inflation, and inflation hits everybody—those who are working and those who are on welfare. The rate of inflation, as announced just the other day, is under 5 percent, and the 4.4 percent that was indicated at the time of the 4 percent GNP, was less than the 5.4 percent. It means that the American buyer is getting a better bargain today because inflation is less.

MR. KRAFT: Mr. President, let me ask you this: There has been an increase in layoffs, and that's something that bothers everybody because even people that have a job are afraid they are going to be fired. Did you predict that increase in layoffs? Didn't that take you by surprise? Hasn't your administration been surprised by this pause? In fact, haven't you been so obsessed with saving money that you didn't even push the Government to spend funds that were allocated?

MR. FORD: Mr. Kraft, I think the record can be put in this way, which is the way that I think satisfies most Americans: Since the depths of the recession, we have added 4 million jobs. Most importantly, consumer confidence, as surveyed by the reputable organization at the University of Michigan, is at the highest since 1972.

In other words, there is growing public confidence in the strength of this economy. And that means that there will be more industrial activity; it means that there will be a reduction in the unemployment; it means that there will be increased hires; it means that there will be increased employment.

Now, we've had this pause but most economists, regardless of their political philosophy, indicate that this pause for a month or two was healthy because we could not have honestly sustained a 9.2 percent rate of growth, which we had in the first quarter of this year.

Now, I'd like to point out as well that the United States economic recovery from the recession of a year ago, is well ahead of the economic recovery of any major free industrial nation in the world today. We are ahead of all of the Western Europe countries. We are ahead of Japan. The United States is leading the free world out of the recession that was serious a year and a half ago.

We are going to see unemployment going down, more jobs available, and the rate of inflation going down. And I think this is a record that the American people understand and will appreciate.

THE MODERATOR: Governor Carter.

MR. CARTER: Well, with all due respect to President Ford, I think he ought to be ashamed of making that statement because we have the highest unemployment rate now than we had at any time between the Great Depression, caused by Herbert Hoover, and the time President Ford took office. We have got 7 1/2 million people out of jobs. Since he has been in office, 2 1/2 million more American people have lost their jobs. In the last 4 months alone, 500,000 Americans have gone on the unemployment rolls. In the last month, we've had a net loss of 163,000 jobs.

Anybody who says that the inflation rate is in good shape now ought to talk to the housewives. One of the overwhelming results that I have seen in places is people feel that you can't plan any more, there is no way to make a prediction that my family might be able to own a home or to put my kids through college. Savings accounts are losing money instead of gaining money. Inflation is robbing us.

Under the present administrations—Nixon's and Ford's—we have had three times the inflation rate that we experienced under President Johnson and President Kennedy. The economic growth is less than half today what it was at the beginning of this year. And housing starts—he compares the housing starts with last year, I don't blame him because in 1975 we had fewer housing starts in this country, fewer homes built than any year since 1940. That's 35 years. And we've got a 35-percent unemployment rate in many areas of this country among construction workers. And Mr. Ford hasn't done anything about it. And I think this shows a callous indifference to the families that have suffered so much. He has vetoed bills passed by Congress within congressional budget guidelines—

job opportunities for 2 million Americans. We will never have a balanced budget, we will never meet the needs of our people, we will never control the inflationary spiral as long as we have 7 1/2 or 8 million people out of work who are looking for jobs. And we have probably got 2 1/2 more million people who are not looking for jobs any more because they've given up hope. That is a very serious indictment of this administration. It's probably the worst one of all.

THE MODERATOR: Mr. Maynard.

MR. MAYNARD: Governor Carter, you entered this race against President Ford with a 20-point lead or better in the polls and now it appears that this campaign is headed for a photo finish. You have said how difficult it is to run against a sitting President, but Mr. Ford was just as much an incumbent in July when you were 20 points ahead as he is now. Can you tell us what caused the evaporation of that lead, in your opinion?

MR. CARTER: Well, that's not exactly an accurate description of what happened. When I was that far ahead it was immediately following the Democratic Convention and before the Republican Convention. At that time 25 or 30 percent of the Reagan supporters said that they would not support President Ford, but as occurred at the end of the Democratic Convention, the Republican Party there was about a 10-point spread. I believe that to be accurate. I had 49 percent; President Ford had 39 percent.

The polls are good indications of fluctuations, but they vary widely one from another, and the only poll I've ever followed is the one that, you know, is taken on Election Day. I was in 30 primaries in the spring and at first it was obvious that I didn't have any standing in the polls. As a matter of fact, I think when Gallup ran their first poll in December 1975, they didn't even put my name on the list. They had 35 people on the list—my name wasn't even there. At the beginning of the year, I had about 2 percent. So the polls, to me, are interesting, but they don't determine my hopes or my despair.

I campaign among people. I have never depended on powerful political figures to put me in office. I have a direct relationship with hundreds of thousands of people around the country who actively campaign for me. In Georgia alone, for instance, I got 84 percent of the vote, and I think there were 14 people in addition to myself on the ballot, and Governor Wallace had been very strong in Georgia. That is an overwhelming support from my own people who know me best. And today we have about 500 Georgians at their own expense, just working people who believe in me, spread around the country involved in the political campaign.

So the polls are interesting, but I don't know how to explain the fluctuations. I think a lot of it depends on current events—sometimes foreign affairs, sometimes domestic affairs. But I think our core of support among those who are crucial to the election has been fairly steady. And my success in the primary season was, I think, notable for a newcomer, from someone who's outside of Washington, who never has been a part of the Washington establishment. And I think that we will have a good result on November 2 for myself and I hope for the country.

THE MODERATOR: President Ford, your response.

MR. FORD: I think the increase in the prospects as far as I am concerned and the less favorable prospects for Governor Carter reflect that Governor Carter is inconsistent in many of the positions that he takes. He tends to distort on a number of occasions. Just a moment ago, for example, he was indicating that in the 1950's, for example, unemployment was very low. He fails to point out that in the 1950's we were engaged in the war in Vietnam—I mean in Korea. We had 3,500,000 young men in the Army, Navy, Air Force, and Marines. That's not the way to end unemployment or to reduce unemployment.

At the present time, we are at peace. We have reduced the number of people in the Army, Navy, Air Force, and Marines from 3,500,000 to 2,100,000. We are not at war. We have reduced the military manpower by 1,400,000. If we had that many more people in the Army, the Navy, the Air Force, and Marines, our unemployment figure would be considerably less.

But this administration doesn't believe the way to reduce unemployment is to go to war or to increase the number of people in the military. So, you cannot compare unemployment, as you sought to, at the present time, with the 1950's, because the then administration had people in the military. They were at war. They were fighting overseas. And this administration has reduced the size of the military by 1,400,000. They are in the civilian labor market, and they are not fighting anywhere around the world today.

THE MODERATOR: Thank you, gentlemen.

This will complete our questioning for this debate. We don't have time for more questions and full answers. So, now each candidate will be allowed up to 4 minutes for a closing statement. And, at the original coin toss in Philadelphia a month ago, it was determined that President Ford would make the first closing statement tonight.

President Ford.

MR. FORD: For 25 years, I served in the Congress under five Presidents. I saw them work, I saw them make very hard decisions. I didn't always agree with their decisions, whether they were Democratic or Republican Presidents. For the last 2 years, I've been the President, and I have found from experience that it's much more difficult to make those decisions than it is to second guess them.

I became President at the time that the United States was in a very troubled time. We had inflation of over 12 percent; we were on the brink of the worst recession in the last 40 years; we were still deeply involved in the problems of Vietnam; the American people had lost faith and trust and confidence in the Presidency itself. That situation called for me to first put the United States on a steady course and to keep our keel well-balanced, because we had to face the difficult problems that had all of a sudden hit America.

I think most people know that I did not seek the Presidency, but I am asking for your help and assistance to be President for the next 4 years. During this campaign, we've seen a lot of television shows, a lot of bumper stickers, and a great many slogans of one kind or another, but those are not the things that count. What counts is that the United States celebrated its 200th birthday on July 4. As a result of that wonderful experience all over the United States, there is a new spirit in America. The American people are healed, are working together. The American people are moving again and moving in the right direction.

We have cut inflation by better than half. We have come out of the recession, and we are well on the road to real prosperity in this country again. There has been a restoration of faith and confidence and trust in the Presidency because I've been open, candid, and forthright. I have never promised. We are at peace— not a single young American is fighting or dying on any foreign soil tonight. We have peace with freedom.

I've been proud to be President of the United States during these very troubled times. I love America just as all of you love America. It would be the highest honor for me to have your support on November 2 and for you to say, "Jerry Ford, you've done a good job; keep on doing it."

Thank you, and good night.

THE MODERATOR: Thank you, President Ford.

Governor Carter.

MR. CARTER: The major purpose of an election for President is to choose a leader, someone who can analyze the depths of feeling in our country, to set a standard for our people to follow, to inspire people to reach for greatness, to correct our defects, to answer difficulties, to bind ourselves together in a spirit of unity.

I don't believe the present administration has done that. We have been discouraged and we've been alienated, sometimes we've been embarrassed, sometimes we've been ashamed. Our people are out of work, and there is a sense of withdrawal.

But our country is innately very strong. Mr. Ford is a good and decent man, but he has been in office now more than 800 days, approaching almost as long as John Kennedy was in office. I would like to ask the American people what has been accomplished. A lot remains to be done.

My own background is different from his. I was a school board member and a library board member, I served on a hospital authority, and I was in the State senate, and I was Governor and I am an engineer, a naval officer, a farmer, a businessman. I believe we require someone who can work harmoniously with the Congress and can work closely with the people of this country, and who can bring a new image and a new spirit to Washington.

Our tax structure is a disgrace and needs to be reformed. I was Governor of Georgia for 4 years. We never increased sales taxes or income tax or property taxes. As a matter of fact, the year before we went out of office we gave a $50 million refund to the property taxpayers of Georgia.

We spend $600 per person in this country—every man, woman, and child— for health care. We still rank 15th among all of the nations in the world in infant mortality, and our cancer rate is higher than any country in the world. We don't have good health care. We could have it.

Employment ought to be restored to our people. We have become almost a welfare state. We spend now 700 percent more on unemployment compensation than we did 8 years ago when the Republicans took over the White House. Our people want to go back to work. Our education system can be improved. Secrecy ought to be stripped away from government, and a maximum of personal privacy ought to be maintained. Our housing programs have gone bad. It used to be that the average family could own a house, but now less than a third of our people can afford to buy their own homes.

The budget was more grossly out of balance last year than ever before in the history of our country—$65 billion—primarily because our people are not at work. Inflation is robbing us, as we've already discussed, and the Government bureaucracy is just a horrible mess.

This doesn't have to be. I don't know all of the answers. Nobody could. But I do know that if the President of the United States and the Congress of the United States and the people of the United States said, "I believe our Nation is greater than what we are now," I believe that if we are inspired, if we can achieve a degree of unity, if we can set our goals high enough and work toward recognized goals with industry and labor and agriculture along with Government at all levels, we can achieve great things.

We might have to do it slowly. There are no magic answers to it, but I believe together we can make great progress, we can correct our difficult mistakes and answer those very tough questions.

I believe in the greatness of our country, and I believe the American people are ready for a change in Washington. We have been drifting too long. We have been dormant too long. We have been discouraged too long. And we have not set an example for our own people, but I believe that we can now establish in the White House a good relationship with Congress, a good relationship with our people, set very high goals for our country, and with inspiration and hard work we can achieve great things and let the world know—that's very important, but more importantly, let the people in our own country realize—that we still live in the greatest Nation on Earth.

Thank you very much.

THE MODERATOR: Thank you, Governor Carter, and thank you, President Ford. I also would like to thank the audience and my three colleagues—Mr. Kraft, Mr. Maynard, and Mr. Nelson, who have been our questioners.

This debate has, of course, been seen by millions of Americans, and in addition tonight is being broadcast to 113 nations throughout the world.

This concludes the 1976 Presidential debates, a truly remarkable exercise in democracy, for this is the first time in 16 years that Presidential candidates have debated. It is the first time ever that an incumbent President has debated his challenger, and the debate included the first between the two Vice-Presidential candidates.

President Ford and Governor Carter, we not only want to thank you but we commend you for agreeing to come together to discuss the issues before the American people.

And our special thanks to the League of Women Voters for making these events possible. In sponsoring these events, the League of Women Voters Education Fund has tried to provide you with the information that you will need to choose wisely.

The election is now only 11 days off. The candidates have participated in presenting their views in three 90-minute debates, and now it's up to the voters, and now it is up to you to participate. The League urges all registered voters to vote on November 2 for the candidate of your choice.

And now, from Phi Beta Kappa Memorial Hall on the campus of the College of William and Mary, this is Barbara Walters wishing you all a good evening.

THE VOTES IN THE 1976 ELECTION

CANDIDATES FOR PRESIDENT AND VICE PRESIDENT
Democratic—Jimmy Carter; Walter Mondale
Republican—Gerald R. Ford; Robert Dole

STATE	Total	Dem.	Rep.	ELECTORAL VOTE	
				D	R
Alabama	1,182,850	659,170	504,070	9	—
Alaska	123,574	44,058	71,555	—	3
Arizona	742,719	295,602	418,642	—	6
Arkansas	767,535	498,604	267,903	6	—
California	7,867,117	3,742,284	3,882,244	—	45
Colorado	1,081,554	460,353	584,367	—	7
Connecticut	1,381,526	647,895	719,261	—	8
Delaware	235,834	122,596	109,831	3	—
Dist. of Col.	168,830	137,818	27,873	3	—
Florida	3,150,631	1,636,000	1,469,531	17	—
Georgia	1,467,458	979,409	483,743	12	—
Hawaii	291,301	147,375	140,003	4	—
Idaho	344,071	126,549	204,151	—	4
Illinois	4,718,914	2,271,295	2,364,269	—	26
Indiana	2,220,362	1,014,714	1,183,958	—	13
Iowa	1,279,306	619,931	632,863	—	8
Kansas	957,845	430,421	502,752	—	7
Kentucky	1,167,142	615,717	531,852	9	—
Louisiana	1,278,439	661,365	587,446	10	—
Maine	483,216	232,279	236,320	—	4
Maryland	1,439,897	759,612	672,661	10	—
Massachusetts	2,547,558	1,429,475	1,030,276	14	—
Michigan	3,653,749	1,696,714	1,893,742	—	21
Minnesota	1,949,931	1,070,440	819,395	10	—
Mississippi	769,361	381,309	366,846	7	—
Missouri	1,953,600	998,387	927,443	12	—
Montana	328,734	149,259	173,703	—	4
Nebraska	607,688	233,692	359,705	—	5
Nevada	201,876	92,479	101,273	—	3
New Hampshire	339,618	147,635	185,935	—	4
New Jersey	3,014,472	1,444,653	1,509,688	—	17
New Mexico	418,409	201,148	211,419	—	4
New York	6,534,170	3,389,558	3,100,791	41	—
North Carolina	1,678,914	927,365	741,960	13	—
North Dakota	297,188	136,078	153,470	—	3
Ohio	4,111,873	2,011,621	2,000,505	25	—
Oklahoma	1,092,251	532,442	545,708	—	8
Oregon	1,029,876	490,407	492,120	—	6
Pennsylvania	4,620,787	2,328,677	2,205,604	27	—
Rhode Island	411,170	227,636	181,249	4	—
South Carolina	802,583	450,807	346,149	8	—
South Dakota	300,678	147,068	151,505	—	4
Tennessee	1,476,345	825,879	633,969	10	—
Texas	4,071,884	2,082,319	1,953,300	26	—
Utah	541,198	182,110	337,908	—	4
Vermont	187,765	80,954	102,085	—	3
Virginia	1,697,094	813,896	836,554	—	12
Washington	1,555,534	717,323	777,732	—	9
West Virginia	750,964	435,914	314,760	6	—
Wisconsin	2,104,175	1,040,232	1,004,987	11	—
Wyoming	156,343	62,239	92,717	—	3
Total	81,555,889	40,830,763	39,147,793	297	241

Election of 1980

JULES WITCOVER is a syndicated political columnist for The Baltimore Evening Sun. *He is the author of* Marathon: The Pursuit of the Presidency, 1972–1976, *and* 85 Days: The Last Campaign of Robert Kennedy. *He is the co-author of* Blue Smoke and Mirrors: How Reagan Won and Why Carter Lost the Election of 1980, *and* Wake Us When It's Over: Presidential Politics of 1984.

Election of 1980

by *Jules Witcover*

After nearly half a century of the Democratic New Deal and successor variations, including three Republican Presidencies that paid lip service to many of its basic tenets, the election of 1980 at last brought a clean and dramatic break. Ronald Reagan became the first true embodiment of classic Republican conservatism to reach the White House since Herbert Hoover had left it in defeat in 1933.

Dwight Eisenhower, Richard Nixon, and Gerald Ford all had voiced the required conservative rhetoric but often bowed to the realities (except in Eisenhower's first two years) of mixed party responsibility in Washington, and of government as adjuster of economic and social inequities. For Reagan, though, the rhetoric was the reality, and his election ushered in a right-wing revolt that had been promised—or threatened—ever since the disastrous presidential candidacy of Barry Goldwater in 1964. Reagan campaigned throughout 1980 to "get the government off the backs of the people" and then proceeded, in his fashion, to try to do just that.

Though the country had been moving gradually toward the right, the election of 1980 was not so much an unvarnished demand for Ronald Reagan and his conservative views as it was a rejection of the Democratic incumbent, Jimmy Carter, whose four years in the Presidency had been indecisive and disappointing. Carter, a one-term governor of Georgia before his surprising rise to power in 1976, was himself essentially an economic conservative who had won election in the aftermath of the Watergate scandal, Nixon's resignation, and Ford's

suspicious pardon of Nixon shortly after the presidential resignation. The movement to the right was thus obscured and Carter was able to ride public disenchantment to his own victory. Carter lost public favor because he was not able
to cope with soaring inflation and unemployment, and because he could not
bring a satisfactory resolution to the major foreign policy crisis of his administration—the holding of fifty-two American hostages in Iran for more than a
year. For a time, Carter's appeal reached such a low that a member of his own
party, Senator Edward M. Kennedy of Massachusetts, youngest brother of the
late President, was able to seriously challenge him for the nomination. Although
Kennedy failed in that endeavor, his challenge further undermined Carter's
strength as the incumbent in the general election. Reagan, after having captured
the Republican nomination with relative ease, had only to demonstrate that he
was an acceptable alternative to the unpopular man in the White House. In this
undertaking, Reagan had the unwitting collaboration of Carter himself in an
election that turned more on personality, style and circumstance, than it did on
ideology and campaign techniques.

At the outset, the election of 1980 promised to be a model of the refinement
of presidential politics as technology. Since Franklin D. Roosevelt's use of radio
to persuade voters, presidential campaigns had increasingly become the domain
of the professional practitioners—consultants, speechwriters, television advertising men, media manipulators. Now, at last, on the Republican side there
appeared to be the perfect marriage: the political technocrats and a candidate,
Reagan, who had been a professional actor. They would write the script, he
would perform it on the stump, and the whole product would be neatly packaged
for the media.

It would be all so tidy and predictable—except that presidential campaigns
and elections seldom follow a precise script. They often are too susceptible to
events and circumstances beyond the foresight or the control of the technocrats,
or of the candidates either, and this fact was particularly true in 1980. And so,
in the end, the contest between Jimmy Carter and Ronald Reagan came down
to the manner in which the man required by his constitutional obligations to
cope with the events and circumstances of the time—President Carter—did so,
or failed to do so. Reagan did, to be sure, enunciate most of the conservative
dogma in the course of the campaign, and later his overwhelming election would
be labeled by many a "revolution" based on ideology. But, in fact, the victory
was based more on public revulsion toward Carter personally, and his performance in office.

Carter's beginnings as President did not presage the crisis of confidence
that brought him down four years later. His campaign in 1976 as a candidate
who put his confidence in the good judgment, and the goodness, of the American
people created an aura of optimism and even intimacy that he augmented with
an unannounced, unprecedented, dramatic walk down Pennsylvania Avenue
after his inauguration. He seemed, in that gesture, to confirm that this President
intended to live up to his campaign words about staying close to the people who
had elected him, and being guided by their wisdom. In his first weeks and months
in office, Carter conspicuously attempted to do so, or at least to nurture that

impression. He made spontaneous visits to government offices to talk to the civil servants who now toiled under him; he took voters' calls phoned into the Oval Office on a special line; dressed in a cozy sweater, he delivered a televised fireside chat to the nation; he sent his young daughter Amy to public school; and he held town meetings in small communities around the country.

These gestures, however, were not enough to navigate the shoals of a Washington about which, as a former small-state governor with a thinly veiled contempt for the federal bureaucracy, he was inadequately informed. Almost at once, he irritated Congress by drawing up a "hit list" of locally cherished federal water projects and attempting to kill them off without consulting Capitol Hill. In a single stroke, this move unveiled Carter's inexperience in dealing with the federal legislature and his disinclination to govern by compromise rather than by force of his own rigid convictions.

Not only did Carter not know his way around the Washington establishment; worse, he surrounded himself with aides, many from his own Georgia, who were equally uninformed about the ways of the capital city, and in some cases even more insensitive to its power brokers. Those cabinet appointees who did know the Washington ropes, and who were selected amid Carter's pledges that they would be independent and would have ready access to him, soon found that the Georgia guard diminished the worth of those promises. Eager to get things done, Carter overloaded congressional circuits with a flood of legislative proposals and then complained impatiently about lack of action, further irritating even members of his own party on the Hill. On top of all this, Carter demonstrated a self-destructive willingness to tolerate and even excuse the ineptness of some aides and the penchant of others to conduct themselves with an arrogance that only complicated the new President's relationships with Congress.

As a candidate, Carter repeatedly emphasized the need to raise government up to the high standard of ethics from which it had fallen during the Watergate nightmare. This outspoken disdain for dishonesty in government returned to haunt him, however, in the summer of 1977 when it was disclosed that his director of the budget, Georgia banker Bert Lance, had been involved in highly questionable banking practices, including the acceptance of large overdrafts by himself, his wife, and other relatives at his own bank. When the comptroller of the currency issued a damning report, Carter incredibly chose to interpret it as a vindication, even to the point of holding a televised press conference with Lance and telling his man: "Bert, I'm proud of you." Additional revelations several weeks later forced Lance to resign. Carter stood by him to the end, and in a teary statement said he didn't think "there's any way that I could find anyone to replace Bert Lance that would be, in my judgment, as competent, as strong, as decent, and as close to me as a friend and adviser as he has been." That statement may have eased the pain for Lance, but it did nothing to stem the erosion of Carter's standards of ethics in government.

One notable irony of the Carter White House years was that a man whose only governmental experience had been in domestic policies as a governor saw his tenure dominated by foreign affairs. Carter's most pressing domestic problems—rising inflation and joblessness—were exacerbated by soaring world oil prices, but after challenging the American people to take on the energy crisis as "the moral equivalent of war," he backed off, leaving confusion and diminished public confidence in his wake. Frustrated by his inability to cope with a debilitating economic picture, the foreign policy neophyte turned his attentions to problems abroad, where ultimately he found the greatest achievement of this White House term, as well as his greatest heartbreak.

At the core of American concerns in the Middle East, beyond the dependency on the region's oil, was the continuing enmity between Israel and the Arab world. Carter considered the conflict at once the most vexing problem and the area of greatest opportunity for American diplomacy, and after private meetings in his first year in office with President Anwar Sadat of Egypt and Prime Minister Menachem Begin of Israel, he worked single-mindedly to bring about a resolution of their differences.

The task seemed an impossible one. But with patience and determination Carter nursed the effort along, until at last Sadat broke the ice with a dramatic visit in November 1977 to Jerusalem. Sadat's discussions with Begin constituted public recognition by Egypt of Israel's right to exist as a state. Throughout the ebb and flow of the tenuous Sadat-Begin relationship in the months that followed, Carter devoted a remarkable amount of his time and energies to the role of peacemaker, finally astonishing the world by bringing the two leaders together for marathon discussions at Camp David, in the Maryland hills north of Washington. Laboring tirelessly himself as mediator over a 13-day period, shuttling between Sadat and Begin for hours on end of reasoning and cajoling, Carter helped hammer out in September 1978 a peace treaty between the two longtime enemy states that was not only historic for the Middle East but the showcase achievement of the Carter Administration.

This triumph raised Carter's stock in the world community, but it did nothing to combat the growing image at home of an Administration incapable of dealing with the critical pocketbook issues that so often determine the outcome of national elections. Unemployment and the inflation rate both continued to rise, and as Carter seemed unable to arrest the trend, the Republicans began to look to the 1980 election with increasing hope. Only five years after the Watergate fiasco that many thought at the time would cripple the GOP for years to come, the party was regrouping to make a serious run at the White House again, with a host of potential candidates in the wings.

Foremost of these was the man who had unsuccessfully challenged incumbent Gerald Ford in 1976, the former governor of California, Ronald Reagan. But because Reagan would be 70 years old in 1981, there were widespread doubts about his electability, and indeed about whether he would even seek the nomination again. A long list of other prospects was forming, including Senate Minority Leader Howard H. Baker of Tennessee; Senator Robert Dole of Kansas, Ford's 1976 running mate; former Secretary of the Treasury (and former Democrat) John B. Connally; former United Nations Ambassador George Bush of Texas; former White House chief of staff General Alexander Haig, now commander of the North Atlantic Treaty Organization; former Secretary of the

Treasury William Simon; and Representatives John B. Anderson and Philip Crane of Illinois and Jack Kemp of New York. Crane in fact had already declared his candidacy in August of 1978, taking a leaf from the book of early-starting Jimmy Carter in 1975.

Faced with irrefutable signs of political as well as economic trouble, Carter in early July 1979 decided that drastic measures were in order. He retreated to Camp David to prepare a speech to the nation that was first billed as yet another proposal to end the energy crisis, by now manifesting itself in waiting lines and heated tempers at the nation's gasoline pumps. But with nothing essentially new to say, Carter at the last hour decided to postpone the speech and instead summoned his closest White House advisers to consult with him. Among them was Patrick Caddell, his young pollster, who reported a rapidly growing pessimism among the American people about the ability of government to solve national problems.

The hours of consultation at Camp David dragged into days, inevitably creating the impression that some major crisis was at hand. That impression was fed by subsequent decisions to call in other important Democrats—first governors meeting in Louisville, then, in no particular order, mayors and members of the House and Senate, old Washington political hands, economists, religious leaders, labor leaders, businessmen, state legislators, and county officials. Over a period of eight days, nearly 150 individuals of various stripes were called in to tell the President of the United States what was wrong with how he was running the country. It was an incredible spectacle that invited ridicule—and got it in spades.

When the presidential speech finally emerged, it was a curious amalgam of *mea culpa* for Carter's own shortcomings and a warning of, as he put it, "a crisis of confidence" among the American people "that strikes at the very heart and soul of our national will." The talk soon became known as Carter's "malaise speech," although the President never used that word and Caddell vowed he had not either. In the shorthand of reporting, the consensus analysis was that Carter was trying to shift the blame for his failures onto the people, and it did not sit at all well with them.

Carter's Vice President, Walter F. Mondale, who had left the Senate to be Carter's running mate in 1976, later insisted that he had opposed the President's handling of the national malaise situation. But Mondale's reported dissent was overruled. Another listener who was particularly distressed at this assessment of the American spirit was Senator Kennedy. Because of fundamental differences he had with the President, Kennedy had for months been considering the idea of challenging Carter for the 1980 Democratic nomination. Kennedy's acknowledged desire to someday regain the White House that tragedy had taken from his brother, John F. Kennedy, was well known.

Others who shared Kennedy's disenchantment with Carter, notably William Winpisinger of the International Association of Machinists, a fiery and profane Carter-hater known to all as "Wimpy," as early as March 1979, had formed a committee to draft Kennedy but the Massachusetts Senator discouraged it and it went nowhere.

Until Carter's malaise speech, Kennedy had always been able to talk himself out of such a challenge to the incumbent, but now it was not so easy. Kennedy's distress increased sharply a couple of days after the speech when Carter suddenly announced that he was requesting the resignations of all the members of his cabinet, cabinet-level officials and senior White House staff—thirty-four individuals in all. The political objective, clearly, was to indicate to the public that Carter meant business and was making a fresh start—while getting rid of some officials, who in the view of Carter and the most influential insiders, were not playing ball. The targets were Secretary of the Treasury W. Michael Blumenthal; Secretary of Health, Education and Welfare Joseph Califano; and Secretary of Transportation Brock Adams. Two others who earlier had indicated they wanted to leave, Secretary of Energy James Schlesinger and Attorney General Griffin Bell, were thrown into the pot to augment the appearance of a major housecleaning. Though intended to demonstrate a sure administrative hand on the national tiller, the action was a failure. Instead, the firings were read as more admissions of presidential mistakes and uncertainty, and nowhere were they read more clearly that way than in the mind of Edward Kennedy.

Thus, as the fall of 1979 arrived, first-term President Jimmy Carter, determined to seek and win reelection in 1980, was threatened both outside and inside his Democratic party. The Republicans openly rejoiced at the picture of confusion and ineffectiveness that his "malaise summit" and accompanying shakeup had painted, and one by one they declared their intent to challenge him. After Crane there came Connally, Baker, Bush, Dole, Anderson, Senator Larry Pressler of South Dakota, and—the final entrant—Ronald Reagan. At the same time, Ted Kennedy seethed at the mess a President from his own party had wrought with notions, Kennedy said later, that "just ran so contrary to everything I believe in and that I was brought up to believe in."

Nor was that all that jeopardized Carter's reelection chances as the election year approached. On the fourth of November, a mob of young Iranians stormed the American embassy in Tehran, angered by a decision by Carter a week earlier to admit the deposed and ailing Shah of Iran, exiled in Mexico, into the United States for emergency medical treatment. The militants took about 90 hostages and eventually held 52 Americans, demanding the return of the Shah under threat that the hostages would be tried, or killed outright.

Nearly nine months earlier, armed men had seized the same embassy and had taken 101 persons hostage, but government forces had freed them within four hours. Consequently the immediate expectation in the Carter White House was that this latest episode, while serious, would be resolved in short order. That expectation, however, proved far off the mark, with disastrous political ramifications at home for Carter.

By this time, Kennedy had already decided to challenge Carter for the Democratic nomination. Although all the early polls indicated that if he ran he would easily defeat the incumbent, once Kennedy began to be perceived as an actual candidate, that prospect plummeted in a startling manner. Ever since the night of July 18, 1969, when Kennedy drove a car off a bridge on the island of Chappaquiddick near Martha's Vineyard in Massachusetts and a young woman passenger drowned, the question of the episode's political impact had hung ominously over Kennedy's career. Now, that question was being put to the acid test. Also being tested was the assumption of many Democrats that a national yearning for a return to the Camelot years of John F. Kennedy would make the youngest brother of the slain President their party's strongest candidate.

Kennedy himself, and those closest to him, apparently shared that assumption at the outset. As early as February of 1979 some of them had been meeting, with and without him, to consider the possibility of a challenge. Significantly, however, as one participant noted later, the prime focus of the discussions was always "not on how one would do it if one decided to do it, but whether one should do it."

Carter, too, assumed that Kennedy thought the nomination would be his for the asking, and to disabuse him of that notion—and in the obvious hope of scaring him off—he sent a direct message to Kennedy through a trusted emissary that he intended to seek reelection no matter what happened. In other words, Carter was saying, Kennedy could not count on a repeat of 1968, when Lyndon Johnson had withdrawn in the face of a challenge. Also, in a Democratic party straw vote in Florida, in which some free-lance Kennedy backers sought to pull an upset, the Carter White House committed heavy resources and administered a two-to-one shellacking to the Kennedy forces. So Kennedy had plenty of reason to know by this time that, if he took on the incumbent President, the challenge would be no waltz.

Yet the polls continued to be a glittering lure to Kennedy. As late as November 1, Carter's general approval rating among all voters in the Gallup Poll was at his all-time low—29 percent—and Kennedy led him by two to one as the choice of Democrats for the presidential nomination. Shored up by such data, and stiffened by his dismay at Carter's policies and pessimistic talk, Kennedy set his formal announcement of candidacy for November 7 in Boston.

Three nights before that occasion, however, an event occurred that further crippled Kennedy's candidacy before it had even begun. Kennedy was the subject of a one-hour television documentary written by and featuring one of the day's outstanding television reporters, Roger Mudd, then of CBS News. The documentary traced Kennedy's political and personal career and included segments of two lengthy interviews Mudd had conducted with Kennedy that were nothing short of disastrous for the prospective candidate.

Kennedy's answers were halting, uncertain and full of vague generalities. One exchange was particularly embarassing to Kennedy. He was asked by Mudd a question every presidential candidate knows to expect: "Why do you want to be President?" Kennedy responded with a rambling discourse about how the country "has more natural resources than any nation in the world, the greatest technology of any country in the world, the greatest capacity for innovation in the world, and the greatest political system in the world. . . . We're facing complex issues and problems in this nation at this time, but we have faced similar challenges at other times. And the energies and the resourcefulness of this nation, I think, should be focused on these problems in a way that brings a sense of restoration in this country by its people—to—in dealing with the problems that we face—primarily the issues on the economy, the problems of inflation, and the problems of energy. And I would basically feel that—that it's imperative for this country to either move forward, that it can't stand still, or otherwise it moves back.''

What made this mushy response especially startling was the fact that it came from a man who for the past 11 years had been confronted almost daily with speculation about an eventual bid for the Presidency. Although subsequent surveys indicated the Mudd documentary had been watched by only 15 percent of the American television audience that night (the hit movie *Jaws* was running opposite it on another network), word of it soon set the political community buzzing, to Kennedy's considerable disadvantage. However, another event halfway around the world at roughly the same time as the telecast proved to be even more destructive to the start of his presidential candidacy—the takeover of the American embassy in Tehran.

In times of foreign policy crisis, Americans historically have rallied around their President, and this episode was no exception. The overwhelming impulse was to close ranks behind the national leader, to demonstrate solidarity to the rest of the world, and especially to the Iranian adversaries who were inflicting insult and indignity on United States citizens. As the siege of the embassy continued for days and stretched into weeks, Carter became the beneficiary of the national concern, with tangible political ramifications. By late November, an ABC News-Louis Harris poll showed for the first time that Carter had moved ahead of Kennedy, 48 to 46 percent, as the choice of Democrats and independents for the Democratic nomination.

Kennedy contributed to his own slide by attacking Carter's decision to admit the Shah of Iran to the United States for medical treatment, saying in a television interview that the Shah "ran one of the most violent regimes in the history of mankind." Kennedy had ample grounds for making the statement, but in the context of the ongoing crisis, and of his political challenge to Carter, it came off as partisan carping that would only undermine Carter in his efforts to obtain the release of the hostages.

Carter, correctly assessing the political advantage that had come his way, soon went on national television and invoked the Iranian crisis as justification for not campaigning. He and his advisers understood that under the circumstances the most effective campaigning he could do was to perform his duties as President. "At the height of the Civil War," he intoned, "Abraham Lincoln said, 'I have but one task and that is to save the Union.'" Then he added with all due modesty, "Now I must devote my considered efforts to resolving the Iranian crisis." He would leave the burden of campaigning to his Vice President, Walter Mondale.

Shortly afterward, Carter's decision to stay off the campaign trail received an added rationale when the Soviet Union invaded Afghanistan. Clearly this was no time for the President of the United States to be out around the country engaging in partisan debate. To the great chagrin of Kennedy and Governor Edmund G. Brown, Jr., of California, who had also decided to challenge the incumbent, Carter withdrew from a scheduled debate in Iowa in advance of the precinct caucuses there that would launch the formal contest for 1980 national convention delegates.

In addition, Kennedy's lack of preparation for a serious candidacy was being confirmed now in his own erratic performance on the stump. Less well-known candidates had the luxury of working the kinks out of their speeches and campaign style in relative obscurity; as a Kennedy, the Massachusetts senator burst upon the presidential campaign as a major figure expected to perform effectively and appealingly from the first day. He didn't, and he paid a heavy price in news-media criticism and even ridicule, while Carter was enjoying the insulation from public censure that came to an American President conspicuously occupied with a national crisis.

While the intraparty challenge to Carter was stumbling, the Republicans were intensifying their own competition for the right to run against this seemingly vulnerable first-term President. Ever since Ronald Reagan's impressive challenge to the previous incumbent, Gerald Ford, Reagan's supporters had been organizing and raising money for another try in 1980. California functionaries of his 1976 campaign formed an "independent" group called Citizens for the Republic in 1977 that raised funds to help conservative Republican candidates for lesser offices and to bankroll Reagan's considerable speechmaking on the political circuit. The effort kept intact the nucleus of the Reagan campaign operation, and bolstered the enthusiasm of his 1976 supporters as well.

In early June of 1978, the voters of Reagan's California, after a long and emotional public debate, pulled off a taypayers' revolt with overwhelming passage of Proposition 13, an initiative that imposed a ceiling on property taxes. It was an idea that Reagan had pushed without success as governor of California and he hailed its passage now as evidence that his goal of "cutting government down to size" was being embraced. Thus encouraged, he continued to tell audiences that the federal government was like a free-spending son. "You can tell him to be less extravagant," Reagan would say, "or you can cut his allowance. Well, it's time to cut the government's allowance." With such appealing if simplistic talk, Reagan remained far ahead of the Republican field in the polls and entered the race in mid-November 1979 as the clear frontrunner for his party's nomination.

Of the challengers—Baker, Connally, Bush, Anderson, Dole, and Crane— only the first three were considered to have much chance to stop Reagan, and the first real test was in Iowa. Even before the caucuses there, however, Baker and Connally both showed political weakness in minor state-party straw polls, and it was Bush who soon emerged as Reagan's only serious obstacle to the nomination.

George Bush had an impressive string of credentials; in addition to having been United Nations Ambassador under Ford, he also had been a member of Congress from Texas, Republican national chairman, director of the Central Intelligence Agency, and special United States representative to the Republic of China. He was regarded outside the Republican party and by its most right-wing elements as a moderate, but he really was as conservative as any of the other candidates except Crane and Reagan. He appealed to many in the party who were unenthusiastic about Reagan because of his age or what was viewed as his ideological rigidity.

Of the three main challengers, Howard Baker was the favorite of the insiders—of the serious observers of the Senate in both the Republican party and in the news media. He was smart, knowledgeable, agreeable and effective as the minority leader. But he was also anathema to many conservatives because he had voted, as they put it, to "give away" the Panama Canal. And he was, it turned out, much too cautious politically. He delayed his entry into the race out of an overriding interest in the Senate's business, in particular the matter of ratification of the second strategic arms limitations treaty with the Soviet Union—called SALT II—which he and much of his party opposed. He rationalized that the debate on this critical issue would dominate foreign policy discussion in the country in the year before the presidential election, and he thus would be well-positioned to benefit politically from his role as Senate minority leader in the vanguard of the fight against it. SALT II, however, never did become the subject of a great debate in the Senate. In fact, when the Soviet Union invaded Afghanistan, Carter withdrew the treaty from consideration for ratification.

As a late starter in the presidential race, Baker looked for an event at which to demonstrate his strength quickly. He chose a straw vote at a presidential forum in Maine, where the popular Republican senator, William Cohen, had endorsed him and where a moderate Republican history in the state promised to be very congenial to him. Reagan, aware of that same history, passed up the presidential forum, in keeping with the basic strategy to remain aloof, above the fray. But the other contenders jumped in. Baker's connections in the state, and a vigorous organizational effort, immediately established him as the favorite—an impression to which aides contributed with optimistic talk. Baker flew into Portland with a planeload of reporters primed to give the country a full account of the launching of the Baker campaign. But he delivered a desultory speech on the heels of rousers from Connally and Bush. When the votes were in, Bush had beaten him by 20 votes out of about 900. It was only a straw vote, but Baker had been humbled by losing the expectations game—failing to meet the standard expected of him.

Two weeks later, the same thing happened to Connally in Florida. A strapping and impressive man, Connally, as Nixon's Secretary of Treasury, had enhanced his already firm reputation as a strong administrator and forceful personality—as well as a wheeler-dealer in the mold of his old close friend, Lyndon Johnson. That latter reputation was augmented by his indictment in 1974 on charges that he had taken a dairy lobby bribe in return for his help in obtaining beneficial price-support legislation. After a long trial, Connally was acquitted in 1975 and he remained a favorite of Republican businessmen. But he proved to be a bit too smooth, and subject to suspicion, for most voters.

With Baker wounded as a result of his conspicuous defeat in the Maine straw vote, Connally looked south for an opportunity to move up just behind Reagan in the Republican pecking order. He decided to make a major effort in a similar straw vote at the Florida state convention two weeks later. Reagan was having some organizational problems in Florida and Connally forces let their hopes get so high that they began to tell reporters their man would run very close to, or even defeat, Reagan. In doing so they, like the Baker aides in Maine, built expectations too high. Reagan beat Connally handily, and the confident Texan suffered a deflation from which he never recovered.

These early setbacks to two of Reagan's three main rivals for the Republican nomination only cemented the strategy of Reagan's campaign manager, former Nixon political adviser John Sears, to keep his frontrunning candidate serenely above the battle. Invited to join all the other Republican candidates in a nationally televised debate in advance of the Iowa precinct caucuses, Reagan declined on grounds that the debate might be "divisive." Thus, the challengers in both major parties were being denied their prime targets in Iowa, Carter having already begged off from the Democratic debate after the Iranian crisis and Afghanistan invasion.

For Carter, not debating was smart politics for an incumbent busy being President at a time of major foreign policy difficulty. Kennedy and Brown could criticize him and his handling of the crises only at their own political peril as the country rallied around him. Each night, as Kennedy and Brown campaigned in Iowa, Carter was seen on the television evening news dealing with the hostage crisis. When caucus night —January 21—arrived, he trounced Kennedy by nearly two to one—59 to 31 percent—with Brown far behind. With that one result, the myth of Kennedy invincibility was shattered.

By this time, the Iowa caucuses had become a major national political story, and Iowans enjoyed the spotlight. They were disappointed, and many were resentful that Reagan—an adopted son by virtue of having worked as a sports announcer on Iowa radio before going to Hollywood—would snub them by declining their invitation. Convinced by the polls that he was well ahead, and confident that the political organization that had been put in place was adequate to the job, Reagan not only passed up the debate but chose not to campaign in the state, except for an antiseptic final weekend rally outside Des Moines for which loyalists were bussed in.

Bush, meanwhile, having weathered the early straw votes and having built an impressive organization of his own in Iowa, campaigned diligently throughout the state. He held his own in the debate that went forward without Reagan, though nothing more than that. He benefited from an organizational effort that was at least the equivalent of Reagan's, and from one other thing—the tremendous interest generated in the caucus process by the invasion of the national news media. On caucus night, more than 110,000 Republicans participated, or more than four times the previous high. The Reagan campaign, confidently basing its grass-roots efforts on a much lower figure, calculated that 30,000 votes would be more than enough for Reagan to win. He received 31,348, but with the much higher turnout than anticipated, it was not quite what was needed. Bush won with 33,530 and suddenly the aloof frontrunner was in trouble.

Reagan, though, was no flash in the pan. As an ideological candidate, a true believer in the conservative dogma and the possessor of the talent and professional training necessary to peddle it to voters, all he really needed was to get out among them and start selling. This he did in the first primary, in New Hampshire, with a zest that belied his age and that contrasted sharply with his earlier frontrunner's strategy of detachment. Ever since the Eisenhower years the Republican party had been moving inexorably, in its heart if not always in its actions, to the right, and in Reagan, Republicans found a candidate who did not temper his views out of any concern that the GOP was the minority party. Indeed, he stoutly believed, and preached, that it could become the majority party only by presenting itself as a clear alternative to the Democrats. The only real question about him among Republican voters was not where he stood, but whether he had the fortitude and stamina at his age to run an effective and winning race against the Democratic nominee. His loss in Iowa forced him to demonstrate that he did, and the New Hampshire primary gave him the opportunity.

One other factor worked to Reagan's advantage in New Hampshire, as a result of what had happened in Iowa. Bush, riding the crest of that upset, suddenly was thrust into the national spotlight, and as it shone down on him, questions about his own leadership abilities, his record, and his proposals multiplied and gained greater prominence. Although Bush, like Reagan, was a longtime conservative, he always seemed so acquiescent, so willing to please, that he came off as a rubbery figure. Also, while Bush emphasized the competitive aspects of the nomination fight—the horse race, in the political parlance—Reagan hammered away at all the ten-strike themes of conservatism, from bloated government and welfare cheating to balanced budgets and the Communist threat. The Iowa defeat had dropped him temporarily behind Bush in the polls, but his more vigorous campaigning—including his participation in a debate with all the other candidates—soon erased the Bush lead. Then, one widely publicized event on the final weekend broke the primary wide open, and, in retrospect, removed the last real barrier to Reagan's nomination.

A local newspaper, the *Nashua Telegraph*, proposed a two-man debate between the frontrunning candidates, Reagan and Bush. Reagan's managers favored the idea because they felt that if Republican voters concluded the choice was between Reagan and the marshmallowy Bush, their man would be the clear winner. Bush's aides, on the other hand, believed that such a debate would confirm Bush's position as the prime, if not only, realistic alternative to Reagan.

The other candidates, however, complained to the Federal Election Commission, which ruled that a two-man debate would be so beneficial to Reagan and Bush that its sponsorship by the newspaper would be an illegal contribution to their campaigns. The Reagan campaign suggested that Reagan and Bush split the costs, and when Bush balked at that idea, Reagan agreed to pay for the whole affair himself. That decision set the stage for one of those dramatic incidents in a campaign that serves to give voters a capsule reading on a candidate, and helps to make him a winner—or a loser.

Reagan campaign manager Sears, still wary about exposing his man in any risk-prone environment and aware that the campaign's internal polls indicated Reagan had already recovered from the Iowa setback, had a brainstorm. Why not diminish the odds of a Reagan mistake in the debate by increasing the number of candidates called upon to provide answers in a limited time period from two to seven? And, at the same time, why not be conciliatory to the five who faced being shut out? As Reagan's press secretary at the time, James Lake, put it later, "We didn't need those other candidates out there bad-mouthing us the last three days."

On the morning of the debate, February 23, Sears and Lake called all the other candidates and invited them to participate that night. All of them except Connally, who was pursuing a southern strategy and was campaigning in South Carolina, agreed to come. The *Nashua Telegraph* still had the role of moderator, and its editors and Bush balked at the idea of expanding the two-man debate, but the Reagan team had made up its mind. A wild scene ensued when Reagan trooped into the high school auditorium debating ground with Dole, Baker, Anderson and Crane in tow. As they lined up behind the debate table, Bush sat woodenly, staring straight ahead. Reagan took his seat and began making his case for including the others. The moderator, Jon Breen, editor of the paper, looked toward a sound technician and snapped: "Turn Mr. Reagan's microphone off!" It was one of the all-time memorable straight lines in presidential politics, because Reagan, as if on cue, flushed angrily, leaned forward and shot back: "I'm paying for this microphone, Mr. Green (sic)!"

Bedlam reigned in the auditorium as spectators cheered, applauded and demanded that chairs be brought out for the four standing candidates. But the newspaper executives and Bush held fast, Bush still staring ahead and looking for all the world like a disapproving teacher's pet in the midst of a blackboard eraser fight. Finally, the rejected four stalked off the platform and the two-man debate went forward, but few remembered afterward what had been said during it. The story was Reagan's heroic attempt to include his four colleagues, and Bush's rigid refusal to let them speak. Not only that; it was a lively, dramatic picture story for television—a great "visual" in the new jargon—with an irate Reagan demanding to be heard in the cause of open debate and a shaken, slightly foolish-looking Bush playing the heavy.

The Nashua scene unfolded on the Saturday night before the primary, and Bush contributed to the damage it inflicted on him by retreating from New Hampshire to spend the final weekend at his home in Texas. On all the Sunday network and local television news shows, and again Monday morning and evening, viewers saw again and again that dramatic segment of "Reagan and the microphone," and then tape of Bush jogging in sunny Houston while Reagan continued to shake hands in snowy New Hampshire. The juxtaposition underscored what was being called a "wimp factor" against Bush in a most emphatic way. Later, after the election, Bush described the whole episode as a "basic sandbag" orchestrated by Sears. But whatever the debate was, George Bush's candidacy was never the same again. On primary day, February 26, Reagan routed him, 50 to 23 percent, with the rest of the field even farther behind.

Baker, who received only 13 percent of the New Hampshire vote, finished fourth in both Massachusetts and Vermont the next week and withdrew from the race. Connally bowed out four days later after losing, 54 to 30 percent, to Reagan in South Carolina. Dole and Crane soon followed suit, leaving only Reagan, Bush, and Anderson in the field.

Anderson, the most moderate of the contenders and a man of droll style and humor, had by this time begun to attract a modest following as the commonsense Republican. In the Iowa debate, he had won the crowd over by explaining how Reagan could, as he proposed, cut taxes, increase defense spending and still balance the budget: "It's simple. You do it with mirrors." It was the kind of remark expected from Anderson by those who knew him. He had spent nearly twenty years in the House and, in his later years, he had been a key figure in the party leadership, admired for his intellectual honesty and political independence. Convinced after nearly two decades in the House that he would rise no higher there, Anderson had decided to make one long-shot bid for the main brass ring before quitting politics altogether.

In the New Hampshire primary, Anderson finished a weak fourth with 10 percent of the vote, but for a brief period thereafter he threatened to replace Bush as Reagan's prime challenger. He ran second to Reagan in Vermont and second to Bush in Massachusetts on March 4, but two weeks later Reagan polished him off in the March 18 Illinois primary. Reagan, with his unerring knack for touching Republican sensitivities, needled Anderson in a televised debate in Chicago for his reluctance to pledge his support for any Republican nominee. "John," Reagan asked in mock sorrow, touching his hand to Anderson's sleeve, "would you really find Ted Kennedy preferable to me?" Reagan beat Anderson in his home state, 48 to 37 percent, and again in neighboring Wisconsin two weeks later. Anderson, persuaded by friends and admirers who took no comfort in the prospect of a Reagan-Carter race in the fall, announced in late April that he would run as an independent candidate at the head of what he called a "National Unity Campaign."

Bush, meanwhile, hung on, winning the March 25 primary in Connecticut (where he had attended Yale and where his father, Prescott Bush, had been a U.S. senator), but losing in the much more important states of New York (March 25) and Pennsylvania (April 22). On the ropes now, Bush primed for Michigan, where the popular Republican governor, William G. Milliken, had no use for Reagan. Milliken had helped Gerald Ford carry his home state against Reagan in 1976 at a time when Reagan was enjoying a string of primary and caucus successes, and he was determined to deny Reagan Michigan again, and possibly stall his march to the nomination. Milliken and his political organization campaigned diligently for Bush and succeeded in upsetting Reagan in Michigan on May 20, but it was too late.

The very night of Bush's Michigan victory, ABC and CBS News announced in their election telecasts that the delegates Reagan had picked up in a losing cause there, and for his victory in the Oregon primary, were enough to assure his nomination. Bush wanted to press on, but his aides, aware that his campaign lacked the money required to continue what was now a useless venture, closed it down and confronted him with a fait accompli he could not reverse. Seven weeks before the Republican national convention opened in Detroit, Ronald Reagan was certain to win the nomination.

On the Democratic side, the issue was not so conveniently, nor so amicably, resolved. Ted Kennedy had entered the contest against incumbent Jimmy Carter ostensibly because he was profoundly disturbed at where Carter was leading the party and the country, at home and abroad. But the two men had no love for each other, either, and the animosity only multiplied as the campaign progressed.

The drubbing Kennedy took from Carter in the Iowa caucuses on January 21 shook him and his campaign to the core. He had to acknowledge that he had embarked on his presidential bid without adequate preparation and that he had committed some early gaffes, such as his criticism of the Shah. But the real problem, he and his chief aides convinced themselves, was the restraint of foreign policy criticism that the hostage crisis and the situation in Afghanistan were imposing on him, and the free ride that Carter the candidate was being given. Kennedy resolved to tackle the problem head-on. In a speech at Georgetown University on January 28, he noted that Hitler's conquest of France and the Low Countries had not stopped public or presidential debate in the 1940s. "If the Vietnam war taught us anything," he said, "it is precisely that when we do not debate our foreign policy, we may drift into deeper trouble."

Kennedy's decision to attack the incumbent's management of foreign affairs in the midst of the Iranian crisis did not adequately gauge the people's inclination to fall in behind their leader under such circumstances. In caucuses in Maine, Kennedy's neighbors rejected him, though narrowly (45 to 39 percent), in favor of Carter. But Kennedy was determined. Attacking Carter in another speech in the same vein at Harvard on February 13, Kennedy chose to interpret the closer Maine result as an indication that "the Presidency can never be above the fray, isolated from the actions and passions of our time. A President cannot afford to posture as the high priest of patriotism."

The next night in a press conference, however, Carter demonstrated the power of the incumbency in political campaigning. "The thrust of what Senator Kennedy has said throughout the last few weeks," the President intoned, "is very damaging to our country and to the establishment of our principles and the maintenance of them, and to the achievement of our goals to keep the peace and get our hostages released."

The force of Carter's indictment was clear in the next primary results, in New Hampshire on February 26: Carter 49 percent, Kennedy 38 percent. Kennedy managed to salvage the primary in his home state of Massachusetts, but Carter resumed his winning ways across the South—South Carolina, Georgia, Florida, Alabama—and capped off these victories by trouncing Kennedy in Illinois on March 18, where the support of Chicago's beleaguered first woman mayor, Jane Byrne, only added to the senator's difficulties.

Finally, all Carter had to do to assure his nomination was to defeat Kennedy in New York. If Kennedy lost there, he would have little rationale for continuing his campaign. But there, for the first time, Carter's foreign policy missteps gave the challenger a chance. By confusion or design, the Carter administration several weeks before the New York primary had cast a vote in the United Nations Security Council that had outraged Israel and the American Jewish community. After having twice abstained on similar votes in 1979, the American ambassador voted for a resolution calling on Israel to dismantle civilian settlements in occupied Arab territories, including Jerusalem. When the uproar came, Carter quickly declared the vote a mistake caused by the American U.N. delegation and the White House's "failure to communicate," and he sought to placate irate Jewish voters.

Kennedy adroitly seized on the Carter misstep not only as a question of Carter's support for Israel but also as a measure of his undependability in the conduct of foreign policy. Kennedy's own tremendous support in the Jewish community, combined with growing doubts about Carter's commitment to the Israeli side in the Middle East, gave him the opening he needed. Campaigning strenuously in the closing days, while Carter continued what by now was called his "Rose Garden strategy" of sticking to his presidential duties, Kennedy upset the incumbent in New York on March 25 by a thumping 16 percentage points. White House political strategists began to consider seriously whether the time was not approaching when Carter would have to take to the stump and override a pledge not to campaign until the hostages in Iran were freed.

Before having to confront that possibility, however, Carter still hoped he could extricate the hostages. A United Nations commission had been negotiating with the Iranian government and on the morning of April 1, hours before voters were to cast ballots in the presidential primaries in Wisconsin and Kansas, Carter called a most unusual early morning televised press conference (7:13 a.m. to be precise) to report a "positive step." Word had come, he said, from Iranian President Abolhassan Bani-Sadr that the hostages would be transferred from the "militants" at the embassy to the government's jurisdiction if the United States ended "all propaganda and agitation" against Iran. Such a step would have been an interim one only, and it never happened, but Carter by his words encouraged the idea that the hostages' outright release might be imminent.

Reporter: "Do you know when they will be actually released and be brought home?"

Carter: "I presume that we will know more about that as the circumstances develop. We do not know the exact time scheduled at this moment."

Carter won the Wisconsin and Kansas primaries handily, but the hostages remained where they were, and pressures on the President to campaign continued. What finally got him out of the Rose Garden and onto the stump, ironically, was not the hostages' release, but a daring military rescue attempt whose abject failure made it more unlikely than ever that they would be set free, but which gave Carter a rationale, however contorted, to start campaigning for renomination.

About three weeks after Carter's false alarm, on his orders six large American transport planes departed on the night of April 24 from a base in southern Egypt and headed for a spot in the Iranian desert, 300 miles southeast of Tehran. There they were to refuel eight American helicopters from the aircraft carrier

Nimitz, which was stationed in the Gulf of Oman. The helicopters were then to proceed, swooping in over the seized embassy, and land troops who would extricate the hostages. But only six helicopters made it to the refueling point and one developed a mechanical problem when it got there. The plan called for a minimum of six helicopters for the raid, so with Carter's approval it was aborted. As the transports and helicopters prepared to leave the site, one helicopter collided with a transport on the ground, causing a fire that killed eight men. The survivors fled, leaving the Iranians with the wreckage and the American dead with which to reap a propaganda bonanza, which they quickly did.

The disaster became a metaphor for Carter's handling of the hostage crisis, if not for his foreign policy in general. And it came at a most unpropitious time politically, because Kennedy in the wake of his New York primary upset was making notable progress in a strategy aimed at establishing a final rationale for his own nomination. Arguing that the Democratic nominee had to be strong in the industrial heartland of the country, Kennedy campaigned aggressively and won the Pennsylvania primary on April 22 and the caucuses in Michigan (by an eyelash) on April 26, and set his sights on the final big-state primaries in California, Ohio and New Jersey on June 3.

Five days before those primaries, Carter finally made his first overt campaign appearance of the year, at a rally in Columbus, Ohio. He won that state, but Kennedy captured California and New Jersey. Carter, however, by virtue of the proportional allocation formula used by the party, picked up enough delegates to assure his nomination—though not without a final row and some embarrassing scenes at the national convention in New York in August.

The Republican convention—or, more accurately, coronation—drew the spotlight first, opening in a rehabilitated downtown Detroit on July 14. With Reagan's nomination certain, the only questions of note were what the platform would say, and who would be Reagan's running mate. The Reagan strategists decided at the outset that the platform would not become a battleground, since it meant very little in the scheme of things, anyway. The only issue that generated any fuss was the Equal Rights Amendment, which the platform committee, dominated by Reaganites, threw out of the party's document of principles. This act, which naturally was greeted by loud and emotional protests from the outnumbered Republican feminists, contravened the Republicans' 40-year-old tradition of support for equal rights for women. As for the selection of a running mate, the convention seemed quite content to leave that matter to the presidential nominee—and was astonished when it learned what he had been contemplating.

Well in advance of the convention, Reagan's pollster, Richard Wirthlin, had been surveying voters about a list of prospective running mates. The list included Bush, Baker, William Simon, former Secretary of Defense Donald Rumsfeld, Senator Richard Lugar of Indiana, Jack Kemp, Representative Guy Vander Jagt of Michigan, Senator Paul Laxalt of Nevada (Reagan's best friend on Capitol Hill), and former President Gerald Ford. Of all these, Ford clearly was the best known and potentially brought more to the ticket than any of the others. But he had flirted earlier with the possibility of running for President again and had turned down the idea. So why would he be interested in running for Vice President, a job he had already held?

Reagan was intrigued by the idea, though, especially because he was cool to the most obvious alternative—Bush. Ever since that scene in the high school auditorium in Nashua, Reagan had been put off by Bush's weak performance. "If he can't stand up to that kind of pressure," he told one intimate at the time, "how could he stand up to the pressure of being President?" And he told another: "I have strong reservations about George Bush. I'm concerned about turning the country over to him." Of all the prospects, Reagan plainly preferred Laxalt, but the senator's small-state base, especially with Nevada's extensive gambling interests, worked against his selection.

Prior to Ford's arrival at the convention, he had received feelers about the vice presidential nomination but had turned them all aside. Nevertheless, Reagan himself broached the subject directly to Ford at private meetings in their Detroit hotel and even arranged to have Ford's secretary of state, Henry Kissinger, discuss with Ford the foreign policy roles he might assume as Reagan's Vice President. Soon Ford and Reagan aides were conferring on the possibility. Ford seemed by now to have more than a passing interest, as discussions advanced into what role he might play as Vice President in the actual governing process. Inevitably, word of the deliberations soon leaked out, and before long the major television commentators were speculating about the possibility of this incredible "dream ticket."

Ford, interviewed by Walter Cronkite on CBS News, fanned the talk with observations that sounded for all the world as if he were on the verge. "I would not go to Washington . . . and be a figurehead Vice President," he said at one point. "If I go to Washington, and I'm not saying that I am accepting, I have to go there with the belief that I will play a meaningful role across the board in the basic and the crucial and the important decisions that have to be made in a four-year period." Was he thinking, Cronkite asked, of "something like a co-presidency?" Ford replied: "That's something Governor Reagan really ought to consider. . . ."

Reagan, watching the interview in his room, was predictably shocked when the term "co-presidency" was used. Later testimony indicated that the word served as a dash of cold water in the faces of all the principals, showing them with clarity what they all had been toying with—and cooling the interest of the Reagan advisers particularly. Nervously, Reagan pressed Ford for an answer, and was greatly relieved when Ford finally declined. Reagan settled in the end on the obvious choice, Bush, who with customary eagerness accepted.

The Reagan-Ford "dream ticket" had proved illusory, but the two principals' lengthy conversations about it did achieve one thing. It diminished the ill feelings between the two men that had existed since Reagan's challenge to Ford for the 1976 nomination, and Reagan's subsequent failure to campaign very extensively for Ford that year. And it laid down a foundation for Ford's active participation as a campaigner for Reagan in the fall of 1980 in a campaign that would play on the public's dissatisfaction with Carter as Ford's successor.

In his acceptance speech on July 17, Reagan asked: "Can you look at the record of this administration and say, 'Well done'? Can anyone compare the state of our economy when the Carter administration took office with where we are today and say, 'Keep up the good work'? Can you look at our reduced standing in the world today and say, 'Let's have four more years of this'?" The Republican convention roared back: "No!"

The Democratic convention, opening in New York on August 11, produced no similar reconciliation of the party's two main figures, except in the most transparently artificial manner. Although Carter came into the convention with more than a majority of the delegates, the Kennedy forces had one more card to play. They were well aware that Carter, still in the throes of economic distress and humbled by the seemingly endless Iranian hostage crisis, was running more than 25 percentage points behind Reagan in the public-opinion polls. If the delegates, elected to the convention under rules that committed them to vote for the candidate to whom they were pledged, were made free of that firm commitment, might they not be persuaded by the polls to switch to Kennedy, or at least to abandon Carter for some other Democrat? It was worth a try.

Under the euphemism "open convention" a campaign was launched to change the party rules and grant "freedom" to the delegates. But the trouble was that most of the Carter delegates did not want to be free in that sense. They had worked hard to get to the convention, often in bitter primary and caucus fights against Kennedy backers, and they were in no mood to switch, especially for Kennedy. The Carter forces easily turned back the rules challenge by roughly a three-to-two ratio, and Carter's nomination bid had passed its final obstacle.

It remained for Kennedy, however, to provide the two emotional highlights of the convention—one very positive, one extremely negative. The first was a speech he delivered the night before the presidential roll call, in which he had the hall roaring with approval as he touched all the old liberal nerves with cheer lines that in many cases mocked the cautious, middle-road brand of Democratic policies espoused by Carter. His own candidacy had been criticized for having been a rerun of tired old liberal ideas, and seemingly in defense of it he told the convention:

"The commitment I seek is not to outworn views, but to old values that will never wear out. Programs may sometimes become obsolete, but the ideal of fairness always endures. Circumstances may change but the work of compassion must continue. It is surely correct that we cannot solve problems by throwing money at them; but it is also correct that we dare not throw national problems onto a scrap heap of inattention and indifference. . . . For those whose cares have been our concern, the work goes on, the cause endures, the hope still lives, the dream shall never die."

The 40-minute demonstration that followed Kennedy's speech was clearly the emotional peak of the convention. Carter's acceptance speech, on August 14 after his nomination for President and that of Walter Mondale for Vice President, was an anticlimax. Rather than defending his four years in office, which was an uneviable task, Carter warned of two futures—one of "security, justice and peace" under a second Carter term, one of "despair . . . surrender . . . risk—the risk of international confrontation, the risk of an uncontrollable, unaffordable and unwinnable nuclear arms race" under Reagan.

Kennedy's negative contribution was his late appearance, at the very close of the convention, at a gathering of party stalwarts on the rostrum for pictures with the newly nominated standard-bearer. For days there had been speculation about whether Kennedy would agree to stand with Carter for the traditional victory pose of hands joined over heads. As the convention and the nationwide television audience watched and waited, Carter prowled the Madison Square Garden platform, greeting other senators, governors, mayors, various party officials—but no Kennedy. The senator explained later that his car had been caught in traffic. When he finally arrived, he shook hands perfunctorily with Carter and then strolled around the rostrum with the President of the United States trotting after him like, a Carter intimate said with dismay later, "a puppy dog." It was not an auspicious end for the convention, nor a good beginning for an extremely difficult campaign ahead.

In spite of the very favorable polls, Reagan's political strategists entered the fall campaign with two major concerns. One had to do with their own candidate—whether he had the self-discipline to navigate the course without self-destructing. His aides were well aware that Reagan had a history of making off-the-cuff observations that got him into trouble. That particular penchant was a product more than anything else of his faith in whatever he read or heard, almost without regard to source, that dovetailed with his rather uncomplicated, rigid view of the world. After eight years as a governor and with two presidential nomination campaigns behind him, the Reagan lore abounded with what came to be known, even within his own campaign, as his "horror stories"—accounts of how welfare recipients had ripped off the system for hundreds of thousands of dollars, to give only one example. Also, he did not always appreciate at once the political ramifications of things he said, so it was imperative that the campaign somehow guard against this problem.

The second concern had to do with the opposition. Jimmy Carter as the incumbent President had the power by virtue of his office to affect events—or to appear to affect them—that could have a decisive impact on the outcome of the election. As early as July, at the Republican convention, Reagan's campaign manager (and later his much-beleaguered director of the Central Intelligence Agency), William Casey, had told reporters that one of his major fears was that on the eve of the election Carter might spring an "October surprise"—some foreign policy coup possibly concerning the hostages—that would bring him immediate, short-term voter support.

To guard against such an eventuality, Casey said then, he was establishing "an intelligence operation" to maintain an "incumbency watch" on the administration. No more was said about it, but such an operation was indeed organized under a Casey aide, who, using retired military and CIA personnel, checked on such things as troop and materiel movements via military transport at major American bases in this country and abroad. The effort was, from all later reports, amateurish and of little value. But its very pursuit underscored the concern within the Reagan camp that Carter might indeed try to pull out the election with some "October surprise."

The fear of Reagan's "horror stories" and lack of political sensitivity proved to be a valid one. In a speech to the Veterans of Foreign Wars, he referred to the Vietnam war as "a noble cause"—and triggered a brief rehash of that political nightmare. He stirred up an educational hornets' nest when he told a conference of evangelists that there were "great flaws" in the theory of evolution, and that it might be a good idea if schools taught the creationist theory as well. As Bush prepared to go to Peking for the Republican ticket, Reagan said he was looking forward to reestablishing official relations with Taiwan. He called Tuscumbia, Alabama, where Carter was kicking off his own campaign, the birthplace of the Ku Klux Klan—it was not. He suggested that volcanic Mount St. Helens in a few months had "probably released more sulfur dioxide into the atmosphere of the world than has been released in the last ten years of auto driving"—a contention immediately rejected by the Environmental Protection Agency, which said man-made sources contributed from 40 to 160 times more pollution each day than did the eruption in Washington State. He said "growing and decaying vegetation" contributed 93 percent of nitrogen oxides that polluted the air, confusing them with nitrous oxides, the natural product of plant respiration. Whereupon he was greeted at one campaign stop by a sign on a tree that said "Chop Me Down Before I Kill Again."

In the midst of these gaffes, which threatened to make Reagan a continuing subject of ridicule and to undermine seriously his credibility, the campaign enlisted the services of one of the Republican party's most politically sensitive professionals, Stuart Spencer, who had helped run Reagan's gubernatorial campaigns as well as the 1976 Ford campaign against him. Spencer traveled with Reagan as a sort of gaffe preventer and was for the most part successful in curbing the "horror stories" and explaining away those that did pop out of Reagan's mouth.

The fear of an "October surprise" could not be dispelled so easily. It continued to hang over the Reagan campaign until the very end, when reports of eleventh-hour efforts by Carter to extricate the hostages before the election did indeed surface and give the Reagan campaign some last-minute anxiety.

Carter's concern going into the fall campaign, plain and simple, was that voters would base their decision on what they thought about him and his record, and not about Reagan. Although Carter was ready and willing to defend his four years in office, the polls showed conclusively that his Administration would require a lot of selling in light of the rising inflation and interest rates at home and the hostage dilemma abroad. No amount of media magic from Carter's campaign technocrats could change the fact that the 1980 election was one in which events, most of them damaging to Carter, were the controlling factors. The best hope for Carter to overtake his challenger was somehow to make the voters think so much less of Reagan or, more specifically, to come to fear his election, that Carter would seem the safer alternative.

Such a strategy was, for obvious reasons, a risky one. Negative campaigning, while demonstrably effective if handled carefully, also can backfire on a candidate, especially if employed against a foe who is well liked by the voters. And asking them to choose the lesser of two evils is in itself a depressant, discouraging voter turnout. The Democrats, as the majority party, usually seek and depend on a large turnout.

This same lesser-of-two-evils approach was dictating the independent candidacy of John Anderson, who was counting on there being enough voters who could not swallow either Carter or Reagan to turn the election his way. This concept seemed to have considerable validity as the fall campaign began, but faded as Reagan demonstrated his acceptability, first in a debate with Anderson in which he held his own, and then with Carter.

Carter's political advisers acknowledged that playing on fears about Reagan was their best bet to divert voters' attention from the Carter record, and they were aware that the ideal way to do so would be to have others, not Carter himself, going after Reagan. One of Carter's remaining strengths was that voters continued to believe that he was a man of great religious conviction and good will, and it was essential that this belief not be tarnished. But that rational judgment did not take into consideration Carter's own frustration, and his conviction that Reagan really was a threat to peace.

Thus, early in the campaign, Carter told a Torrance, California, audience on September 22 that the election "will help to decide whether we have war or peace." Reagan, warned by his own advisers in advance that Carter would try to "demonize" him in the campaign, responded with appropriate indignation. "To assume that anyone would deliberately want a war," he lamented, "is beneath decency." In short order, the nation's news media were commenting not only on "the war-and-peace issue" but also on "the meanness issue"—a disturbing penchant by Carter to accuse Reagan of being a heartless wretch and, indeed, a demon. Nevertheless, internal polls did indicate that Carter's negative campaigning was cutting into Reagan's lead.

The President finally went too far in a talk to party workers in Chicago on October 6, warning them that their votes would "literally decide the lives of millions of people in our country and indeed throughout the world. . . . You'll determine whether or not this America will be unified or, if I lose the election, whether Americans might be separated black from white, Jew from Christian, North from South, rural from urban."

The indictment of Reagan as a polarizer proved in time to have considerable validity, but in the context of the campaign it was taken as another example of "meanness" by a desperate incumbent. Reagan, playing the situation for all it was worth, professed sorrow that his opponent could have stooped so low. "I can't be angry," he said. "I'm saddened that anyone, particularly someone who has held that position, could intimate such a thing. I'm not asking for an apology from him. . . . But I think he owes the country an apology."

Such was the political climate when, a week before the election and after much wrangling over arrangements, Carter and Reagan finally met on October 28 in a nationally televised debate in Cleveland. The Reagan strategy earlier had been to avoid any debates, but when, by mid-October, the negative campaigning against Reagan had begun to take its toll, the decision was made to chance it. Also, as the campaign approached its conclusion, Anderson was sinking badly, and the Reagan campaign feared Carter would win over many of Anderson's former supporters unless Reagan did something to woo straying Republicans back into the fold. And, finally, a late debate would give Reagan an opportunity to counter an "October surprise" if Carter were to spring one on him.

As for Carter, the old axiom that incumbents should not debate, endorsed by his advisers, in the end went out the window; he had to get Reagan on the same platform and demonstrate conclusively who was the better risk for the future.

As is almost always the case in presidential debates, it was the incumbent who had more to lose and the challenger everything to gain. By this time, Reagan's polls indicated, a negative judgment on Carter already had been made by the voters, but they still had to be convinced that Reagan was up to the job. Merely by holding his own in debate with the incumbent, Reagan would be able to make that point, and he did so. One reason that the challenger did so well, the Democrats argued later, was that the Reagan campaign had managed to get hold of extensive briefing papers prepared for Carter as he readied himself for the debate. Disclosure of this fact after the election led to a lengthy investigation and eventually a court order for the appointment of an independent investigator to determine how the Reagan campaign obtained the papers, and how they were used in preparing Reagan for the debate. A higher court, however, voided that order and effectively shelved the investigation.

In the debate, Carter tried to fan concern about Reagan in handling foreign policy, from the use of military force to nuclear arms control and proliferation of nuclear weapons. He made a strong case that Reagan's policies threatened an acceleration of the arms race, but he undercut his own performance with an inexplicable comment. "I had a discussion with my daughter Amy the other day, before I came here," Carter said at one point, "to ask her what the most important issue was. She said she thought nuclear weaponry and the control of nuclear arms." The notion of relying on the judgment of an eight-year-old in such a matter was, on its face, both baffling and ludicrous, and the ridicule the comment later brought Carter diverted attention from his own reasoned arms-control criticism of Reagan, which later proved quite warranted.

On another occasion, when Carter had Reagan dead to rights in saying that he "began his career campaigning around this nation against Medicare," which was true, Reagan sidestepped by saying, simply, "There you go again"—intimating that here was Carter up to his old tricks of unfair allegations. Finally, Reagan scored the forensic coup of the evening with a simple concluding question to the television audience: "Are you better off than you were four years ago?" If so, he said, vote for Carter. If not, vote for him.

Although Reagan's pollsters contended later their man had begun to widen his lead even before the debate, there was no doubt that his ability to more than hold his own against the incumbent President finally broke the logjam of concern about him and led to his overwhelming victory a week later.

Arrangements for a debate among the vice presidential candidates got nowhere. It did not matter. Walter Mondale, George Bush and former Wisconsin Governor Patrick J. Lucey, running with Anderson, all campaigned vigorously but unspectacularly in the shadow of the men who had selected them, and about whom the voters would make their judgment on Election Day.

There remained, however, one final hope for Carter to turn the tables on the last weekend of the campaign. It was the first day of November, but the possibility after all of an October surprise—a few days late—now presented itself. After more months of intrigue and threats in Tehran, the parliament of Iran was meeting to consider the fate of the hostages. There was no telling what their release just three days before the election might do to the emotions of American voters as they faced the choice between Carter and Reagan. For the Reagan campaign, traveling in Michigan and Ohio, the prospect was the only political cloud on the horizon; for the Carter campaign, in Chicago, it was the one event that might yet bail out the desperate incumbent.

Just before four o'clock Sunday morning, November 2, Carter received a phone call from the deputy secretary of state, Warren Christopher, informing him that the Iranian parliament had agreed to release the hostages provided the United States met four demands: pledge noninterference in Iranian affairs, free all frozen Iranian assets in the United States, cancel all American public and private claims against Iran, and return the Shah's wealth to Iran. The demands were extreme, but Carter could not afford not to consider them, or at least to use them as a starting point for further negotiations. He decided to return to Washington immediately to be better able, his aides said, to appraise the situation with expert advice and superior communications. But Carter's camp was also thinking about the potential political impact of the President conspicuously rushing back to his desk in the Oval Office to grapple personally with the opportunity. It was just the sort of campaign climax Reagan's strategists had most feared.

That Sunday, as the nation anxiously awaited the outcome of this latest hopeful development—and as its people watched television network reviews of the hostage crisis, now approaching its first anniversary—Carter and his closest aides considered his response. It was determined almost at once that the terms were unacceptable, and to say so was only going to confirm Carter's year-long failure to obtain the hostages' release. Yet there was no real alternative; indeed, the Reagan campaign had so effectively conditioned the voters by now to be wary of some eleventh-hour gimmick by Carter concerning the hostages that it was difficult even to put the best face on the bad situation.

In the end, Carter went on television and reported that while the Iranian proposal was "a significant development" that appeared to offer "a positive basis" for further negotiations for the hostages, "I know also that all Americans will want their return to be on a proper basis, which is worthy of the suffering and sacrifices which the hostages have endured." In other words, they were not coming out, and Reagan was home free. Up to the last hour, the campaign of 1980 was the captive not of the new breed of political managers who were said to be taking over the electoral process, but of events outside the control even of the incumbent President.

Carter spent the final day before the election on a mad dash from east coast to west and back again, but to no avail. On election day, November 4, Americans in every section of the country expressed their clear preference for Reagan, if they voted at all. A turnout of just over 52 percent of the eligible voting-age population confirmed that the general apathy of the post-John F. Kennedy years was continuing.

Nationwide, Reagan won 51 percent of the vote to only 41 percent for Carter and 7 percent for Anderson, with the rest split among minor candidates. Reagan won comfortably in the East (5 percentage points), South (8 percent against a Southern candidate), and Midwest (10 percent) and routed Carter in the West (20 percent). He carried 44 states to Carter's 6 and won 489 electoral votes to 49 for Carter.

According to a New York Times-CBS News survey of voters leaving their polling places, white males, Catholics, Protestants, independents and defecting Democrats, and voters age 30 and older with incomes in excess of $15,000 a year and advanced education were Reagan's strongest backers. Whites supported him 55 percent to 36 percent, while blacks backed Carter, 82–14, and Hispanics supported the losing incumbent by 54–36. Males preferred Reagan, 54–37, women by only 46–45. Catholics went 51–40 for Reagan, Protestants 56–37; even Jews, a traditional anchor in the Democratic constituency, gave him 39 percent, to 45 percent for Carter. Independents favored Reagan 50–34 and 26 percent of Democrats switched to him. Only the 18–21 age group chose Carter, and very narrowly—44–43. Reagan's popularity was demonstrated in direct proportion to voters' increased age, income, and education, with a slight falloff of the Social Security-conscious, 60-plus age group, which also backed him, 54–40. Reagan cracked the normally Democratic blue-collar vote in this survey, 47–46, and trailed Carter only slightly, 44–47, among union-household voters surveyed.

What was more, the Republicans gained control of the Senate for the first time since Eisenhower's first-term election 28 years earlier—strong evidence that a conservative tide was indeed gripping the country. No less than seven liberal Democratic stalwarts were ousted, including the 1972 party standard-bearer, George McGovern of South Dakota.

A major factor in this development was the role played by political action committees (PACs)—groups raising and spending money on behalf of candidates of their choice, or against those to whom they objected. With the direct presidential campaigns financed with federal funds, the PACs either made "independent expenditures" for their presidential choice or for congressional and senatorial campaigns, and in both cases the Republican candidates were by far the major beneficiaries. Whereas in 1976 Federal Election Commission records indicated that corporate PACs, most of them backing Republicans, had outnumbered Democratic-oriented labor PACs, 450 to 303, the ratio had mushroomed by 1980: 1,226 corporate and business PACs to only 318 run by labor unions. Also, eight of the ten largest PAC givers to congressional candidates were corporate or conservative political groups.

Yet, so focused had the election year been on Jimmy Carter—his failures and, in the general election, on his personal demeanor as a candidate—that it was debatable whether Reagan's victory meant the country really wanted and expected his undiluted brand of conservatism. He had used the same extravagantly conservative rhetoric in getting elected governor of California, after all, and had turned out to be more moderate and accommodating in his actions than his campaign oratory had suggested he would be.

Polls before and after the election confirmed that voters did, in fact, want to "get the government off our backs," but only in general terms of excessive spending, taxation and regulation. When it came to government services of nearly every description, they still wanted government to perform them—services from Social Security and hospital care to welfare and unemployment benefits that were the very essence of the New Deal. It would not be until Ronald Reagan took office in January of 1981, and he began to convert his rhetoric to sweeping changes in government policy and thought, that the voters who so soundly rejected Jimmy Carter would appreciate what their dislike of the first elected incumbent to be defeated for reelection in nearly three decades had wrought.

In his inaugural address, Reagan repeated a statement that had come to sum up his whole attitude in more than twenty years of political preaching. "In this present crisis," he said, "government is not the solution to our problem; government is the problem. . . . It is my intention to curb the size and influence of the federal establishment. . . . It's not my intention to do away with government. It is rather to make it work—work with us, not over us; to stand by our side, not ride on our back." And, it turned out for good or ill, Ronald Reagan really meant what he said.

Appendix

Acceptance Speech by Governor Ronald Reagan
Detroit, July 17, 1980

In his acceptance speech Reagan blamed the Carter Administration for runaway inflation, high taxes, and mediocre leadership. He asked the delegates, "Can you look at our reduced standing in the world today and say, 'Let's have four more years of this'?" The Republican convention roared back, "No."

MR. CHAIRMAN, delegates to this convention, my fellow citizens of this great nation:

With a deep awareness of the responsibility conferred by your trust, I accept your nomination for the Presidency of the United States. I do so with deep gratitude.

I am very proud of our party tonight. This convention has shown to all America a party united, with positive programs for solving the nation's problems; a party ready to build a new consensus with all those across the land who share a community of values embodied in these words: family, work, neighborhood, peace and freedom.

I know we have had a quarrel or two in our party, but only as to the method of attaining a goal. There was no argument about the goal. As President, I will establish a liaison with the fifty Governors to encourage them to eliminate, wherever it exists, discrimination against women. I will monitor Federal laws to insure their implementation and to add statutes if they are needed.

More than anything else, I want my candidacy to unify our country, to renew the American spirit and sense of purpose. I want to carry our message to every American, regardless of party affiliation, who is a member of this community of shared values.

Never before in our history have Americans been called upon to face three grave threats to our very existence, any one of which could destroy us. We face a disintegrating economy, a weakened defense and an energy policy based on the sharing of scarcity.

The major issue of this campaign is the direct political, personal, and moral responsibility of Democratic Party leadership—in the White House and in Congress—for this unprecedented calamity which has befallen us. They tell us they have done the most that humanly could be done. They say that the United States has had its days in the sun, that our nation has passed its zenith. They expect you to tell your children that the American people no longer have the will to cope with their problems, that the future will be one of sacrifice and few opportunities.

My fellow citizens, I utterly reject that view. The American people, the most generous on earth, who created the highest standard of living, are not going to accept the notion that we can only make a better world for others by moving backwards ourselves. Those who believe we *can* have no business leading the nation.

I will not stand by and watch this great country destroy itself under mediocre leadership that drifts from one crisis to the next, eroding our national will and purpose. We have come together here because the American people deserve better from those to whom they entrust our nation's highest offices, and we stand united in our resolve to do something about it.

We need a rebirth of the American tradition of leadership at *every* level of government and in private life as well. The United States of America is unique in world history because it has a genius for leaders—many leaders—on many levels. But, back in 1976, Mr. Carter said, "Trust *me*." And a lot of people did. Now, many of those people are out of work. Many have seen their savings eaten away by inflation. Many others on fixed incomes, especially the elderly, have watched helplessly as the cruel tax of inflation wasted away their purchasing power. And, today, a great many who trusted Mr. Carter wonder if we can survive the Carter policies of national defense.

"Trust me" government asks that we concentrate our hopes and dreams on one man, that we trust him to do what's best for us. My view of government places trust not in one person or one party, but in those values that transcend persons and parties. The trust is where it belongs—in the people. The responsibility to live up to that trust is where it belongs, in their elected leaders. That kind of relationship, between the people and their elected leaders, is a special kind of *compact*, an agreement among themselves to build a community and abide by its laws.

Three hundred and sixty years ago, in 1620, a group of families dared to cross a mighty ocean to build a future for themselves in a new world. When they arrived at Plymouth, Massachusetts, they formed what they called a "compact," an agreement among themselves to build a community and abide by its law.

The single act—the voluntary binding together of free people to live under the law—set the pattern for what was to come.

A century and a half later, the descendants of those people pledged their lives, their fortunes and their sacred honor to found this nation. Some forfeited their fortunes and their lives; none sacrificed honor.

Four score and seven years later, Abraham Lincoln called upon the people of all America to renew their dedication and their commitment to a government of, for and by the people.

Isn't it once again time to renew our compact of freedom, to pledge to each other all that is best in our lives, all that gives meaning to them—for the sake of this, our beloved and blessed land?

Together, let us make this a new beginning. Let us make a commitment to care for the needy, to teach our children the values and virtues handed down to us by our families, to have the courage to defend those values and the willingness to sacrifice for them.

Let us pledge to restore, in our time, the American spirit of voluntary service, of cooperation, of private and community initiative, a spirit that flows like a deep and mighty river through the history of our nation.

As your nominee, I pledge to restore to the federal government the capacity to do the people's work without dominating their lives. I pledge to you a government that will not only work well, but wisely, its ability to act tempered by prudence, and its willingness to do good balanced by the knowledge that government is never more dangerous than when our desire to have it help us blinds us to its great power to harm us.

The first Republican President once said, "While the people retain their virtue and their vigilance, no Administration by any extreme of wickedness or folly can seriously injure the government in the short space of four years."

If Mr. Lincoln could see what's happened in these last three and a half years, he might hedge a little on that statement. But, with the virtues that are our legacy as a free people and with the vigilance that sustains liberty, we still have time to use our renewed compact to overcome the injuries that have been done to America these past three and a half years.

First, we must overcome something the present Administration has cooked up: a new and altogether indigestible economic stew, one part inflation, one part high unemployment, one part recession, one part runaway taxes, one part deficit spending and seasoned by an energy crisis. It's an economic stew that has turned the national stomach. It is as if Mr. Carter had set out to prove, once and for all, that economics is indeed a "dismal science."

Ours are not problems of abstract economic theory. These are problems of flesh and blood, problems that cause pain and destroy the moral fiber of real people who should not suffer the further indignity of being told by the White House that it is all somehow their fault. We do not have inflation because—as Mr. Carter says—we have lived too well.

The head of a government which has utterly refused to live within its means and which has, in the last few days, told us that this year's deficit will be $60 billion, dares to point the finger of blame at business and labor, both of which have been engaged in a losing struggle just trying to stay even.

High taxes, we are told, are somehow good for us, as if, when government spends our money it isn't inflationary, but when we spend it, it is.

Those who preside over the worst energy shortage in our history tell us to use less, so that we will run out of oil, gasoline and natural gas a little more slowly. Conservation is desirable, of course, for we must not waste energy. But conservation is not the sole answer to our energy needs.

America must get to work producing more energy. The Republican program for solving economic problems is based on growth and productivity.

Large amounts of oil and natural gas lay beneath our land and off our shores, untouched because the present Administration seems to believe the American people would rather see more regulation, taxes and controls than more energy.

Coal offers great potential. So does nuclear energy produced under rigorous safety standards. It could supply electricity for thousands of industries and millions of jobs and homes. It must not be thwarted by a tiny minority opposed to economic growth which often finds friendly ears in regulatory agencies for its obstructionist campaigns.

Make no mistake. We will not permit the safety of our people or our environmental heritage to be jeopardized, but we are going to reaffirm that the economic prosperity of our people is a fundamental part of our environment.

Our problems are both acute and chronic, yet all we hear from those in positions of leadership are the same tired proposals for more government tinkering, more meddling and more control—all of which led us to this state in the first place.

Can anyone look at the record of this Administration and say, "Well done"? Can anyone compare the state of our economy when the Carter administration took office with where we are today and say, "Keep up the good work"? Can anyone look at our reduced standing in the world today and say, "Let's have four more years of this"?

I believe the American people are going to answer these questions the first week of November and their answer will be, "No—we've had enough." And, when the American people *have* spoken, it will be up to us—beginning next January 20th—to offer an Administration and Congressional leadership of competence and more than a little courage.

We must have the clarity of vision to see the difference between what is essential and what is merely desirable, and then the courage to use this insight to bring our government back under control and make it acceptable to the people.

We Republicans believe it is essential that we maintain both the forward momentum of economic growth and the strength of the safety net beneath those in society who need help. We also believe it is essential that the integrity of all aspects of Social Security be preserved.

Beyond these essentials, I believe it is clear our federal government is overgrown and overweight. Indeed, it is time for our government to go on a diet. Therefore, my first act as Chief Executive will be to impose an immediate and thorough freeze on federal hiring. Then, we are going to enlist the very best minds from business, labor and whatever quarter to conduct a detailed review of every department, bureau and agency that lives by federal appropriation. We are also going to enlist the help and ideas of many dedicated and hard-working government employees at all levels who want a more efficient government as much as the rest of us do. I know that many are demoralized by the confusion and waste they confront in their work as a result of failed and failing policies.

Our instructions to the groups we enlist will be simple and direct. We will remind them that government programs exist at the sufferance of the American taxpayer and are paid for with money earned by working men and women. Any program that represents a waste of their money—a theft from their pocketbooks—must have that waste eliminated or the program must go—by Executive Order where possible, by Congressional action where necessary. Everything that can be run more effectively by state and local government we shall turn over to state and local government, along with the funding sources to pay for it. We are going to put an end to the money merry-go-round where our money becomes Washington's money, to the way the federal bureaucrats tell them to.

I will not accept the excuse that the federal government has grown so big and powerful that it is beyond the control of any President, any Administration or Congress. We are going to put an end to the notion that the American taxpayer exists to fund the federal government. The federal government exists to serve the American people and to be accountable to the American people. On January 20th, we are going to reestablish that truth.

Also on that date we are going to initiate action to get substantial relief for our taxpaying citizens and action to put people back to work. None of this will be based on any new form of monetary tinkering of fiscal sleight of hand. We will simply apply to government the common sense we all use in our daily lives.

Work and family are at the center of our lives, the foundation of our dignity as a free people. When we deprive people of what they have earned, or take away their jobs, we destroy their dignity and undermine their families. We cannot support our families unless there are jobs, and we cannot have jobs unless people have both money to invest and the faith to invest it.

These are concepts that stem from the foundation of an economic system that for more than two hundred years has helped us master a continent, create a previously undreamed of prosperity for our people and has fed millions of others around the globe. That system will continue to serve us in the future if our government will stop ignoring the basic values on which it was built and stop betraying the trust and good will of the American workers who keep it going.

The American people are carrying the heaviest peacetime tax burden in our nation's history—and it will grow even heavier, under present law, next January. This burden is crushing our ability and incentive to save, invest and produce. We are taxing ourselves into economic exhaustion and stagnation.

This must stop. We must halt this fiscal self-destruction and restore sanity to our economic system.

I have long advocated a 30 percent reduction in income tax rates over a period of three years. This phased tax reduction would begin with a 10 percent "down payment" tax cut in 1981, which the Republicans in Congress and I have already proposed.

A phased reduction of tax rates would go a long way toward easing the heavy burden on the American people. But, we should not stop here.

Within the context of economic conditions and appropriate budget priorities during each fiscal year of my Presidency, I would strive to go further. This would include improvement in business depreciation taxes so we can stimulate investment in order to get plants and equipment replaced, put more Americans back to work and put our nation back on the road to being competitive in world commerce. We will also work to reduce the cost of government as a percentage of our Gross National Product.

The first task of national leadership is to set honest and realistic priorities in our policies and our budget and I pledge that my Administration will do that.

When I talk of tax cuts, I am reminded that every major tax cut in this century has strengthened the economy, generated renewed productivity and ended up yielding new revenues for the government by creating new investment, new jobs and more commerce among our people.

The present Administration has been forced by us Republicans to play follow-the-leader with regard to a tax cut. But, we must take with the proverbial "grain of salt" any tax cut proposed by those who have given us the greatest tax increase in our history. When those in leadership give us tax increases and tell us we must also do with less, have they thought about those who have always had less—especially the minorities? This is like telling them that just as they step on the first rung of the ladder of opportunity, the ladder is being pulled up. That may be the Democratic leadership's message to the minorities, but it won't be ours. Our message will be: we have to move ahead, but we're not going to leave anyone behind.

Thanks to the economic policies of the Democratic Party, millions of Americans find themselves out of work. Millions more have never even had a fair chance to learn new skills, hold a decent job, seize the opportunity to climb the ladder and secure for themselves and their families a share in the prosperity of this nation.

It is time to put America back to work, to make our cities and towns resound with the confident voices of men and women of all races, nationalities and faiths bringing home to their families a decent paycheck they can cash for honest money.

For those without skills, we'll find a way to help them get skills.

For those without job opportunities we'll stimulate new opportunities, particularly in the inner cities where they live.

For those who have abandoned hope, we'll restore hope and we'll welcome them into a great national crusade to make America great again!

When we move from domestic affairs and cast our eyes abroad, we see an equally sorry chapter in the record of the present Administration.

—A Soviet combat brigade trains in Cuba, just 90 miles from our shores.

—A Soviet army of invasion occupies Afghanistan, further threatening our vital interests in the Middle East.

—America's defense strength is at its lowest ebb in a generation, while the Soviet Union is vastly outspending us in both strategic and conventional arms.

—Our European allies, looking nervously at the growing menace from the East, turn to us for leadership and fail to find it.

—And, incredibly more than 50 of our fellow Americans have been held captive for over eight months by a dictatorial foreign power that holds us up to ridicule before the world.

Adversaries large and small test our will and seek to confound our resolve, but the Carter Administration gives us weakness when we need strength, vacillation when the times demand firmness.

Why? Because the Carter Administration lives in the world of make-believe. Every day, it dreams up a response to that day's troubles, regardless of what happened yesterday and what will happen tomorrow. The Administration lives in a world where mistakes, even very big ones, have no consequence.

The rest of us, however, live in the real world. It is here that disasters are overtaking our nation without any real response from the White House.

I condemn the Administration's make-believe, its self-deceit and—above all—its transparent hypocrisy.

For example, Mr. Carter says he supports the volunteer army, but he lets military pay and benefits slip so low that many of our enlisted personnel are actually eligible for food stamps. Re-enlistment rates drop and, just recently, after he fought all week against a proposal to increase the pay of our men and women in uniform, he helicoptered out to our carrier the *U.S.S. Nimitz*, which was returning from long months of duty. He told the crew that he advocated better pay for them and their comrades! Where does he really stand, now that he's back on shore?

I'll tell you where I stand. I do not favor a peacetime draft or registration, but I do favor pay and benefit levels that will attract and keep highly motivated men and women in our volunteer forces and an active reserve trained and ready for an instant call in case of an emergency.

An Annapolis graduate may be at the helm of the ship of state, but the ship has no rudder. Critical decisions are made at times almost in Marx Brothers fashion, but who can laugh? Who was not embarrassed when the Administration handed a major propaganda victory in the United Nations to the enemies of Israel, our staunch Middle East ally for three decades, and then claimed that the American vote was a "mistake," the result of a "failure of communication" between the President, his Secretary of State and his U.N. Ambassador?

Who does not feel a growing sense of unease as our allies, facing repeated instances of an amateurish and confused Administration, reluctantly conclude that America is unwilling or unable to fulfill its obligations as leader of the free world?

Who does not feel rising alarm when the question in any discussion of foreign policy is no longer, "Should we do something?", but "Do we have the capacity to do anything?"

The Administration which has brought us to this state is seeking your endorsement for four more years of weakness, indecision, mediocrity and incompetence. No American should vote until he or she has asked, "Is the United States stronger and more respected now than it was three and a half years ago? Is the world today a safer place in which to live?"

It is the responsibility of the President of the United States, in working for peace, to insure that the safety of our people cannot successfully be threatened by a hostile foreign power. As President, fulfilling that responsibility will be my Number One priority.

We are not a warlike people. Quite the opposite. We always seek to live in peace. We resort to force infrequently and with great reluctance—and only after we have determined that it is absolutely necessary. We are awed—and rightly so—by the forces of destruction at loose in the world in this nuclear era. But neither can we be naive or foolish. Four times in my lifetime America has gone to war, bleeding the lives of its young men into the sands of beachheads, the fields of Europe and the jungles and rice paddies of Asia. We know only too well that war comes not when the forces of freedom are strong but when they are weak. It is then that tyrants are tempted.

We simply cannot learn these lessons the hard way again without risking our destruction.

Of all the objectives we seek, first and foremost is the establishment of lasting world peace. We must always stand ready to negotiate in good faith, ready to pursue any reasonable avenue that holds forth the promise of lessening tensions and furthering the prospects of peace. But let our friends and those who may wish us ill take note: the United States has an obligation to its citizens and to the people of the world never to let those who would destroy freedom dictate the future course of human life on this planet. I would regard my election as proof that we have renewed our resolve to preserve world peace and freedom. This nation will once again be strong enough to do that.

This evening marks the last step—save one—of a campaign that has taken Nancy and me from one end of this great land to the other, over many months and thousands and thousands of miles. There are those who question the way we choose a President, who say that our process imposes difficult and exhausting burdens on those who seek the office. I have not found it so.

It is impossible to capture in words the splendor of this vast continent which God has granted as our portion of his creation. There are no words to express the extraordinary strength and character of this breed of people we call Americans.

Everywhere we have met thousands of Democrats, Independents and Republicans from all economic conditions and walks of life bound together in that community of shared values of family, work, neighborhood, peace and freedom. They are concerned, yes, but they are not frightened. They are disturbed, but not dismayed. They are the kind of men and women Tom Paine had in mind when he wrote—during the darkest days of the American Revolution—"We have it in our power to begin the world over again."

Nearly one hundred and fifty years after Tom Paine wrote those words, an American President told the generation of the Great Depression that it had a "rendezvous with destiny." I believe this generation of Americans today also has a rendezvous with destiny.

Tonight, let us dedicate ourselves to renewing the American Compact. I ask you not simply to "Trust *me*," but to trust your values—our values—and to hold me responsible for living up to them. I ask you to trust that American spirit which knows no ethnic, religious, social, political, regional or economic boundaries, the spirit that burned with zeal in the hearts of millions of immigrants from every corner of the earth who came here in search of freedom.

Some say that spirit no longer exists. But I have seen it—I have felt it—all across the land, in the big cities, the small towns and in rural America. The American spirit is still there, ready to blaze into life if you and I are willing to do what has to be done, the practical, down-to-earth things that will stimulate our economy, increase productivity and put America back to work.

The time is now to limit federal spending, to insist on a stable monetary reform and to free ourselves from imported oil.

The time is now to resolve that the basis of a firm and principled foreign policy is one that takes the world as it is and seeks to change it by leadership and example, not by lecture and harangue.

The time is now to say that while we shall seek new friendships and expand and improve others, we shall not do so by breaking our word or casting aside old friends and allies.

And, the time is now to redeem promises once made to the American people by another candidate, in another time and another place. He said,

". . . For three long years I have been going up and down this country preaching that government—federal, state and local—costs too much. I shall not stop that preaching. As an immediate program of action, we must abolish useless offices. We must eliminate unnecessary functions of government. . . .

". . . We must consolidate subdivisions of government and, like the private citizen, give up luxuries which we can no longer afford.

"I propose to you, my friends, and through you that government of all kinds, big and little be made solvent and that the example be set by the President of the United States and his cabinet."

So said Franklin Delano Roosevelt in his acceptance speech to the Democratic National Convention in July, 1932.

The time is now, my fellow Americans, to recapture our destiny, to take it into our own hands. But, to do this will take many of us, working together, I ask you tonight to volunteer your help in this cause so we can carry our message throughout the land.

Yes, isn't now the time that we, the people, carried out these unkept promises? Let us pledge to each other and to all America on this July day forty-eight years later, we intend to do just that.

I've thought of something that is not part of my speech and I'm worried over whether I should do it.

Can we doubt that only a Divine Providence placed this land, this island of freedom, here as a refuge for all those people in the world who yearn to breathe freely: Jews and Christians enduring persecution behind the Iron Curtain, the boat people of Southeast Asia, of Cuba and Haiti, the victims of the drought in Africa, the freedom fighters of Afghanistan and our own countrymen held in savage captivity?

I'll confess that I've been a little afraid to suggest what I'm going to suggest— I'm more afraid not to—that we begin our crusade joined together in a moment of silent prayer. God bless America.

Acceptance Speech by President Jimmy Carter
New York, August 14, 1980

Rather than defend his four years in office, President Carter chose to contrast the future, as he saw it, under Republican and Democratic leadership. The GOP, he assured the convention, would provide a future characterized by "the despair of millions," "massive tax cuts for the rich," and an "unwinnable nuclear arms race." His vision of the future under continued Democratic rule included security, justice, peace, and a good life for all Americans.

FELLOW DEMOCRATS, fellow citizens:

I thank you for the nomination you've offered me. And I especially thank you for choosing as my running mate the best partner any president ever had—Fritz Mondale.

With gratitude and with determination, I accept your nomination.

And I am proud to run on a progressive and sound platform that you have hammered out at this convention.

Fritz and I will mount a campaign that defines the real issues—a campaign that responds to the intelligence of the American people—a campaign that talks sense—and we're going to beat, whip the Republicans in November.

We'll win because we are the party of a great president who knew how to get reelected—Franklin D. Roosevelt. And we're the party of a courageous fighter who knew how to "give 'em hell"—Harry Truman. And as Truman said, he just told the truth and they thought it was hell.

And we're the party of a gallant man of spirit—John Fitzgerald Kennedy. And we're the party of a great leader of compassion—Lyndon Baines Johnson.

And the party of a great man who should have been president and would have been one of the greatest presidents in history—Hubert Horatio Hornblower Humphrey. I have appreciated what this convention has said about Senator Humphrey, a great man who epitomized the spirit of the Democratic Party, and I would like to say that we're also the party of Governor Jerry Brown and Senator Edward M. Kennedy.

I'd like to say a personal word to Senator Kennedy. Ted, you're a tough competitor and a superb campaigner and I can attest to that. Your speech before this convention was a magnificent statement of what the Democratic Party is and what it means to the people of this country—and why a Democratic victory is so important this year. I reach out to you tonight and I reach out to all those who have supported you in your valiant and passionate campaign.

Ted, your party needs—and I need—you and your idealism and dedication working for us. There is no doubt that even greater service lies ahead of you—and we are grateful to you and to have your strong partnership now in the larger cause to which your own life has been dedicated.

I thank you for your support. We'll make great partners this fall in whipping the Republicans.

We're Democrats and we have had our differences, but we share a bright vision of America's future—a vision of good life for all our people—a vision of a secure nation, a just society, a peaceful world, a strong America—confident and proud and united.

And we have a memory of Franklin Roosevelt forty years ago when he said that there are times in our history when concerns over our personal lives are overshadowed by concern for "what will happen to the country we have known." This is such a time—and I can tell you that the choice to be made this year can transform our own personal lives and the life of our country as well.

During the last presidential campaign, I crisscrossed this country and I listened to thousands and thousands of people—housewives and farmers, teachers and small business leaders, workers and students, the elderly and the poor—people of every race and every background and every walk of life. It was a powerful experience—a total immersion in the human reality of America.

And I have now had another kind of total immersion—being president of the United States of America. Let me talk for a moment about what that job is like—and what I have learned from it.

I've learned that only the most complex and difficult tasks come before me in the Oval Office. No easy answers are found there—because no easy questions come there.

I've learned that for a president, experience is the best guide to the right decisions. I'm wiser tonight than I was four years ago.

And I have learned that the presidency is a place of compassion. My own heart is burdened for the troubled Americans. The poor and the jobless and the afflicted—they've become part of me. My thoughts and my prayers for our hostages in Iran are as though they were my own sons and daughters.

The life of every human being on Earth can depend on the experience and judgment and vigilance of the person in the Oval Office. The president's power for building and his power for destruction are awesome. And the power is greatest exactly where the stakes are highest—in matters of war and peace. And I have learned something else—something that I have come to see with extraordinary clarity. Above all, I must look ahead—because the president of the United States is the steward of the nation's destiny.

He must protect our children—and the children they will have—and the children of generations to follow. He must speak and act for them. That is his burden—and his glory.

And that is why a president cannot yield to short-sighted demands, no matter how rich or powerful the special interests might be that make those demands. And that is why the president cannot bend to the passions of the moment, however popular they might be. And that is why the president must sometimes ask for sacrifice when his listeners would rather hear the promise of comfort.

The president is a servant of today. But his true constituency is the future. That is why the election of 1980 is so important.

Some have said it makes no difference who wins this election. They are wrong.

This election is a stark choice between two men, two parties, two sharply different pictures of what America is and what the world is. But it is more than that.

It is a choice between two futures. The year 2000 is just less than 20 years away—just four presidential elections after this one. Children born this year will come of age in the 21st century.

The time to shape the world of the year 2000 is now. The decisions of the next few years will set our course, perhaps an irreversible course—and the most important of all choices will be made by the American people at the polls less than three months from tonight.

The choice could not be more clear—nor the consequences more crucial.

In one of the futures we can choose—the future that you and I have been building together—I see security and justice and peace.

I see a future of security that will come from tapping our own great resources of oil and gas, coal and sunlight—and from building the tools, the technology and factories for a revitalized economy based on jobs and stable prices for everyone.

I see a future of justice—the justice of good jobs, decent health care, quality education, and the full opportunity for all people, regardless of color or language or religion: the simple human justice of equal rights for all men—and for all women, guaranteed equal rights at last—under the Constitution of the United States of America.

And I see a future of peace—a peace born of wisdom and based on the fairness toward all countries of the world—a peace guaranteed both by American military strength and by American moral strength as well.

That is the future I want for all people—a future of confidence and hope and a good life. It is the future America must choose—and with your help and with your commitment, it is the future America will choose.

But there is another possible future.

In that other future, I see despair—the despair of millions who would struggle for equal opportunity and a better life—and struggle alone.

And I see surrender—the surrender of our energy future to the merchants of oil, the surrender of our economic future to a bizarre program of massive tax cuts for the rich, service cuts for the poor and massive inflation for everyone.

And I see risk—the risk of international confrontation: the risk of an uncontrollable, unaffordable, and unwinnable nuclear arms race.

No one, Democrat or Republican leader, consciously seeks such a future. And I do not claim that my opponent does. But I do question the disturbing commitments and policies already made by him and by those with him who have now captured control of the Republican Party.

The consequences of those commitments and policies would drive us down the wrong road. It's up to all of us to make sure America rejects this alarming, and even perilous, destiny.

The only way to build a better future is to start with realities of the present. But while we Democrats grapple with the real challenges of a real world, others talk about a world of tinsel and make-believe.

Let's look for a moment at their make-believe world.

In their fantasy America, inner-city people and farm workers and laborers do not exist. Women, like children, are to be seen but not heard. The problems of working women are simply ignored. The elderly do not need Medicare. The young do not need more help in getting a better education. Workers do not require the guarantee of a healthy and a safe place to work.

In their fantasy world, all the complex global changes of the world since World War II have never happened. In their fantasy America, all problems have simple solutions. Simple—and wrong.

It is a make-believe world. A world of good guys and bad guys, where some politicians shoot first and ask questions later.

No hard choices. No sacrifice. No tough decisions. It sounds too good to be true—and it is.

The path of fantasy leads to irresponsibility. The path of reality leads to hope and peace. The two paths could not be more different. Nor could the futures to which they lead.

Let's take a hard look at the consequences of our choice.

You and I have been working toward a secure future by rebuilding our military strength—steadily, carefully and responsibly. The Republicans talk about military strength—but they were in office for eight out of the last 11 years—and in the face of a growing Soviet threat they steadily cut real defense spending by more than a third.

We've reversed the Republican decline in defense. Every year since I've been president, we've had real increases in our commitment to a stronger nation—increases which are prudent and rational. There is no doubt that the United States of America can meet any threat from the Soviet Union.

Our modernized strategic forces, a revitalized NATO, the Trident submarine, the cruise missile, Rapid Deployment Force—all these guarantee that we will never be second to any nation. Deeds, not words—fact, not fiction.

We must and we will continue to build our own defenses. We must and we will continue to seek balanced reductions in nuclear arms.

The new leaders of the Republican Party, in order to close the gap between their rhetoric and their record, have now promised to launch an all-out nuclear arms race. This would negate any further effort to negotiate a strategic arms limitation agreement.

There can be no winners in such an arms race—and all the people of the Earth can be the losers.

The Republican nominee advocates abandoning arms control policies which have been important and supported by every Democratic president since Harry Truman and also by every Republican president since Dwight D. Eisenhower. This radical and irresponsible course would threaten our security—and could put the whole world in peril.

You and I must never let this come to pass.

It's simple to call for a new arms race. But when armed aggression threatens world peace, tough-sounding talk like that is not enough. A president must act—responsibly. When Soviet troops invaded Afghanistan, we moved quickly to take action. I suspended some grain sales to the Soviet Union. I called for draft registration. We joined wholeheartedly with the Congress. And I joined whole-heartedly with the Congress and with the U.S. Olympics Committee and led more that 60 other nations in boycotting the big propaganda show in Russia— the Moscow Olympics.

The Republican leader opposed two of these forceful but peaceful actions and he waffled on the third. But when we asked him what he would do about aggression in Southwest Asia, he suggested blockading Cuba. Even his running mate wouldn't go along with that.

He doesn't seem to know what to do with the Russians. He's not sure if he wants to feed them or play with them or fight with them.

As I look back on my first term, I'm grateful that we've had a country with a full four years of peace. And that's what we're going to have for the next four years—peace.

It's only common sense that if America is to stay secure and at peace, we must encourage others to be peaceful as well.

As you know, we've helped in Zimbabwe-Rhodesia, where we stood firm for racial justice and democracy. And we have also helped in the middle East. Some have criticized the Camp David accords and they've criticized some delays in the implementation of the Middle East peace treaty.

Well, before I became president there was no Camp David accord and there was no Middle East peace treaty. Before Camp David, Israel and Egypt were poised across barbed wire, confronting each other with guns and tanks and planes. But afterward, they talked face-to-face with each other across a peace table—and they also communicated through their own ambassadors in Cairo and Tel Aviv.

Now that's the kind of future we're offering—of peace to the Middle East if the Democrats are reelected in the fall.

I am very proud that nearly half the aid that our country has ever given to Israel in the 32 years of her existence has come during my administration. Unlike our Republican predecessors, we have never stopped nor slowed that aid to Israel. And as long as I am president, we will never do so. Our commitment is clear: security and peace for Israel: peace for all the peoples of the Middle East.

But if the world is to have a future of freedom as well as peace, America must continue to defend human rights.

Now listen to this: The new Republican leaders oppose our human rights policy. They want to scrap it. They seem to think it's naive for America to stand up to freedom and—for freedom and democracy. Just what do they think we should stand up for?

Ask the former political prisoners who now live in freedom if we should abandon our stand on human rights.

Ask the dissidents in the Soviet Union about our commitment to human rights.

Ask the Hungarian-Americans, ask the Polish-Americans. Listen to Pope John Paul II.

Ask those who are suffering for the sake of justice and liberty around the world.

Ask the millions who've fled tyranny if America should stop speaking out for human principles.

Ask the American people. I tell you that as long as I am president, we will hold high the banner of human rights, and you can depend on it.

Here at home the choice between two futures is equally important.

In the long run, nothing is more crucial to the future of America than energy—nothing was so disastrously neglected in the past.

Long after the 1973 Arab oil embargo, the Republicans in the White House had still done nothing to meet the threat to national security of our nation. Then, as now, their policy was dictated by the big oil companies.

We Democrats fought hard to rally our nation behind a comprehensive energy program and a good program—a new foundation for challenging and exciting progress. Now, after three years of struggle, we have that program.

The battle to secure America's energy future has been fully and finally joined. Americans have cooperated with dramatic results.

We've reversed decades of dangerous and growing dependence on foreign oil. We are now importing 20 percent less oil. That is one and a half million barrels of oil every day less than the day I took office.

And with our new energy policy now in place, we can discover more, produce more, create more, and conserve more energy—and we will use American resources, American technology, and millions of American workers to do it with.

Now what do the Republicans propose?

Basically their energy program has two parts.

The first part is to get rid of almost everything that we've done for the American public in the last three years.

They want to reduce or abolish the synthetic fuels program. They want to slash the solar energy incentives, the conservation programs, aid to mass transit, aid to the elderly Americans to help pay their fuel bills.

They want to eliminate the fifty-five mile speed limit. And while they're at it, the Republicans would like to gut the Clean Air Act. They never liked it to begin with.

That's one part of the program.

The other part is worse.

To replace what we have built, this is what they propose: to destroy the windfall profits tax, and to "unleash" the oil companies and let them solve the energy problem for us.

That's it. That's the whole program. There is no more.

Can this nation accept such an outrageous program? No! We Democrats will fight it every step of the way, and we'll begin tomorrow morning with the campaign for reelection in November.

When I took office, I inherited a heavy load of serious economic problems besides energy—and we've met them all head-on. We've slashed government regulation and put free enterprise back into the airlines, the trucking and the financial systems of our country—and we're now doing the same thing for the railroads. This is the greatest change in the relationship between government and business since the New Deal.

We've increased our exports dramatically. We've reversed the decline in the basic research and development. And we have created more than 8 million new jobs—the biggest increase in the history of our country.

But the road's bumpy, and last year's skyrocketing OPEC price increases have helped to trigger a worldwide inflation crisis.

We took forceful action, and interest rates have now fallen, the dollar is stable and, although we still have a battle on our hands, we are struggling to bring inflation under control.

We are now at a critical turning point in our economic history. Because we made the hard decisions—because we guided our economy through a rough but essential period of transition—we have laid the groundwork for a new economic age.

Our economic renewal program for the 1980s will meet our immediate need for jobs by attacking the very same long-term problems that caused unemployment and inflation in the first place. It will move America simultaneously towards our five great economic goals—lower inflation, better productivity, revitalization of American industry, energy security and jobs.

It is time to put all America back to work—not in make work, but in real work.

There is real work modernizing American industry and creating new industries for America.

Here are just a few things we will build together.

New industries turn our coal and shale and farm products into fuel for our cars and trucks, and to turn the light of the sun into heat and electricity for our homes; A modern transportation system for railbeds and ports to make American coal into a powerful rival of OPEC oil;

Industries that will provide the convenience of communications and futuristic computer technology to serve millions of American homes, offices and factories;

Job training for workers displaced by economic changes;

New investment pinpointed in regions and communities where jobs are needed most;

Better mass transit in our cities and between cities;

And a whole new generation of American jobs to make homes and vehicles and buildings that will house us and move us in comfort—with a lot less energy.

This is important, too: I have no doubt that the ingenuity and dedication of the American people can make every single one of these things happen. We are talking about the United States of America—and those who count this country out as an economic superpower are going to find out just how wrong they are.

We are going to share in the exciting enterprise of making the 1980s a time of growth for America.

The Republican alternative is the biggest tax giveaway in history. They call it "Reagan-Kemp-Roth." I call it a free lunch Americans cannot afford.

The Republican tax program offers rebates to the rich, deprivation for the poor and fierce inflation for all of us. Their party's own vice presidential nominee said that "Reagan-Kemp-Roth" would result in an inflation rate of more than

30 percent. He called it "voodoo economics." He suddenly changed his mind toward the end of the Republican convention, but he was right the first time.

Along with this gigantic tax cut, the new Republican leaders promise to protect retirement and health programs, and to have massive increases in defense spending.

And they claim they can balance the budget.

If they are serious about these promises—and they say they are—then a close analysis shows that the entire rest of the government would have to abolish—everything from education to farm programs, from the G.I. Bill to the night watchman at the Lincoln Memorial. And the budget would still be in the red.

The only alternative would be to build more printing presses to print cheap money. Either way the American people lose. But the American people will not stand for it.

The Democratic Party has always embodied the hope of our people for justice, opportunity and a better life. And we've worked in every way possible to strengthen the American family, to encourage self-reliance, and to follow the Old Testament admonition: "Defend the poor and fatherless: give justice to the afflicted and needy." (Psalms 82:3)

We have struggled to assure that no child in America ever goes to bed hungry, that no elderly couple in America has to live in a substandard home, and that no young person in America is excluded from college because his family is poor.

What have the Republicans proposed? Just an attack on everything we have done in the achievement in social justice and decency that we've won in the last 50 years—ever since Franklin Delano Roosevelt's first term. They would make Social Security voluntary. They would reverse our progress on the minimum wage, full employment laws, safety in the work place and a healthy environment.

Lately, as you know, the Republicans have been quoting Democratic presidents, but who can blame them? Would you rather quote Herbert Hoover or Franklin Delano Roosevelt? Would you rather quote Richard Nixon or John Fitzgerald Kennedy?

The Republicans have always been the party of privilege, but this year their leaders have gone even further. In their platform, they have repudiated the best traditions of their own party.

Where is the conscience of Lincoln in the party of Lincoln? What's become of that traditional Republican commitment to fiscal responsibility? What's happened to their commitment to a safe and sane arms control?

Now I don't claim perfection for the Democratic Party. I don't claim that every decision that we have made has been right or popular. Certainly they've not all been easy. But I will say this:

We've been tested under fire. We've neither ducked nor hidden. And we've tackled the great, central issues in our time, the historic challenges of peace and energy which had been ignored for years.

We've made tough decisions and we've taken the heat for them. We've made mistakes and we've learned from them. So we have built the foundation now for a better future.

We've done something clse—perhaps even more important. In good times and bad, in the valleys and on the peaks, we've told people the truth—the hard truth—the truth that sometimes hurts.

One truth that we Americans have learned is that our dream has been earned for progress and for peace. Look what our land has been through within our own memory—a great depression, a world war, the technological explosion, the civil rights revolution, the bitterness of Vietnam, the shame of Watergate, the twilight peace of nuclear terror.

Through each of these momentous experiences we've learned the hard way about the world and about ourselves. For we've matured and we've grown as a nation. And we've grown stronger.

We've learned the uses and the limitations of power. We've learned the beauty and responsibility of freedom. We've learned the value and the obligation of justice—and we have learned the necessity of peace.

Some would argue that to master these lessons is somehow to limit our potential. That is not so. A nation which knows its true strengths, which sees its true challenges, which understands legitimate constraints—that nation, our nation—is far stronger than one which takes refuge in wishful thinking or nostalgia.

The Democratic Party—the American people—have understood these fundamental truths.

All of us can sympathize with the desire for easy answers. There's often the temptation to substitute idle dreams for hard reality.

The new Republican leaders are hoping that our nation will succumb to that temptation this year. But they profoundly misunderstand and underestimate the character of the American people.

Three weeks after Pearl Harbor, Winston Churchill came to North America—and he said: "We've not journeyed all this way across the centuries, across the oceans, across the mountains, across the prairies because we are made of sugar candy."

We Americans have courage.

Americans have always been on the cutting edge of change. We've always looked forward with anticipation and confidence. I still want the same thing that all of you want—a self-reliant neighborhood and strong families: work for the able-bodied and good medical care for the sick, opportunity for our youth and dignity for our old, equal rights and justice for all people.

I want teachers eager to explain what a civilization really is—and I want students to understand their own needs and their own aims, but also the needs and yearnings of their neighbors. I want women free to pursue without limit the full life of what they want for themselves.

I want our farmers growing crops to feed our nation and the world, secure in the knowledge that the family farm will thrive and with a fair return on the good work they do for all of us. I want workers to see meaning in the labor they perform—and work enough to guarantee a job for every worker in this country.

And I want the people in business free to pursue with boldness and freedom new ideas. And I want minority citizens fully to join the mainstream of American life, and I want from the bottom of my heart to remove the blight of racial and other discrimination from the face of our nation, and I'm determined to do it.

I need for all of you to join me in fulfilling that vision. The choice—the choice between the two futures—could not be more clear. If we succumb to a dream world, then we'll wake up to a nightmare. But if we start with reality and fight to make our dreams a reality—then Americans will have a good life, a life of meaning and purpose in a nation that's strong and secure.

Above all, I want us to be what the founders of our nation meant us to become—the land of freedom, the land of peace, and the land of hope.

Thank you very much.

Presidential Debate
Cleveland, October 28, 1980

On October 28, 1980, television sets in more than 60 million American households were tuned to the second Carter-Reagan debate. It lasted 90 minutes. During this period, the debate attracted more than 100 million listeners, the largest political audience in American history.

Ms. RUTH HINERFELD, League of Women Voters Education Fund: Good evening, I'm Ruth Hinerfeld of the League of Women Voters Education Fund. Next Tuesday is Election Day. Before going to the polls, voters want to understand the issues and know the candidates' positions. Tonight, voters will have an opportunity to see and hear the major party candidates for the presidency state their views on issues that affect us all. The League of Women Voters is proud to present this Presidential Debate. Our moderator is Howard K. Smith.

MR. HOWARD K. SMITH, ABC News: Thank you, Mrs. Hinerfeld. The League of Women Voters is pleased to welcome to the Cleveland Ohio Convention Center Music Hall President Jimmy Carter, the Democratic Party's candidate for reelection to the presidency, and Governor Ronald Reagan of California, the Republican Party's candidate for the presidency. The candidates will debate questions on domestic, economic, foreign policy, and national security issues.

The questions are going to be posed by a panel of distinguished journalists who are here with me. They are: Marvin Stone, the editor of *U.S. News and World Report;* Harry Ellis, national correspondent of the *Christian Science Monitor;* William Hilliard, assistant managing editor of the *Portland Oregonian;* Barbara Walters, correspondent, ABC News.

The ground rules for this, as agreed by you gentlemen, are these: Each panelist down here will ask a question, the same question, to each of the two candidates. After the two candidates have answered, a panelist will ask follow-up questions to try to sharpen the answers. The candidates will then have an opportunity each to make a rebuttal. That will constitute the first half of the debate, and I will state the rules for the second half later on.

Some other rules: The candidates are not permitted to bring prepared notes to the podium, but are permitted to make notes during the debate. If the candidates exceed the allotted time agreed on, I will reluctantly but certainly interrupt. We ask the Convention Center audience here to abide by one ground rule. Please do not applaud or express approval or disapproval during the debate.

Now, based on a toss of the coin, Governor Reagan will respond to the first question from Marvin Stone.

MR. MARVIN STONE: Governor, as you're well aware, the question of war and peace has emerged as a central issue in this campaign in the give and take of recent weeks. President Carter has been criticized for responding late to aggressive Soviet impulses, for insufficient build-up of our armed forces, and a paralysis in dealing with Afghanistan and Iran. You have been criticized for being all too quick to advocate the use of lots of muscle—military action—to deal with foreign crises. Specifically, what are the differences between the two of you on the uses of American military power?

GOVERNOR REAGAN: I don't know what the differences might be, because I don't know what Mr. Carter's policies are. I do know what he has said about mine. And I'm only here to tell you that I believe with all my heart that our first priority must be world peace, and that use of force is always and only a last resort, when everything else has failed, and then only with regard to our national security.

Now, I believe, also, that this meeting . . . this mission, this responsibility for preserving the peace, I believe, is a responsibility peculiar to our country, and that we cannot shirk our responsibility as a leader of the Free World because we're the only ones that can do it. Therefore, the burden of maintaining the peace falls on us. And to maintain that peace requires strength. America has never gotten in a war because we were too strong. We can get into a war by letting events get out of hand, as they have in the last three and a half years under the foreign policies of this Administration of Mr. Carter's, (sic) until we're faced each time with a crisis. And good management in preserving the peace requires that we control the events and try to intercept before they become a crisis.

I have seen four wars in my lifetime. I'm a father of sons, I have a grandson. I don't ever want to see another generation of young Americans bleed their lives into sandy beachheads in the Pacific, or rice paddies and jungles in the . . . in Asia or the muddy battlefields of Europe.

MR. SMITH: Mr. Stone, do you have a follow-up question for the Governor?

MR. STONE: Yes. Governor, we've been hearing that the defense build-up that you would associate yourself with would cost tens of billions of dollars more than is now contemplated. Assuming that the American people are ready to bear this cost, they nevertheless keep asking the following question: How do you reconcile huge increases in military outlays with your promise of substantial tax cuts and of balancing the budget, which in this fiscal year, the one that just ended, ran more than $60 billion in the red?

GOVERNOR REAGAN: Mr. Stone, I have submitted an economic plan that I have worked out in concert with a number of fine economists in this country, all of whom approve it, and believe that over a five-year projection, this plan can permit the extra spending for needed refurbishing of our defensive posture, that it can provide for a balanced budget by 1983 if not earlier, and that we can afford—along with the cuts that I have proposed in government spending—we can afford the tax cuts I have proposed and probably mainly because Mr. Carter's economic policy has built into the next five years, and on beyond that, a tax increase that will be taking $86 billion more out of the people's pockets than was taken this year. And my tax cut does not come close to eliminating that $86 billion increase. I'm only reducing the amount of the increase. In other words, what I'm talking about is not putting government back to getting less money than government's been getting, but simply cutting the increase in . . . in spending.

MR. SMITH: The same question now goes to President Carter. President Carter, would you like to have the question repeated?

MR. STONE: Yes, President Carter, the question of war and peace, a central issue in the campaign. You've been criticized for, in the give and take, for responding late to aggressive Soviet impulses, for an insufficient build-up of our armed forces, and a paralysis in dealing with Afghanistan and Iran. Governor Reagan, on the other hand, has been criticized for being all too quick to advocate the use of lots of muscle—military action—to deal with foreign crises such as I have mentioned. Specifically, what are the differences between the two of you on the uses of American military power?

PRESIDENT CARTER: Mr. Stone, I've had to make thousands of decisions since I've been president, serving in the Oval Office. And with each one of those decisions that affect the future of my country, I have learned in the process. I think I'm a much wiser and more experienced man than I was when I debated four years ago against President Ford. I've also learned that there are no simple answers to complicated questions. H.L. Mencken said that for every problem there's a simple answer. It would be neat and plausible and wrong.

The fact is that this nation, in the eight years before I became president, had its own military strength decreased. Seven out of eight years, the budget commitments for defense went down, 37 percent in all. Since I've been in office, we've had a steady, carefully planned, methodical but very effective increase in our commitment for defense.

But what we've done is use that enormous power and prestige and military strength of the United States to preserve the peace. We've not only kept peace for our own country, but we've been able to extend the benefits of peace to others. In the Middle East, we've worked for a peace treaty between Israel and Egypt, successfully, and have tied ourselves together with Israel and Egypt in a common defense capability. This is a very good step forward for our nation's security, and we'll continue to do as we have done in the past.

I might also add that there are decisions that are made in the Oval Office by every president which are profound in nature. There are always trouble spots in the world, and how those troubled areas are addressed by a president alone in that Oval Office affects our nation directly, the involvement of the United States and also our American interests. That is a basic decision that has to be made so frequently, by every president who serves. That is what I have tried to do successfully by keeping our country at peace.

MR. SMITH: Mr. Stone, do you have a follow-up for . . .

MR. STONE: Yes. I would like to be a little more specific on the use of military power, and let's talk about one area for a moment. Under what circumstances would you use military forces to deal with, for example, a shut-off of the Persian Oil Gulf, if that should occur, or to counter Russian expansion beyond Afghanistan into either Iran or Pakistan? I ask this question in view of charges that we are woefully unprepared to project sustained—and I emphasize the word sustained—power in that part of the world.

PRESIDENT CARTER: Mr. Stone, in my State of the Union address earlier this year, I pointed out that any threat to the stability or security of the Persian Gulf would be a threat to the security of our own country. In the past, we have not had an adequate military presence in that region. Now we have two major carrier task forces. We have access to facilities in five different areas of that region. And we've made it clear that working with our allies and others, that we are prepared to address any foreseeable eventuality which might interrupt commerce with that crucial area of the world.

But in doing his, we have made sure that we address this question peacefully, not injecting American military forces into combat, but letting the strength of our nation be felt in a beneficial way. This, I believe, has assured that our interests will be protected in the Persian Gulf region, as we have done in the Middle East and throughout the world.

MR. SMITH: Governor Reagan, you have a minute to comment or rebut.

GOVERNOR REAGAN: Well yes, I question the figure about the decline in defense spending under the two previous Administrations in the preceding eight years to this Administration. I would call to your attention that we were in a war that wound down during those eight years, which of course made a change in military spending because of turning from war to peace. I also would like to point out that Republican presidents in those years, faced with a Democratic majority in both houses of the Congress, found that their requests for defense budgets were very often cut.

Now, Gerald Ford left a five-year projected plan for a military build-up to restore our defenses, and President Carter's Administration reduced that by 38 percent, cut 60 ships out of the Navy building program that had been proposed, and stopped the . . . the B-1, delayed the Cruise missile, stopped the production line for the Minuteman missile, stopped the Trident or delayed the Trident submarine, and now is planning a mobile military force that can be delivered to various spots in the world, which does make me question his assaults on whether I am the one who is quick to look for use of force.

MR. SMITH: President Carter, you have the last word on this question.

PRESIDENT CARTER: Well, there are various elements of defense. One is to control nuclear weapons, which I hope we'll get to later on because that is the most important single issue in this campaign. Another one is how to address troubled areas of the world. I think, habitually, Governor Reagan has advocated the injection of military forces into troubled areas, when I and my predecessors— both Democrats and Republicans—have advocated resolving those troubles and those difficult areas of the world peacefully, diplomatically, and through negotiation. In addition to that, the build-up of military forces is good for our country because we've got to have military strength to preserve the peace. But I'll always remember that the best weapons are the ones that are never fired in combat, and the best soldier is one who never has to lay his life down on the field of battle. Strength is imperative for peace, but the two must go hand in hand.

MR. SMITH: Thank you, gentlemen. The next question is from Harry Ellis to President Carter.

MR. HARRY ELLIS: Mr. President, when you were elected in 1976, the Consumer Price Index stood at 4.8 percent. It now stands at more than 12 percent. Perhaps more significantly, the nation's broader, underlying inflation rate has gone up from 7 percent to 9 percent. Now, a part of that was due to external factors beyond U.S. control, notably the more than doubling of oil prices by OPEC last year. Because the United States remains vulnerable to such external shocks, can inflation in fact be controlled? If so, what measures would you pursue in a second term?

PRESIDENT CARTER: Again it's important to put the situation in perspective. In 1974, we had a so-called oil shock, wherein the price of OPEC oil was raised to an extraordinary degree. We had an even worse oil shock in 1979. In 1974, we had the worst recession, the deepest and most penetrating recession since the Second World War. The recession that resulted this time was the briefest since the Second World War.

In addition, we've brought down inflation. Earlier this year, in the first quarter, we did have a very severe inflation pressure brought about by the OPEC price increase. It averaged about 18 percent in the first quarter of this year. In the second quarter, we had dropped it down to about 13 percent. The most recent figures, the last three months, on the third quarter of this year, the inflation rate is 7 percent—still too high, but it illustrates very vividly that in addition to providing an enormous number of jobs—nine million new jobs in the last three and a half years—that the inflationary threat is still urgent on us.

I notice that Governor Reagan recently mentioned the Reagan-Kemp-Roth proposal, which his own running mate, George Bush, described as voodoo economics, and said that it would result in a 30 percent inflation rate. And *Business Week,* which is not a Democratic publication, said that this Reagan-Kemp-Roth proposal—and I quote them, I think—was completely irresponsible and would result in inflationary pressures which would destroy this nation.

So our proposals are very sound and very carefully considered to stimulate jobs, to improve the industrial complex of this country, to create tools for American workers, and at the same time would be anti-inflationary in nature. So to add nine million new jobs, to control inflation, and to plan for the future with an energy policy now intact as a foundation is our plan for the years ahead.

MR. SMITH: Mr. Ellis, do you have a follow-up question for Mr. Carter?

MR. ELLIS: Yes. Mr. President, you have mentioned the creation of nine million new jobs. At the same time, the unemployment rate still hangs high, as does the inflation rate. Now, I wonder, can you tell us what additional policies you would pursue in a second administration in order to try to bring down that inflation rate? And would it be an act of leadership to tell the American people they are going to have to sacrifice to adopt a leaner life-style for some time to come?

PRESIDENT CARTER: Yes. We have demanded that the American people sacrifice, and they have done very well. As a matter of fact, we're importing today about one-third less oil from overseas than we did just a year ago. We've had a 25 percent reduction since the first year I was in office. At the same time, as I have said earlier, we have added about nine million net new jobs in that period of time—a record never before achieved.

Also, the new energy policy has been predicated on two factors: one is conservation, which requires sacrifice, and the other one, increase in production of American energy, which is going along very well—more coal this year than ever before in American history, more oil and gas wells drilled this year than ever before in history.

The new economic revitalization program that we have in mind, which will be implemented next year, would result in tax credits which would let business invest in new tools and new factories to create even more new jobs—about one million in the next two years. And we also have planned a youth employment program which would encompass 600,000 jobs for young people. This has already passed the House, and it has an excellent prospect to pass the Senate.

MR. SMITH: Now, the same question goes to Governor Reagan. Governor Reagan, would you like to have the question repeated?

MR. ELLIS: Governor Reagan, during the past four years, the Consumer Price Index has risen from 4.8 percent to currently over 12 percent. And perhaps more significantly, the nation's broader, underlying rate of inflation has gone up from 7 percent to 9 percent. Now, a part of that has been due to external factors beyond U.S. control, and notably, the more than doubling of OPEC oil prices last year, which leads me to ask you whether, since the United States remains vulnerable to such external shocks, can inflation in fact be controlled? If so, specifically what measures would you pursue?

GOVERNOR REAGAN: Mr. Ellis, I think this idea that has been spawned here in our country, that inflation somehow came upon us like a plague and therefore it's uncontrollable and no one can do anything about it, is entirely spurious and it's dangerous to say this to the people. When Mr. Carter became president, inflation was 4.8 percent, as you said. It had been cut in two by President Gerald Ford. It is now running at 12.7 percent.

President Carter also has spoken of the new jobs created. Well, we always, with the normal growth in our country and increase in population, increase the number of jobs. But that can't hide the fact that there are eight million men and women out of work in America today, and two million of those lost their jobs in just the last few months. Mr. Carter had also promised that he would not use unemployment as a tool to fight against inflation. And yet, his 1980 economic message stated that we would reduce productivity and gross national product and increase unemployment in order to get a handle on inflation, because in January, at the beginning of the year, it was more than 18 percent. Since then, he has blamed the people for inflation, OPEC, he has blamed the Federal Reserve system, he has blamed the lack of productivity of the American people, he has then accused the people of living too well and that we must share in scarcity, we must sacrifice and get used to doing with less. We don't have inflation because the people are living too well. We have inflation because the government is living too well. And the last statement, just a few days ago, was a speech to the effect that we have inflation because government revenues have not kept pace with government spending.

I see my time is running out here. I'll have to get this out very fast. Yes, you can lick inflation by increasing productivity and decreasing the cost of government to the place that we have balanced budgets, and are no longer grinding out printing press money, flooding the market with it because the government is spending more than it takes in. And my economic plan calls for that. The President's economic plan calls for increasing taxes to the point that we finally take so much money away from the people that we can balance the budget in that way. But we will have a very poor nation and a very unsound economy if we follow that path.

MR. ELLIS: Yes. You have centered on cutting government spending in what you have just said about your own policies. You have also said that you would increase defense spending. Specifically, where would you cut government spending if you were to increase defense spending and also cut taxes, so that, presumably, federal revenues would shrink?

GOVERNOR REAGAN: Well, most people, when they think about cutting government spending, they think in terms of eliminating necessary programs or wiping out something, some services that government is supposed to perform. I believe that there is enough extravagance and fat in government. As a matter of fact, one of the secretaries of HEW under Mr. Carter testified that he thought there was $7 billion worth of fraud and waste in welfare and in the medical programs associated with it. We've had the General Accounting Office estimate that there are probably tens of billions of dollars that are lost in fraud alone, and they have added that waste adds even more to that.

We have a program for gradual reduction of government spending based on these theories, and I have a task force now that has been working on where those cuts could be made. I'm confident that it can be done and that it will reduce inflation because I did it in California. And inflation went down below the national average in California when we returned the money to the people and reduced government spending.

MR. SMITH: President Carter.

PRESIDENT CARTER: Governor Reagan's proposal, the Reagan-Kemp-Roth proposal, is one of the most highly inflationary ideas that ever has been presented to the American public. He would actually have to cut government spending by at least $130 billion in order to balance the budget under this ridiculous proposal. I notice that his task force that is working for his future plans had some of their ideas revealed in the *Wall Street Journal* this week. One of those ideas was to repeal the minimum wage, and several times this year, Governor Reagan has said that the major cause of unemployment is the minimum wage. This is a heartless kind of approach to the working families of our country, which is typical of many Republican leaders of the past, but I think has been accentuated under Governor Reagan.

In California—I'm surprised Governor Reagan brought this up—he had the three largest tax increases in the history of that state under his administration. He more than doubled state spending while he was governor—122 percent increase—and had between a 20 percent and 30 percent increase in the number of employees . . .

MR. SMITH: Sorry to interrupt, Mr. Carter.

PRESIDENT CARTER: . . . in California. Thank you, sir.

MR. SMITH: Governor Reagan has the last word on this question.

GOVERNOR REAGAN: Yes. The figures that the President has just used about California is a distortion of the situation there, because while I was Governor of California, our spending in California increased less per capita than the spending in Georgia while Mr. Carter was Governor of Georgia in the same four years. The size of government increased only one sixth in California of what it increased in proportion to the population in Georgia.

And the idea that my tax-cut proposal is inflationary: I would like to ask the President why is it inflationary to let the people keep more of their money and spend it the way that they like, and it isn't inflationary to let him take that money and spend it the way he wants?

MR. SMITH: I wish that question need not be rhetorical, but it must be because we've run out of time on that. Now, the third question to Governor Reagan from William Hilliard.

MR. WILLIAM HILLIARD: Yes, Governor Reagan, the decline of our cities has been hastened by the continual rise in crime, strained race relations, the fall in the quality of public education, persistence of abnormal poverty in a rich nation, and a decline in the services to the public. The signs seem to point toward a deterioration that could lead to the establishment of a permanent underclass in the cities. What, specifically, would you do in the next four years to reverse this trend?

GOVERNOR REAGAN: I have been talking to a number of Congressmen who have much the same idea that I have, and that is that in the inner city areas, that in cooperation with the local government and with national government, and using tax incentives and with cooperating with the private sector, that we have development zones. Let the local entity, the city, declare this particular area, based on the standards of the percentage of people on welfare, unemployed, and so forth, in that area. And then, through tax incentives, induce the creation of businesses providing jobs and so forth in those areas. The elements of government through these tax incentives . . . . For example, a business that would not have, for a period of time, an increase in the property tax reflecting its development of the unused property that it was making wouldn't be any loss to the city because the city isn't getting any tax from that now. And there would simply be a delay, and on the other hand, many of the people who wouldn't be given jobs are presently wards of the government, and it wouldn't hurt to give them a tax incentive, because they . . . that wouldn't be costing government anything either.

I think there are things to do in this regard. I stood in the South Bronx on the exact spot that President Carter stood on in 1977. You have to see it to believe it. It looks like a bombed-out city—great, gaunt skeletons of buildings, windows smashed out, painted on one of them "Unkept promise," on another, "Despair." And this was the spot at which President Carter had promised that he was going to bring in a vast program to rebuild this department. There are whole . . . or this area . . . there are whole blocks of land that are left bare, just bulldozed down flat. And nothing has been done, and they are now charging to take tourists there to see this terrible desolation. I talked to a man just briefly there who asked me one simple question: "Do I have reason to hope that I can someday take care of my family again? Nothing has been done."

MR. SMITH: Follow-up, Mr. Hilliard?

MR. HILLIARD: Yes, Governor Reagan. Blacks and other non-whites are increasing in numbers in our cities. Many of them feel that they are facing a hostility from whites that prevents them from joining the economic mainstream of our society. There is racial confrontation in the schools, on jobs, and in housing, as non-whites seek to reap the benefits of a free society. What do you think is the nation's future as a multi-racial society?

GOVERNOR REAGAN: I believe in it. I am eternally optimistic, and I happen to believe that we've made great progress from the days when I was young and when this country didn't even know it had a racial problem. I know those things can grow out of despair in an inner city, when there's hopelessness at home, lack of work, and so forth. But I believe that all of us together, and I believe the presidency is what Teddy Roosevelt said it was. It's a bully pulpit. And I think that something can be done from there, because a goal for all of us should be that one day things will be done neither because of nor in spite of any of the differences between us—ethnic differences or racial differences, whatever they may be—that we will have total equal opportunity for all people. And I would do everything I could in my power to bring that about.

MR. SMITH: Mr. Hilliard, would you repeat your question for President Carter?

MR. HILLIARD: President Carter, the decline of our cities has been hastened by the continual rise in crime, strained race relations, the fall in the quality of public education, persistence of abnormal poverty in a rich nation, and a decline in services to the public. The signs seem to point toward a deterioration that could lead to the establishment of a permanent underclass in the cities. What, specifically, would you do in the next four years to reverse this trend?

PRESIDENT CARTER: Thank you, Mr. Hilliard. When I was campaigning in 1976, everywhere I went, the mayors and local officials were in despair about the rapidly deteriorating central cities of our nation. We initiated a very fine urban renewal program, working with the mayors, the governors, and other interested officials. This has been a very successful effort. That's one of the main reasons that we've had such an increase in the number of people employed. Of the nine million people put to work in new jobs since I've been in office, 1.3 million of those has been among black Americans, and another million among those who speak Spanish.

We now are planning to continue the revitalization program with increased commitments of rapid transit, mass transit. Under the windfall profits tax, we expect to spend about $43 billion in the next ten years to rebuild the transportation systems of our country. We also are pursuing housing programs. We've had a 73 percent increase in the allotment of federal funds for improved education. These are the kinds of efforts worked on a joint basis with community leaders, particularly in the minority areas of the central cities that have been deteriorating so rapidly in the past.

It's very important to us that this be done with the full involvement of minority citizens. I have brought into the top level, top levels of government, into the White House, into administrative offices of the Executive branch, into the judicial system, highly qualified black and Spanish citizens and women who in the past had been excluded.

I noticed that Governor Reagan said that when he was a young man that there was no knowledge of a racial problem in this country. Those who suffered from discrimination because of race or sex certainly knew we had a racial problem. We have gone a long way toward correcting these problems, but we still have a long way to go.

MR. SMITH: Follow-up question?

MR. HILLIARD: Yes. President Carter, I would like to repeat the same follow-up to you. Blacks and other non-whites are increasing in numbers in our cities. Many of them feel that they are facing a hostility from whites that prevents them from joining the economic mainstream of our society. There is racial confrontation in the schools, on jobs, and in housing, as non-whites seek to reap the benefits of a free society. What is your assessment of the nation's future as a multi-racial society?

PRESIDENT CARTER: Ours is a nation of refugees, a nation of immigrants. Almost all of our citizens came here from other lands and now have hopes, which are being realized, for a better life, preserving their ethnic commitments, their family structures, their religious beliefs, preserving their relationships with their relatives in foreign countries, but still holding themselves together in a very coherent society, which gives our nation its strength.

In the past, those minority groups have often been excluded from participation in the affairs of government. Since I've been president, I've appointed, for instance, more than twice as many black federal judges as all previous presidents in the history of this country. I've done the same thing in the appointment of women, and also Spanish-speaking Americans. To involve them in the administration of government and the feeling that they belong to the societal structure that makes decisions in the judiciary and in the executive branch is a very important commitment which I am trying to realize and will continue to do so in the future.

MR. SMITH: Governor Reagan, you have a minute for rebuttal.

GOVERNOR REAGAN: Yes. The President talks of government programs, and they have their place. But as governor, when I was at the end of the line and receiving some of these grants for government programs, I saw that so many of them were dead-end. They were public employment for these people who really want to get out into the private job market where there are jobs with a future.

Now, the President spoke a moment ago about . . . that I was against the minimum wage. I wish he could have been with me when I sat with a group of teenagers who were black, and who were telling me about their unemployment problems, and that it was the minimum wage that had done away with the jobs that they once could get. And indeed, every time it has increased you will find there is an increase in minority unemployment among young people. And therefore, I have been in favor of a separate minimum for them.

With regard to the great progress that has been made with this government spending, the rate of black unemployment in Detroit, Michigan, is 56 percent.

MR. SMITH: President Carter, you have the last word on this question.

PRESIDENT CARTER: It's obvious that we still have a long way to go in fully incorporating the minority groups into the mainstream of American life. We have made good progress, and there is no doubt in my mind that the commitment to unemployment compensation, the minimum wage, welfare, national health insurance, those kinds of commitments that have typified the Democratic party since ancient history in this country's political life are a very important element of the future. In all those elements, Governor Reagan has repeatedly spoken out against them, which, to me, shows a very great insensitivity to giving deprived families a better chance in life. This, to me, is a very important difference between him and me in this election, and I believe the American people will judge accordingly.

There is no doubt in my mind that in the downtown central cities, with the, with the new commitment on an energy policy, with a chance to revitalize homes and to make them more fuel efficient, with a chance for our synthetic fuels program, solar power, this will give us an additional opportunity for jobs which will pay rich dividends.

MR. SMITH: Now, a question from Barbara Walters.

MS. WALTERS: Mr. President, the eyes of the country tonight are on the hostages in Iran. I realize this is a sensitive area, but the question of how we respond to acts of terrorism goes beyond this current crisis. Other countries have policies that determine how they will respond. Israel, for example, considers hostages like soldiers and will not negotiate with terrorists. For the future, Mr. President, the country has a right to know, do you have a policy for dealing with terrorism wherever it might happen, and, what have we learned from this experience in Iran that might cause us to do things differently if this, or something similar, happens again?

PRESIDENT CARTER: Barbara, one of the blights on this world is the threat and the activities of terrorists. At one of the recent economic summit conferences between myself and the other leaders of the Western world, we committed ourselves to take strong action against terrorism. Airplane hijacking was one of the elements of that commitment. There is no doubt that we have seen in recent years—in recent months—additional acts of violence against Jews in France and, of course, against those who live in Israel, by the PLO and other terrorist organizations.

Ultimately, the most serious terrorist threat is if one of those radical nations, who believe in terrorism as a policy, should have atomic weapons. Both I and all my predecessors have had a deep commitment to controlling the proliferation of nuclear weapons. In countries like Libya, or Iraq, we have even alienated some of our closest trade partners because we have insisted upon the control of the spread of nuclear weapons to those potentially terrorist countries.

When Governor Reagan has been asked about that, he makes the very disturbing comment that non-proliferation, or the control of the spread of nuclear weapons, is none of our business. And recently when he was asked specifically about Iraq, he said there is nothing we can do about it.

This ultimate terrorist threat is the most fearsome of all, and it's part of a pattern where our country must stand firm to control terrorism of all kinds.

MR. SMITH: Ms. Walters, a follow up?

Ms. WALTERS: While we are discussing policy, had Iran not taken American hostages, I assume that, in order to preserve our neutrality, we would have stopped the flow of spare parts and vital war materials once war broke out between Iraq and Iran. Now we're offering to lift the ban on such goods if they let our people come home. Doesn't this reward terrorism, compromise our neutrality, and possibly antagonize nations now friendly to us in the Middle East?

PRESIDENT CARTER: We will maintain our position of neutrality in the Iran and Iraq war. We have no plans to sell additional materiel or goods to Iran, that might be of a warlike nature. When I made my decision to stop all trade with Iran as a result of the taking of our hostages, I announced then, and have consistently maintained since then, that if the hostages are released safely, we would make delivery on those items which Iran owns—which they have bought and paid for—also, that the frozen Iranian assets would be released. That's been a consistent policy, one I intend to carry out.

MR. SMITH: Would you repeat the question now for Governor Reagan, please, Ms. Walters?

Ms. WALTERS: Yes. Governor, the eyes of the country tonight remain on the hostages in Iran, but the question of how we respond to acts of terrorism goes beyond this current crisis. There are other countries that have policies that determine how they will respond. Israel, for example, considers hostages like soldiers and will not negotiate with terrorists.

For the future, the country has the right to know, do you have a policy for dealing with terrorism wherever it might happen, and what have we learned from this experience in Iran that might cause us to do things differently if this, or something similar, should happen again?

GOVERNOR REAGAN: Barbara, you've asked that question twice. I think you ought to have at least one answer to it. I have been accused lately of having a secret plan with regard to the hostages. Now, this comes from an answer that I've made at least 50 times during this campaign to the press, when I am asked have you any ideas of what you would do if you were there? And I said, well, yes. And I think that anyone that's seeking this position, as well as other people, probably, have thought to themselves, what about this, what about that? These are just ideas of what I would think of if I were in that position and had access to the information, and which I would know all the options that were open to me.

I have never answered the question, however, second; the one that says, well, tell me, what are some of those ideas? First of all, I would be fearful that I might say something that was presently under way or in negotiations, and thus expose it and endanger the hostages, and sometimes, I think some of my ideas might require quiet diplomacy where you don't say in advance, or say to anyone, what it is you're thinking of doing.

Your question is difficult to answer, because, in the situation right now, no one wants to say anything that would inadvertently delay, in any way, the return of those hostages if there . . . if there is a chance that they're coming soon, or that (it) might cause them harm. What I do think should be done, once they are safely here with their families, and that tragedy is over—we've endured this humiliation for just lacking one week of a year now—then, I think, it is time for us to have a complete investigation as to the diplomatic efforts that were made in the beginning, why they have been there so long, and when they come home, what did we have to do in order to bring that about—what arrangements were made? And I would suggest that Congress should hold such an investigation. In the meantime, I'm going to continue praying that they'll come home.

MR. SMITH: Follow-up question.

MS. WALTERS: I would like to say that neither candidate answered specifically the question of a specific policy for dealing with terrorism, but I will ask Governor Reagan a different follow-up question. You have suggested that there would be no Iranian crisis had you been president, because we would have given firmer support to the Shah. But Iran is a country of 37 million people who were resisting a government that they regarded as dictatorial.

My question is not whether the Shah's regime was preferable to the Ayatollah's, but whether the United States has the power or the right to try to determine what form of government any country will have, and do we back unpopular regimes whose major merit is that they are friendly to the United States?

GOVERNOR REAGAN: The degree of unpopularity of a regime when the choice is total authoritarianism . . . totalitarianism, I should say, in the alternative government . . . makes one wonder whether you are being helpful to the people. And we've been guilty of that. Because someone didn't meet exactly our standards of human rights, even though they were an ally of ours, instead of trying patiently to persuade them to change their ways, we have, in a number of instances, aided a revolutionary overthrow which results in complete totalitarianism, instead, for those people. I think that this is a kind of a hypocritical policy when, at the same time, we're maintaining a detente with the one nation in the world where there are no human rights at all—the Soviet Union.

Now, there was a second phase in the Iranian affair in which we had something to do with that. And that was, we had adequate warning that there was a threat to our embassy, and we could have done what other embassies did—either strengthen our security there, or remove our personnel before the kidnap and the takeover took place.

MR. SMITH: Governor, I'm sorry, I must interrupt. President Carter, you have a minute for rebuttal.

PRESIDENT CARTER: I didn't hear any comment from Governor Reagan about what he would do to stop or reduce terrorism in the future. What the Western allies did decide to do is to stop all air flights—commercial air flights—to any nation involved in terrorism or the hijacking of airplanes, or the harboring of hijackers. Secondly, we all committed ourselves, as have all my predecessors in the Oval Office, not to permit the spread of nuclear weapons to a terrorist nation, or to any other nation that does not presently have those weapons or capabilities for explosives. Third, not to make any sales of materiel or weapons to a nation which is involved in terrorist activities. And, lastly, not to deal with the PLO until and unless the PLO recognizes Israel's right to exist and recognizes U.N. Resolution 242 as a basis for Middle East peace.

These are a few of the things to which our nation is committed, and we will continue with these commitments.

MR. SMITH: Governor Reagan, you have the last word on that question.

GOVERNOR REAGAN: Yes, I have no quarrel whatsoever with the things that have been done, because I believe it is high time that the civilized countries of the world made it plain that there is no room worldwide for terrorism; there will be no negotiation with terrorists of any kind. And while I have a last word here, I would like to correct a misstatement of fact by the President. I have never made the statement that he suggested about nuclear proliferation and nuclear proliferation, or the trying to halt it, would be a major part of a foreign policy of mine.

MR. SMITH: Thank you, gentlemen. That is the first half of the debate. Now, the rules for the second half are quite simple. They're only complicated when I explain them. In the second half, the panelists with me will have no follow-up questions. Instead, after the panelists have asked a question, and the candidates have answered, each of the candidates will have two opportunities to follow up, to question, to rebut, or just to comment on his opponent's statement.

Governor Reagan will respond, in this section, to the first question from Marvin Stone.

MR. STONE: Governor Reagan—arms control: The President said it was the single most important issue. Both of you have expressed the desire to end the nuclear arms race with Russia, but by methods that are vastly different. You suggest that we scrap the Salt II treaty already negotiated, and intensify the build-up of American power to induce the Soviets to sign a new treaty—one more favorable to us. President Carter, on the other hand, says he will again try to convince a reluctant Congress to ratify the present treaty on the grounds it's the best we can hope to get.

Now, both of you cannot be right. Will you tell us why you think you are?

GOVERNOR REAGAN: Yes. I think I'm right because I believe that we must have a consistent foreign policy, a strong America, and a strong economy. And then, as we build up our national security, to restore our margin of safety, we at the same time try to restrain the Soviet build-up, which has been going forward at a rapid pace, and for quite some time.

The Salt II treaty was the result of negotiations that Mr. Carter's team entered into after he had asked the Soviet Union for a discussion of actual reduction of nuclear strategic weapons. And his emissary, I think, came home in 12 hours having heard a very definite nyet. But taking that one no from the Soviet Union, we then went back into negotiations on their terms, because Mr. Carter had cancelled the B-1 bomber, delayed the MX, delayed the Trident submarine, delayed the Cruise missile, shut down the Missile Man—the three—the Minute Man missile production line, and whatever other things that might have been done. The Soviet Union sat at the table knowing that we had gone forward with unilateral concessions without any reciprocation from them whatsoever.

Now, I have not blocked the Salt II treaty, as Mr. Carter and Mr. Mondale suggest that I have. It has been blocked by a Senate in which there is a Democratic majority. Indeed, the Senate Armed Services Committee voted 10 to 0, with seven abstentions, against the Salt II treaty, and declared that it was not in the national security interests of the United States. Besides which, it is illegal, because the law of the land, passed by Congress, says that we cannot accept a treaty in which we are not equal. And we are not equal in this treaty for one reason alone—our B-52 bombers are considered to be strategic weapons; their Backfire bombers are not.

MR. SMITH: Governor, I have to interrupt you at that point. The time is up for that. But the same question now to President Carter.

MR. STONE: Yes. President Carter, both of you have expressed the desire to end the nuclear arms race with Russia, but through vastly different methods. The Governor suggests we scrap the Salt II treaty which you negotiated in Vienna . . . or signed in Vienna, intensify the build-up of American power to induce the Soviets to sign a new treaty, one more favorable to us. You, on the other hand, say you will again try to convince a reluctant Congress to ratify the present treaty on the grounds it is the best we can hope to get from the Russians.

You cannot both be right. Will you tell us why you think you are?

PRESIDENT CARTER: Yes, I'd be glad to. Inflation, unemployment, the cities are all very important issues, but they pale into insignificance in the life and duties of a president when compared with the control of nuclear weapons. Every president who has served in the Oval Office since Harry Truman has been dedicated to the proposition of controlling nuclear weapons.

To negotiate with the Soviet Union a balanced, controlled, observable, and then reducing levels of atomic weaponry, there is a disturbing pattern in the attitude of Governor Reagan. He has never supported any of those arms control agreements—the limited test ban, Salt I, nor the Antiballistic Missile Treaty, nor the Vladivostok Treaty negotiated with the Soviet Union by President Ford—and now he wants to throw into the wastebasket a treaty to control nuclear weapons on a balanced and equal basis between ourselves and the Soviet Union, negotiated over a seven-year period, by myself and my two Republican predecessors.

The Senate has not voted yet on the Strategic Arms Limitation Treaty. There have been preliminary skirmishings in the committees of the Senate, but the Treaty has never come to the floor of the Senate for either a debate or a vote. It's understandable that a senator in the preliminary debates can make an irresponsible statement, or maybe, an ill-advised statement. You've got 99 other senators to correct that mistake, if it is a mistake. But when a man who hopes to be president says, take this treaty, discard it, do not vote, do not debate, do not explore the issues, do not finally capitalize on this long negotiation—that is a very dangerous and disturbing thing.

MR. SMITH: Governor Reagan, you have an opportunity to rebut that.

GOVERNOR REAGAN: Yes, I'd like to respond very much. First of all, the Soviet Union . . . if I have been critical of some of the previous agreements, it's because we've been out-negotiated for quite a long time. And they have managed, in spite of all of our attempts at arms limitation, to go forward with the biggest military build-up in the history of man.

Now, to suggest that because two Republican presidents tried to pass the Salt treaty—that puts them on its side—I would like to say that President Ford, who was within 90 percent of a treaty that we could be in agreement with when he left office, is emphatically against this Salt treaty. I would like to point out also that senators like Henry Jackson and Hollings of South Carolina—they are taking the lead in the fight against this particular treaty.

I am not talking of scrapping. I am talking of taking the treaty back, and going back into negotiations. And I would say to the Soviet Union, we will sit and negotiate with you as long as it takes, to have not only legitimate arms limitation, but to have a reduction of these nuclear weapons to the point that neither one of us represents a threat to the other. That is hardly throwing away a treaty and being opposed to arms limitation.

MR. SMITH: President Carter?

PRESIDENT CARTER: Yes. Governor Reagan is making some very misleading and disturbing statements. He not only advocates the scrapping of this treaty— and I don't know that these men that he quotes are against the treaty in its final form—but he also advocates the possibility, he said it's been a missing element, of playing a trump card against the Soviet Union of a nuclear arms race, and is insisting upon nuclear superiority by our own nation, as a predication for negotiation in the future with the Soviet Union.

If President Brezhnev said, we will scrap this treaty, negotiated under three American presidents over a seven-year period of time, we insist upon nuclear superiority as a basis for future negotiations, and we believe that the launching of a nuclear arms race is a good basis for future negotiations, it's obvious that I, as president, and all Americans, would reject such a proposition. This would mean the resumption of a very dangerous nuclear arms race. It would be very disturbing to American people. It would change the basic tone and commitment that our nation has experienced ever since the Second World War, with all presidents, Democratic and Republican. And it would also be very disturbing to our allies, all of whom support this nuclear arms treaty. In addition to that, the adversarial relationship between ourselves and the Soviet Union would undoubtedly deteriorate very rapidly.

This attitude is extremely dangerous and belligerent in its tone, although it's said with a quiet voice.

MR. SMITH: Governor Reagan?

GOVERNOR REAGAN: I know the President's supposed to be replying to me, but sometimes, I have a hard time in connecting what he's saying with what I have said or what my positions are. I sometimes think he's like the witch doctor that gets mad when a good doctor comes along with a cure that'll work.

My point I have made already, Mr. President, with regard to negotiating: it does not call for nuclear superiority on the part of the United States. It calls for a mutual reduction of these weapons, as I say, that neither of us can represent a threat to the other. And to suggest that the Salt II treaty that your negotiators negotiated was just a continuation, and based on all of the preceding efforts by two previous presidents, is just not true. It was a new negotiation because, as I say, President Ford was within about 10 percent of having a solution that could be acceptable. And I think our allies would be very happy to go along with a fair and verifiable Salt agreement.

MR. SMITH: President Carter, you have the last word on this question.

PRESIDENT CARTER: I think, to close out this discussion, it would be better to put into perspective what we're talking about. I had a discussion with my daughter, Amy, the other day, before I came here, to ask her what the most important issue was. She said she thought nuclear weaponry—and the control of nuclear arms.

This is a formidable force. Some of these weapons have ten megatons of explosion. If you put 50 tons of TNT in each one of railroad cars, you would have a carload of TNT—a trainload of TNT stretching across this nation. That's one major war explosion in a warhead. We have thousands, equivalent of megaton, or million tons, of TNT warheads. The control of these weapons is the single major responsibility of a president, and to cast out this commitment of all presidents, because of some slight technicalities that can be corrected, is a very dangerous approach.

MR. SMITH: We have to go to another question now, from Harry Ellis to President Carter.

MR. ELLIS: Mr. President, as you have said, Americans, through conservation, are importing much less oil today than we were even a year ago. Yet U.S. dependence on Arab oil as a percentage of total imports is today much higher than it was at the time of the 1973 Arab oil embargo, and for some time to come, the loss of substantial amounts of Arab oil could plunge the U.S. into depression.

This means that a bridge must be built out of this dependence. Can the United States develop synthetic fuels and other alternative energy sources without damage to the environment, and will this process mean steadily higher fuel bills for American families?

PRESIDENT CARTER: I don't think there's any doubt that, in the future, the cost of oil is going to go up. What I've had as a basic commitment since I've been president is to reduce our dependence on foreign oil. It can only be done in two ways: one, to conserve energy—to stop the waste of energy—and, secondly, to produce more American energy. We've been very successful in both cases. We've now reduced the importing of foreign oil in the last year alone by one third. We imported today two million barrels of oil less than we did the same date just a year ago.

This commitment has been opening up a very bright vista for our nation in the future, because with the windfall profits tax as a base, we now have an opportunity to use American technology and American ability and American natural resources to expand rapidly the production of synthetic fuels, yes; to expand rapidly the production of solar energy, yes; and also to produce the traditional kinds of American energy. We will drill more oil and gas wells this year than any year in history. We'll produce more coal this year than any year in history. We are exporting more coal this year than any year in history.

And we have an opportunity now, with improved transportation systems and improved loading facilities in our ports, to see a very good opportunity on a world international market, to replace OPEC oil with American coal as a basic energy source. This exciting future will not only give us more energy security, but will also open up vast opportunities for Americans to live a better life and to have millions of new jobs associated with this new and very dynamic industry now in prospect because of the new energy policy that we've put into effect.

MR. SMITH: Would you repeat the question now for Governor Reagan?

MR. ELLIS: Governor Reagan, Americans, through conservation, are importing much less oil today than we were even a year ago. And yet, U.S. reliance on Arab oil as a percentage of total imports is much higher today than it was during the 1973 Arab oil embargo. And the substantial loss of Arab oil could plunge the United States into depression.

The question is whether the development of alternative energy sources, in order to reduce this dependence, can be done without damaging the environment, and will it mean for American families steadily higher fuel bills?

GOVERNOR REAGAN: I'm not so sure that it means steadily higher fuel costs, but I do believe that this nation has been portrayed for too long a time to the people as being energy-poor when it is energy-rich. The coal that the President mentioned—yes, we have it—and yet one eighth of our total coal resources is not being utilized at all right now. The mines are closed down; there are 22,000 miners out of work. Most of this is due to regulations which either interfere with the mining of it or prevent the burning of it. With our modern technology, yes, we can burn our coal within the limits of the Clean Air Act. I think, as technology improves, we'll be able to do even better with that.

The other thing is that we have only leased out—begun to explore—2 percent of our outer continental shelf for oil, where it is believed, by everyone familiar with that fuel and that source of energy, that there are vast supplies yet to be found. Our government has, in the last year or so, taken out of multiple use millions of acres of public lands that once were—well, they were public lands subject to multiple use—exploration for minerals and so forth. It is believed that probably 70 percent of the potential oil in the United States is probably hidden in those lands, and no one is allowed to even go and explore to find out if it is there. This is particularly true of the recent efforts to shut down part of Alaska.

Nuclear power: There were 36 power plants planned in this country. And let me add the word safety; it must be done with the utmost of safety. But 32 of those have given up and cancelled their plans to build, and again, because government regulations and permits, and so forth, take—make it take—more than twice as long to build a nuclear plant in the United States as it does to build one in Japan or in Western Europe.

We have the sources here. We are energy rich, and coal is one of the great potentials we have.

MR. SMITH: President Carter, your comment?

PRESIDENT CARTER: To repeat myself, we have this year the opportunity, which we'll realize, to produce 800 million tons of coal—an unequalled record in the history of our country. Governor Reagan says that this is not a good achievement, and he blames restraints on coal production on regulations—regulations that affect the life and the health and safety of miners, and also regulations that protect the purity of our air and the quality of our water and our land. We cannot cast aside those regulations. We have a chance in the next 15 years, insisting upon the health and safety of workers in the mines, and also preserving the same high air and water pollution standards, to triple the amount of coal we produce.

Governor Reagan's approach to our energy policy, which has already proven its effectiveness, is to repeal, or to change substantially, the windfall profits tax—to return a major portion of $227 billion back to the oil companies; to do away with the Department of Energy; to short-circuit our synthetic fuels program; to put a minimal emphasis on solar power; to emphasize strongly nuclear power plants as a major source of energy in the future. He wants to put all our eggs in one basket and give that basket to the major oil companies.

MR. SMITH: Governor Reagan.

GOVERNOR REAGAN: That is a misstatement, of course, of my position. I just happen to believe that free enterprise can do a better job of producing the things that people need than government can. The Department of Energy has a multi-billion-dollar budget in excess of $10 billion. It hasn't produced a quart of oil or a lump of coal, or anything else in the line of energy. And for Mr. Carter to suggest that I want to do away with the safety laws and with the laws that pertain to clean water and clean air, and so forth: as Governor of California, I took charge of passing the strictest air pollution laws in the United States—the strictest air quality law that has ever been adopted in the United States. And we created an OSHA—an Occupational Safety and Health Agency—for the protection of employees before the federal government had one in place. And to this day, not one of its decisions or rulings has ever been challenged.

So, I think some of those charges are missing the point. I am suggesting that there are literally thousands of unnecessary regulations that invade every facet of business, and indeed, very much of our personal lives, that are unnecessary; that government can do without; that have added $130 billion to the cost of production in this country; and that are contributing their part to inflation. And I would like to see us a little more free, as we once were.

MR. SMITH: President Carter, another crack at that?

PRESIDENT CARTER: Sure. As a matter of fact, the air pollution standard laws that were passed in California were passed over the objections of Governor Reagan, and this is a very well-known fact. Also, recently, when someone suggested that the Occupational Safety and Health Act should be abolished, Governor Reagan responded, amen.

The offshore drilling rights is a question that Governor Reagan raises often. As a matter of fact, in the proposal for the Alaska land legislation, 100 percent of all the offshore lands would be open for exploration, and 95 percent of all the Alaska lands, where it is suspected or believed that minerals might exist. We have, with our five-year plan for the leasing of offshore lands, proposed more land to be drilled than has been opened up for drilling since this program first started in 1954. So we're not putting restraints on American exploration, we're encouraging it in every way we can.

MR. SMITH: Governor Reagan, you have the last word on this question.

GOVERNOR REAGAN: Yes: If it is a well-known fact that I opposed air pollution laws in California, the only thing I can possibly think of is that the President must be suggesting the law that the federal government tried to impose on the State of California—not a law, but regulations—that would have made it impossible to drive an automobile within the city limits of any California city, or to have a place to put it if you did drive it against their regulations. It would have destroyed the economy of California, and, I must say, we had the support of Congress when we pointed out how ridiculous this attempt was by the Environmental Protection Agency. We still have the strictest air control, or air pollution laws in the country.

As for offshore oiling, only 2 percent now is so leased and is producing oil. The rest, as to whether the lands are going to be opened in the next five years or so—we're already five years behind in what we should be doing. There is more oil now, in the wells that have been drilled, than has been taken out in 121 years that they've been drilled.

MR. SMITH: Thank you, Governor. Thank you, Mr. President. The next question goes to Governor Reagan from William Hilliard.

MR. HILLIARD: Governor Reagan, wage earners in this country—especially the young—are supporting a Social Security system that continues to affect their income drastically. The system is fostering a struggle between the young and the old and is drifting the country toward a polarization of these two groups. How much longer can the young wage earner expect to bear the ever-increasing burden of the Social Security system?

GOVERNOR REAGAN: The Social Security system was based on a false premise, with regard to how fast the number of workers would increase and how fast the number of retirees would increase. It is actuarially out of balance, and this first became evident about 16 years ago, and some of us were voicing warnings then. Now, it is trillions of dollars out of balance, and the only answer that has come so far is the biggest single tax increase in our nation's history—the payroll tax increase for Social Security—which will only put a bandaid on this and postpone the day of reckoning by a few years at most.

What is needed is a study that I have proposed by a task force of experts to look into this entire problem as to how it can be reformed and made actuarially sound, but with the premise that no one presently dependent on Social Security is going to have the rug pulled out from under them and not get their check. We cannot frighten, as we have with the threats and the campaign rhetoric that has gone on in this campaign, our senior citizens—leave them thinking that in some way they're endangered and they would have no place to turn. They must continue to get those checks, and I believe that the system can be put on a sound actuarial basis. But it's going to take some study and some work, and not just passing a tax increase to let the load—or the roof—fall in on the next administration.

MR. SMITH: Would you repeat that question for President Carter?

MR. HILLIARD: Yes, President Carter, Wage earners in this country, especially the young, are supporting a Social Security system that continues to affect their income drastically. The system is fostering a struggle between young and old and is drifting the country toward a polarization of these two groups. How much longer can the young wage earner expect to bear the ever-increasing burden of the Social Security system?

PRESIDENT CARTER: As long as there is a Democratic president in the White House, we will have a strong and viable Social Security system, free of the threat of bankruptcy. Although Governor Reagan has changed his position lately, on four different occasions, he has advocated making Social Security a voluntary system, which would, in effect, very quickly bankrupt it. I noticed also in the *Wall Street Journal* early this week that a preliminary report of his task force advocates making Social Security more sound by reducing the adjustments in Social Security for the retired people to compensate for the impact of inflation.

These kinds of approaches are very dangerous to the security, the well-being and the peace of mind of the retired people of this country and those approaching retirement age. But no matter what it takes in the future to keep Social Security sound, it must be kept that way. And although there was a serious threat to the Social Security system and its integrity during the 1976 Campaign and when I became president, the action of the Democratic Congress working with me has been to put Social Security back on a sound financial basis. That is the way it will stay.

MR. SMITH: Governor Reagan?

GOVERNOR REAGAN: Well, that just isn't true. It has, as I said, delayed the actuarial imbalance falling on us for just a few years with that increase in taxes, and I don't believe we can go on increasing the tax, because the problem for the young people today is that they are paying in far more than they can ever expect to get out. Now, again this statement that somehow I wanted to destroy it and I just changed my tune, that I am for voluntary Social Security, which would mean the ruin of it.

Mr. President, the voluntary thing that I suggested many years ago was that with a young man orphaned and raised by an aunt who died, his aunt was ineligible for Social Security insurance because she was not his mother. And I suggested that if this is an insurance program, certainly the person who is paying in should be able to name his own beneficiary. That is the closest I have ever come to anything voluntary with Social Security. I, too, am pledged to a Social Security program that will reassure these senior citizens of ours that they are going to continue to get their money.

There are some changes that I would like to make. I would like to make a change in the regulation that discriminates against a wife who works and finds that she then is faced with a choice between her father's or her husband's benefits, if he dies first, or what she has paid in, but it does not recognize that she has also been paying in herself, and she is entitled to more than she presently can get. I'd like to change that.

MR. SMITH: President Carter's rebuttal now.

PRESIDENT CARTER: These constant suggestions that the basic Social Security system should be changed does call for concern and consternation among the aged of our country. It is obvious that we should have a commitment to them, that Social Security benefits should not be taxed and that there would be no peremptory change in the standards by which Social Security payments are made to retired people. We also need to continue to index Social Security payments, so that if inflation rises, the Social Security payments would rise a commensurate degree to let the buying power of a Social Security check continue intact.

In the past, the relationship between Social Security and Medicare has been very important to providing some modicum of aid for senior citizens in the retention of health benefits. Governor Reagan, as a matter of fact, began his political career campaigning around this nation against Medicare. Now, we have an opportunity to move toward national health insurance, with an emphasis on the prevention of disease; an emphasis on out-patient care, not in-patient care; an emphasis on hospital cost containment to hold down the cost of hospital care for those who are ill; an emphasis on catastrophic health insurance, so that if a family is threatened with being wiped out economically because of a very high medical bill, then the insurance would help pay for it. These are the kinds of elements of a national health insurance, important to the American people. Governor Reagan, again, typically is against such a proposal.

MR. SMITH: Governor?

GOVERNOR REAGAN: When I opposed Medicare, there was another piece of legislation meeting the same problem before the Congress. I happened to favor the other piece of legislation and thought that it would be better for the senior citizens and provide better care than the one that was finally passed. I was not opposing the principle of providing care for them. I was opposing one piece of legislation versus another.

There is something else about Social Security. Of course, it doesn't come out of the payroll tax. It comes out of a general fund, but something should be done about it. I think it is disgraceful that the Disability Insurance Fund in Social Security finds checks going every month to tens of thousands of people who are locked up in our institutions for crime or for mental illness, and they are receiving disability checks from Social Security every month while a state institution provides for all of their needs and their care.

MR. SMITH: President Carter, you have the last word on this question.

PRESIDENT CARTER: I think this debate on Social Security, Medicare, national health insurance typifies, as vividly any other subject tonight, the basic historical differences between the Democratic party and Republican party. The allusions to basic changes in the minimum wage is another, and the deleterious comments that Governor Reagan has made about unemployment compensation. These commitments that the Democratic party has historically made to the working families of this nation have been extremely important to the growth in their stature and in a better quality of life for them.

I noticed recently that Governor Reagan frequently quotes Democratic presidents in his acceptance address. I have never heard a candidate for president, who is a Republican, quote a Republican president, but when they get in office, they try to govern like Republicans. So, it is good for the American people to remember that there is a sharp, basic historical difference between Governor Reagan and me on these crucial issues—also, between the two parties that we represent.

MR. SMITH: Thank you, Mr. President, Governor Reagan. We now go to another question—a question to President Carter by Barbara Walters.

MS. WALTERS: Thank you. You have addressed some of the major issues tonight, but the biggest issue in the minds of American voters is yourselves—your ability to lead this country. When many voters go into that booth just a week from today, they will be voting their gut instinct about you men. You have already given us your reasons why people should vote for you, now would you please tell us for this, your final question, why they should not vote for your opponent, why his presidency could be harmful to the nation and, having examined both your opponent's record and the man himself, tell us his greatest weakness.

PRESIDENT CARTER: Barbara, reluctant as I am to say anything critical about Governor Reagan, I will try to answer your question. First of all, there is the historical perspective that I just described. This is a contest between a Democrat in the mainstream of my party, as exemplified by the actions that I have taken in the Oval Office the last four years, as contrasted with Governor Reagan, who in most cases does typify his party, but in some cases, there is a radical departure by him from the heritage of Eisenhower and others. The most important crucial difference in this election campaign, in my judgment, is the approach to the control of nuclear weaponry and the inclination to control or not to control the spread of atomic weapons to other nations who don't presently have it, particularly terrorist nations.

The inclination that Governor Reagan has exemplified in many troubled times since he has been running for president—I think since 1968—to inject American military forces in places like North Korea, to put a blockade around Cuba this year, or in some instances, to project American forces into a fishing dispute against the small nation of Ecuador on the west coast of South America. This is typical of his long-standing inclination, on the use of American power, not to resolve disputes diplomatically and peacefully, but to show that the exercise of military power is best proven by the actual use of it.

Obviously, no president wants war, and I certainly do not believe that Governor Reagan, if he were president, would want war, but a president in the Oval Office has to make a judgment on almost a daily basis about how to exercise the enormous power of our country for peace, through diplomacy, or in a careless way in a belligerent attitude which has exemplified his attitudes in the past.

MR. SMITH: Barbara, would you repeat the question for Governor Reagan?

MS. WALTERS: Yes, thank you. Realizing that you may be equally reluctant to speak ill of your opponent, may I ask why people should not vote for your opponent, why his presidency could be harmful to the nation, and having examined both your opponent's record and the man himself, could you tell us his greatest weakness?

GOVERNOR REAGAN: Well, Barbara, I believe that there is a fundamental difference—and I think it has been evident in most of the answers that Mr.

Carter has given tonight—that he seeks the solution to anything as another opportunity for a federal government program. I happen to believe that the federal government has usurped powers of autonomy and authority that belong back at the state and local level. It has imposed on the individual freedoms of the people, and there are more of these things that could be solved by the people themselves, if they were given a chance, or by the levels of government that were closer to them.

Now, as to why I should be and he shouldn't be; when he was a candidate in 1976, President Carter invented a thing he called the misery index. He added the rate of unemployment and the rate of inflation, and it came, at that time, to 12.5 percent under President Ford. He said that no man with that size misery index had a right to seek reelection to the presidency. Today, by his own decision, the misery index is in excess of 20 percent, and I think this must suggest something.

But, when I had quoted a Democratic president, as the President says, I was a Democrat. I said many foolish things back in those days. But the president that I quoted had made a promise, a Democrat promise, and I quoted him because it was never kept. And today, you would find that that promise is at the very heart of what Republicanism represents in this country today. That's why I believe there are going to be millions of Democrats that are going to vote with us this time around, because they too want that promise kept. It was a promise for less government and less taxes and more freedom for the people.

MR. SMITH: President Carter?

PRESIDENT CARTER: I mentioned the radical departure of Governor Reagan from the principles or ideals of historical perspective of his own party. I don't think this can be better illustrated than in the case of guaranteeing women equal rights under the Constitution of our nation. For 40 years, the Republican party platforms called for guaranteeing women equal rights with a constitutional amendment. Six predecessors of mine who served in the Oval Office called for this guarantee of women's rights. Governor Reagan and his new Republican party have departed from this commitment—a very severe blow to the opportunity for women to finally correct discrimination under which they have suffered.

When a man and a woman do the same amount of work, a man gets paid $1.00, a woman only gets paid 59 cents. And the Equal Rights Amendment only says that equality of rights shall not be abridged for women by the federal government or by the state governments. That is all it says—a simple guarantee of equality of opportunity which typifies the Democratic party, and which is a very important commitment of mine, as contrasted with Governor Reagan's radical departure from the long-standing policy of his own party.

MR. SMITH: Governor Reagan?

GOVERNOR REAGAN: Yes, Mr. President, once again, I happen to be against the amendment, because I think the amendment will take this problem out of the hands of elected legislators and put it in the hands of unelected judges. I am for equal rights, and while you have been in office for four years and not one single state—and most of them have a majority of Democratic legislators—has added to the ratification or voted to ratify the Equal Rights Amendment.

While I was governor, more than eight years ago, I found 14 separate instances where women were discriminated against in the body of California law, and I had passed and signed into law 14 statutes that eliminated those discriminations, including the economic ones that you have just mentioned—equal pay and so forth.

I believe that if in all these years that we have spent trying to get the amendment, that we had spent as much time correcting these laws, as we did in California—and we were the first to do it. If I were president, I would also now take a look at the hundreds of federal regulations which discriminate against women and which go right on while everyone is looking for an amendment. I would have someone ride herd on those regulations, and we would start eliminating those discriminations in the federal government against women.

MR. SMITH: President Carter?

PRESIDENT CARTER: Howard, I'm a Southerner, and I share the basic beliefs of my region about an excessive government intrusion into the private affairs of American citizens and also into the private affairs of the free enterprise system. One of the commitments that I made was to deregulate the major industries of this country. We've been remarkably successful, with the help of a Democratic Congress. We have deregulated the air industry, the rail industry, the trucking industry, financial institutions. We're now working on the communications industry.

In addition to that, I believe that this element of discrimination is something that the South has seen so vividly as a blight on our region of the country which has now been corrected—not only racial discrimination but discrimination against people that have to work for a living—because we have been trying to pick ourselves up by our bootstraps, since the long depression years, and lead a full and useful life in the affairs of this country. We have made remarkable success. It is part of my consciousness and of my commitment to continue this progress.

So, my heritage as a Southerner, my experience in the Oval Office, convinces me that what I have just described is a proper course for the future.

MR. SMITH: Governor Reagan, yours is the last word.

GOVERNOR REAGAN: Well, my last word is again to say this: we were talking about this very simple amendment and women's rights. And I make it plain again: I am for women's rights. But I would like to call the attention of the people to the fact that that so-called simple amendment could be used by mischievous men to destroy discriminations that properly belong, by law, to women respecting the physical differences between the two sexes, labor laws that protect them against things that would be physically harmful to them. Those would all, could all be challenged by men. And the same would be true with regard to combat service in the military and so forth.

I thought that was the subject we were supposed to be on. But, if we're talking about how much we think about the working people and so forth, I'm the only fellow who ever ran for this job who was six times president of his own union and still has a lifetime membership in that union.

MR. SMITH: Gentlemen, each of you now has three minutes for a closing statement. President Carter, you're first.

PRESIDENT CARTER: First of all, I'd like to thank the League of Women Voters for making this debate possible. I think it's been a very constructive debate and I hope it's helped to acquaint the American people with the sharp differences between myself and Governor Reagan. Also, I want to thank the people of Cleveland and Ohio for being such hospitable hosts during these last few hours in my life.

I've been president now for almost four years. I've had to make thousands of decisions, and each one of those decisions has been a learning process. I've seen the strength of my nation, and I've seen the crises it approached in a tentative way. And I've had to deal with those crises as best I could.

As I've studied the record between myself and Governor Reagan, I've been impressed with the stark differences that exist between us. I think the result of this debate indicates that that fact is true. I consider myself in the mainstream of my party. I consider myself in the mainstream even of the bipartisan list of presidents who served before me. The United States must be a nation strong. The United States must be a nation secure. We must have a society that's just and fair. And we must extend the benefits of our own commitment to peace, to create a peaceful world.

I believe that since I've been in office, there have been six or eight areas of combat evolved in other parts of the world. In each case, I alone have had to determine the interests of my country and the degree of involvement of my country. I've done that with moderation, with care, with thoughtfulness; sometimes consulting experts. But, I've learned in this last three and a half years that when an issue is extremely difficult, when the call is very close, the chances are the experts will be divided almost 50-50. And the final judgment about the future of the nation—war, peace, involvement, reticence, thoughtfulness, care, consideration, concern—has to be made by the man in the Oval Office. It's a lonely job, but with the involvement of the American people in the process, with an open Government, the job is a very gratifying one.

The American people now are facing, next Tuesday, a lonely decision. Those listening to my voice will have to make a judgment about the future of this country. And I think they ought to remember that one vote can make a lot of difference. If one vote per precinct had changed in 1960, John Kennedy would never have been president of this nation. And if a few more people had gone to the polls and voted in 1968, Hubert Humphrey would have been president, Richard Nixon would not.

There is a partnership involved in our nation. To stay strong, to stay at peace, to raise high the banner of human rights, to set an example for the rest of the world, to let our deep beliefs and commitments be felt by others in other nations, is my plan for the future. I ask the American people to join me in this partnership.

MR. SMITH: Governor Reagan?

GOVERNOR REAGAN: Yes, I would like to add my words of thanks, too, to the ladies of the League of Women Voters for making these debates possible. I'm sorry that we couldn't persuade the bringing in of the third candidate, so that he could have been seen also in these debates. But still, it's good that at least once, all three of us were heard by the people of this country.

Next Tuesday is Election Day. Next Tuesday all of you will go to the polls, will stand there in the polling place and make a decision. I think when you make that decision, it might be well if you would ask yourself, are you better off than you were four years ago? Is it easier for you to go and buy things in the stores than it was four years ago? Is there more or less unemployment in the country than there was four years ago? Is America as respected throughout the world as it was? Do you feel that our security is as safe, that we're as strong as we were four years ago? And if you answer all of those questions "yes", why then, I think your choice is very obvious as to whom you will vote for. If you don't agree, if you don't think that this course that we've been on for the last four years is what you would like to see us follow for the next four, then I could suggest another choice that you have.

This country doesn't have to be in the shape that it is in. We do not have to go on sharing in scarcity with the country getting worse off, with unemployment growing. We talk about the unemployment lines. If all of the unemployed today were in a single line allowing two feet for each of them, that line would reach from New York City to Los Angeles, California. All of this can be cured and all of it can be solved.

I have not had the experience the President has had in holding that office, but I think in being Governor of California, the most populous state in the Union—if it were a nation, it would be the seventh-ranking economic power in the world—I, too, had some lonely moments and decisions to make. I know that the economic program that I have proposed for this nation in the next few years can resolve many of the problems that trouble us today. I know because we did it there. We cut the cost—the increased cost of government—in half over the eight years. We returned $5.7 billion in tax rebates, credits and cuts to our people. We, as I have said earlier, fell below the national average in inflation when we did that. And I know that we did give back authority and autonomy to the people.

I would like to have a crusade today, and I would like to lead that crusade with your help. And it would be one to take government off the backs of the great people of this country, and turn you loose again to do those things that I know you can do so well, because you did them and made this country great. Thank you.

MR. SMITH: Gentlemen, ladies and gentlemen, for 60 years the League of Women Voters has been committed to citizen education and effective participation of Americans in governmental and political affairs. The most critical element of all in that process is an informed citizen who goes to the polls and who votes. On behalf of the League of Women Voters, now, I would like to thank President Carter and Governor Reagan for being with us in Cleveland tonight. And, ladies and gentlemen, thank you and good night.

THE VOTES IN THE 1980 ELECTION

CANDIDATES FOR PRESIDENT AND VICE PRESIDENT
Democratic—Jimmy Carter; Walter Mondale
Republican—Ronald Reagan; George Bush
Independent—John Anderson; Patrick Lucey

STATE	Total	Dem.	Rep.	Ind.	ELECTORAL VOTE D	ELECTORAL VOTE R
Alabama.........	1,341,929	636,730	654,192	15,885	—	9
Alaska	158,445	41,842	86,112	8,564	—	3
Arizona	873,945	246,843	529,688	76,604	—	6
Arkansas	837,582	398,041	403,164	21,057	—	6
California........	8,587,063	3,083,661	4,524,858	727,871	—	45
Colorado	1,184,415	367,973	652,264	130,579	—	7
Connecticut	1,406,285	541,732	677,210	168,260	—	8
Delaware	235,900	105,754	111,252	16,344	—	3
Dist. of Col.	175,237	131,113	23,545	14,971	3	—
Florida	3,686,930	1,419,475	2,046,951	178,569	—	17
Georgia	1,596,695	890,733	654,168	35,896	12	—
Hawaii	303,287	135,879	130,112	32,021	4	—
Idaho	437,431	110,192	290,699	27,142	—	4
Illinois...........	4,749,721	1,981,413	2,358,049	344,886	—	26
Indiana..........	2,242,033	844,197	1,255,656	107,729	—	13
Iowa	1,317,661	508,672	676,026	114,589	—	8
Kansas	979,795	326,150	566,812	67,535	—	7
Kentucky	1,294,627	616,417	635,274	30,519	—	9
Louisiana	1,548,591	708,453	792,853	26,198	—	10
Maine	523,011	220,974	238,522	53,450	—	4
Maryland	1,540,496	726,161	680,606	113,452	10	—
Massachusetts	2,524,298	1,053,802	1,057,631	382,044	—	14
Michigan	3,909,725	1,661,532	1,915,225	272,948	—	21
Minnesota	2,051,980	954,174	873,268	169,960	10	—
Mississippi	892,620	429,281	441,089	11,826	—	7
Missouri	2,099,824	931,182	1,074,181	76,488	—	12
Montana.........	363,952	118,032	206,814	28,159	—	4
Nebraska	640,854	166,851	419,937	44,025	—	5
Nevada..........	247,885	66,666	155,017	17,580	—	3
New Hampshire ..	383,990	108,864	221,705	49,295	—	4
New Jersey	2,975,684	1,147,364	1,546,557	224,173	—	17
New Mexico	456,971	167,826	250,779	28,404	—	4
New York	6,201,959	2,728,372	2,893,831	441,341	—	41
North Carolina ...	1,855,833	875,635	915,018	52,364	—	13
North Dakota	301,545	79,189	193,695	22,921	—	3
Ohio	4,283,603	1,752,414	2,206,545	255,521	—	25
Oklahoma	1,149,708	402,026	695,570	38,051	—	8
Oregon	1,181,516	456,890	571,044	109,894	—	6
Pennsylvania	4,561,501	1,937,540	2,261,872	288,588	—	27
Rhode Island.....	416,072	198,342	154,793	56,213	4	—
South Carolina ...	894,071	430,385	441,841	14,114	—	8
South Dakota	327,703	103,855	198,343	21,342	—	4
Tennessee	1,617,616	783,051	787,761	35,921	—	10
Texas	4,541,636	1,881,147	2,510,705	109,747	—	26
Utah	604,222	124,266	439,687	30,041	—	4
Vermont.........	213,299	81,952	94,628	31,071	—	3
Virginia	1,866,032	752,174	989,609	93,813	—	12
Washington	1,742,394	650,193	865,244	166,180	—	9
West Virginia	737,715	367,462	334,206	31,156	6	—
Wisconsin........	2,273,221	981,584	1,088,845	159,793	—	11
Wyoming	176,713	49,427	110,700	12,350	—	3
Total...........	86,515,221	35,483,883	43,904,153	5,588,014	49	489

Election of 1984

WILLIAM SHANNON, former columnist and member of the editorial board of The New York Times, *served as Ambassador to Ireland from 1977 to 1981. He currently teaches at Boston University.*

Election of 1984

by *William V. Shannon*

The 1984 election was a contest between a President and a party.

Ronald Reagan, attractive and articulate, relaxed and amiable, was a highly skilled campaigner running for reelection in a time of peace and rising prosperity. His political base was relatively narrow and the Republican party weak in much of the country, but in an age of media politics, Reagan's strength as a television campaigner was to prove an enormous asset.

Opposing Reagan was the powerful, heterogeneous, and often uneasy coalition known as the Democratic party. Beginning with their capture of the House of Representatives in the mid-term election of 1930 and benefiting from the inspired leadership of Franklin D. Roosevelt during the ordeals of the Great Depression and World War II, the Democrats supplanted the Republicans as the nation's majority party. By 1984 events had eroded the dominance they had once enjoyed. Still, as the year opened, the Democrats controlled the House of Representatives as they had for 50 of the previous 54 years, and seemed likely to retain that control in November, regardless of the outcome in the presidential race. With 45 seats in the Senate, they were favored to make gains that, if not large enough to recapture the majority they had lost in 1980, would probably put them in position to do so in 1986. The Democrats controlled 35 of the 50 governorships, and 34 of the state legislatures completely and one of the two chambers in four other states.

The Democrats in the mid-term election of 1982 regained 26 of the 33 House seats they had lost two years earlier. This strong showing had damaged the theory, tentatively advanced by some commentators, that 1980 might be a "critical election," heralding the return of the Republicans as the natural majority party.* In terms of expressed political preference, the Gallup Poll in 1983 reported that 44 percent of voters were Democrats, 25 percent were Republicans, and 31 percent were independents.

Reagan's political strength was similar to that of Dwight D. Eisenhower. It was a personal, not a party, phenomenon. Without Reagan, the Republicans would be much weaker. The first major political event of the year, therefore, was Reagan's decision to seek reelection despite his age. At 73, he was already the oldest man ever to serve in the White House. The Democrats dared not make Reagan's advanced age an issue; his evident physical vigor and unbroken record of good health made the fact of his age a matter for public admiration rather than concern. This admiration was bolstered by the President's insouciant response to the shooting attempt on his life in March 1981. "I forgot to duck," he joked to his wife. As he was about to undergo surgery for removal of the bullet, he wisecracked to the surgeons, "I hope you are all Republicans."

If reporters noted that Reagan worked only five or six hours a day, spent long weekends at Camp David, and took frequent vacations, this too, was not circumstance the Democrats could easily convert into an issue. After President Carter's long hours and studious work, and the earlier crises of the Nixon and Johnson years, Americans seemed relieved to have a President who coped with the job without strain and with unfailing equanimity and good humor. Reagan had hung President Calvin Coolidge's portrait in the Cabinet Room as a symbol of his esteem for that Republican predecessor. Like Coolidge's famous naps, Reagan's relaxed approach to the Presidency was not only acceptable to the country but actually reassuring. It was as if the man at the top was signalling the nation that things were not as bad as the news media would have the public believe.

Reagan's administrative style was not an accommodation to his advancing years. It was a continuation of the way he had governed California for eight years from 1967 to 1975. He viewed himself as a chairman of the board, rather than as an active executive. He delegated to senior aides most of his administrative power over appointments, legislation, the budget, and supervision of departments and agencies. He involved himself on a day-to-day basis in only a few issues. He was content to provide broad policy direction and to serve as his Administration's most persuasive spokesman. At the middle and upper levels of his Administration, there were frequent struggles for power and for control of policy among cabinet officers and factions of the White House staff. Rivals waged ideological and personal feuds through "leaks" to the press. These conflicts did the President no political harm; Reagan stayed above these battles, clearly unconcerned about any inefficiency or loss of morale that in-fighting might produce, and serenely confident of his ability to impose his will if and when he chose to do so. Since the huge expansion of the activities of the federal

*V.O. Key had described the elections of 1800, 1828, 1860, 1896 and 1932 as "critical" because they registered in each instance a new balance of social forces and set the political pattern for the next several decades.

government had begun under Franklin Roosevelt a half-century earlier, no President had governed with such a loose rein.

Reagan was unfamiliar with the details or even the main issues in many disputes, both foreign and domestic. Indeed, the breadth of his ignorance was sometimes startling. In October, 1983, for example, at a time when U.S.-Soviet arms control negotiations were breaking down, *The New York Times* reported that Reagan told a group of visitors that he had only recently learned that most of the Soviet nuclear deterrent force was in land-based rather than submarine-based missiles. Surprisingly this disclosure evoked relatively little public comment.

Like Eisenhower, but to an even greater extent, Reagan stayed politically popular by distancing himself in public from his own administration. Scandals occurred and controversies flared, but the President, not ever having involved himself closely with most of these appointees or the problems confronting them, was untouched.

Having been elected as an opponent of big government, Reagan said in his inaugural address: "Government is not the solution to our problem. Government is the problem." Once in office, he continued in speeches around the country to attack "Washington" and "the bureaucracy." He fostered the belief that he and his fellow citizens were allies against the government rather than that he had been chosen by them to direct the affairs of that government.

Reagan's detached style of governing, his distancing himself from his own appointees and the career bureaucracy, and his blithe cheerfulness and imperturbable optimism were central to the political problem faced by the Democrats in 1984. Reagan was dubbed "the Teflon President: nothing sticks to him." It was significant that in the fourth year of his Presidency there were no anti-Reagan jokes of the kind that normally circulate about Presidents. There seemed to be no audience for them. Politicians of both parties reported that many constituents disagreed with the President's policies, distrusted his intentions, or questioned his competence, and yet avowed that they liked him personally. Democrats in Congress and at the state level were consequently reluctant to mount against him the kind of sustained attacks that had weakened other recent Presidents.

This liking for Reagan did not have the firm foundation of respect for past accomplishments that undergirded the liking for Eisenhower in the 1950s. Nor was there the profound gratitude and loyalty from broad masses of people that Franklin D. Roosevelt's innovative programs had evoked. Still less was Reagan a hero who inspired emulation and enthusiasm, particularly among younger voters, as John F. Kennedy did. The liking for Reagan was a reflection of his sunny disposition, a reciprocation of his positive approach. It also correlated closely with the trend of the economy.

Reagan came to office committed to a counterrevolution in economic and social policy and in foreign affairs. He sought to reverse the growth in big government and to abolish or reduce the size of the government programs in education, health care, job training, housing, legal aid, and environmental protection. Some of the programs had originated in the Roosevelt New Deal of the 1930s and others in the Kennedy-Johnson Administrations of the 1960s.

Reagan was a "born again" conservative. As a Hollywood actor, he had been well known in the Democratic party and active in liberal causes. He voted four times for Roosevelt and for Harry Truman in 1948. He shifted sharply to the right during the 1950s. By the time he reemerged on the political scene as a television evangelist for Barry Goldwater in the 1964 campaign, Reagan had adopted the free-market economics and minimal-government theory last espoused in the White House by Herbert Hoover. Reagan, first as a paid lecturer and television program host for the General Electric Company and then as a candidate for state and national office, preached his new beliefs in simple terms and with the fresh enthusiasm of a convert. He was that rare figure in any nation's politics: an ideologue with charm. He mixed the economics of Herbert Hoover with the jokes of Bob Hope; he softened and warmed the stark creed of competitive individualism with sentimental stories and happy-ending anecdotes from the *Reader's Digest.*

Interpreting his 1980 mandate broadly, Reagan proposed in 1981 a fundamental reshaping of the relationship between the federal government and the individual citizen in a way that had not been attempted since the New Deal. He pushed through a budget that tightened eligibility standards and cut appropriations for Medicaid, food stamps, student loans, job training, student lunch programs, aid to the handicapped, and aid to the arts and humanities. In subsequent budgets, he continued this downward pressure. In his first three years in office, for example, government spending on job training and public employment programs fell from $9.2 billion to $5.2 billion.

Reagan recommended abolition of the Department of Education, which had been established in 1979, but Congress resisted this change. The first Reagan budget reduced federal spending for elementary, secondary and vocational education programs from $7 billion to $6.5 billion. In subsequent years, Congress rejected even steeper cuts that he proposed. In the resulting compromises, spending for all education programs stayed approximately level with 1981 figures which, as critics pointed out, was a concealed cut in real terms since spending did not take account of inflation.

Reagan persuaded Congress to consolidate 30 health programs, previously targeted for specific categories of people and administered under strict federal regulations, into three block grants; states received wide discretion as to their administration. Critics argued that since these grants were not indexed for inflation, the change would mean a decline in the quality of health assistance for low-income individuals, particularly in the poorer states, which would not out of state funds make up the shortfall in federal money.

Reagan in 1981 proposed cutting Social Security benefits and gradually raising the retirement age to 68 by the year 2000. These proposals reflected his longstanding preoccupation with the "actuarial unsoundness" of the Social Security system.* When his recommendations aroused a storm of protest from

---

*His provocative remarks about Social Security had alarmed elderly Republican voters in the New Hampshire and Florida primaries in 1976 and probably cost Reagan victory over President Gerald Ford in the contest for the nomination that year.

Congress and the senior-citizens lobby, Reagan backed off. Eventually, a bipartisan commission worked out a compromise which Congress approved in 1983. It raised the system's revenues and at least temporarily defused Social Security as a political issue.

The Reagan counterrevolution in domestic policy was more than offset in its fiscal effect by a dramatic rise in defense spending. Reagan raised the defense budget in his first year by $30 billion—about 14 percent—to a level of $222 billion, and increased it by smaller but still substantial percentages in each subsequent year. By 1984, defense spending had reached $284 billion.

A major feature of Reagan's program was the 1981 tax bill, which cut personal income taxes by 25 percent over a three-year period and provided in dollar terms the largest income tax reduction in history. The bill reduced the surtax on the highest incomes from 70 percent to 50 percent, lowered the capital gains tax, and greatly reduced estate and gift taxes. By liberalizing amortization and depreciation schedules, the bill provided a huge tax reduction to corporations. Reagan professed confidence that, as with the much smaller Kennedy-Johnson tax cut enacted in 1964, lower rates would actually produce higher revenues by stimulating business activity.

When during the 1980 primary campaign Reagan had promised to reduce taxes, increase defense spending, and also balance the budget, his party rivals said these objectives were so self-contradictory that they would be impossible to achieve. George Bush, later to become Reagan's Vice President, deprecated the agenda as "voodoo economics." When Congress actually voted this program into effect in the spring and summer of 1981, many from both parties voted for it while suspending their disbelief. Senator Howard Baker, the Senate Republican floor leader, described the Reagan economic program as a "riverboat gamble."

For a lengthy period, it looked as if Reagan had lost this gamble. Coincidentally with his signing of the budget and tax bills, a severe recession began. This deepened in 1982 to become the worst economic decline the nation had experienced in the 40 years since the end of the Great Depression. Twelve million persons, or more than 10 percent of the work force, were unemployed. Business bankruptcies and farm foreclosures reached 50-year highs. Reagan won his 1980 debate with Carter when he urged viewers to ask themselves: "Am I better off today than I was four years ago?" At the end of Reagan's first year, an opinion poll asking Americans the same question reported that 67 percent said no and only 32 percent said yes. Reagan's own job approval rating as President slipped by December 1982 to 41 percent, well below the levels of his modern predecessors at a comparable point in their first term; it was the most precipitous decline in popularity any President had experienced in his first two years in office.

Reagan had the confidence of a true believer. He stubbornly refused to change course. In the winter of 1982–83, when his political fortunes were at low ebb and commentators spoke of him as a one-term President and of his need to "revitalize" his failing Administration, Reagan cheerily assured the nation that the worst was over and an upturn was sure to begin. That winter the economy began a modest recovery which quickened as the year progressed and turned in 1984 into a roaring boom. Unemployment fell to the 7 percent it had been when Carter left office. Gross national product spurted ahead at an 8 percent rate. An international glut of oil and a worldwide collapse in commodity prices brought the inflation rate in early 1984 to 3 percent, the lowest rate since 1972, when the Nixon-imposed price controls were in effect. Reagan looked like a prophet. His popularity ratings moved steadily upward in the spring of 1984.

One large, awkward problem remained. As his critics had foreseen and his own supporters had feared, "supply side" economics did not produce a budget miracle. Deficits reached the $200 billion range and seemed likely to stay there for the next several years, even if full employment were achieved. Because of the deficit, interest rates remained at 12 percent, abnormally high for a recovery period by historical standards. For decades, Reagan had preached that huge deficits were dangerous and sinful. As recently as September 25, 1982 in a radio broadcast, he declared, "There's only one major cause of our economic problems: government spending more than it takes in and sending you the bill. There's only one permanent cure: bringing government spending in line with government revenues."

Now Reagan tactically shifted his ideological ground. While taking credit for the brisk economic recovery, he deprecated the importance of deficits. This dispute was to provide a major theme in the subsequent campaign.

In the early years of his Administration, Reagan disappointed one section of his supporters by his refusal to allow the so-called "social issues" to compete for congressional attention with his economic program. As 1984 drew near, Reagan gave these issues increasing prominence in his speeches. He supported a constitutional amendment to outlaw abortions and another to restore organized prayer in the public schools. He urged tax credits for parents paying tuition for church-related and other private schools. None of these measures could muster the necessary majorities in Congress.

These social issues were the political fallout from the liberal decisions of the Supreme Court under the leadership of Chief Justice Earl Warren and (on the question of abortion) under Chief Justice Warren Burger. Previous conservative Republican candidates, Goldwater, Nixon and Ford, had made use of these issues. Reagan, a more skillful public speaker than any of his recent Republican predecessors, was unusual in his ability to dramatize these issues and in the prominence that he chose to give them. These issues enabled him to appeal to two separate constituencies: conservative Roman Catholics in the big cities and suburbs of the North and fundamentalist "Moral Majority" Protestants, largely in the South.

Critics saw a certain irony in Reagan's championship of these fundamentalist causes, pointing out that he was unique among recent Presidents in that he attended religious services only once or twice a year. Also, before going to Washington, Reagan had spent years associating with people in Hollywood circles whose sophisticated lifestyles reflected values sharply different from those of conservative Catholics and fundamentalist Protestants.

Reagan's support for government legislation on specific social issues involved him in obvious philosophical paradoxes and inconsistencies. For instance, though he argued for limiting government's responsibilities in the economic sphere, he endorsed government intervention in family life to decide the question of abortion. Likewise, though he had previously taken the view that the legal age for drinking alcoholic beverages should be left to the states to determine, he reversed himself in July 1984 and signed a federal law designed to compel the states to establish 21 as the minimum drinking age, a measure intended to reduce deaths caused by young drunken drivers. Again, though he deplored violent street crime, he opposed further legislation controlling handguns.

In decided contrast to his elaborate domestic agenda, Reagan entered office with only a few simple notions about international problems and rather hazy ideas about the rest of foreign affairs. His fundamental convictions were that the Soviet Union was responsible for creating most international problems and for worsening those that it did not create. He felt that the Communist leaders understood only the language of power, and consequently, that it was necessary for the United States to have a large and rapid buildup of military weapons.

Reagan's most famous statement of his world view came on March 8, 1983, in an address to a convention in Orlando, Florida of the National Association of Evangelicals, the largest organization of fundamentalist Protestants, representing approximately 3 million people. Reagan declared that Soviet Communism is "the focus of evil in the modern world." He denounced the proposal for a freeze of nuclear weapons at existing levels without prior Soviet arms reductions as "a very dangerous fraud." He said:

> That is merely the illusion of peace. The reality is that we must find peace through strength. . . In your discussion of the nuclear freeze proposals, I urge you to beware the temptation of pride—the temptation of blithely declaring yourselves above it all and label both sides equally at fault, to ignore the facts of history and the aggressive impulses of an evil empire.

As he usually did in his speeches, Reagan illustrated these remarks with homely stories. He told of hearing a young father discussing Communism with his daughters. He quoted the father approvingly: "I would rather see my little girls die now, still believing in God, than have them grow up under Communism and one day die no longer believing in God."

Urging his listeners to "pray for the salvation of all those who live in that totalitarian darkness," Reagan said, "There is sin and evil in the world, and we are enjoined by Scripture and the Lord Jesus to oppose it with all our might."

His audience interrupted Reagan frequently with strong applause. At the end the crowd rose in a standing ovation as the orchestra played, "Onward Christian Soldiers."

Many observers, including some who shared Reagan's perception of the essential character of the Soviet regime and of the importance of American military strength in undergirding American foreign policy, were nonetheless dismayed at the ineptitude and sterility which marked his Administration's conduct of foreign affairs. After eighteen months in office, Reagan fired his first secretary of state, General Alexander Haig. Having served as deputy national security adviser under Henry Kissinger and then as White House chief of staff in the Nixon Administration, Haig was accustomed to serving a President deeply interested in foreign affairs. He could never adapt to the reality that Reagan, preoccupied with domestic issues, had only a modest interest in the subject. In his memoir, *Caveat,* Haig repeatedly complained that Reagan refused to set aside an hour a week for the two men to confer in private, that his daily reports to the President went unanswered, and that his conversations and memoranda on sensitive topics often appeared "leaked" in the next day's *Washington Post* or *New York Times.* Reagan allowed his senior White House staff to treat Haig in the dismissive and manipulative manner that Nixon's senior aides had treated most cabinet officers in charge of domestic departments.

Blaming his difficulties on hostile intrigues by White House aides overly concerned with politics and with the cosmetic effects of foreign policy, Haig wrote in his memoir: "The impulse to view the Presidency as a public relations opportunity and to regard government as a campaign for reelection (which, of course, it is, but within limits) distorts balance, frustrates consistency, and destroys credibility." When Haig protested once too often against these presidential aides and threatened in June 1982 to resign, Reagan accepted a resignation that Haig had not yet actually submitted.

George Shultz, Haig's successor, had earned a high reputation for competence and political finesse in the Nixon Administration, in which he served successively as secretary of labor, budget director, and secretary of the treasury. After Haig's stormy tenure, Shultz restored calm and harmony to relations between the State Department and the White House.

As 1984 opened, though, the Reagan administration was still seeking in vain for its first foreign policy success. Reagan, who had mounted strong attacks on many of his predecessor's foreign policy achievements, spent much of his time in office backing away from his earlier statements. Friendly relations between the United States and China were impaired because Reagan's sympathies for the old nationalist regime in Taiwan aroused Chinese suspicions. After three years of negotiations, Reagan was able to visit China in 1984 and lay most of these suspicions to rest. Reagan made no effort to disturb the Panama Canal treaties; in July, 1984, he warmly welcomed the president-elect of Panama to the White House. On this occasion, Bernard Gwertzman, longtime diplomatic correspondent of *The New York Times,* wrote:

> As the Reagan Administration struggles with its Central American policy, the solid relations between the United States and Panama, one of the side benefits from the treaties, are a major source of satisfaction to the Administration. Imagine the Administration's problems, if in addition to El Salvador and Nicaragua, it also had to worry about protecting the Panama Canal against a hostile Panama.

Despite his harsh rhetoric toward Communism, Reagan paradoxically followed a softer policy toward the Soviet Union than Carter had adopted in his last year in office after the Soviet invasion of Afghanistan. A few weeks after taking office, Reagan lifted the Carter-imposed embargo on grain sales to the Soviet Union. When the Soviet Union used the Polish army as a proxy to crack down on the Solidarity movement in Poland, Reagan shied away from using strong measures, such as declaring Poland in default on its foreign debt. Reagan Administration efforts to block the construction of a Soviet natural gas pipeline to Western Europe had to be abandoned when America's European allies refused to cooperate.

Reagan achieved a success of sorts when the European members of the NATO alliance resisted Soviet pressure and went ahead in December 1983 with the installation of intermediate-range ballistic missiles in Britain, Germany, and Italy in response to the prolonged Soviet buildup of similar missiles. This carried through a NATO decision negotiated by Carter in December 1979 that provided for the installation of these missiles unless an agreement to limit them had been reached with the Soviet Union within four years. Whether a different Administration from that of Reagan could have achieved such an agreement is a moot question. The Reagan Administration had difficulty making up its collective mind as to whether any compromise with the Soviet Union was possible. In January 1983 the President fired Eugene Rostow, director of the Arms Control and Disarmament Agency, on the grounds that he had exceeded his authority in trying to reach an agreement with the Russians. Rostow's ouster confirmed a widely held impression that Reagan was not interested in an arms control agreement unless it involved sweeping Soviet concessions. In the absence of such concessions, he believed a continuation of the American military buildup would put useful pressure on the Soviet Union and eventually produce a more conciliatory Soviet policy. In the autumn of 1983 the Soviet government made good on its longstanding threat to withdraw from arms control talks if the Western powers installed intermediate-range ballistic missiles. All arms control negotiations came to a halt.

Reagan's political strategists had hoped that he would be able in 1984 to emulate Nixon's 1972 strategy. That is, they wanted him to attend a summit meeting with the head of the Soviet government, sign an arms-control agreement, and enter the campaign having effectively deprived the Democrats of the peace issue. As part of this attempt to reach an election-year thaw, Reagan in July 1984 lifted the ban Carter had imposed in 1980 on Soviet trawlers fishing within 200 miles of the U.S. coastline; the old 3-mile limit was restored. The Russians, however, appeared to take the President's strident anti-Communist rhetoric more seriously than his own political staff did. Despite repeated Reagan overtures, they refused during the first half of the year to signal any willingness to meet with him before the election.

Reagan encountered his most spectacular setback in the Middle East. His initial hopes to construct an anti-Soviet consensus that would include both Israel and its Arab neighbors soon flickered out. In the spring of 1982, the Administration offered only modest warnings when Israel began to move militarily into southern Lebanon to push back the army of the Palestine Liberation Organization. Some critics contended that then Secretary of State Haig actually encouraged this Israeli move, but the evidence now available is inconclusive. What is clear is that as the Israeli army expanded its operations and eventually reached the Lebanese capital of Beirut, the Reagan Administration became alarmed by the number of civilian casualties in Lebanon and the resulting bad publicity the invasion received on American television.

As the fighting around Beirut neared its climax, Haig, because of his difficulties in dealing with the President, was dismissed from office. His successor, Secretary Shultz, and the roving U.S. ambassador in the region, Philip Habib, then put maximum pressure on the fragile Lebanese government and on Israel to reach an agreement providing for Israeli withdrawal from Beirut following the departure of the shattered PLO army into exile. The Reagan Administration was unduly confident of its ability to persuade Syria to make a complementary military withdrawal from Lebanon once the Israelis backed off. Instead, the Soviets used this time to reequip its defeated Syrian client. Syria, thus strengthened, proved adamant in resisting American diplomatic pressure and reasserted its presence in Lebanon.

Some 1400 U.S. Marines had been stationed around the Beirut Airport as part of an international peacekeeping force. They became hostage to a policy the political foundations of which had disintegrated; there was no strong Lebanese government for the peacekeeping force to support. Lebanese Moslem factions backed by Syrian firepower began attacking the Marine position. In November 1983 a suicide terrorist drove a bomb-laden truck into the Marine encampment and set off an explosion that killed 249 Marines and wounded many others. Even after this catastrophe, Reagan continued to defend his placing the Marines in this tactically vulnerable and politically pointless position, and to question the courage of those who urged a withdrawal. Then he reversed course. The *Wall Street Journal* reported that "on February 7 (1984), the day the Administration announced the withdrawal of U.S. Marines from Beirut, the President was heading for California to begin a vacation. He delayed the start of his holiday for only about 20 minutes to review a statement disclosing the abrupt policy switch, and he never appeared in public to announce the withdrawal."

Eight Democratic party figures sought their party's nomination to oppose Reagan. Although they varied in experience and the extent of their familiarity to the public, none was a frivolous candidate and each could stake out some plausible claim to party leadership. As a group, they represented the range of political sentiment among Democrats: radical, liberal, moderate, conservative.

The two best-known candidates were former Vice President Walter F. "Fritz" Mondale of Minnesota and Senator John Glenn of Ohio. Mondale carried the heavy burden of being identified with the unpopular, rejected Carter Administration. As against that negative, Mondale was personally well known and warmly supported by the leaders of the many different interest groups traditionally identified with the Democratic Party: the AFL-CIO, the teachers' associations, the black, Jewish, and Hispanic communities, women's rights activists, environmentalists, the elderly, and peace organizations. Under the changed rules for the 1984 convention that gave members of Congress, governors, and party officials a large bloc of guaranteed seats, Mondale had an added advantage. Insofar as a party establishment could be said to exist, Mondale was its favorite because many governors, big-city mayors, and members of Congress had found him a sympathetic and knowledgeable ally in Washington during the Carter years. Mondale also had kept together an able political staff regarded by many as the best since John F. Kennedy's group in 1960.

Glenn's assets were the converse of Mondale's. Except in the Deep South, Glenn had little support in the party establishment or the traditional interest groups. His political staff was made up of "hired guns" who had worked in many previous campaigns, but they were not a team and were not used to working with Glenn or with one another. As the first man to orbit the earth, a Marine Corps hero, and a ruggedly handsome man from a small town, Glenn projected an Eisenhoweresque image that would be attractive to conservative Democrats and Republican-leaning independents in the Middle West and South where national Democratic candidates had been weak. His success in winning reelection to the Senate from Ohio by a margin of more than one million votes in the face of the Reagan victory in 1980 underscored Glenn's broad, almost nonpartisan appeal. If nominated, one supposed he might be a formidable candidate.

Three U.S. senators of widely diversified backgrounds competed with Mondale and Glenn for the party's middle ground. Alan Cranston of California rivaled Glenn as a spectacularly successful vote-getter in his own state. As assistant floor leader, he was an acknowledged master of parliamentary maneuvers and legislative coalition-building in the Senate. At 69, Cranston was three years younger than Reagan, and as a longtime runner, he was in superb physical condition. Yet, with his bald head and severely lean face, Cranston looked older than the President, and his personal style was colorless. Making arms control and the nuclear freeze the dominant theme of his campaign, Cranston gambled that he could ride the peace issue to the nomination as George McGovern had done a dozen years earlier.

Senator Gary Hart of Colorado had been McGovern's manager in the 1972 campaign. Since coming to the Senate in 1974, he had positioned himself closer to his party's center. His appeal in 1984 was generational and nonideological. He stressed the need for new ideas, for a party commitment to the overriding importance of economic growth, and for emancipation of the party from old interest-group alignments. He spoke of promoting new technologies and assisting an economy in transition from heavy industry to information and services. Hart made a conscious effort to evoke memories of John F. Kennedy. Indeed, Hart's cool, reserved personality did remind some people of the young JFK; the co-chairman of his national campaign committee was Kennedy's longtime associate, Theodore C. Sorensen. As the 1984 campaign began, Hart was an unknown factor. Many politicians and media people thought he was conducting a dry run for a more serious campaign in 1988.

Senator Fritz Hollings of South Carolina at 62 was a veteran of 18 years in the Senate. An unclassifiable independent in his thinking, he could be termed a moderate liberal. He was a critic of the oil industry, attacking the depletion allowance as excessive and supporting the Carter Administration's windfall profits tax. He had been a crusader against hunger and malnutrition in the 1960s and had made a name for himself as a supporter of civil rights legislation, and as a strong proponent of the federal programs of nutritional assistance for women, infants and children. Hollings, however, was also a staunch advocate of big military budgets, not a popular position among liberal activists who were influential in northern and western presidential primaries. Hollings urged a one-year, across-the-board budget freeze of everything from military spending to Social Security as a way of scaling back the Reagan deficit. He argued that only if the Democrats made themselves credible to the country as the party that could manage the economy and the national defense could they hope to regain power. Tall, handsome, white-haired and blessed with a rich baritone voice, Hollings looked like Hollywood's vision of a U.S. Senator.

Former Governor Reubin Askew of Florida was the second Southerner in the race. Highly esteemed in eight years as governor, he had served in the last two years of the Carter Administration as U.S. Special Trade Representative. He was the conservative candidate in the Democratic field, the only one opposing abortion and homosexual rights and openly critical of the AFL-CIO. On education, civil rights and economic issues, however, Askew was not conservative by the standard of Reagan supporters. Askew had declined McGovern's invitation in 1972 to be his vice presidential running mate. Had he accepted, he would have entered the 1984 campaign better known. As it was, he was unfamiliar to most voters and never overcame his initial invisibility.

At the opposite end of the political spectrum from Askew were former Senator George McGovern and the Reverend Jesse Jackson. Against the advice of most of his former supporters, McGovern entered the race, frankly recognizing that he had almost no chance. Instead of becoming the comic Harold-Stassen-type figure that his admirers feared, McGovern made his brief participation in the 1984 campaign a successful blend of idealism and nostalgia. He criticized what he regarded as excessive defense spending, assailed cold war attitudes in foreign policy in Central America and elsewhere, and unequivocally advocated New Deal and New Frontier social programs. His candor and undiminished eloquence won renewed respect from many Democrats. Also, his posture as a peacemaker among his rivals responded to the anxiety of many Democrats who feared that the long and difficult string of state primaries was breeding party disunity. McGovern was handicapped, however, by a lack of funds and by the media's low expectations for him.

Jackson, a black minister, was the youngest, least predictable and most controversial of the eight candidates. He was not the first black to seek the Democratic presidential nomination; Representative Shirley Chisholm of New York had been a candidate in 1972 without attracting any significant support. Born and reared in South Carolina, Jackson was a Baptist minister, and black churches were the support network for his primary campaign. Having served on the staff of the Reverend Martin Luther King, Jr., until the latter's assassination, Jackson then formed his own Chicago-based organization, PUSH (People United to Save Humanity). He lectured widely in churches and schools, urging young blacks to better themselves through education and hard work. He used threats of black consumer boycotts to persuade some organizations to sign "economic covenants," opening up more jobs to blacks.

Jackson made his debut in national politics at the Miami Beach convention in 1972 where he led the Illinois delegation that was seated in place of one headed by Chicago's Mayor Richard Daley. During the Carter years, Jackson had been an outsider; United Nations Ambassador Andrew Young was the nation's most prestigious black leader. Carter also dealt regularly with Mrs. Coretta King, the widow of the slain civil rights leader, and with black big-city mayors, led by Coleman Young of Detroit. In 1978 Jackson accepted an invitation from William Brock, then chairman of the Republican National Committee, to address the organization. If the GOP leadership would work with him, Jackson said, he would deliver blacks out of their "bondage" to the Democratic party. Nothing came of this overture.

In 1983 Jackson began positioning himself to seek the Democratic nomination. By the time he announced his candidacy in the autumn of that year, most of the nation's black mayors and other leaders of the black political establishment had aligned themselves with Mondale. Jackson proved a formidable competitor. The most effective orator in the campaign, he delivered lengthy talks containing applause lines that he had crafted and polished in the course of hundreds of speeches over the previous 15 years. Like William Jennings Bryan's "cross of gold" speech at the 1896 convention, Jackson's principal speech was a work of art that had been years in the making. In a way that no other black leader had succeeded in doing, he mixed the bravado, the knowingness, and the "street smarts" of alienated, working-class, big-city blacks with the more traditional rhetoric of moral uplift and Biblical imagery familiar to church-going blacks. His radicalism also appealed to some left-wing white Democrats. Where his rivals called for slowing down the rate of increase in the Pentagon budget, Jackson urged a sharp reduction in military spending. Where his rivals coupled calls for a peaceful solution in Central America with denunciation of Communism, Jackson (and McGovern) called for restoration of diplomatic relations with Cuba and for cooperation with the Sandinista government in Nicaragua. Of the 3 million votes he polled in the primaries, Jackson received 22 percent of them from whites.

Jackson was a master at manipulating the media: he anticipated its needs, had a flair for creating news, and dressed up his opinions in provocative language. He began his campaign with a publicity coup. He flew to Syria and negotiated the release of Lieutenant Robert Goodman, Jr., a black Navy flier who had been shot down and captured while bombing Syrian positions in Lebanon. Though criticized in advance for going outside normal diplomatic channels, Jackson demonstrated that he could negotiate as skillfully with an Arab head of state as with Chicago politicians or corporate executives.

The political season began in what seemed preordained fashion when Mondale—well organized, well financed and far ahead in the opinion polls—swept to victory in the Iowa caucuses. Hart was a distant second, McGovern third, and Cranston fourth. Within a few days, however, private polling in New Hampshire showed that Mondale's previously huge lead was rapidly shrinking. The movement was toward Hart. On February 28, the voters confirmed the pollsters' reports. Hart won with 41 percent of the vote. This was followed within a few days by Hart victories in the Maine caucuses and the Vermont primary. The field suddenly narrowed to five as Cranston, Hollings, and Askew withdrew.

March 13 was the first "super Tuesday" of the campaign; Massachusetts, Rhode Island, Georgia, Florida, and Alabama voted on that day. If Mondale's nominal support in New England had materialized, this was the day on which his managers had hoped he would preempt the nomination. As it was, it became the day on which he had to make a comeback or see his campaign collapse. Increasingly, Mondale looked as if he might go the way of Edmund S. Muskie in 1972, another respected candidate of the party leaders but one who failed to ignite voter enthusiasm.

When a *Boston Globe* poll showed him trailing Hart in Massachusetts by 15 points, Mondale chose to make his stand in the South. This decision underscored the uselessness of endorsements by elected officials. In Massachusetts, Mondale had the endorsement of Governor Michael Dukakis, other state officials, and three influential congressmen. In Maine he had been backed by Governor Joseph Brennan and Senator George Mitchell. Ignoring endorsements, voters were looking for a "new face."

The South was critical not only for Mondale but also for Glenn and Jackson, neither of whom had scored well in Iowa or New England. Glenn had to demonstrate that in the South, the nation's most conservative region, he had political muscle as a war hero and astronaut. Jackson had to do well among blacks in the South or his campaign would lose its credibility. Hart, Mondale, Glenn, and Jackson spent two weeks crisscrossing the neighboring states of Georgia, Florida, and Alabama in what became a regional primary. With Massachusetts and Rhode Island now conceded to Hart, it became essential for Mondale to win at least two of the three southern states.

He barely managed to do so. Mondale carried Georgia with 31 percent of the vote to Hart's 27 percent. (Jackson 21 percent, Glenn 18.) He carried Alabama more decisively with 34 percent, while Glenn edged Hart for second place, each getting 21 percent while Jackson was close behind with 19 percent. Hart carried Florida with a shade under 40 percent of the vote (Mondale 33, Jackson 12, Glenn 11).

Glenn's failure to win any of the three southern states destroyed his candidacy. McGovern, having made his continuance in the race contingent on carrying Massachusetts, the only state to support him over Nixon in 1972, also withdrew when he polled only 21 percent of the vote, finishing third behind Hart and Mondale. The first super Tuesday thus narrowed the field to three and, in effect, to two, since no one expected the party to nominate Jackson.

The March 13 primaries came very close to making Hart the nominee. Had Mondale failed to carry Georgia where he had the support of former President Carter and where he was widely and favorably known, the former Vice President might well have withdrawn from the race, making Hart the *de facto* winner four months in advance of the convention. The imponderables could be argued either way. If Jackson had not entered the race, many black voters would have supported Mondale. If Glenn had withdrawn sooner, his supporters might have gone to Hart and given him a clean sweep in the South.

Although Hart carried more states and polled more votes on March 13, Mondale did well enough to reestablish his candidacy. He told his cheering supporters that evening, "When this race began, it looked like Mondale doing a 100-yard dash. Then it looked like Hart doing a 100-yard dash. But tonight that's all changed. It's going to be a marathon all the way."

It proved an accurate forecast.

Illinois was the next primary state. There, on March 20, Mondale turned the preconvention contest around. Polls taken for both candidates on March 15 and 16 showed Hart six to eight points ahead. It was his victory to win if he could hold his lead.

Since leaping into national prominence, Hart had been harrassed by news stories pointing out that his family name had originally been Hartpence and that he had shortened it to Hart, that various documents and biographical listings had reported him to be a year younger than he actually was, and that he had changed his religion from that of his parents. None of these personal details should have caused Hart any serious difficulty, but he complicated matters by giving confusing, defensive, and sometimes inconsistent explanations. In Illinois he highlighted these questions by attacking Mondale for running a television advertisement about them. When it turned out that no such Mondale advertisement existed, Hart had to apologize. More serious was his uncertainty as to how to handle Cook County Democratic Chairman Edward Vrdolyak. For months, Hart had been assailing Mondale as the candidate of established interests and of party insiders like Vrdolyak. In Illinois, a week before the primary, the Hart campaign ran a television commercial attacking Mondale and Vrdolyak. Then Hart had second thoughts. Vrodlyak was engaged in a bitter feud with Chicago Mayor Harold Washington, a black. Although Washington and Jackson were not personally or politically close, there was little doubt that the city's large black vote would go heavily to Jackson. What black votes Jackson did not get would go mostly to Mondale, who was favorably known in the black community for his civil rights record. If Hart antagonized those white voters sympathetic to Vrdolyak, he would have little support in Chicago. On the Friday before the primary, the Hart organization announced that the television commercial was an error and would be withdrawn, although some stations continued to run it over the weekend.

These mix-ups over the nonexistent Mondale advertisement and the ill-advised anti-Vrdolyak advertisement could both be explained by the fatigue of a candidate who had been campaigning without pause and under intense pressure for several weeks. They could also be explained by the inexperience of his staff, most of whom had never participated in a national campaign. Whatever the explanation, these tactical errors damaged Hart's reputation for competence and leadership among the voters who were his base: the students, the independents, and the young urban professionals frequently referred to as "Yuppies."

Hart carried these voters in Illinois by much narrower margins than he had in New England and in Florida. Mondale won the primary with 40 percent to Hart's 35 percent and Jackson's 20 percent.

The New York primary occurred two weeks later. Hart again seriously miscalculated. In other states, he had shown courage and consistency in defending controversial votes he had cast as a senator from Colorado that might not be universally popular. In Michigan, for example, he defended to automobile workers his vote against the government rescue of the Chrysler Corporation and his opposition to "domestic content" legislation which would restrict the importation of Japanese automobiles. In New York he began with an analogous problem. He was on record against moving the United States embassy from Tel Aviv to Jerusalem. Israel had proclaimed Jerusalem as its capital but most nations were reluctant to acknowledge the change because of conflicting Arab claims to the city. In New York approximately 30 percent of the voters in a Democratic primary are Jewish. Mondale had long cultivated Jewish support and was on record in favor of moving the embassy to Jerusalem. Rather than stand his ground, Hart repudiated an earlier statement as having been written in error by a staff member, and then changed his position to conform with that of Mondale. Many voters felt the "staff mistake" explanation was implausible. Others, including a sizable number of Jews, felt the significance of the embassy issue had been grossly exaggerated and constituted pandering for Jewish votes.

In a debate in New York, Mondale sprang on Hart what became the most famous line of the primary season: "Where's the beef?" Hart had been stressing the need for new ideas and a new politics. By borrowing the punch line from a popular, well-known television commercial for a chain of fast-food restaurants, Mondale epitomized in three words his telling argument that Hart's ideas were not new and had little substance.

For the first time, Mondale benefited directly from the support of a major officeholder. Governor Mario Cuomo of New York not only endorsed him but also lent his son Andrew to manage the Mondale campaign in the state, recruited the principal state campaign aides, and imposed his own television consultant and his own television advertising strategy. The resulting landslide victory (Mondale 621,802, Hart 380,298, Jackson 355,315) enhanced Cuomo's prestige and restored Mondale as the man to beat for the nomination.

The New York disaster was followed by major defeats for Hart in Pennsylvania, Missouri, Tennessee and Texas. By early May, Mondale had more than 1,500 of the 1,967 delegates needed to win while Hart had only half as many. Technically, Mondale could still be stopped, but it was now certain that Hart could not go to the convention as the leader on the first ballot. Still, Hart refused to yield. On May 8, while Mondale was winning Maryland and North Carolina, Hart caused a renewed flurry of interest with close, upset victories in Ohio and Indiana.

True to its grueling marathon quality, the primary season came to a hard-fought conclusion on June 5 when Mondale carried New Jersey, while Hart won in California. The steady drift of uncommitted delegates to join the probable winner enabled Mondale to claim the nomination on the following day.

In the interval between his long-delayed proclamation of triumph and the Democratic convention, Mondale faced two delicate political problems. One was a rapprochement with Jesse Jackson and the other was the choice of a running mate.

Although never in serious contention for the nomination, Jackson, by his stylish performance in the debates and on television talk shows and by his convincing display of voting strength in black neighborhoods across the country, had achieved a major objective. He had established himself as the foremost spokesman of the black community, a position of leadership that no one had occupied since the death sixteen years earlier of Martin Luther King. He had polled more than 3 million votes, won the primaries in South Carolina, Louisiana, and the District of Columbia, and carried several cities including Philadelphia.

Jackson claimed to be leading a "rainbow coalition" of minorities and disadvantaged groups. In reality, Mondale was the true leader of a rainbow coalition. He drew some black support in every state (always doing much better in this regard than Hart). When it counted, as in Texas, Hispanic voters preferred him over Jackson by a wide margin. Although Jackson received 22 percent of his votes from whites, the powerful thrust of his candidacy came from blacks. His candidacy was a black show of strength.

In rallying that strength, Jackson had aroused fear and distrust among Jewish voters. In what he apparently regarded as a private conversation with aides but overheard by reporters, Jackson early in the year used the terms "Hymie" and "Hymietown" to refer to Jews and to New York City. After first denying the comment, Jackson in an appearance at a synagogue in New Hampshire in February expressed regret and said of his use of these derogatory terms, "It was wrong."

This controversy had barely subsided when Louis Farrakhan, a Chicago-based leader of a splinter Black Muslim group known as "The Nation of Islam," leaped from obscurity to notoriety. Farrakhan, a Jackson supporter, made a threat of physical retaliation against the black reporter for *The Washington Post* who was the source of the story about Jackson's earlier remarks. In subsequent speeches and interviews, Farrakhan referred to Judaism as a "gutter religion," described Adolf Hitler as "wickedly great," and termed the establishment of Israel an "outlaw act."

Jackson refused at first to repudiate Farrakhan. He apparently calculated that Jews and others who were offended by these remarks were not going to vote for him anyway, while if he denounced Farrakhan, he would lose prestige among those isolated and alienated inner-city blacks to whom the Black Muslim movement appeals. Eventually, under intense pressure from Jewish organizations and from adverse editorial comment in the media, Jackson characterized Farrakhan's statements as "reprehensible and morally indefensible," but he was careful not to reject Farrakhan and his following.

Independent of these controversies, Jackson was a suspect figure in the Jewish community because of his attitude toward Middle East issues. He repeatedly called for the creation of an independent Palestinian Arab state. In

1979, when Andrew Young was forced to resign as U.S. Ambassador to the United Nations because of his unauthorized contacts with the Palestine Liberation Organization (PLO) representative in New York, Jackson attributed his removal to "Jewish pressure." Subsequently, Jackson visited the Middle East, met with Yassir Arafat, the head of the PLO, and publicly embraced him.

Mondale, who had always enjoyed strong support from both the black and Jewish communities, was eager to diminish the antagonism swirling around Jackson without offending either group. Timothy F. Hagan, co-chairman of the Mondale campaign in Ohio, and Rabbi Marvin Hier of Los Angeles co-authored a proposed plank in the Democratic platform. It read: "The Democratic Party takes this opportunity to reaffirm its adherence to pluralistic principles and to repudiate and completely dissociate itself from people who promote all forms of hatred, bigotry, racism, and anti-Semitism."

Although this proposed language seemed so banal as to be unobjectionable to anyone, some Jackson supporters did object. Representative Mickey Leland of Texas, chairman of the Black Caucus in the Democratic National Committee, saw it as an attack on Farrakhan and therefore an oblique attempt to embarrass Jackson. Leland said: "I think it's very divisive. It's obviously taking a shot at Farrakhan. We give Farrakhan credence by doing that."

Since the resolution had been put forward too late to meet the Platform Committee's deadline, it required a two-thirds majority of the delegates to bring it up for a vote. To avoid even the possibility of an embarrassing black-Jewish clash on television, the Mondale managers persuaded the authors of the resolution to withhold it until the meeting of the Democratic National Committee on the day after the convention. It was then approved unanimously. Meanwhile, in his address to the convention on the third evening, Jackson included conciliatory language toward his Jewish critics.

"If in my low moments, in word, deed or attitude, through some error of temper or tone, I have caused discomfort, created pain or revived someone's fears, that was not my intention," he said.

Recalling many joint efforts of blacks and Jews in behalf of "social justice at home and peace abroad," he declared, "When all is said and done, we must forgive each other, redeem each other and move on."

Jackson's words were warmly received by most Jewish leaders and Jewish delegates and did much to dispel the gathering rancor.

Jackson's speech was a personal triumph, and he left San Francisco with enhanced prestige. He had failed, however, to extract any substantial concessions on the platform from Mondale. The nominee resisted Jackson's proposals for an outright endorsement of affirmative action and racial quotas in employment, for the abolition of two-stage primaries in which the candidate who fails to achieve a majority faces a runoff, and for a substantial federal program of public works and public jobs to relieve unemployment.

As the general campaign proceeded, Jackson faded in importance. Because of their pronounced hostility to Reagan's domestic policies, black voters clearly had no impluse to shift from their traditional Democratic loyalty. Jackson's support for the Democratic ticket and his efforts to register new voters were positive influences, but it soon became clear that the Democrats had serious problems with white voters. Unless Mondale could overcome them, no outpouring of black support could possibly save him.

Fundamental pessimism about the outlook for victory in November dominated Mondale's choice of a running mate. First, he concluded that he could not break Reagan's grip on the South and West. The President would have an unshakable base of more than 200 of the 270 electoral votes needed to win. This assumption meant that it would make little sense to choose a conservative Southerner such as Senator Sam Nunn of Georgia or Senator Lloyd Bentsen of Texas to achieve a conventional north-south regional balance. No Southerner in second place on the ticket could prevent Reagan from winning most of the South. If victory could be achieved for the Democrats, it could probably only come about by doing exceptionally well in traditional Democratic strongholds in the Northeast and the industrial Middle West. A possible pattern for victory envisaged by Mondale and his strategists was modeled approximately on John Kennedy's narrow victory in 1960 and on Hubert Humphrey's near-miss in 1968. It presumed Mondale would win four of the six New England states (Maine, Massachusetts, Rhode Island, and Connecticut), all of the Middle Atlantic states (New York, New Jersey, Pennsylvania, Delaware, Maryland, West Virginia and the District of Columbia), six states in the Middle West (Ohio, Michigan, Illinois, Missouri, Wisconsin and Minnesota), three in the South (Georgia, Arkansas and Texas), and one in the Far West (Hawaii). This combination would produce 275 electoral votes.

This minimal strategy argued for choosing a popular figure from the Northeast to complement Mondale's presumed strength as a Middle Westerner. Mondale had been impressed by Governor Cuomo's effectiveness in the New York primary. However, rejecting repeated overtures, Cuomo convinced Mondale that he was not available to run.

A second pessimistic calculation was that Mondale's personality failed to excite and motivate voters. His political skills, notably his alertness and self-discipline as a debater, had enabled him to take advantage of Hart's weaknesses and inconsistencies. Those skills, together with his solid support from interest-group constituencies, had won him the nomination, but they would not suffice in a general election. He needed to do something dramatic to dispel his gray image. Proceeding on this assumption, Mondale decided that if Cuomo was not available, he should choose a running mate who would be a "first"—the first woman or the first black or the first Hispanic.

Polling data indicated that only one candidate would add discernible strength to a Mondale ticket. That was Hart, but Hart had no interest in the Vice Presidency and refused to make any of the tactical and rhetorical concessions needed to ease the way toward an accommodation. Mondale did not want Hart urgently enough to make a firm offer. Polls also suggested that of the kinds of candidates who would represent an historic "first," a woman would attract additional votes for Mondale. A majority responded that a black or Hispanic vice presidential candidate would be acceptable, but the number of "Don't know" and "Undecided" voters was sufficiently large to provide no clear guidance. Mondale was not matched up with particular candidates in trial runs because none of the candidates under consideration was sufficiently well known nationally to make a reliable poll possible.

In late June and early July at his home in North Oaks, Minnesota, Mondale interviewed Tom Bradley, the black mayor of Los Angeles, Henry Cisneros, the Hispanic-American mayor of San Antonio, and Dianne Feinstein, the mayor of San Francisco. Finally, he met with Representative Geraldine Ferraro of New York, the chairperson of the Platform Committee. She was a protegé of House Speaker Thomas P. O'Neill and also came strongly recommended by Cuomo, who argued that she would appeal to Italian-American as well as women voters.

Mondale's aides were closely divided between Feinstein and Ferraro. Two calculations tipped the decision in favor of Ferraro. Mondale did not believe even a Californian on his ticket could deprive Reagan of the electoral votes of his home state, whereas Ferraro would help in New York, a state indispensable to the Democrats. Secondly, Feinstein, once divorced, once widowed, and now married for the third time, was serving as mayor of a city known as the "gay capital of America." She would project traditional family and neighborhood values less successfully than Ferraro, a Roman Catholic, a wife for 24 years, a mother of three children, and a former assistant prosecutor. A final touch in Ferraro's favor was that the racially and ethnically mixed district in Queens which she had represented in Congress for six years was the photographic back-drop used in the "All in the Family" television series. With Reagan making inroads among normally Democratic blue-collar and lower middle-class Catholic voters in the big cities and suburbs, Mondale judged Ferraro's religion and ethnic background as important assets.

"This is an exciting choice!" Mondale exclaimed when he revealed his choice of Ferraro one week before the convention opened. His decision achieved its immediate objective of creating a burst of excitement and favorable publicity in the days leading up to the San Francisco convention. Regardless of the outcome of the election, Mondale had lowered a historic barrier against women participating at the highest level of national politics.

The large imponderable was whether Ferraro would widen the "gender gap" between male and female voters to an extent that would help the Democrats significantly. In 1980, six million more women voted than did men. Reagan, who won the white male vote decisively, barely edged out Carter among the women, 46 percent to 45 percent. Polls throughout the subsequent four years had consistently showed that a majority of women had less confidence in Reagan than did men because they viewed his foreign policy as bellicose and his domestic policies as lacking in compassion.

Having made his bold move on the Vice Presidency, Mondale then committed an astonishing lapse of political judgment. On the weekend before the convention opened, he announced that he was dismissing Charles Manatt as Democratic national chairman and naming Bert Lance to direct his campaign. After having to resign as director of the Office of Management and Budget in the Carter Administration in 1977, Lance was indicted for alleged violations of Federal banking laws. A jury acquitted him on most of the charges but failed to reach a verdict on three. Deciding these were not sufficiently weighty to justify a second trial, the judge dismissed them. Lance resumed his banking career and made a political comeback as chairman of the Georgia Democratic party. He had been helpful in rallying support to Mondale in the crucial Georgia primary in March and had a wide, friendly acquaintance with other southern politicians. Having passed over the South in the choice of a running mate, Mondale wanted to make a gesture to that region. Other politicians and political commentators, however, found it hard to understand why Mondale would want to revive memories of the "Bert Lance affair" and underscore his own association with the Carter Administration. Adverse reaction to the Lance appointment undercut the euphoria over the Ferraro selection. Mondale backed away from his mistake, allowing Manatt to remain as national chairman and Lance to withdraw. This bungling harmed Mondale's prospects in Georgia, one of the few southern states where he might have been competitive against Reagan. It also for the first time stirred doubts in the political community as to whether Mondale's senior staff, a tightly closed group made up mostly of younger Minnesotans, was as astute as their reputation had suggested.

The platform on which the Mondale-Ferraro ticket campaigned was unequivocally liberal. When contrasted with the program adopted the following month by the Republicans at their Dallas convention, the Democratic platform drew the philosophical line between the two parties more sharply than at any time since the Johnson vs. Goldwater contest twenty years earlier.

On defense spending and military power, the Republican platform praised the Reagan military buildup and pledged "to do everything necessary so that, in case of conflict, the United States would clearly prevail." The Democrats stated: "We will reduce the rate of increase in defense spending. . . . True national security requires urgent measures to freeze and reverse the arms race, not the pursuit of the phantom of nuclear superiority or futile Star Wars' schemes."

On Central America, the Republican platform declared: "The entire region . . . is gravely threatened by Communist expansion, inspired and supported by the Soviet Union and Cuba. . . . We support continued assistance to the democratic freedom fighters in Nicaragua." The Democratic platform said: "We need to develop relations based on mutual respect and mutual benefit. Beyond essential security concerns, these relations must emphasize diplomacy, development and respect for human rights. . . . We must terminate our support for the contras and paramilitary groups in Nicaragua."

With regard to the income tax, the Republicans pledged themselves to "eliminate the incentive-destroying effects of graduated tax rates. . . . We therefore support tax reform that will lead to a . . . modified flat tax." The Democrats countered: "We will enhance the progressivity of our personal income tax code."

Concerning health care, the Republicans stated: "Many health problems arise within the family and should be dealt with there. . . . We will not tolerate the use of federal funds, taxed away from parents, to abrogate their role in family health care." The Democrats said: "We reaffirm our commitment to the long-term goal of comprehensive national health insurance."

On education, the Republican platform stated: "We believe that education is a local function, a state responsibility, and a federal concern. The federal role in education should be limited." The Democratic platform said: "While education is the responsibility of local government, local governments already strapped for funds by this administration cannot be expected to bear alone the burden. . . . We call for the immediate restoration of the cuts in funding of education programs by the Reagan Administration."

With regard to nuclear power, the GOP platform stated: "We will work to eliminate unnecessary regulatory procedures so that nuclear plants can be brought on line quickly, efficiently, and safely." The Democratic plank: "The Democratic Party strongly opposes the Reagan Administration's policy of aggressively promoting the further subsidizing of nuclear power." The Democrats also promised to "revitalize" the Environmental Protection Agency, while the Republicans were silent on that scandal-ridden agency.

Several perennial issues reappeared in one or both platforms. The Democrats said that ratification of the Equal Rights Amendment would be "a top priority." The Republican platform was silent on the ERA. With regard to "right to work," the Democrats promised to repeal section 14(b) of the Taft-Hartley Act. The Republicans said: "We reaffirm our longstanding support for the right of states to enact 'right to work' laws under section 14(b) of the Taft-Hartley Act." The Republicans also made a cautious bow toward the restoration of the gold standard, saying that it "may be a useful mechanism . . . to sustain price stability." The Democrats were silent on the gold standard.

These opposing planks contradicted the myth that the two major parties had few serious differences and were becoming indistinguishable. Since Ferraro had chaired the Platform Committee and Mondale's aides had carefully monitored the platform's language, the adoption of the platform and the nomination of Ferarro for Vice President expressed the liberal consensus and ideological harmony that, for better or worse, prevailed among the Democrats.

The Democrats were well aware that the images projected at the convention to the television audience would probably influence voters far more than the platform that was adopted. In terms of imagery, the San Francisco convention was an almost unqualified success. Governor Cuomo as keynote speaker demonstrated that he was Reagan's equal in the art of talking both to the live audience in the hall and the vastly larger audience watching on television. He expressed emotional force and evoked enthusiasm from his immediate listeners without losing the conversational tone and psychological intimacy necessary to hold the attention of television viewers. He challenged Reagan directly by taking back for the Democrats the now fashionable themes of family, neighborhood, and community and using them to justify not the individualism and competition of the marketplace but the caring and compassion of government acting with social responsibility. He said:

> The difference between Democrats and Republicans has always been measured in courage and confidence. The Republicans believe the wagon train will not make it to the frontier unless some of our old, some of our young,

and some of our weak are left behind by the side of the trail. The strong
will inherit the land!

We Democrats believe that we can make it all the way with the whole family
intact. We have. More than once. Ever since Franklin Roosevelt lifted himself from his wheelchair to lift this nation from its knees. Wagon train after
wagon train. To new frontiers of education, housing, peace. The whole family
aboard. Constantly reaching out to extend and enlarge that family. Lifting
them up into the wagon on the way. Blacks and Hispanics, people of every
ethnic group, and Native Americans—all those struggling to build their families and claim some small share of America. For nearly 50 years we carried
them to new levels of comfort, security, dignity, even affluence.

Some of us are in this convention to remind ourselves where we come from
and to claim the future for ourselves and for our children.

The bitter rivals of 1980, former President Carter and Senator Edward M.
Kennedy, made supportive appearances. Carter addressed the delegates briefly
on opening night; Kennedy introduced Mondale for his acceptance speech. Hart
and Jackson both made major speeches before the balloting began. Although
their remarks were conciliatory and Mondale's first ballot victory was assured,
neither withdrew. Mondale was nominated with 2191 votes, while Hart had 1200
1/2 and Jackson had 465 1/2.

In accepting, Mondale made a direct appeal to those who had voted for
Reagan four years earlier:

I heard you. And our party heard you. After we lost, we didn't tell the
American people that they were wrong. Instead, we began asking you what
our mistakes had been. . . . Tonight we come to you with a new realism:
ready for the future, and recapturing the best in our tradition.

We know that America must have a strong defense, and a sober view of the
Soviets. We know that government must be as well-managed as it is well-
meaning. We know that a healthy, growing private economy is the key to
our future.

Look at our platform. There are no defense cuts that weaken our security;
no business taxes that weaken our economy; no laundry lists that raid our
treasury. We are wiser, stronger, and focussed on the future.

Assailing Reagan's budget deficit and promising to cut it by two-thirds,
Mondale promised to raise taxes.

Let's tell the truth. Mr. Reagan will raise taxes, and so will I. He won't tell
you. I just did.

This was a move almost as unorthodox as choosing a woman for a running
mate. Though known for his caution, Mondale had made two bold moves,
knowing that he had to go for broke if he was to have any chance of winning.

The Mondale staff had distributed thousands of small American flags to
the delegates and visitors. The television cameras closed out the convention on
a living tableau of massed thousands linking arms, waving flags, and singing

"God Bless America." If patriotism could be reclaimed from Reagan and the Republicans, the Democrats were making the effort.

A Gallup poll taken for *Newsweek* immediately after the convention put Mondale ahead of Reagan 48 percent to 46 percent. The Ferraro nomination and the well-managed convention seemed to have paid off.

The Republicans gathered for their national convention in Dallas on August 20 under ideal circumstances for the party in power. The nation was at peace. The economy was booming. (The gross national product which had been rising since the recession ended in late 1982 leaped ahead at an annual rate of 7.6 percent in the second quarter of 1984). The incumbent President was personally popular and politically in command of his party. For observers with long memories, the Reagan "coronation" in Dallas was strongly reminiscent of the San Francisco convention that renominated Dwight D. Eisenhower in 1956.

No serious controversies marred the prevailing mood of optimism and triumph. None of the other speakers competed with Reagan for admiration or attention in the way that Cuomo and Jackson had rivalled Mondale. The keynote speaker was U.S. Treasurer Katherine Ortega, chosen not for her oratorical skills but for her symbolism as a woman and a Hispanic. The stronger speech on the first evening was delivered by Jeane Kirkpatrick, the ambassador to the United Nations and still nominally a Democrat, who berated her party for departing from the stress on military strength and anti-Communism that had characterized the Democratic Administrations of Truman, Kennedy and Johnson. Vice President Bush and his prospective rivals in 1988, Senators Howard Baker and Robert Dole and Representative Jack Kemp, made speeches, none of which notably stirred the delegates.

Senator Barry Goldwater took the delegates on a stroll down memory lane. He did not have to remind them that it was with a speech in his campaign twenty years earlier that Reagan had made his national political debut. Reagan's triumph was the delayed justification of the conservative crusade that Goldwater had begun a quarter-century earlier. Goldwater savored the moment and revived half-forgotten rhetoric and campaign themes. He blamed four wars in the 20th century on "the foreign policy and defense weakness of Democratic Administrations." Quoting from his own acceptance speech of 1964, he said: "Let me remind you, extremism in the defense of liberty is no vice."

After his speech, Goldwater in an interview with ABC News disclosed that on some issues the Republican party had drifted to a more extreme position than his own. He deplored the platform's rejection of abortion in all circumstances and its demand for a constitutional amendment to restore prayer in the schools.

"I don't think it [abortion] should be in politics at all," Goldwater said. "Then we get into school prayer. The decision of the Supreme Court on school prayer was a proper one. No government should write a prayer, and make my children use it—or anybody's children use it."

It was precisely on these "social issues" that Reagan and the convention managers overreached themselves and lost votes that they might otherwise have won. At an ecumenical prayer breakfast on August 23, the last day of the convention, Reagan said, "The truth is, politics and morality are inseparable, and as morality's foundation is religion, religion and politics are necessarily related. We need religion as a guide."

He asserted that the desire of a majority of Americans to have voluntary prayer in public schools was being frustrated by opponents "in the name of tolerance, freedom, and openmindedness."

"Isn't the real truth that they are intolerant of religion? They refuse to tolerate its importance in our lives."

Fundamentalist evangelical Protestants dominated the prayer breakfast. Their clergymen such as the Reverend Jerry Falwell, the founder of the Moral Majority movement, and the Reverend Wallie Amos Criswell, a leader of the conservative wing of the Southern Baptist Convention, were prominent among the clergymen who opened and closed the convention sessions with prayer.

Although Reagan, at the prayer breakfast and in appearances later in the campaign before Mormon and Jewish groups, was careful to note that he was neutrally benevolent toward all religions, his remarks in Dallas and his association with fundamentalist Protestants set off shock waves among Jewish voters. As a small minority in a nation with a Christian majority, Jews had been sensitized by the tragic history of their people in other countries to react whenever a political leader began to identify the state with ideals of the dominant religion. Elsewhere, it had often been the signal for the onset of anti-Semitic persecution.

In the Democratic primaries in the spring, the anti-Semitic overtones of the Jackson campaign had opened up for Republican strategists the prospect that Reagan could further enhance the support he had gained among Jewish voters in 1980. As the campaign developed, however, Jackson faded from the news, and the fear of fundamentalist Protestant influence on Reagan became the dominant concern for many Jewish voters. (On Election Day, Jews by a margin of 66 percent to 32 percent would return to their traditional Democratic allegiance. This contrasted with the 1980 results: Carter 45 percent, Reagan 39 percent, and Anderson 15 percent.)

But at the GOP convention in August, the depth of Reagan's overall popular support was evident. Senator Paul Laxalt of Nevada made the nominating speech for Reagan as he had four years earlier. Reagan was in effect presented to the convention for his acceptance speech by an 18-minute film starring himself. The Columbia Broadcasting System and the American Broadcasting Company declined to show the film on the grounds that it was propaganda, not news, but the National Broadcasting Company put it on the air as did the Cable News Network. (The three major networks had refused to run a similar film about Mondale shown at the Democratic convention.) The theme of the Reagan film was that his administration represented a new morning, a new beginning for America. In a rapid sequence of images, none of them lasting longer than a few seconds, Americans in different walks of life and from different ethnic backgrounds were shown at sunrise and at flag-raisings. There were numerous pictures featuring the American flag as Reagan's voice spoke of a "reawakening of patriotism in our country." A singer with a husky male voice sang a song, "God Bless the U.S.A." Its lyrics were in part:

If tomorrow all the things were gone
I've worked for all my life,
And I had to start again
With just my children and my wife,
I'd thank my lucky stars to be living here today,
'Cause the flag still stands for freedom,
And they can't take that away.
And I'm proud to be an American. . . .

And there ain't no doubt I love this place.
God bless the U.S.A.

The film included excerpts from dramatic and ceremonial moments in the previous four years. News footage on the attempted assassination of 1981 was shown, and the President's voice was heard saying that Cardinal Terence Cooke of New York had visited him in the hospital and said, "God must have been sitting on your shoulder."

"And I told him," Reagan is heard saying on the film, "He must have been. I told him, 'Whatever time I've got left, it now belongs to someone else.' "

The film had several scenes of Reagan's trip to Normandy battlefields of World War II on the 40th anniversary of D-Day. It moved on to show Reagan surrounded by the U.S. Olympic team. After a huge close-up of Reagan and a brief silence, there was the sound of "Ruffles and Flourishes." Then an announcer's voice on the soundtrack said: "Ladies and gentlemen, the President of the United States."

Time magazine described the Reagan film as "something of a cross between a Pepsi-Cola commercial (happy young people, catchy music) and [the 1984 film] *The Natural* (mythic baseball heroism inspired by love and personal fidelity, backlighted by the sun, awash with violins). That was no surprise: the 18-minute movie was crafted, in large part, by Phil Dusenberry, co-author of the screenplay for *The Natural* and vice chairman and executive creative director of the BBDO, Inc., advertising agency, which handles the Pepsi account."

Reagan, who had made his living as a film actor and then as the host of a television program, was the first President since Kennedy to bring television successfully into the service of his political ends. Television was to Reagan what radio had been to Franklin Roosevelt. In the film about Reagan shown at the Dallas convention, which was also narrated by Reagan, the blending of television and politics, and the use of television as simultaneously a medium for entertainment, for advertising, and for political propaganda, were brought to the highest peak of craftmanship yet reached.

Reagan's acceptance speech, although highly effective in evoking applause from his audience, was regarded by most commentators as anti-climactic. It was devoted largely to a point-by-point response to criticisms levelled by Mondale and other speakers at the Democratic convention. Reagan heavily underscored the contrasts as he saw them between America in 1984 and four years earlier. He set forth his central message in this paragraph near the end of his address:

> We promised we'd reduce the growth of the Federal Government, and we have. We said we intended to reduce interest rates and inflation, and we have. We said we would reduce taxes to provide incentives for individuals and business to get our economy moving again, and we have. We said there must be jobs with a future for our people, not government make-work programs. And, in the last 19 months, six and a half million new jobs in the private sector have been created. We said we would once again be respected throughout the world, and we are. We said we would restore our ability to protect our freedom on land, sea and in the air, and we have.
>
> We bring to the American citizens in this election year a record of accomplishment and the promise of continuation.

Polls taken as the Republican convention ended showed that the Reagan-Bush ticket had regained the considerable lead that it had enjoyed in June. Between the two conventions, the Olympic Games had been held in Los Angeles, games which Reagan had opened and which Mondale had not attended. The many gold medals won by American athletes indirectly reinforced Reagan's theme of revitalized American patriotism and self-confidence. Unless Reagan stumbled badly, he appeared to be headed for a decisive victory.

Democratic planning for the fall campaign was not complicated by a third party in the field. John Anderson in the spring had abandoned his effort to keep a third party alive, and he endorsed Mondale after his nomination. Democrats hoped to develop a partisan theme that would reinvigorate the Democratic coalition, hold the 41 percent of the total vote that Carter had won in 1980, and add at least two-thirds of the 6.7 percent of the vote that Anderson had attracted. In addition, they planned a registration drive to maximize their black support. If they could stay in contention in the last two months of the campaign with their support at, say, 46 or 47 percent, they would be in a position to close the gap if they received one or two lucky breaks.

It was soon apparent that the Democrats were unable to present an effective campaign theme and that luck was running against them. From an intellectual standpoint, the lack of a unifying theme was understandable. What theme could tie together such national and world problems as the budget deficits, arms control, the Middle Eastern stalemate, the Nicaraguan revolution, and the Soviet invasion of Afghanistan? But what was intellectually defensible was politically disadvantageous. In an age of television, presidential campaigns had to a large extent become media events, with candidates' speeches written and campaign events planned to play well on the network evening news shows. The news that a candidate generated and the commercials that his campaign paid for were designed to reinforce one another.

Reagan achieved this synergistic effect. His theme was confidence, optimism, America is back and standing tall. His advertising replayed patriotic and upbeat images from the film shown at the Dallas convention. The news programs showed him delivering the same message in highly simplified form: "We think in America every day is the 4th of July. Our opponents think every day is April 15!"

Mondale unveiled his plan to reduce deficits by increasing taxes on corporations and well-to-do individuals, but unless and until voters experienced the effect of the deficit in their own lives, the deficit remained a problem that was difficult to grasp. Having defended Keynesian deficits for two generations, the Democrats were ill at ease in their new role as budget balancers. Few Democratic candidates at the state and local levels associated themselves with Mondale's tax increase and budget deficit proposals.

Polling by the Gallup Organization showed that his tax increase proposal seriously eroded popular support for the national Democratic ticket and that this began to be apparent within a few days of the end of the Democratic convention. The Reagan managers were later astonished to learn that Mondale had made this critically important decision without "market testing" it by advance polling. There was abundant polling evidence of a widespread public uneasiness about the size of the Reagan deficits but no specific information as to how the public would react to a Democratic call for higher taxes.

Data from the polls also indicated that Reagan was perceived as favoring the rich, and Democrats had hoped to exploit the "fairness" issue. In reality, it seemed only to arouse black and Hispanic voters, who were already heavily Democratic and who traditionally did not register or vote in as high proportions as other groups.

Mondale stressed the importance of arms control, promised to freeze nuclear weapons, and urged annual summit meetings with Soviet leaders. He warned against the danger of becoming embroiled in a Vietnam-style conflict in Central America. In the absence of any immediate crisis in U.S.-Soviet relations or of any situation in which American troops were engaged in combat, these peace issues did not catch on with any voters except convinced liberals.

The Soviet leadership blunted the arms-control issue in September when it sent Foreign Minister Andrei Gromyko to visit President Reagan at the White House. This was interpreted as a signal that the Russians foresaw a Reagan victory and were prepared to do business with him on arms control in his second Administration, notwithstanding his harsh anti-Communist rhetoric and their own walkout from the Geneva conference in 1983. Many voters may have concluded that Reagan's tough talk and sustained arms buildup would pay more dividends than the Democrats' conciliatory approach.

The Mondale campaign's lack of a cohesive theme was reflected in the fumbling of its television advertising. The choice of a political consultant or an advertising firm to produce the Mondale commercials was one of the fundamental decisions of the campaign. Yet by the beginning of September, a selection had not been made. When one campaign manager finally chose to split the advertising budget among five different firms, three of them rejected the offer, insisting that they wanted total control or they would not participate. The upshot was that the Mondale advertising limped through the campaign. This failure was a major reason for the magnitude of Mondale's defeat. He and his senior staff, most of them lawyers, had shown themselves in the primaries and conventions to be skillful political organizers on a state-by-state basis, but once a presidential candidate is nominated, the general election campaign is not a state campaign writ large. As he demonstrated in the two debates, Mondale was a competent television performer, but his own and his staff's inability to conceive of the fall campaign in television terms was a critical weakness.

Meanwhile, Lady Luck was riding the Reagan plane. Not only did Gromyko choose to come to Reagan's assistance but two successive misfortunes hit Geraldine Ferraro. The first involved her family finances. During her six years in Congress, she had sought to separate her political career from her husband's real estate business. She had filed separate income tax returns and had refused to include his earnings on the annual financial disclosure statement required of members of Congress. When challenged on these practices after her nomination, Ferraro impulsively said that she would make public both her own and her husband's tax returns. This went beyond the legal requirement of the Federal election laws and beyond normal political practice. When Senator Dole was the Republican vice presidential candidate in 1976, for example, he had not disclosed the tax returns of his wife, who pursued her own career.

Ferraro's husband, John Zaccaro, balked at fulfilling his wife's promise because, as he claimed, full disclosure might embarrass him in the conduct of his real estate operations. She tried to pass off this refusal with a light remark, telling reporters that anyone married to an Italian husband would know how stubborn such a man could be. Predictably, this remark failed to settle the matter. The press began to investigate Zaccaro's business activities vigorously on the possibility that he was hiding something scandalous. One impropriety did turn up. As court-appointed conservator of the property of a wealthy senile woman, Zaccaro had borrowed (and later repaid with 12-percent interest) $175,000 from the estate to invest in one of his own real estate deals, a practice frowned upon by probate courts but not explicitly forbidden by law in New York. When this episode became news, the court removed Zaccaro as conservator. Meanwhile, he had relented and agreed to allow his wife to make his income tax returns public.

The returns of Ferraro and her husband were released to reporters one day in advance of a news conference that she had called. She answered questions from 200 reporters for an hour and 40 minutes. The session was televised live. Her performance was a spectacular personal triumph. *Time* magazine reflected the consensus view when it wrote: "The questions, about her family finances and personal ethics, were complicated and often barbed, yet she managed to seem neither combative nor defensive. Her manner was precise and serious, but relaxed and good-humored too. Her answers were lucid and carefully organized, anecdotal and unpretentious."

Ferraro had no sooner battled back on that front when she was attacked on another. Archbishop John J. O'Connor of New York denounced her for her views on abortion. Ferraro in 1982 had sent a letter to approximately 50 Catholic colleagues in the House of Representatives enclosing a pamphlet from a group, Catholics for a Free Choice, and inviting them to a briefing. In her letter, she wrote: "Catholic lawmakers . . . have experienced moral and political doubt and concern. That is what the briefing and this monograph are all about. They show us that the Catholic position on abortion is not monolithic and that there can be a range of personal and political responses to the issue."

Referring to this letter, Archbishop O'Connor accused her in September 1984 of giving "the world to understand that Catholic teaching is divided on the subject" of abortion. "There is no variance, there is no flexibility, there is no leeway," he declared. He repeated this charge in televised interviews and news conferences over the next week. He climaxed these criticisms with the comment, "Her quarrel is not with me but with the Pope."

During this same period in the first half of September, Archbishop Bernard Law of Boston and 18 other bishops in New England issued a joint statement describing abortion as "the critical issue" of the campaign, and Cardinal John Krol of Philadelphia introduced President Reagan at a Polish festival and extolled his views. Antiabortion demonstrators from the Right to Life movement attended every Ferraro rally, chanting "baby killer."

The effect of this clerical cannonading was to throw Ferraro again on the defensive and distract public attention from the anti-Reagan message she was trying to deliver. Ferraro's position on the abortion issue was no different from that of Governor Cuomo, Senator Kennedy, and many other Catholic political leaders who had refused to join their church's crusade for a constitutional amendment outlawing abortion. She had not ever been publicly criticized by the archbishop of her own diocese of Brooklyn and Queens. That she was attacked so vociferously by Archbishop O'Connor in the neighboring Manhattan diocese and implicitly by Archbishop Law of Boston was an example of the bad luck that shadowed the Democratic campaign. Both these prelates had been appointed only a few months earlier; their predecessors, Cardinal Cooke of New York and Cardinal Humberto Medeiros of Boston, were lower-keyed figures who had generally avoided public battles with political figures.

The abortion controversy was particularly damaging because it undercut much of the rationale for choosing Ferraro. As a wife and mother, a Catholic and an Italian American, she was expected to appeal particularly to socially conservative Catholic Democrats who in recent presidential elections had begun to stray from the party of their parents. Insofar as such voters were influenced by the opinion of leading bishops, she had been effectively neutralized. Columnist Mary McGrory noted the irony: "Here she is, a lifelong Catholic, a product of Catholic schools and colleges. She goes to Mass every Sunday, and the hierarchy of her church is acting like an arm of the Reagan re-election committee. Ronald Reagan, who never puts a foot inside a church, is acclaimed as the nation's spiritual leader, introduced by cardinals and invited to ring monastery bells."

By early October the gap between Reagan and Mondale was widening. All Democratic hopes of turning the election around or even making it reasonably close now depended upon the two televised debates, scheduled for Sunday, October 7, in Louisville, Kentucky, and October 21 in Kansas City, Missouri. The Democrats had originally pressed for six debates but, realistically, had settled for two between Mondale and Reagan and one between Ferraro and

Bush. There was some risk for Reagan in agreeing to any. Since the modern practice of presidential debates had begun, debates had worked in favor of the challenger (Kennedy over Vice President Nixon in 1960, Carter over President Ford in 1976, and Reagan over President Carter in 1980). His agreement to debate was a measure of Reagan's confidence in his communication skills and his conviction that the major issues of peace and prosperity were working in his favor.

The Louisville debate was confined to domestic affairs. The outcome fulfilled Mondale's hopes and interjected a dash of doubt into the rising Republican euphoria. Mondale came across on television as relaxed, self-confident and occasionally witty. He kept Reagan on the defensive through much of the 90 minutes. The President had been heavily briefed and at times sounded almost like Jimmy Carter in rattling off facts and statistics. Mondale, by contrast, adopted the Reaganesque approach of being personally mellow and putting forward his ideas in broad, philosophical terms. This reversal of roles was striking in the closing statements of the two candidates.

Reagan framed the debate by asking again the question he had asked four years earlier: "Are you better off than you were four years before?" He then gave a fact-laden memorized answer in which he said in part:

> Well, let's put it this way, in the first half of 1980 gross national product was down a minus 3.7 percent. The first half of '84 it's up 8.5%. Productivity in the first half of 1980 was down a minus 2 percent. Today it is up a plus 4 percent. Personal earnings after taxes per capita have gone up almost $3,000 in these four years. In 1980 or 1979 the person with a fixed income of $8,000 was $500 above the poverty line, and this maybe explains why there are the numbers still in poverty. By 1980 that same person was $500 below the poverty line.

Mondale responded:

> The President's favorite question is, "Are you better off?" Well, if you're wealthy, you're better off. If you're middle income, you're about where you were, and if you're of modest income, you're worse off. That's what the economists tell us. But is that really the question that should be asked. Isn't the real question, "Will we be better off? Will our children be better off?" . . .
>
> Are we better off with this arms race? Will we be better off if we start this "Star Wars" escalation into the heavens? Are we better off when we de-emphasize our values in human rights? Are we better off when we load our children with this fantastic debt? Would fathers and mothers feel proud of themselves if they loaded their children with debts like this nation is now, over a trillion dollars, on the shoulders of our children? Can we be—say, really say, that we will be better off when we pull away from sort of that basic American instinct of decency and fairness?
>
> I would rather lose a campaign about decency than win a campaign about self-interest. I don't think this nation is composed of people who care only for themselves.

Reagan had earlier used another famous line from his 1980 debate: "There you go again." He used it this time to deny Mondale's charge that he had a secret plan to raise taxes if he were reelected.

Mondale was prepared. Resting an elbow on the lectern and turning to face the President, he asked:

> Remember the last time you said that? You said it when President Carter said you were going to cut Medicare, and you said, "Oh, no, there you go again, Mr. President." And what did you do right after the election? You went out and tried to cut $20 billion out of Medicare. And so when you say, "There you go again," people remember this.

Reagan looked surprised and angry. At other times in the debate, he paused and visibly groped for facts that he needed to complete a sentence but could not quite remember. For the first time, Reagan's age and his often shaky grasp of information seemed to come together and to put in question his fitness to serve as President for another four years. *The Wall Street Journal,* by coincidence, ran a long front-page story on Reagan's age and mental and physical fitness on the day following the debate. This story provided television commentators that evening with an armory of facts and examples on this theme. These stories and commentaries reinforced the impression of telephone polls, taken on Sunday evening and on the next day, that Mondale had won the debate decisively.

"Today we have a brand new race," Mondale said exultantly on October 8 as he marched up Fifth Avenue in the Columbus Day parade, cheered by newly-heartened Democrats. But it was not quite as dramatic as that. His good showing enabled him to cut into the President's pre-debate lead of 15 to 20 points in various opinion polls. A second, even more decisive victory in the Kansas City debate would be necessary to bring him genuinely into contention.

It was not to be, despite the fact that, if anything, Mondale outdebated Reagan on foreign policy issues on October 21 more clearly than he had on domestic issues two weeks earlier. On the very first question, Reagan misspoke about the Central Intelligence Agency's role in Nicaragua and had to correct himself. In the middle of the debate, he gave a long, rambling answer about Biblical prophecies regarding Armageddon. In his closing statement, he ran out of time before he could complete a metaphorical journey down the coastal highway of California.

But these vagaries did not count as much with the public and most commentators as did the fact that, unlike the first debate, Reagan appeared relaxed and confident. When a reporter raised the issue of age, Reagan brought down the house with this reply: "I want you to know that also I will not make age an issue of this campaign. I am not going to exploit for political purposes my opponent's youth and inexperience."

Reagan effectively attacked Mondale's voting record in the Senate on defense issues: "He has a record of weakness with regard to our national defense that is second to none." He also counterattacked skillfully on the human rights issue, asserting that the greatest losses of human rights occur when a country is lost to Communism or extremism and that Afghanistan and Iran had not been "lost on my watch."

Mondale once again was crisp and cogent, making his points firmly and yet not crossing the line into personal attacks on Reagan. On issues such as the failure to protect the Marines in Lebanon and the failure to achieve arms control with the Soviet Union, he poked holes in the Administration's record. But he did not demolish Reagan's credibility nor did Reagan oblige him by shooting himself in the foot as President Ford had done in the 1976 debate when he asserted that Poland was not under Russian dominaton.

Opinion polls and press reaction indicated that the debate was regarded as a draw or possibly even a Reagan victory. Gloom settled upon Mondale and his entourage. Although his crowds grew to huge size in the last two weeks as loyal partisans turned out to wish him well, Mondale knew that he could not overtake Reagan. In the end, the debates had made no difference. The majority of the people felt comfortable with Reagan and were determined to reelect him, barring some extraordinary event that shook their confidence. Mondale had earned respect by his highly competent performance in the two debates but he had not shaken the public's loyalty to the incumbent.

On November 6 Ronald Reagan achieved one of the great political triumphs of American history. He carried 49 states, losing only Mondale's home state of Minnesota and the District of Columbia. His total of 525 electoral votes surpassed Roosevelt's modern record of 523 in 1936. His popular vote margin of 59 percent to 41 percent placed him close behind Harding, Roosevelt, Johnson and Nixon among landslide winners. His immense triumph, however, was, like Nixon's in 1972, a personal rather than a party success. His party lost two seats in the Senate, reducing its margin to 53 to 47 while it gained 14 seats in the House, where Democrats remained in control, 253 to 182.

The indifferent results in Congress suggested to many analysts that 1984 was probably no more a "critical election" than was 1980. But others argued that Reagan's election demonstrated retroactively that Nixon's first victory in 1968 had been a classic "critical election." They held that Nixon's slight margin over Humphrey had masked that election's significance but that his victory did, in fact, mark a definite turn to the right in American politics. If the vote for George C. Wallace, a nonliberal and implicitly racist candidate, were added to that of Nixon, together they represented 57 percent of the electorate. Nixon alone obtained 61 percent in 1972. Reagan's 59 percent of the popular vote in 1984 conformed closely to this pattern.

Kevin Phillips, author of *The Emerging Republican Majority,* pointed out that Nixon and Reagan drew from the same sources of strength. In a *New York Times* article in 1985, he wrote: "The regional, Protestant fundamentalist, ethnic and racial contours of Nixon's 1972 victory all closely foreshadowed those of Reagan's 1984 triumph."

Phillips argued further that:

. . . major realigning elections seem to occur every 28 to 36 years—in 1800, 1828, 1860, 1896 and 1932. Another was due around 1968, and it came. The five realignment periods all shared a common pattern: in each case, the party newly ascending to power invariably controlled the White House for at least 16 of the first 20 years following the watershed, and such 16 to 20-year party hegemonies have occurred only in these circumstances. By January, 1989, the Republicans will have controlled the Presidency for 16 of the previous 20 years. . . . What we are seeing now is the last great crest of a much older [than 1980] political wave: a "conservative" (or more appropriately, non-liberal) national era that began some 17 or 18 years ago and is now in late middle age.

Seen in the context of GOP victories in four out of the last five presidential elections, Carter's narrow win in 1976 could be regarded as a fluke event attributable to post-Watergate malaise. But how was one to explain continued Democratic predominance in the House of Representatives and control or near-parity in the Senate? Perhaps this could be accounted for by the split-level politics of the South. At the presidential level, white Southerners—and notably, white male voters—had shifted to overwhelming opposition to the national Democratic party. Even in the two Carter campaigns, a majority of white Southerners had voted for the Republican candidate in preference to a native Georgian. Only Carter's strong support from black voters had enabled him to win 10 of the 11 southern states in 1976. In 1984, Reagan carried 72 percent of the white vote in the South. But at the local and congressional level, Southerners remained faithful to the Democrats. In a generation, the GOP had managed to make itself competitive in most southern states in campaigns for the U.S. Senate. In 1962, there was only one Republican senator from the region—John Tower of Texas. After the 1984 election, Republicans held 10 of the South's 22 seats in the Senate. Logic suggests that it would be only a matter of time until white Southerners abandoned their split-level approach to politics and begin voting Republican in House elections as well. If this development were to occur, it would bring to an end the half-century of national Democratic dominance in the House of Representatives.

A radically different and, for the Democrats, a potentially less gloomy interpretation was offered by the young political writer, Sidney Blumenthal. In *The Permanent Campaign,* he debunked the "critical election" theory:

American politics is not necessarily about to experience a completion and rebirth at once; history is not a drama with a recurring fourth act. The realignment theory is useful today, but mostly as a counter-model. For it is a good guide to what is not happening.

A majority of the electorate, in fact, has not been formed into a new coalition, and the party system has not been revitalized. Instead, there is a dealignment of voters; their partisan loyalties are shallower with each succeeding election. They do not adhere to the faith of their fathers. They are often willing to take a chance with a fresh face who seems to articulate their concerns of the moment. They are less committed to party than to personalities, and their commitment to personalities is ephemeral. . . .

The media have taken over much of the role of the party as the intermediary between politicians and public. . . . Politicians are no longer able to rely on

the security of the party machinery. They are obliged to wage individualized
campaigns that become permanent in the attempt to govern.

If Blumenthal's analysis was sound, the Democrats did not need to fear
that they were victims of an inexorable cyclical trend, whether it began in 1968
or 1980. Rather, they needed only to seek and find a new leader who understood
the potential of television as a political tool. A fresh personality with a new
style who could project appealing media images could capture the drifting voters
in the dealigned center of American politics and manufacture his own landslide.
In terms of this analysis, Democrats in 1984 made a fundamental error in
nominating the "old politics" Mondale rather than the "new politics" Hart. In
March, 1984, after his early primary victories, Hart defeated Reagan in a Gallup
Poll matchup, 52 percent to 43 percent. This is tantalizing if inconclusive evidence for the theory that Reagan, even with the powers of incumbency and the
issues of peace and prosperity working in his favor, was vulnerable to the appeal
of a new face capable of attracting the fickle loyalties of millions of restless
political consumers.

The "critical elections" theory and the media-as-master theory would be
best seen as complementary interpretations. The political realignment of the
South which resulted from the civil rights revolution of the 1960s was a major
influence in the Republican presidential victories after 1964. To that extent, it
had given the political era since 1968 a distinctive character. During this period,
the rise in political importance of television and the decline in power of state
and local party organizations created a new volatility in the nation's politics.
Television bred the cult of novelty: new faces, new styles, new advertising
slogans. Party organizations were forces for stability, stressing loyalty as against
the lure of change and retarding rapid swings of opinion. As television surged
and the parties ebbed, landslide victories became more frequent. Public opinion
polling, which tended to give ephemeral moods an air of authority and nascent
trends an air of inevitability, reinforced the destabilizing effects of television.

Reagan's significance could ultimately be more cultural than political, more
as a totem than a chief. He became genial host to a vast national audience of
balance-the-budget conservatives, "supply side" radicals, and monetary zealots;
of Right-to-Life moralists and "swinging single" urban young people; of those
comfortable with change as well as of those yearning for a restoration of stability.
By its very nature, this union of divergent social tendencies is destined to be
temporary. There cannot be a permanent coming together of those who seek a
restoration of old pieties and a reinvigoration of old inhibitions and those who
delight in sexual and social freedoms. Any shift in the balance of forces may
bring disillusionment either to fundamentalist or Yuppie and dissolve a fragile
equilibrium into incoherence.

If Calvin Coolidge in the 1920s was a puritan in Babylon, Reagan in the
1980s could be seen as a neo-Victorian in an age of liberation. His moralistic
rhetoric looked backward to the stern moral code of the past, to an idealization
of work, faith, family, and neighborhood. His philosophy of economics and
government looked forward to a loosening of public restraints and communal

responsibility, to an exaltation of individualism and libertarian self-fulfillment. Like Coolidge, Reagan could perform his symbolic moral role and reconcile irreconcilable forces in the culture only as long as prosperity smothered conflict and sustained a public mood of optimism. The 1984 election was an act of hope that Reagan's luck would hold and swelling affluence validate his optimism.

Appendix

First Presidential Debate
Louisville, October 7, 1984

Most political analysts considered Walter Mondale a clear winner of the first presidential debate of 1984. Discussing domestic affairs, the Democratic candidate appeared relaxed and well-prepared. President Reagan, on the other hand, seemed at times quite inarticulate and groping for facts.

The following people participated in last night's Presidential debate in Louisville:

MODERATOR: Barbara Walters, correspondent, ABC News.

PANELISTS: Diane Sawyer, correspondent, CBS News; Fred Barnes, Washington correspondent, *The Baltimore Sun,* and James G. Wieghart, political correspondent, Scripps-Howard Newspapers.

DOROTHY RIDINGS: Good evening from the Kentucky Center of the Arts in Louisville, Ky. I'm Dorothy Ridings, president of the League of Women Voters, the sponsor of tonight's first Presidential debate between Republican Ronald Reagan and Democrat Walter Mondale.

Tonight's debate marks the third consecutive presidential election in which the league is presenting the candidates for the nation's highest office in face-to-face debate.

Our panelists are James Wieghart, national political correspondent for Scripps-Howard News Service; Diane Sawyer, correspondent for the CBS program "60 Minutes," and Fred Barnes, national political correspondent for *The Baltimore Sun.*

Barbara Walters of ABC News, who is appearing in her fourth Presidential debate is our moderator. Barbara:

MODERATOR: A few words as we begin tonight's debate, about the format. The position of the candidates, that is, who answers questions first, and who gives the last statement was determined by a toss of the coin between the two candidates. Mr. Mondale won. And that means that he chose to give the final closing statement. It means, too, that the President will answer the first question first. I hope that's clear. If it isn't, it will become clear as the debate goes on.

Further, the candidates will be addressed as they each wanted and will therefore be called Mr. President and Mr. Mondale. Since there will also be a second debate between the two Presidential candidates tonight will focus primarily on the economy and other domestic issues.

The debate itself is built around questions from the panel. In each of its segments a reporter will ask the candidates the same general question. Then—and this is important—each candidate will have the chance to rebut what the other has said. In the final segment of the debate will be the closing segment and the candidates will each have four minutes for their closing statement. And as I have said, Mr. Mondale will be the last person on the program to speak.

And now I would like to add a personal note, if I may. As Dorothy Ridings pointed out, I have been involved now in four Presidential debates, either as a moderator or as a panelist. In the past there was no problem in selecting panelists. Tonight, however, there were to have been four panelists participating in this debate. The candidates were given a list of almost 100 qualified journalists from all the media and could agree on only these three fine journalists.

As moderator and on behalf of my fellow journalists I very much regret as does the League of Women Voters that this situation has occurred. And now let us begin the debate with the first question from James Wieghart. Mr. Wieghart.

WIEGHART: Mr. President, in 1980, you promised the American people, in your campaign, a balanced budget by 1983. We've now had more and bigger deficits in the four years you've been in office. Mr. President, do you have a secret plan to balance the budget some time in the second term, and if so, would you lay out that plan for us tonight?

REAGAN: I have a plan. Not a secret plan. As a matter of fact, it is the economic recovery program that we presented when I took office in 1981. It is true that earlier, working with some very prominent economists, I had come up, during the campaign, with an economic program that I thought could rectify the great problems confronting us: the double-digit inflation, the high tax rates that I think were hurting the economy, the stagflation that we were undergoing. Before even the Election Day, something that none of those economists had even predicted had happened, that the economy was so worsened that I was openly saying that what we had thought the basis of our plan could have brought a balanced budget: that was no longer possible.

So the plan that we have had and that we're following, is a plan that is based on growth in the economy, recovery without inflation, and reducing the share of the, that the Government is taking from the gross national product, which has become a drag on the economy. Already we have a recovery that has been going on for about 21 months, to the point that we can now call it an expansion. Under that, this year, we have seen a $21 billion reduction in the deficit from last year, based mainly on the increased revenues the government is getting without raising tax rates.

Our tax cut, we think, was very instrumental in bringing about this economic recovery. We have reduced inflation to about a third of what it was. The interest rates have come down about 9 or 10 points, and we think must come down further. In the last 21 months, more than six million people have gotten jobs. There have been created new jobs for those people to where there are now 105 million civilians working where there were only 99 million before, 107 if you count the military.

So we believe that as we continue to reduce the level of Government spending, the increase, rate of increase in Government spending, which has come down from 17 to 6 percent, and at the same time as the growth in the economy increases the revenues the Government gets without raising taxes, those two lines will meet. And when they meet, that is a balanced budget.

WIEGHART: Mr. President, the Congressional Budget Office has some bad news. The lines aren't about to meet according to their projection; they project that the budget deficit will continue to climb. In the year 1989 they project a budget deficit of $273 billion. In view of that and in view of the economic recovery we are now enjoying, would it make sense to propose a tax increase or take some other fiscal measures to reduce that deficit now when times are relatively good?

REAGAN: The deficit is a result, it is a result of excessive Government spending. I do not, and very frankly, take seriously the Congressional Budget Office projections because they have been wrong on virtually all of them, including the fact that our recovery wasn't going to take place to begin with. But it has taken place. But as I said we have the rate of increase in Government spending down to 6 percent. If the rate of increase in Government spending can be held to 5 percent—we're not far from there—by 1989 that would have reduced the budget deficits down to a $30 billion or $40 billion level. At the same time if we can have a 4 percent recovery continue through that same period of time, that will mean without an increase in tax rates, that will mean $400 billion more in Government revenues. And so I think that the lines can meet. Actually, in constant dollars, in the domestic side of the budget there has been no spending increase in the four years that we have been here.

WIEGHART: Mr. Mondale, the Carter-Mondale Administration didn't come close to balancing the budget in its four years in office either, despite the fact that President Carter did promise a balanced budget during his term. You have proposed a plan combining tax increases and budgetary cuts and other changes in the administration of the Government that would reduce the projected budget deficit by two-thirds to approximately $87 billion in 1989. That still is an enormous deficit that we'll be running for these four years. What other steps do you think should be taken to reduce this deficit and position the country for economic growth?

MONDALE: One of the key tests of leadership is whether one sees clearly the nature of the problem confronted by our nation. And perhaps the dominant domestic issue of our times is what do we do about these enormous deficits.

I respect the President. I respect the Presidency and I think he knows that.

But the fact of it is every estimate by this Administration about the size of the deficit has been off by billions and billions of dollars. As a matter of fact, over four years, they've missed the mark by nearly $600 billion. We were told we would have a balanced budget in 1983. It was $200 billion deficit instead. And now we have a major question facing the American people as to whether we'll deal with this deficit and get it down for the sake of a healthy recovery. Virtually every economic analysis that I've heard of, including the distinguished Congressional Budget Office, which is respected by, I think, almost everyone, says that even with historically high levels of economic growth, we will suffer a $263 billion deficit. In other words, it doesn't converge, as the President suggests. It gets larger, even with growth.

What that means is that we will continue to have devastating problems with foreign trade. This is the worst trade year in American history, by far. Our rural and farm friends will have continued devastation. Real interest rates, the real cost of interest, will remain very very high. And many economists are predicting that we're moving into a period of very slow growth because the economy is tapering off and may be a recession.

I get it down to a level below 2 percent of gross national product with a policy that's fair. I've stood up and told the American people that I think it's a real problem, that it can destroy long-term economic growth, and I've told you what I think should be done.

I think this is a test of leadership and I think the American people know the difference.

WIEGHART: Mr. Mondale, one other way to attack the deficit is further reductions in spending. The President has submitted a number of proposals to Congress to do just that, and in many instances the House, controlled by the Democrats, has opposed them.

Isn't it one aspect of leadership for prominent Democrats such as yourself to encourage responsible reductions in spending and thereby reduce the deficit?

MONDALE: Absolutely. And I have proposed over $100 billion in cuts in Federal spending over four years. But I am not going to cut it out of Social Security and Medicare and student assistance and things that people need.

These people depend upon all of us for the little security that they have. And I'm not going to do it that way. The rate of defense spending increase can be slowed; certainly we can find a coffee pot that costs something less than $7,000.

And there are other ways of squeezing this budget without constantly picking on our senior citizens and the most vulnerable in American life.

And that's why the Congress, including the Republicans, have not gone along with the President's recommendations.

MODERATOR: I would like to ask the audience please to refrain from applauding either side. It just takes away from the time for your candidates. And now it is time for the rebuttal, Mr. President: one minute of rebuttal.

REAGAN: Yes, I don't believe that Mr. Mondale has a plan for balancing the budget. He has a plan for raising taxes. As a matter of fact, the biggest single tax increase in the nation's history took place in 1977, and for the five years previous to our taking office, taxes doubled in the United States and the budget's increased $318 billion, so there is no ratio between taxing and balancing a budget. Whether you borrow the money or whether you simply tax it away from the people, you're taking the same amount of money out of the private sector unless and until you bring down Government's share of what it is taking.

With regard to Social Security I hope there'll be more time than just this win it—minute—to mention that, but I will say this: A President should never say never. But I'm going to violate that rule and say "never." I will never stand for a reduction of the Social Security benefits to the people that are now getting them.

MODERATOR: Mr. Mondale.

MONDALE: That's exactly the commitment that was made to the American people in 1980. He would never reduce benefits. And of course what happens right after the election is they proposed to cut Social Security benefits by 25 percent, reducing the adjustment for inflation, cutting out minimum benefits for the poorest on Social Security, removing educational benefits for dependents whose widows were trying, with widows trying to get them through college. Everybody remembers that. People know what happened. There's a difference. I have fought for Social Security and Medicare and for things to help people who are vulnerable all my life, and I will do it as President of the United States.

MODERATOR: Thank you very much. We will now begin with segment No. 2 with my colleague, Diane Sawyer. Miss Sawyer.

SAWYER: Mr. President, Mr. Mondale. The public opinion polls do suggest that the American people are most concerned about the personal leadership characteristics of the two candidates, and each of you has questioned the other's leadership ability. Mr. President, you have said that Mr. Mondale's leadership would take the country down the path of defeatism and despair and Vice President Bush has called him whining and hoping for bad news. And Mr. Mondale, you have said that President Reagan offers showmanship, not leadership, that he has not mastered what he must know to command his Government. I'd like to ask each of you to substantiate your claims. Mr. Mondale first. Give us specifics to support your claim that President Reagan is a showman, not a leader, has not mastered what he must know to be President after four years, and than second, tell us what personal leadership characteristics you have that he does not.

MONDALE: Well first of all, I think the first answer this evening suggests exactly what I'm saying. There is no question that we face this massive deficit. And almost everybody agrees unless we get it down the chances for long-term healthy growth are nil. And it's also unfair to dump these tremendous bills on our children. The President says it will disappear overnight because of some reason; no one else believes that's the case. I do and I'm standing up to the issue with an answer that's fair. I think that's what leadership is all about.

There's a difference between being a quarterback and a cheerleader and when there's a real problem, a President must confront it. What I was referring to, of course, in the comment that you referred to, was the situation in Lebanon. Now, for three occasions, one after another, our Embassies were assaulted in the same way by a truck with demolition. The first time, and I did not criticize the President because these things can happen once, and sometimes twice, the second time the barracks in Lebanon were assaulted as we all remember. There was two or three commission reports, recommendations by the C.I.A., the State Department and the others, and the third time there was even a warning from the terrorists themselves.

Now I believe that a President must command that White House and those who work for him. It's the toughest job on earth. And you must master the facts and insist that things must be done, are done. I believe the way in which I will approach the Presidency is what's needed. Because all my life that has been the way in which I have sought to lead. And that's why in this campaign I am telling you exactly what I want to do; I am answering your questions; I am trying to provide leadership now before the election so that the American people can participate in that decision.

SAWYER: You have said, Mr. Mondale, that the polls have given you lower ratings on leadership than President Reagan because your message has failed to get through. Given that you have been in public office for so many years, what accounts for the failure of your message to get through?

MONDALE: Well, I think we're getting better all the time, and I think tonight, as we contrast for the first time our different approach to government, to values, to the leadership in this country, I think as this debate goes forward, the American people will have, for the first time, a chance to weigh the two of us against each other. And I think as a process, as a part of that process, what I am trying to say will come across. And that is that we must lead, we must command, we must direct, and a President must see it like it is. He must stand for the values of decency that the American people stand for, and he must use the power of the White House to try to control these nuclear weapons and lead this world toward a safer world.

SAWYER: Mr. President, the issue is leadership in personal terms. First, do you think, as Vice President Bush said, that Mr. Mondale's campaign is one of whining and hoping for bad news. And, second, what leadership characteristics do you possess that Mr. Mondale does not?

REAGAN: Well, whether he does or not, let me suggest my own idea about the leadership factor, and since you've asked it. And incidentally, I might say that with the regard to the 25 percent cuts of Social Security before I get to the answer of your question the only 25 percent cut that I know of was accompanying that huge 1977 tax increase was a cut of 25 percent in the benefits for every American who was born after 1916.

Now, leadership. First of all, I think you must have some principles you believe in. In mine, I happen to believe in the people and believe that the people are supposed to be dominant in our society. That they, not government, are to have control of their own affairs to the greatest extent possible with an orderly society.

Now, having that, I think also that in leadership, well, I believe that you find the people—positions such as I'm in—who have the talent and ability to do the things that are needed in the various departments of government.

I don't believe that a leader should be spending his time in the Oval Office deciding who's going to play tennis on the White House court. And you let those people go with the guidelines of overall policy, and not looking over their shoulder and nitpicking the manner in which they go at the job. You are ultimately responsible, however, for that job.

But I also believe something else about that. I believe that—and when I became Governor of California I started this and I continue it in this office— that any issue that comes before me I have instructed Cabinet members and staff they are not to bring up any of the political ramifications that might surround the issue. I don't want to hear them. I want to hear only arguments as to whether it is good or bad for the people. Is it morally right.

And on that basis, and that basis alone, we make a decision on every issue.

Now, with regard to my feeling about why I thought that his record bespoke his possible taking us back to the same things that we knew under the previous Administration, his record is that he spoke in praise of deficits several times. Said they weren't to be abhorred. That as a matter of fact he at one time said he wished the deficit could be doubled because they stimulate the economy and help reduce unemployment.

SAWYER: As a follow-up, let me draw in another specific if I could, a specific that the Democrats have claimed about your campaign; that it is essentially based on imagery. And one specific that they allege is that, for instance, that recently you showed up at the opening ceremony of a Buffalo old age housing project when in fact your policy was to cut Federal housing subsidies for the elderly, yet you were there to have your picture taken with them.

REAGAN: Our policy was not to cut subsidies. We have believed in partnership and that was an example of a partnership between not only local government and the Federal Government but also between the private sector that built that particular structure. And this is what we've been trying to do is involve the Federal Government in such partnerships. We are today subsidizing housing for more that 10 million people, and we're going to continue along that line. We have no thought of throwing people out into the snow, whether because of age or need. We have preserved the safety net for the people with true need in this country and it has been pure demagoguery that we have in some way shut off all the charitable programs or many of them for the people who have real need. The safety net is there and we're taking care of more people than has ever been taken care of before by any administration in this country.

MODERATOR: Mr. Mondale—an opportunity for you to rebut.

MONDALE: Well, I guess I'm reminded a little bit of what Will Rogers once said about Hoover. He said it's not what he doesn't know that bothers me, it's what he knows for sure just ain't so. The fact of it is, the fact of it is the President's budget sought to cut Social Security by 25 percent. It's not an opinion; it's a fact, and when the President was asked the other day, 'What do you want to cut in the budget?' he said, 'Cut those things I asked for but didn't get.' That's Social Security and Medicare.

The second fact is that the housing unit for senior citizens that the President dedicated in Buffalo was only made possible through a Federal assistance program for senior citizens that the President's budget sought to terminate. So if he'd had his way, there wouldn't have been any housing project there at all. This Administration has taken a meat cleaver out in terms of Federal-assisted housing, and the record is there. We have to see the facts before we can draw conclusions.

REAGAN: Well, let me just respond with regard to Social Security.

When we took office we discovered that the program that the Carter-Mondale Administration had said would solve the fiscal problems of Social Security for the next 50 years, wouldn't solve them for 5. Social Security was due to go bankrupt before 1983. Any proposals that I made at that time were at the request of the chairman, a Democrat, of one of the leading committees, who said we have to do something before the program goes broke and the checks bounce.

And so we made a proposal. And then in 1982 they used that proposal in a demagogic fashion for the 1982 campaign. And three days after the election in 1982 they came to us and said, Social Security, we know, is broke. Indeed, we had to borrow $17 billion to pay the checks.

And then I asked for a bipartisan commission, which I'd asked for from the beginning, to sit down and work out a solution, and so the whole matter of what to do with Social Security has been resolved by bipartisan legislation and it is on a sound basis now for as far as you can see into the next century.

MODERATOR: We begin segment No. 3 with Fred Barnes.

BARNES: Mr. President, would you describe your religious beliefs, noting particularly whether you consider yourself a born-again Christian and explain how these beliefs affect your Presidential decisions?

REAGAN: Well, I was raised to have a faith and a belief and have been a member of a church since I was a small boy. In our particular church we didn't use that term born-again so I don't know whether I would fit that—that particular term.

But I have, thanks to my mother, God rest her soul, the firmest possible belief and faith in God. And I don't believe—believe, I should say, as Lincoln once said, that I could not—I would be the most stupid man in the world if I thought I could confront the duties of the office I hold if I could not turn to someone who was stronger and greater than all others; and I do resort to prayer.

At the same time, however, I have not believed that prayer could be introduced into an election or be a part of a political campaign, or religion a part of that campaign. As a matter of fact I think religion became a part of this campaign when Mr. Mondale's running mate said I wasn't a good Christian. So, it does play a part in my life. I have no hesitancy in saying so. And as I say, I don't believe that I could carry on unless I had a belief in a higher authority and a belief that prayers are answered.

BARNES: Given those beliefs, Mr. President, why don't you attend services regularly, either by going to church or by inviting a minister to the White House, as President Nixon used to do, or someone to Camp David, as President Carter used to do.

REAGAN: The answer to your question is very simple—about why I don't go to church. I start—I have gone to church regularly all my life. And I started to here in Washington. And now, in the position I hold and in the world in which we live, where embassies do get blown up in Beirut, we're supposed to talk about that in the—on the debate the 21st, I understand.

But I pose a threat to several hundred people if I go to church. I know the threats are made against me. We all know the possibility of terrorism. We have seen the barricades that have had to built around the White House.

And therefore, I don't feel—and my minister knows this and supports me in this position. I don't feel that I have a right to go to church, knowing that my being there could cause something of the kind that we have seen in other places; in Beirut, for example.

And I miss going to church but I think the Lord understands.

MODERATOR: May I ask the audience please to refrain from applause. Can we have your second question?

BARNES: Mr. Mondale, would you describe your religious beliefs and mention whether you consider yourself a born-again Christian and explain how those beliefs would affect your decisions as President.

MONDALE: First of all, I accept President Reagan's affirmation of faith. I'm sure that we all accept and admire his commitment to his faith and we are strengthened all of us by that fact.

I am a son of a Methodist minister, my wife is the daughter of a Presbyterian minister, and I don't know if I've been born again, but I know I was born into a Christian family, and I believe I've sung at more weddings and more funerals than anybody ever to seek the Presidency. Whether that helps or not I don't know. I have a deep religious faith, our family does, it is fundamental, it's probably the reason I'm in politics. I think our faith tells us, instructs us about the moral life that we should lead, and I think we're all together on that.

What bothers me is this growing tendency to try to use one's own personal interpretation of faith politically, to question others' faith, and to try to use instrumentalities of government to impose those views on others. All history tells us that that's a mistake.

When the Republican platform says that from here on out we're going to have a religious test for judges before they're selected for the Federal court and then Jerry Falwell announces that that means they get at least two Justices of the Supreme Court, I think that's an abuse of faith in our country. This nation is the most religious nation on earth. More people go to church and synagogues than any other nation on earth, and it's because we kept the politicians and the state out of the personal exercise of our faith. That's why faith in the United States is pure and unpolluted by the intervention of politicians, and I think if we want to continue as I do to have a religious nation, let's keep that line and never cross it.

MODERATOR: Thank you. Mr. Barnes, a question? We have time for rebuttal now.

BARNES: I think I have a follow-up.

MODERATOR: Yes, I asked you if you did. I'm sorry I thought you waived it.

BARNES: Yes. Mr. Mondale, you've complained just now about Jerry Falwell, and you've complained other times about other fundamentalists in politics. Correct me if I'm wrong, but I don't recall your ever complaining about ministers who are involved in the civil rights movement, in the anti-Vietnam War demonstrations or about black preachers who've been so involved in American politics. Is it only conservative ministers that you object to?

MONDALE: No. What I object to—what I object to—what I object to is someone seeking to use his faith to question the faith of another or to use that faith and seek to use the power of Government to impose it on others. A minister who is in civil rights or in the conservative movement because he believes his faith instructs him to do that, I admire. The fact that the faith speaks to us and that we are moral people hopefully I accept and rejoice in. It's when you try to use that to undermine the integrity of private political—or private religious faith and the use of the state is where for the most personal decisions in American life—that's where I draw the line.

MODERATOR: Thank you. Now, Mr. President. Rebuttal.

REAGAN: Yes, it's very difficult to rebut, because I find myself in so much agreement with Mr. Mondale. I, too, want that wall that is in the Constitution, separation of church and state, to remain there. The only attacks I have made are on people who apparently would break away at that wall from the Government side using the Government, using the power of the courts and so forth, to hinder that part of the Constitution that says the Government shall not only not establish a religion, it shall not inhibit the practice of religion, and they have been using these things to have Government, through court orders, inhibit the practice of religion.

A child wants to say grace in a school cafeteria, and a court rules that they can't do it. And because it's school property.

These are the types of things that I think have been happening in a kind of a secular way that have been eroding that separation, and I am opposed to that. With regard to a platform in the Supreme Court, I can only say one thing about that. I don't—I have appointed one member of the Supreme Court, Sandra Day O'Connor, I'll stand on my record on that, and if I have the opportunity to appoint any more, I'll do it in the same manner that I did in selecting her.

MODERATOR: Mr Mondale, your rebuttal, please.

MONDALE: The platform to which the President refers in fact calls for a religious test in the selection of judges. And Jerry Falwell says that means we get two or three judges. And it would involve a religious test for the first time in American life.

Let's take the example that the President cites. I believe in prayer. My family prays. We've never had any difficulty finding time to pray. But do we want a constitutional amendment adopted on the kind proposed by the President that gets the local politicians into the business of selecting prayers that our children must either recite in school or be embarrassed and ask to excuse themselves? Who would write the prayer? What would it say? How would it be resolved when those disputes occurred?

It seems to me that a moment's reflection tells you why the United States Senate turned that amendment down. Because it will undermine the practice of honest faith in our country by politicizing it. We don't want that.

MODERATOR: Thank you, Mr. Mondale. Time is up for this round; we go into the second round of our questioning—begin again with Jim Wieghart. Jim.

WIEGHART: After that discussion, this may be like going from the sublime to the ridiculous, but here goes: I have a political question for you, Mr. Mondale. Polls indicate a massive change in the electorate, away from the coalition that has long made the Democratic Party a majority. Blue-collar workers, young professionals, their children and much of the middle class now regard themselves as independents or Republican instead of Democrats. And the gap, the edge the Democrats had in party registration, seems to be narrowing.

I'd like to ask you, Mr. Mondale, what is causing this? Is the Democratic Party out of synch with the majority of Americans? And will it soon be replaced as the majority party by the Republicans? What do you think needs to be done about it as a Democrat?

MONDALE: My answer is that this campaign isn't over yet. And when people vote, I think you're going to see a very strong verdict by the American people that they favor the approach that I'm talking about.

The American people want arms control; they don't want this arms race. And they don't want this deadly new effort to bring weapons into the heavens. And they want an American foreign policy that leads toward a safer world.

The American people see this debt, and they know it's got to come down. And if it won't come down, the economy's going to slow down, maybe go into a recession. They see this tremendous influx and swamping of cheap foreign imports in this country that has cost over three million jobs, given farmers the worst year in American history.

And they know this debt must come down, as well, because it's unfair to our children.

The American people want this environment protected. They know that these toxic waste dumps should have been cleaned up a long time ago. And they know that people's lives and health are being risked because we've had an Administration that has been totally insensitive to the law and the demands for the protection of the environment.

The American people want their children educated; they want to get our edge back in science, and they want a policy, headed by the President, that helps close this gap that's widening between the United States and Europe and Japan.

The American people want to keep opening doors. They want those civil rights laws enforced; they want the equal rights amendment ratified; they want equal pay for comparable effort for women. And they want it because they've understood from the beginning that when we open doors, we're all stronger. Just as we were at the Olympics.

I think as you make the case, the American people will increasingly come to our cause.

WIEGHART: Mr. Mondale, isn't it possible that the American people have heard your message and they are listening but they are rejecting it?

MONDALE: Well, tonight we had the first debate over the deficit. The President says it will disappear automatically. I've said it's going to take some work. I think the American people will draw their own conclusions. Secondly, I've said that I will not support the cuts in Social Security and Medicare and the rest that the President's proposed. The President answers that it didn't happen or if it did, it was resolved later in a commission. As the record develops I think it's going to become increasingly clear that what I am saying and where I want to take this country is exactly where the country wants to go, and the comparison of approaches is such that I think will lead to further strength.

WIEGHART: Mr. President, you and your party are benefiting from what appears to be an erosion of the old Democratic coalition, but you have not laid out a specific agenda to take this shift beyond Nov. 6. What is your program for America for the next decade with some specificity?

REAGAN: Well, again, I am running on the record. I think sometimes Mr. Mondale's running away from his, but I'm running on the record of what we have asked for, will continue to try and get things that we didn't get in the program that has already brought the rate of spending of Government down from 17 percent to 6.1 percent, a program of returning authority and autonomy to the local and state governments that has been unjustly seized by the Federal Government and you might find those words in the Democratic platform of some years ago. I know because I was a Democrat at that time. And I left the party eventually because I could no longer follow the turn in the Democratic leadership that took us down an entirely different path, a path of centralizing authority in the Federal Government, lacking trust in the American people.

I promised when we took office that we would reduce inflation. We have to one-third of what it was. I promised that we would reduce taxes. We did, 25 percent across the board. That barely held even with—if it did that much—with the gigantic tax increased imposed in 1977. But at least it took that burden away from them. I said that we would create jobs for our people, and we did, six million in the last 20 or 21 months. I said that we would become respected in the world again and that we would refurbish our national defense to the place that we could deal on the world scene and then seek disarmaments, reduction of arms, and hopefully an elimination of nuclear weapons. We have done that.

All of the things that I said we would do, from inflation being down, interest rates being down, unemployment falling—all of those things we have done. And I think that this is something the American people see. I think they also know that we have.

We had a commission that came in a year ago with a recommendation on education, on excellence in education, and today without the Federal Government being involved other than passing on to them, the school districts, the words from that commission, we find 35 states with task forces now dealing with their educational problems, we find that schools are extending the curriculum to now have forced teaching of mathematics and science and so forth. All of these things have brought an improvement in the college entrance exams for the first time in some 20 years. So I think that many Democrats are seeing the same thing this Democrat saw. The leadership isn't taking us where we want to go.

WIEGHART: Mr. President, there's a—much of what you said affects the quality of life of many Americans—their income, the way they live and so forth. But there's an aspect to quality of life that lies beyond the private sector which has to do with our neighborhoods, with our cities, our streets, our parks, our environment. In those areas I have a difficulty seeing what your program is and what you feel the Federal responsibility is in these areas of the quality of life in the public sector that affects everybody. And even enormous wealth by one individual can't create the kind of environment that he might like.

REAGAN: There are tasks that Government legitimately should enforce and tasks that Government performs well, and you've named some of them. Crime has come down the last two years for the first time in many, many decades that it has come down or, since we kept records, two consecutive years, and last year it came down—the biggest drop in crime that we've had. I think that we've had something to do with that, just as we have with the drug problem nationwide.

The environment, yes, I feel as strongly as anyone about the preservation of the environment. When we took office we found that the national parks were so dirty and contained so many hazards, lack of safety features that we stopped buying additional parkland until we had rectified this with what was to be a five-year program, but it's just about finished already—a billion dollars—and now we're going back to budgeting for additional lands for our parks.

We have added millions of acres to the wilderness lands, to the game refuges. I think that we're out in front of most, and I see that the red light is blinking so I can't continue but I got more.

MODERATOR: Well, you'll have a chance when your rebuttal time comes up perhaps, Mr. President. Mr. Mondale, now it's your turn for rebuttal.

MONDALE: The President says that when the Democratic Party made its turn he left it. The year that he decided we had lost our way was the year that John F. Kennedy was running against Richard Nixon. I was chairman of Minnesotans for Kennedy. Reagan was chairman of a thing called Democrats for Nixon. Now maybe we made a wrong turn with Kennedy, but I'll be proud of supporting him all our life—all of my life. And I'm very happy that John Kennedy was elected, because John Kennedy looked at the future with courage, saw what needed to be done, and understood his own Government.

The President just said that his Government is shrinking. It's not. It's now the largest peacetime Government ever in terms of the take from the total economy and instead of retreating, instead of being strong where we should be strong, he wants to make it strong and intervene in the most private and personal questions in American life. That's where Government should not be.

MODERATOR: Mr. President.

REAGAN: Before I campaigned as a Democrat for a Republican, I had already voted for Dwight Eisenhower to be President of the United States so my change had come earlier than that. I hadn't gotten around to re-registering as yet. I found that was rather difficult to do but I finally did it.

There are some other things that have been said here, back—and you said that I might be able to dredge them up. Mr. Mondale referred to the farmer's worst year. The farmers are not the victims of anything this Administration has done. The farmers were the victims of the double-digit inflation and the 21 1/2 percent interest rates of the Carter-Mondale Administration and the grain embargo which destroyed our reliability nationwide as a supplier.

All of these things are presently being rectified and I think that we are going to salvage the farmers—as a matter of fact, the—there has been less than one-quarter of 1 percent of foreclosures of the 270,000 loans from government the farmers have.

MODERATOR: Thank you, Mr. President. We'll now turn to Diane Sawyer for her round of questions. Diane.

SAWYER: I'd like to turn to an area that I think few people enjoy discussing. But that we probably should tonight because the positions of the two candidates are so clearly different and lead to very different policy consequences. And that is abortion and right to life. I'm exploring for your personal views of abortion. And specifically how you would want them applied as public policy.

First, Mr. President, do you consider abortion murder or a sin? And second, how hard would you work, what kind of priority would you give in your second term legislation to make abortion illegal? And specifically, would you make certain, as your party platform urges, that Federal justices that you appoint be pro-life?

REAGAN: I have believed that, in the appointment of judges, that all that was specified in the party platform was that they have a, they respect the sanctity of human life. Now that, I would want to see in any judge, and with regard to any issue having to do with human life.

But with regard to abortion, and I have a feeling that this is, there's been some reference, without naming it here in remarks of Mr. Mondale, tied to injecting religion into government.

With me, abortion is not a problem of religion. It's a problem of the Constitution. I believe that until and unless someone can establish that the unborn child is not a living human being, then that child is already protected by the Constitution, which guarantees life, liberty and the pursuit of happiness to all of us.

And I think this is—what we should concentrate on, is trying—I know there was weeks and weeks of testimony before a Senate committee. There were medical authorities, there were religious, there were clerics there, everyone talking about this matter, of pro-life. And at the end of all of that, not one shred of evidence was introduced that the unborn child was not alive. We have seen premature births that are now grown up happy people going around.

Also there is a strange dichotomy in this whole position about our court's ruling that abortion is not the taking of a human life.

In California, some time ago, a man beat a woman so savagely that her unborn child was born dead with a fractured skull. And the California state legislature unanimously passed a law that was signed by the then Democratic Governor, signed a law that said that any man who so abuses a pregnant woman that he causes the death of her unborn child shall be charged with murder. Now isn't it strange that that same woman could have taken the life of her unborn child and it was abortion and not murder but if somebody else does it, that's murder. And it recognizes, it used the term death of the unborn child.

So this has been my feeling about abortion, that we have a problem now to determine. And all the evidence so far comes down on the side of the unborn child being a living human being.

SAWYER: A two-part follow-up. Do I take it from what you've said about the platform, then, that you don't regard the language and don't regard in your own appointments' abortion position a test of any kind for justices that it should be? And also, if abortion is made illegal, how would you want it enforced? Who would be the policing units that would investigate? And would you want the women who have abortions to be prosecuted?

REAGAN: The laws regarding that always were state laws. It was only when the Supreme Court handed down a decision that the Federal Government intervened in what had always been a state policy. Our laws against murder are state laws. So I would think this would be the point of enforcement on this.

I, as I say, I feel that we have a problem here to resolve, and no one has approached it from that matter. It does not happen that the church I belong to had that as part of its dogma; I know that some churches do.

Now, it is a sin if you're taking a human life. On the same time in our Judeo-Christian tradition, we recognize the right of taking a human life in self-defense. And therefore I've always believed that a mother, if medically it is determined that her life is at risk if she goes through with the pregnancy, she has a right then to take the life of even her own unborn child in defense of her own.

SAWYER: Mr. Mondale, to turn to you, do you consider abortion a murder or a sin? And bridging from what President Reagan said, he has written that if society doesn't know whether life does—human life—in fact does begin at conception, as long as there is a doubt, that the unborn child should at least be given the benefit of the doubt and that there should be protection for that unborn child.

MONDALE: This is one of the most emotional and difficult issues that could possibly be debated. I think your questions, however, underscore the fact there is probably no way that Government should, or could, answer this question in every individual case and in the private lives of the American people.

The Constitutional Amendment proposed by President Reagan would make it a crime for a woman to have an abortion if she had been raped or suffered from incest.

Is it really the view of the American people, however you feel on the question of abortion, that Government ought to be reaching into your livingrooms and making choices like this?

I think it cannot work, won't work and will lead to all kinds of cynical evasions of the law. Those who can afford to have them will continue to have them. The disadvantaged will go out in the back alley as they used to do.

I think these questions are inherently personal and moral. And every individual instance is different. Every American should be aware of the seriousness of the step but there are some things that Government can do and some things they cannot do.

Now the example that the President cites has nothing to do with abortion. Somebody went to a woman and nearly killed her. That's always been a serious crime and always should be a serious crime. But how does that compare with the problem of a woman who is raped? Do we really want those decisions made by judges who've been picked because they will agree to find the person guilty? I don't think so and I think it's going in exactly the wrong direction.

In America, on basic moral questions we have always let the people decide in their own personal lives. We haven't felt so insecure that we've reached for the club of state to have our point of view. It's been a good instinct and we're the most religious people on earth.

One final point: President Reagan, as Governor of California, signed a bill which is perhaps the most liberal pro-abortion bill of any state in the Union.

SAWYER: But if I can get you back for a moment on my point which was the question of when human life begins, a two-part follow-up. First of all, at what point do you believe that human life begins in the growth of a fetus? And second of all, you said that government shouldn't be involved in the decision, yet there are those who would say that government is involved and the consequence of the involvement was 1.5 million abortions in 1980. And how do you feel about that?

MONDALE: The basic decision of the Supreme Court is that each person has to make this judgment in her own life, and that's the way it's been done. And it's a personal and private moral judgment. I don't know the answer to when life begins.

And it's not that simple either. You've got another life involved. And if it's rape, how do you draw moral judgments on that? If it's incest, how do you draw moral judgments on that? Does every woman in America have to present herself before some judge picked by Jerry Falwell to clear her personal judgment? It won't work.

MODERATOR: I'm sorry to do this but I really must talk to the audience. You're all invited guests. I know I'm wasting time in talking to you but it really is very unfair of you to applaud sometimes louder, less loud, and I ask you as people who were invited here and polite people to refrain. We have our time now for rebuttal. Mr. President.

REAGAN: Yes. But with regard to this being a personal choice, isn't that what a murderer is insisting on? His or her right to kill someone because of whatever fault they think justifies that. Now, I'm not capable and I don't think you are, any of us, to make this determination that must be made with regard to human life. I am simply saying that I believe that that's where the effort should be directed to make that determination. I don't think that any of us should be called upon here to stand and make a decision as to what other things might come under the self-defense tradition. That, too, would have to be worked out then when you once recognize that we're talking about a life. But in this great society of ours wouldn't it make a lot more sense, in this gentle and kind society, if we had a program that made it possible for when incidents come along which someone feels they must do away with that unborn child, that instead we make it available to the adoption, there are a million-and-a-half people out there standing in line waiting to adopt children who can't have them any other way.

MODERATOR: Mr. Mondale?

MONDALE: I agree with that, and that's why I was a principal sponsor of a liberal adoption law so that more of these children could come to term so that the young mothers were educated, so we found an option, an alternative. I'm all for that. But the question is whether this other option proposed by the President should be pursued, and I don't agree with it. Since I've got about 20 seconds, let me just say one thing.

The question of agriculture came up a minute ago, and that farm income is off 50 percent in the last three years, and every farmer knows it, and the effect of these economic policies is like a massive grain embargo which has caused farm exports to drop 20 percent. It's been a big failure. I opposed the grain embargo in my Administration; I'm opposed to these policies as well.

MODERATOR: I'm sitting here like the great school teacher letting you both get away with things. Because one did it, the other one did it. May I ask in the future that the rebuttals stick to what the rebuttal is and also, foreign policy will be the next debate. Stop dragging it in by its ear into this one. Now having admonished you, I would like to say to the panel, you are allowed one question and one follow-up. Would you try as best you could not to ask two and three. I know it's something we all want to do, two or three questions as part one, and two and three as part two. Having said that, Fred, it's yours.

BARNES: Thank you. Mr. Mondale, let me ask you about middle class Americans and the taxes they pay. I'm talking about—not about the rich or the poor. I know your views on their taxes. But about families earning $25,000 to $45,000 a year. Do you think that those families are overtaxed or undertaxed by the Federal Government?

MONDALE: In my opinion as we deal with this deficit, people from about $70,000 a year on down have to be dealt with very, very carefully because they are the ones who didn't get any relief the first time around. Under the 1981 tax bill people making $200,000 a year got $60,000 in tax relief over three years while people making $30,000 a year, all taxes considered, got no relief at all or their taxes actually went up. That's why my proposal protects everybody from $25,000 a year or less against any tax increases and treats those $70,000 and under in a way that is more beneficial than the way the President proposes with a sales tax or a flat tax.

What does this mean in real life? Well, the other day Vice President Bush disclosed his tax returns to the American people. He's one of the wealthiest Americans and he's our Vice President. In 1981 I think he paid about 40 percent in taxes. In 1983 as a result of these tax preferences he paid a little over 12 percent, 12.8 percent in taxes. That meant that he paid a lower percent in taxes than the janitor who cleaned up his office or the chauffeur who drives him to work.

I believe we need some fairness, and that's why I propose what I think is a fair and responsible proposal that helps protect these people who've already gotten no relief or actually got a tax increase.

BARNES: It sounds as if you were saying you think a group of taxpayers making $25,000 to $45,000 a year is already overtaxed, yet your tax proposal would increase their taxes. I think your agent said those earning about $25 to $35,000, their tax rate would go up and their tax bill would go up $100, and from $35,000 to $45,000 more than that, several hundred dollars. Wouldn't that stifle their incentive to work and invest and so on, and also hurt the recovery?

MONDALE: The first thing is everybody $25,000 or under would have no tax increase. Mr. Reagan after the election is going to have to propose a tax increase. And you will have to compare what he proposes, and his Secretary of the Treasury said he's studying a sales tax or a value-added tax; they're the same thing to hit middle and moderate income Americans and leave wealthy Americans largely untouched. Up until about $70,000, as you go up the ladder, my proposals will be far more beneficial. As soon as we get the economy on a sound ground, as well, I would like to see the total repeal of indexing. I don't think we can do that for a few years but at some point we want to do that as well.

BARNES: Mr. President, let me try this on you. Do you think middle-income Americans are overtaxed or undertaxed?

REAGAN: You know, I wasn't going to say this at all, but I can't help it: There you go again. I don't have a plan to tax or increase taxes; I'm not going to increase taxes. I can understand why you are, Mr. Mondale, because as a Senator you voted 16 times to increase taxes. Now, I believe that our problem has not been that anybody in our country is undertaxed, it's that Government is overfed.

And I think that most of our people—this is why we had a 25 percent tax cut across the board which maintained the same progressivity of our tax structure in the—brackets on up.

And as a matter of fact, it just so happens that in the quirks of administering these taxes, those above $50,000 actually did not get quite as big a tax cut percentage-wise, as did those from $50,000 down. From $50,000 down those people paid two-thirds of the taxes and those people got two-thirds of the tax cut.

Now the Social Security tax of '77—this, indeed, was a tax that hit people in the lower brackets the hardest. It had two features: it had several tax increases phased in over a period of time; there are two more yet to come between now and 1989. At the same time, every year it increased the amount of money—virtually every year, there may have been one or two that we're skipping there—that was subject to that tax. Today it is up to about $38,000 of earnings that is subject to the payroll tax for Social Security. And that tax, there are no deductions, so a person making anywhere from $10, $15, $20, they're paying that tax on the full gross earnings that they have after they have already paid an income tax on that same amount of money.

Now I don't think that to try and say that we were taxing the rich and not the other way around, it just doesn't work out that way. The system is still where it was with regard to the progressivity, as I've said, and that has not been changed. But if you take it in numbers of dollars, instead of percentage, yes you can say, well that person got 10 times as much as this other person. Yes, but he paid 10 times as much also. But if you take it in percentages then you find out that it is fair and equitable across the board.

BARNES: I thought I caught, Mr. President, a glimmer of a stronger statement there in your answer than you've made before. I think the operative position you had before was that you would only raise taxes in a second term as a last resort, and I thought you said flatly that "I'm not going to raise taxes." Is that what you meant to say, that you will not—that you will flatly not raise taxes in your second term as President?

REAGAN: Yes, I had used—last resort would always be with me. If you got the Government down to the lowest level that you yourself could say it could not go any lower and still perform the services for the people. And if the recovery was so complete that you knew you were getting the ultimate amount of revenues that you could get through that growth, and there was still some slight difference there between those two lines, then I had said once that yes, you would have to then look to see if taxes should not be adjusted. I don't foresee those things happening. So I say with great confidence, I'm not going to—I'm not going to go for a tax.

With regard to assailing Mr. Bush about his tax problems and the difference from the tax he once paid and then the later tax he paid, I think if you looked at the deductions, there were great legal expenses in there. It had to do possibly with the sale of his home and they had to do with his setting up of a blind trust. All of those are legally deductions—the deductible in computing your tax. And it was a one-year thing with him.

MODERATOR: Mr. Mondale, here we go again; this time for rebuttal.

MONDALE: Well first of all, I gave him the benefit of the doubt on the house deal. I'm just talking about the 12.8 percent that he paid—and that's what's happening all over this country with wealthy Americans. They've got so many loopholes, they don't have to pay much in taxes.

Now, Mr. President, you said: "There you go again." Right. Remember the last time you said that?

REAGAN: Um hmm.

MONDALE: You said it when President Carter said that you were going to cut Medicare. And you said: "Oh, no, there you go again, Mr. President." And what did you do right after the election? You went out and tried to cut $20 billion out of Medicare.

And so when you say, "There you go again," people remember this, you know. And people will remember that you signed the biggest tax increase in the history of California, and the biggest tax increase in the history of the United States.

And what are you going to do? You've got $260 billion deficit. You can't wash it away. You won't slow defense spending; you refuse to do that.

MODERATOR: Mr. Mondale, I'm afraid your time is up.

MONDALE: Sorry.

MODERATOR: Mr. President.

REAGAN: Yes. With regard to Medicare, no. But it's time for us to say that Medicare is in pretty much the same condition that Social Security was, and something is going to have to be done in the next several years to make it fiscally sound.

And, no, I never proposed any $20 billion should come out of Medicare. I have proposed that the program—we must treat with that particular problem.

And maybe part of that problem is because during the four years of the Carter-Mondale Administration, medical costs in this country went up 87 percent.

MODERATOR: We can't keep going back for other rebuttals. There'll be time later. We now go to our final round. The way things stand now we have time for only two sets of questions and by lot it will be Jim and Diane and we'll start with Jim.

WEIGHART: Mr. President, the economic recovery is real but uneven. The Census Bureau just a month ago reported that there are more people living under poverty now—a million more people—than when you took office. There have been a number of studies, including studies by the Urban Institute and other non-political organizations, that say that the impact of the tax and budget cuts in your economic policies have impacted severely on certain classes of Americans—working mothers, head of households, minority groups, elderly poor. In fact, they're saying that the rich are getting richer and the poor are getting poorer under your policies. What relief can you offer to the working poor, to the minorities and to the women heads of households who have borne the brunt of these economic programs. What can you offer them in the future in your next term?

REAGAN: Some of those facts and figures don't stand up. Yes, there has been an increase in poverty but it is a lower rate of increase than it was in the preceding years before we got here. It has begun to decline, but it is still going up. On the other hand, women heads of households, single women, heads of households, have for the first time—there's been a turn down in the rate of poverty for them. We have found also in our studies that in this increase of poverty it all had to do with their private earnings. It had nothing to do with the transfer payments from government, by way of many programs. We are spending now 37 percent more on food for the hungry in all the various types of programs than was spent in 1980. We're spending a third more on all the programs of human service. We have more people receiving food stamps than were ever receiving them before—2,300,000 more are receiving them even though we took 850,000 off the food stamp rolls because they were making an income that was above anything that warranted their fellow citizens having to support them. We found people making 185 percent of the poverty level were getting Government benefits. We have set a line at 130 percent so that we can direct that aid down to the truly needy.

Some time ago Mr. Mondale said something about education and college students and help of that kind—half, one out of two of full-time college students in the United States are receiving some form of Federal aid, but there again we found people that there were—under the previous Administration—families that had no limit to income were still eligible for low-interest college loans. We didn't think that was right. And so we have set a standard that those loans and those grants are directed to the people who otherwise could not go to college, their family incomes were so low.

So there are a host of other figures that reveal that the grant programs are greater than they have ever been, taking care of more people than they ever have—7.7 million elderly citizens who were living in the lowest 20 percent of earnings, 7.7 million have moved up into another bracket since our Administration took over, leaving only 5 million of the elderly in that bracket when there had been more than 13 million.

WEIGHART: Mr. President, in a visit to Texas, in Brownsville, I believe it was, in the Rio Grande Valley, you did observe that the economic recovery was uneven. In that particular area of Texas unemployment was over 14 percent whereas statewide it was the lowest in the country, I believe 5.6 percent. And you made the comment that, however, that man does not live by bread alone. What did you mean by that comment and, if I interpret it correctly, it would be a comment more addressed to the affluent who, who obviously can look beyond just the bread they need to sustain them with their wherewithal.

REAGAN: That had nothing to do with the other thing of talking about their needs or anything. I remember distinctly I was segueing into another subject. I was talking about the things that have been accomplished and that was referring to the revival of patriotism and optimism, the new spirit that we're finding all over America. And it is a wonderful thing to see when you get out there among the people. So that was the only place that that was used.

I did avoid, I'm afraid, in my previous answer also, the idea of uneven, yes, there is no way that the recovery is, even across the country, just as in the depths of the recession there were some parts of the country that were worse off but some that didn't even feel the pain of the recession.

We're not going to rest, and not going to be happy, until every person in this country who wants a job can have one, until the recovery is complete across the country.

WEIGHART: Mr. Mondale, as you can gather from the question of the President the celebrated war on poverty obviously didn't end the problem of poverty, although it may have dented it. The poor and the homeless and the disadvantaged are still with us. What should the Federal Government's role be to turn back the growth in the number of people living below the poverty level, which is now 35 million in the United States and to help deal with the structural unemployment problems that the President was referring to in an uneven recovery?

MONDALE: No. 1, we've got to get the debt down, to get the interest rates down so the economy will grow and people will be employed. No. 2, we have to work with cities and others to help generate economic growth in those communities—to the Urban Development Action Grant program. I don't mind those enterprise zones, let's try them, but not as a substitute for the others. Certainly education and training is crucial. If these young Americans don't have the skills that make them attractive to employees, they're not going to get jobs.

The next thing is to try to get more entrepreneurship in business within the reach of minorities so that these businesses are located in the communities in which they're found. The other thing is we need the business community as well as government heavily involved in these communities to try to get economic growth. There is no question that the poor are worse off. I think the President genuinely believes that they're better off. But the figures show that about 8 million more people are below the poverty line than four years ago. How you can cut school lunches, how you can cut student assistance, how you can cut housing, how you can cut disability benefits, how you can do all of these things and then the people receiving them—for example the disabled who have no alternative, how they're going to do better, I don't know. Now we need a tight budget, but there's no question that this Administration has singled out things that affect the most vulnerable in American life, and they're hurting.

One final point if I might. There's another part of the lopsided economy that we're in today, and that is that these heavy deficits have killed exports and are swamping the nation with cheap imports. We are now $120 billion of imports, 3 million jobs lost and farmers are having their worst year. That's another reason to get the deficit down.

WEIGHART: Mr. Mondale, is it possible that the vast majority of Americans who appear to be prosperous have lost interest in the kinds of programs you're discussing to help those less privileged than they are?

MONDALE: I think the American people want to make certain that that dollar is wisely spent. I think they stand for civil rights. I know they're all for education in science and training, which I strongly support.

They want these young people to have a chance to get jobs and the rest. I think the business community wants to get involved. I think they're asking for new and creative ways to try to reach it, and with everyone involved. I think that's part of it.

I think also that the American people want a balanced program that gives us long-term growth, so that they're not having to take money that's desperate to themselves and their families and give it to someone else. I'm opposed to that, too.

MODERATOR: And now it is time for our rebuttal for this period. Mr. President.

REAGAN: Yes, the connection that's been made again between the deficit and the interest rates—there is no connection between them. There is a connection between interest rates and inflation.

But I would call to your attention that in 1981, while we were operating still on the Carter-Mondale budget that we inherited, that the interest rates came down from 21 1/2 toward the 12 or 13 figure and while they were coming down, the deficits had started their great increase: they were going up.

Now, if there was a connection, I think that there would be a different parallel between deficit getting larger and interest rates going down.

The interest rates are based on inflation. And right now, I have to tell you, I don't think there is any excuse for the interest rates being as high as they are, because we have brought inflation down so low. I think it can only be that they're anticipating or hope—expecting, not hoping—that maybe we don't have a control of inflation and it's going to go back up again.

Well, it isn't going to go back up. We're going to see that it doesn't.

MODERATOR: Mr. President.

And I haven't got time to answer with regard to—

MODERATOR: Thank you, Mr. President. Mr. Mondale.

MONDALE: Mr. President, if I heard you correctly, you said that these deficits don't have anything to do with interest rates. I will grant you that interest rates were too high in 1980 and we can have another debate as to why—energy prices and so on. There is no way of glossing around that. But when these huge deficits went in place in 1981, what's called the real interest rates, the spread between inflation and what a loan costs you, doubled. And that's still the case today, and the result is interest costs that have never been seen before in terms of real charges and it's attributable to the deficit.

Everybody, every economist, every businessman believes that. Your own Council of Economic Advisers, Mr. Feldstein in his report, told you that. Every chairman of the Finance and Ways and Means committees, Republican leaders in the Senate and the House, are telling you that. That deficit is ruining the long-term hopes for this economy. It's causing high interest rates, it's ruining us in trade, it's given us the highest small-business failure in 50 years, the economy is starting downhill, with housing . . .

MODERATOR: Thank you Mr. Mondale. You're both very obedient, I have to give you credit for that. We now start our final round of questions. We do want to have time for your rebuttal and we start with Diane: Diane Sawyer.

SAWYER: Since we are reaching the end of the question period, and since in every Presidential campaign the candidates tend to complain that the opposition candidate is not held accountable for what he or she says, let me give you a chance to do that. Mr. Mondale, beginning with you, what do you think the most outrageous thing is your opponent said in this debate tonight?

MONDALE: You want to give me some suggestions? I'm going to use my time a little differently. I'm going to give the President some credit. I think the President has done some things to raise the sense of spirit and morale, good feeling, in this country. And he's entitled to credit for that.

What I think we need, however, is not just that but to move forward not just congratulating ourselves, but challenging ourselves to get on with the business of dealing with America's problems.

I think in education, when he lectured the country about the importance of discipline, I didn't like it at first but I think it helped a little bit.

But now we need both that kind of discipline and the resources and the consistent leadership that allows this country to catch up in education and science and training.

I like President Reagan and—this is not personal—there are deep differences about our future and that's the basis of my campaign.

SAWYER: Follow up in a similar vein then. What remaining question would you most like to see your opponent forced to answer?

MONDALE: Without any doubt, I've stood up and told the American people that that $263 billion deficit must come down. And I've done what no candidate for President's ever done, I told you before the election what I'd do.

Mr. Reagan, as you saw tonight, President Reagan takes the position it will disappear by magic. It was once called voodoo economics. I wish the President would say, yes, the C.B.O. is right. Yes, we have a $263 billion deficit. This is how I'm going to get it done. Don't talk about growth because even though we need growth, that's not helping, it's going to go in the other direction as they've estimated. And give us a plan.

What will you cut? Whose taxes will you raise? Will you finally touch that defense budget? Are you going to go after Social Security and Medicare and student assistance and the handicapped again, as you did last time?

If you'd just tell us what you're going to do, then the American people could compare my plan for the future with your plan. And that's the way it should be. The American people would be in charge.

SAWYER: Mr. President, the most outrageous thing your opponent has said in the debate tonight?

REAGAN: Well, now, I have to start with a smile since his kind words to me. I'll tell you what I think has been the most outrageous thing in political dialogue both in this campaign and the one in '82, and that is the continued discussion and claim that somehow I am the villain who is going to pull the Social Security checks out from those people who are dependent on them. And why I think it is outrageous; first of all, it isn't true. But why it is outrageous is because for political advantage, every time they do that, they scare millions of senior citizens who are totally dependent on Social Security, have no place to turn, and they have to live and go to bed at night thinking is it true; is someone going to take our check away from us and leave us destitute? And I don't think that that should be a part of political dialogue. Now, to—I just have a minute here?

SAWYER: You have more time. You can keep going.

REAGAN: O.K. All right. Now, Social Security, let's lay it to rest once and for all. I told you never would I do such a thing. But I tell you also now Social

Security has nothing to do with the deficit. Social Security is totally funded by the payroll tax levied on employer and employee. If you reduce the outgo of Social Security, that money would not go into the general fund to reduce a deficit. It would go into the Social Security Trust Fund. So Social Security has nothing to do with balancing a budget or erasing or lowering the deficit.

Now, again to get to whether I have—am depending on magic—I think I have talked in straight economic terms about a program of recovery that was—I was told wouldn't work and then after it worked, I was told that lowering taxes would increase inflation and none of these things happened. It is working and we're going to continue on that same line. As to what we might do and find in further savings cuts, no, we're not going to starve the hungry. But we have 2,478 specific recommendations from a commission of more than 2,000 business people in this country through the Grace Commission, that we're studying right now and we've already implemented 17 percent of them that are recommendations as to how to make Government more efficient, more economic.

SAWYER: And to keep it even. What remaining question would you most like to see your opponent forced to answer?

REAGAN: The deficits are so much of a problem for him now, but that in 1976 when the deficit was $52 billion and everyone was panicking about that, he said, no, that he thought it ought to be bigger because a bigger deficit would stimulate the economy and would help do away with unemployment. In 1979 he made similar statements, the same effect, that the deficits—there was nothing wrong with having deficits. Remember there was a trillion dollars in debt before we got here. That's got to be paid by our children, and grandchildren too, if we don't do it. And I'm hoping we can start some payments on it before we get through here. That's why I want another four years.

MODERATOR: Well, we have time now, if you'd like to answer the President's question or whatever rebuttal.

MONDALE: Well, we've just finished almost the whole debate and the American people don't have the slightest clue about what President Reagan will do about these deficits. And yet that's the most important single issue of our time. I did support the '76 measure that he told about, because we were in a deep recession and we need some stimulation. But I will say, as a Democrat, I was a real piker, Mr. President. In 1979 we ran a $29 billion deficit, all year. This Administration seems to run that every morning, and the result is exactly what we see: This economy is starting to run downhill. Housing is off, last report on new purchases is the lowest since 1982, our growth is a little over 3 percent now, many people are predicting a recesssion, and the flow of imports into this country is swamping the American people. We've got to deal with this problem, and those of us who want to be your President should tell you now what we're going to do so you can make a judgment.

MODERATOR: Thank you very much. We must stop now. I want to give you time for your closing statements. It's indeed time for that from each of you. We will begin with President Reagan.

*   *   *

MODERATOR: I'm sorry, Mr. Reagan you had your rebuttal and I've just cut you off because our time was going. You have a chance now for rebuttal before your closing statement. Is that correct?

REAGAN: No, I might as well just go with. . .

MODERATOR: Do you want to go with—

REAGAN: I don't think so.

MODERATOR: Do you want to wait?

REAGAN: I'm all confused now.

MODERATOR: Technically, you did. I have little voices that come in my ear. You don't get those same voices, I'm not hearing it from here, I'm hearing it from here. You have waived your rebuttal. You can go with your closing statement.

REAGAN: Well, we'll include it in that.

Four years ago in similar circumstances to this I asked you, the American people, a question. I asked, are you better off than you were four years before. The answer to that obviously was no, and as a result I was elected to this office and promised a new beginning. Now, maybe I'm expected to ask that same question again. I'm not going to because I think that all of you or not everyone, those people that have—are in those pockets of poverty and haven't caught up, they couldn't answer the way I would want them to. But I think that most of the people in this country would say yes they are better off than they were four years ago.

The question I think should be enlarged. Is America better off than it was four years ago? And I believe the answer to that has to also be yes.

I promised a new beginning. So far it is only a beginning. If the job were finished, I might have thought twice about seeking reelection to this job. But we now have an economy that for the first time—well, let's put it this way, in the first half of 1980 gross national product was down a minus 3.7 percent. The first half of '84 it's up 8.5 percent. Productivity in the first half of 1980 was down a minus 2 percent. Today it is up a plus 4 percent. Personal earnings after taxes per capita have gone up almost $3,000 in these four years. In 1980 or 1979 the person with a fixed income of $8,000 was $500 above the poverty line, and this maybe explains why there are the numbers still in poverty. By 1980 that same person was $500 below the poverty line.

We have restored much of our economy with regard to a business investment. It is higher than it has been since 1949. So there seems to be no shortage of investment capital. We have, as I said, cut the taxes but we have reduced inflation and for two years now it has stayed down there, not a double digit but in the range of 4 or below.

We believe that we had also promised that we would make our country more secure. Yes, we have an increase in the defense budget. But back then we had planes that couldn't fly for lack of spare parts or pilots. We had navy vessels that couldn't leave harbor, because of lack of crew or again, lack of spare parts. Today we're well on our way to a 600-ship navy. We have 543 at present. We have—our military, the morale is high, I think the people should understand that two-thirds of the defense budget pays for pay and salary—or pay and pension. And then you add to that food and wardrobe and all the other things and you only have a small portion going for weapons. But I am determined that if ever our men are called on they should have the best that we can provide in the manner of tools and weapons. There has been reference to expensive spare parts, hammers costing $500. Well, we are the ones who found those.

I think we've given the American people back their spirit. I think there is an optimism in the land and a patriotism and I think that we're in a position once again to heed the words of Thomas Paine who said: "We have it in our power to begin the world over again."

MODERATOR: Thank you Mr. Reagan. Mr. Mondale, the closing words are now yours.

MONDALE: I want to thank the League of Women Voters and the city of Louisville for hosting this evening's debate. I want to thank President Reagan for agreeing to debate. He didn't have to and he did, and we all appreciate it.

The President's favorite question is "Are you better off?" Well, if you're wealthy, you're better off. If you're middle income, you're about where you were, and if you're of modest income, you're worse off. That's what the economists tell us. But is that really the question that should be asked. Isn't the real question, "Will we be better off? Will our children be better off? Are we building the future that this nation needs?"

I believe that if we ask those questions that bear on our future—not just congratulate ourselves but challenge us to solve those problems—you'll see that we need new leadership.

Are we better off with this arms race? Will we be better off if we start this star wars escalation into the heavens? Are we better off when we de-emphasize our values in human rights? Are we better off when we load our children with this fantastic debt? Would fathers and mothers feel proud of themselves if they loaded their children with debts like this nation is now, over a trillion dollars, on the shoulders of our children? Can we be—say, really say, that we will be better off when we pull away from sort of that basic American instinct of decency and fairness?

I would rather lose a campaign about decency than win a campaign about self-interest. I don't think this nation is composed of people who care only for themselves. And when we sought to assault Social Security and Medicare, as the record shows we did, I think that was mean spirited. When we terminated 400,000 desperate, hopeless, defenseless Americans who were on disability, confused and unable to defend themselves, and just laid them out on the street as we did for four years, I don't think that's what America is all about. America is a fair society, and it is not right that Vice President Bush pays less in taxes than the janitor who helps him. I believe there's fundamental fairness crying out that needs to be achieved in our tax system.

I believe that we will be better off if we protect this environment. And contrary to what the President says I think their record on the environment is inexcusable and often shameful. These laws are not being enforced, have not been enforced and the public health and the air and the water are paying the price. That's not fair for our future.

I think our future requires the President to lead us in an all-out search to advance our education, our learning and our science and training, because this world is more complex and we're being pressed harder all the time.

I believe in opening doors. We won the Olympics in part because we've had civil rights laws and the laws that prohibit discrimination against women. I have been for those efforts all my life. The President's record is quite different.

The question is our future. President Kennedy once said in response to similar arguments, we are great but we can be greater. We can be better if we face our future, rejoice in our strengths, face our problems and by solving them build a better society for our children.

Thank you.

MODERATOR: Thank you Mr. Mondale, and thank you Mr. President, and our thanks to our panel members as well. And so we bring to a close this first of the League of Women Voters Presidential debates of 1984. You two can go at each other again in the final League debate on Oct. 21 in Kansas City, Mo., and this Thursday night, Oct. 11, at 9 P.M. Eastern daylight time, Vice President Bush will debate Congresswoman Geraldine Ferraro in Philadelphia. And I hope that you will all watch once again; no matter what the format, these debates are very important. We all have an extremely vital decision to make. Once more gentlemen, our thanks, once more to you our thanks, and now this is Barbara Walters wishing you a good evening.

Second Presidential Debate
Kansas City, Missouri, October 21, 1984

In the eyes of the public, if not in the minds of forensic experts, President Reagan held his own in the second presidential debate of 1984. When the issue of age was raised, the President quipped to great effect: "I will not make age an issue of this campaign. I am not going to exploit for political purposes my opponent's youth and inexperience." Even Walter Mondale was forced to smile.

The following people participated in last night's Presidential debate in Kansas City:

MODERATOR: Edwin Newman, syndicated columnist.

PANELISTS: Georgie Anne Geyer, syndicated colunmist; Marvin Kalb, chief diplomatic correspondent, NBC News; Morton Kondracke, executive editor, *The New Republic,* and Henry Trewhitt, diplomatic correspondent, *The Baltimore Sun.*

DOROTHY S. RIDINGS: Good evening from the Municipal Auditorium in Kansas City. I am Dorothy Ridings, the president of the League of Women Voters, the sponsor of this final Presidential debate of the 1984 campaign between Republican Ronald Reagan and Democrat Walter Mondale.

Our panelists for tonight's debate on defense and foreign policy issues are Georgie Anne Geyer, syndicated columnist for Universal Press Syndicate, Marvin Kalb, chief diplomatic correspondent for NBC News, Morton Kondracke, executive editor of *The New Republic* magazine and Henry Trewhitt, diplomatic correspondent for *The Baltimore Sun.*

Edwin Newman, formerly of NBC News and now a syndicated columnist for King Features is our moderator. Ed.

MODERATOR: Dorothy Ridings, thank you. A brief word about our procedure tonight. The first question will go to Mr. Mondale. He'll have two and a half minutes to reply. Then the panel member who put the question will ask the followup. The answer to that will be limited to one minute. After that, the same question will be put to President Reagan. Again, there will be a followup and then each man will have one minute for rebuttal.

The second question will go to President Reagan first. After, the alternating will continue. At the end there will be four-minute summations with President Reagan going last.

We have asked the questioners to be brief.

Let's begin. Miss Geyer, your question to Mr. Mondale.

GEYER: Mr. Mondale, two related questions on the crucial issue of Central America. You and the Democratic Party have said that the only policy toward the horrendous civil wars in Central America should be on economic developments and negotiations with, perhaps a quarantine of, Marxist Nicaragua.

336

Do you believe that these answers would in any way solve the bitter conflicts there? Do you really believe that there is no need to resort to force at all? Are not these solutions to Central America's gnawing problems simply again too weak and too late?

MONDALE: I believe that the question oversimplifies the difficulties of what we must do in Central America. Our objectives ought to be to strengthen the democracy, to stop Communist and other extremist influences and stabilize the community in that area.

To do that, we need a three-pronged attack. One is military assistance to our friends who are being pressured. Secondly, a strong and sophisticated economic aid program and human rights program that offers a better life and a sharper alternative to the alternative offered by the totalitarians who oppose us. And finally, a strong diplomatic effort that pursues the possibilities of peace in the area.

That's one of the big disagreements that we have with the President, that they have not pursued the diplomatic opportunities either within El Salvador or as between the country and have lost time during which we might have been able to achieve peace.

This brings up the whole question of what Presidential leadership is all about. I think the lesson in Central America, this recent embarrassment in Nicaragua where we are giving instructions for hired assassins, hiring criminals and the rest—all of this has strengthened our opponent.

A President must not only assure that we're tough. But we must also be wise and smart in the exercise of that power. We saw the same thing in Lebanon where we spent a good deal of America's assets but the leadership of this government did not pursue wise policies, we have been humiliated and our opponents are stronger.

The bottom line of national strength is that the President must command. He must lead. And when a President doesn't know that submarine missiles are recallable, says that 70 percent of our strategic forces are conventional, discovers three years into his Administration that our arms control efforts have failed because he didn't know that most Soviet missiles were on land—these are things a President must know to command. A President is called the Commander in Chief. And he's called that because he's supposed to be in charge of facts and run our government and strengthen our nation.

GEYER: Mr. Mondale, if I could broaden the question just a little bit. Since World War II, every conflict that we as Americans have been involved with has been in nonconventional or irregular terms and yet we keep fighting in conventional or traditional military terms. The Central American wars are very much in the same pattern as China, as Lebanon, as Iran, as Cuba in the early days. Do you see any possibility that we are going to realize the change in warfare in our time or react to it in those terms?

MONDALE: We absolutely must, which is why I responded to your first question the way I did. It's much more complex. You must understand the region, you must understand the politics in the area, you must provide a strong alternative and you must show strength—and all at the same time. That's why I object to the covert action in Nicaragua. That's a classic example of a strategy that's embarrassed us, strengthened our opposition and undermined the moral authority of our people and our country in the region.

Strength requires knowledge, command. We've seen in the Nicaraguan example a policy that has actually hurt us, strengthened our opposition and undermined the moral authority of our country in that region.

GEYER: Mr. President, in the last few months it has seemed more and more that your policies in Central America were beginning to work. Yet just at this moment we are confronted with the extraordinary story of the C.I.A. guerilla manual for the anti-Sandinista Contras, whom we are backing, which advocates not only assassinations of Sandinistas but the hiring of criminals to assassinate the guerillas we are supporting in order to create martyrs. Is this not in effect our own state-supported terrorism?

REAGAN: No, but I'm glad you asked that question because I know it's on many people minds. I have ordered an investigation; I know that the C.I.A. is already going forward with one. We have a gentleman down in Nicaragua who is on contract to the C.I.A., advising supposedly on military tactics, the Contras. And he drew up this manual. It was turned over to the agency head of the C.I.A. in Nicaragua to be printed, and a number of pages were excised by that agency head there, the man in charge, and he sent it on up here to C.I.A., where more pages were excised before it was printed. But some way or other, there were 12 of the original copies that got out down there and were not submitted for this printing process by the C.I.A. Now those are the details as we have them, and as soon as we have an investigation and find out where any blame lies for the few that did not get excised or changed, we certainly are going to do something about that. We'll take the proper action at the proper time.

I was very interested to hear about Central America and our process down there, and I thought for a moment that instead of a debate I was going to find Mr. Mondale in complete agreement with what we're doing because the plan that he has outlined is the one we've been following for quite some time, including diplomatic processes throughout Central America and working closely with the Contadora Group. So I can only tell you, about the manual, that we're not in the habit of assigning guilt before there has been proper evidence produced in proof of that guilt; but if guilt is established, whoever is guilty, we will treat with that situation then and they will be removed.

GEYER: Well, Mr. President, you are implying then that the C.I.A. in Nicaragua is directing the Contras there. I'd also like to ask whether having the C.I.A. investigate its own manual in such a sensitive area is not sort of like sending the fox into the chicken coop a second time.

REAGAN: I'm afraid I misspoke when I said a C.I.A. head in Nicaragua. There's not someone there directing all of this activity. There are, as you know, C.I.A. men stationed in other countries in the world, and certainly in Central America, and so it was a man down there in that area that this was delivered to. And he recognized that what was in that manual was a direct contravention of my own executive order in December of 1981, that we would have nothing to do with regard to political assassinations.

MODERATOR: Mr. Mondale, your rebuttal?

MONDALE: What is a President charged with doing when he takes his oath of office? He raises his right hand and takes an oath of, oath of office to take care, to faithfully execute the laws of the land. Presidents can't know everything but a President has to know those things that are essential to his leadership and the enforcement of our laws.

This manual, several thousands of which were produced, was distributed ordering political assassination, hiring of criminals and other forms of terrorism. Some of it was excised but the part dealing with political terrorism was continued.

How can this happen? How can something this serious occur in an Administration and have a President of the United States in a situation like this say he didn't know. A President must know these things.

I don't know which is worse—not knowing or knowing and not stopping it.

And what about the mining of the harbors in Nicaragua, which violated international law? This has hurt this country and a President's supposed to command.

MODERATOR: Mr. President, your rebuttal.

REAGAN: Yes. I have so many things to respond to I'm going to pick out something you said earlier.

You've been all over the country repeating something that I will admit the press has also been repeating—that I believe that nuclear missiles could be fired and then called back. I never conceived of such a thing. I never said any such thing.

In a discussion of our strategic arms negotiations, I said that submarines carrying missiles and airplanes carrying missiles were more conventional-type weapons, not as destabilizing as the land-based missiles and that they were also weapons that, or carriers, that, if they were sent out and there was a change, you could call them back before they had launched their missiles. But I hope that from here on, you will no longer be saying that particular thing, which is absolutely false. How anyone could think that any sane person would believe you could call back a nuclear missile I think is as ridiculous as the, as the whole concept has been.

So, thank you for giving me a chance to straighten the record. I'm sure that you appreciate that.

MODERATOR: Mr. Kalb, your question to President Reagan.

KALB: Mr. President, you have often described the Soviet Union as a powerful evil empire intent on world domination. But this year, you have said, and I quote: "If they want to keep their Mickey Mouse system, that's O.K. with me." Which is it, Mr. President. Do you want to contain them within their present borders and perhaps try to reestablish détente or what goes for détente or do you really want to roll back their empire?

REAGAN: I have said, on a number of occasions, exactly what I believe about the Soviet Union. I retract nothing that I have said. I believe that many of the things they have done are evil in any concept of morality that we have. But I also recognize that as the two great superpowers in the world, we have to live with each other. And I told Mr. Gromyko we don't like their system. They don't like ours. And we're not gonna change their system and they sure better not try to change ours. But, between us, we can either destroy the world or we can save it. And I suggested that certainly it was to their common interest, along with ours, to avoid a conflict and to attempt to save the world and remove the nuclear weapons. And I think perhaps we established a little better understanding.

I think that in dealing with the Soviet Union, one has to be realistic. I know that Mr. Mondale, in the past, just people like ourselves and if we were kind and good and did something nice, they would respond accordingly. And the result was unilateral disarmament. We canceled the B-1 under the previous Administration. What did we get for it? Nothing.

The Soviet Union has been engaged in the biggest military buildup in the history of man at the same time that we tried the policy of unilateral disarmament, of weakness, if you will. And now, we are putting up a defense of our own. And I've made it very plain to them. We seek no superiority. We simply are going to provide a deterrent so that it will be too costly for them if they are nursing any ideas of aggression against us. Now they claim they're not. And I made it plain to them that we're not. But, this, there's been no change in my attitude at all. I just thought when I came into office it was time that there was some realistic talk to and about the Soviet Union. And we did get their attention.

KALB: Mr. President, on perhaps the other side of the coin, a related question, sir. Since World War II, the vital interests of the United States have always been defined by treaty commitments and by Presidential proclamations. Aside from what is obvious, such as NATO, for example, which countries, which regions in the world do you regard as vital national interests of this country, meaning that you would send American troops to fight there if they were in danger?

REAGAN: Ah, well now you've added a hypothetical there at the end, Mr. Kalb, about that where we would send troops in to fight. I am not going to make the decision as to what the tactics could be, but obviously there are a number of areas in the world that are of importance to us.

One is the Middle East. And that is of interest to the whole Western world and the industrialized nations, because of the great supply of energy upon which so many depend there.

The—our neighbors here in America are vital to us. We're working right now in trying to be of help in southern Africa with regard to the independence of Namibia and the removal of the Cuban surrogates, the thousands of them, from Angola.

So, I can say there are a great many interests. I believe that we have a great interest in the Pacific basin. That is where I think the future of the world lies.

But I am not going to pick out one and in advance and hypothetically say, oh, yes, we would send troops there. I don't—

MODERATOR: Sorry, Mr. President. Sorry, your time was up.

KALB: Mr. Mondale, you have described the Soviet leaders as, and I'm quoting, cynical, ruthless and dangerous, suggesting an almost total lack of trust in them. In that case, what makes you think that the annual summit meetings with them that you've proposed will result in agreements that would satisfy the interests of this country?

MONDALE: Because the only type of agreements to reach with the Soviet Union are the types that are specifically defined, so we know exactly what they must do, subject to full verification. Which means we know every day whether they're living up to it, and follow-ups wherever we find suggestions that they're violating it, and the strongest possible terms.

I have no illusions about the Soviet Union leadership or the nature of that state. They are a tough and a ruthless adversary, and we must be prepared to meet that challenge. And I would.

Where I part with the President is that despite all of those differences, we must, as past Presidents before this one have done, meet on the common ground of survival.

And that's where the President has opposed practically every arms control agreement, by every President of both political parties, since the bomb went off.

And he now completes this term with no progress toward arms control at all, but with a very dangerous arms race underway instead.

There are now over 2,000 more warheads pointed at us today than there were when he was sworn in, and that does not strengthen us.

We must be very, very realistic in the nature of that leadership, but we must grind away and talk to find ways of reducing these differences, particularly where arms races are concerned and other dangerous exercises of Soviet power.

There will be no unilateral disarmament under my Administration. I will keep this nation strong. I understand exactly what the Soviets are up to. But that, too, is part of national strength.

To do that, a President must know what is essential to command and to leadership and to strength. And that's where the President's failure to master, in my opinion, the essential elements of arms control has cost us dearly.

These four years—three years into this Administration he said he just discovered that most Soviet missiles are on land and that's why his proposal didn't work.

I invite the American people tomorrow, because I will issue the statement quoting President Reagan. He said exactly what I said he said. He said that these missiles were less dangerous than ballistic missiles because you could fire them and you could recall them if you decided there'd been a miscalculation. A President must know those things.

MODERATOR: I'm sorry.

KALB: A related question, Mr. Mondale, on Eastern Europe: Do you accept the conventional diplomatic wisdom that Eastern Europe is a Soviet sphere of influence, and if you do, what could a Mondale Administration realistically do to help the people of Eastern Europe achieve the human rights that were guaranteed to them as a result of the Helsinki accords.

MONDALE: I think the essential strategy of the United States ought not to accept Soviet control over Eastern Europe. We ought to deal with each of these countries separately, we ought to pursue strategies with each of them—economic and the rest—that help them pull away from their dependence upon the Soviet Union.

Where the Soviet Union has acted irresponsibly, as they have in many of those countries—especially recently in Poland—I believe we ought to insist that Western credits extended to the Soviet Union bear the market rate, make the Soviets pay for their irresponsibility. That is a very important objective to make certain that we continue to look forward to progress toward greater independence by these nations and work with each of them separately.

MODERATOR: Mr. President, your rebuttal.

REAGAN: Yes, I'm not going to continue trying to respond to these repetitions of the falsehoods that have already been stated here, but with regard to whether Mr. Mondale would be strong, as he said he would be, I know that he has a commercial out where he is appearing on the deck of the Nimitz and watching the F-14's take off, and that's an image of strength—except that if he had had his way when the Nimitz was being planned he would have been deep in the water out there because there wouldn't have been any Nimitz to stand on. He was against it.

He was against the F-14 fighter, he was against the M-1 tank, he was against the B-1 bomber, he wanted to cut the salary of all of the military, he wanted to bring home half of the American forces in Europe, and he has a record of weakness with regard to our national defense that is second to none. Indeed, he was on that side virtually throughout all his years in the Senate and he opposed even President Carter when toward the end of his term President Carter wanted to increase the defense budget.

MODERATOR: Mr. Mondale, your rebuttal.

MONDALE: Mr. President, I accept your commitment to peace, but I want you to accept my commitment to a strong national defense. I propose a budget, I have proposed a budget, which would increase our nation's strength by, in real terms, by double that of the Soviet Union. I tell you where we disagree. It is true, over 10 years ago I voted to delay production of the F-14 and I'll tell you why. The plane wasn't flying the way it was supposed to be, it was a waste of money.

Your definition of national strength is to throw money at the Defense Department. My definition of national strength is to make certain that a dollar spent buys us a dollar's worth of defense. There's a big difference between the two of us. A President must manage that budget. I will keep us strong, but you'll not do that unless you command that budget and make certain we get the strength that we need. When you pay $500 for a $5 hammer, you're not buying strength.

MODERATOR: I would ask the audience not to applaud. All it does is take up time that we would like to devote to the debate. Mr. Kondracke, your question to Mr. Mondale.

KONDRACKE: Mr. Mondale, in an address earlier this year you said that before this country resorts to military force, and I'm quoting, American interests should be sharply defined, publicly supported, Congressionally sanctioned, militarily feasible, internationally defensible, open to independent scrutiny and alert to regional history. Now aren't you setting up such a gauntlet of tests here that adversaries could easily suspect that as President you would never use force to protect American interests?

MONDALE: No; as a matter of fact, I believe every one of those standards is essential to the exercise of power by this country. And we can see that in both Lebanon and in Central America. In Lebanon this President exercised American power all right, but the management of it was such that our marines were killed, we had to leave in humiliation, the Soviet Union became stronger, terrorists became emboldened, and it was because they did not think through how power should be exercised, did not have the American public with them on a plan that worked, that we ended up the way we did.

Similarly, in Central America, what we're doing in Nicaragua with this covert war which the Congress, including many Republicans, have tried to stop is finally end up with the public definition of American power that hurts us, where we get associated with political assassins and the rest. We have to decline for the first time in modern history jurisdiction of the World Court because they'll find us guilty of illegal actions, and our enemies are strengthened from all of this.

We need to be strong. We need to be prepared to use that strength, but we must understand that we are a democracy; we are a government by the people, and when we move, it should be for very severe and extreme reasons that serve our national interest and end up with a stronger country behind us. It is only in that way that we can persevere.

KONDRACKE: You've been quoted as saying that you might quarantine Nicaragua. I'd like to know what that means. Would you stop Soviet ships as President Kennedy did in 1962 and wouldn't that be more dangerous than President Reagan's covert war?

MONDALE: What I'm referring to there is the mutual self-defense provisions that exist in the inter-American treaty, the so-called Rio Pact, that permits the nations, our friends in that region, to combine to take steps, diplomatic and otherwise, to prevent Nicaragua when she acts irresponsibly in asserting power in other parts outside of her border, to take those steps, whatever they might be, to stop it.

The Nicaraguans must know that it is the policy of our Government that those people, that that leadership must stay behind the boundaries of their nation, not interfere in other nations. And by working with all of the nations in the region, unlike the policies of this Administration and unlike the President said they have not supported negotiations in that region, we will be much stronger because we'll have the moral authority that goes with those efforts.

KONDRACKE: President Reagan, you introduced U.S. forces into Lebanon as neutral peacekeepers but then you made them combatants on the side of the Lebanese Government. Eventually you were forced to withdraw them under fire and now Syria, a Soviet ally, is dominant in the country. Doesn't Lebanon represent a major failure on the part of your Administration and raise serious questions about your capacity as a foreign policy strategist and as Commander in Chief?

REAGAN: No, Morton, I don't agree to all of those things. First of all, when we and our allies, the Italians, the French and the United Kingdom, went into Lebanon, we went in there at the request of what was left of the Lebanese Government, to be a stabilizing force while they tried to establish a government. But first, pardon me, the first time we went in, we went in at their request because the war was going on right in Beirut between Israel and the P.L.O. terrorists. Israel could not be blamed for that. Those terrorists had been violating their northern border consistently and Israel chased them all the way to there.

Then, we went in, with the multinational force, to help remove and did remove more than 13,000 of those terrorists from Lebanon. We departed and then the Government of Lebanon asked us back in as a stabilizing force while they established a government and sought to get the foreign forces all the way out of Lebanon and that they could then take care of their own borders. And we were succeeding. We were there for the better part of a year. Our position happened to be at the airport or there were occasional snipings and sometimes some artillery fire, but we did not engage in conflict that was out of line with our mission.

I will never send troops anywhere on a mission of that kind without telling them that if somebody shoots at them they can darn well shoot back. And this is what we did. We never initiated any kind of action, we defended ourselves there. But, we were succeeding to the point that the Lebanese Government had been organized, if you will remember there were the meetings in Geneva in which they began to meet with the hostile factional forces and try to put together some kind of a peace plan. We were succeeding and that was why the terrorist acts began. There are forces there—and that includes Syria, in my mind—who don't want us to succeed, who don't want that kind of a peace with a dominant Lebanon, dominant over its own territory. And so the terrorist acts began and led to the one great tragedy when they were killed in that suicide bombing of the building. Then the multi-lateral force withdrew for only one reason. We withdrew because we were no longer able to carry out the mission for which we had been sent in. But we went in in the interest of peace and to keep Israel and Syria from getting into the sixth war between them. And I have no apologies for our going on a peace mission.

KONDRACKE: Mr. President, four years ago you criticized President Carter for ignoring ample warning that our diplomats in Iran might be taken hostage. Haven't you done exactly the same thing in Lebanon, not once, but three times, with 300 Americans, not hostages, but dead? And you vowed swift retaliation against terrorists but doesn't our lack of response suggest that you're just bluffing?

REAGAN: Morton, no. I think there's a great difference between the Government of Iran threatening our diplomatic personnel and there is a Government that you can see and can put your hand on. In the terrorist situation there are terrorist factions all over—in a recent 30 day period 37 terrorist actions in 20 countries have been committed. The most recent has been the one in Brighton. In dealing with terrorists, yes, we want to retaliate, but only if we can put our finger on the people responsible and not endanger the lives of innocent civilians there in the various communities and in the city of Beirut where these terrorists are operating. I have just signed legislation to add to our ability to deal, along with our allies, with this terrorist problem, and it's going to take all the nations together, just as when we banded together we pretty much resolved the problem of skyjackings some time ago. Well, the red light went on—I could have gone on forever.

MODERATOR: Mr. Mondale, your rebuttal?

MONDALE: Groucho Marx said, who do you believe, me or your own eyes? And what we have in Lebanon is something that the American people have seen. The Joint Chiefs urged the President not to put our troops in that barracks because they were undefensible. They urged—they went to him five days before they were killed and said please take them out of there. The Secretary of State admitted that this morning. He did not do so. The report following the explosion in the barracks disclosed that we had not taken any of the steps that we should have taken. That was the second time. Then the embassy was blown up a few weeks ago and once again none of the steps that should have been taken were taken and we were warned five days before that explosives were on their way and they weren't taken. The terrorists have won each time. The President told the terrorists he was going to retaliate. He didn't. They called their bluff. And the bottom line is the United States left in humiliation and our enemies are stronger.

MODERATOR: Mr. President, your rebuttal?

REAGAN: Yes, first of all, Mr. Mondale should know that the President of the United States did not order the Marines into that barracks. That was a command decision made by the commanders on the spot and based with what they thought was best for the men there. That is one. On the other things that you've just said about the terrorists—I'm tempted to ask you what you would do. These are unidentified people, and after the bomb goes off they're blown to bits because they are suicidal individuals who think that they're going to go to paradise if they perpetrate such an act and lose their life in doing it. We are going to, as I say—we are busy trying to find the centers where these operations stem from and retaliation will be taken, but we are not going to simply kill some people to say, oh look, we got even. We want to know when we retaliate that we're retaliating with those who are responsible for the terrorist acts. And terrorist acts are such that our own United States Capitol in Washington has been bombed twice.

MODERATOR: Mr. Trewhitt, your question to President Reagan?

TREWHITT: Mr. President, I want to raise an issue that I think has been lurking out there for two or three weeks, and cast it specifically in national security terms. You already are the oldest President in history, and some of your staff say you were tired after your most recent encounter with Mr. Mondale. I recall, yes, that President Kennedy, who had to go for days on end with very little sleep during the Cuba missile crisis. Is there any doubt in your mind that you would be able to function in such circumstances?

REAGAN: Not at all, Mr. Trewhitt and I want you to know that also I will not make age an issue of this campaign. I am not going to exploit for political purposes my opponent's youth and inexperience.

If I still have time, I might add, Mr. Trewhitt, I might add that it was Seneca or it was Cicero, I don't know which, that said if it was not for the elders correcting the mistakes of the young, there would be no state.

TREWHITT: Mr. President, I'd like to head for the fence and try to catch that one before it goes over but—without going to another question. The—you and Mr. Mondale have already disagreed about what you had to say about recalling submarine-launched missiles. There's another similar issue out there that relates to your—you said at least that you were unaware that the Soviet retaliatory power was based on land-based missiles. First, is that correct? Secondly, if it is correct, have you informed yourself in the meantime and, third, is it even necessary for the President to be so intimately involved in strategic details?

REAGAN: Yes. This had to do with our disarmament talks and the whole controversy about land missiles came up because we thought that the strategic nuclear weapons—the most destabilizing are the land-based. You put your thumb on a button and somebody blows up 20 minutes later.

So we thought that it would be simpler to negotiate first with those, and then we made it plain, a second phase, take up the submarine-launched—the airborne missiles. The Soviet Union, to our surprise and not just mine—made it plain when we brought this up that they placed, they thought, a greater reliance on the land-based missiles and therefore they wanted to take up all three and we agreed. We said all right, if that's what you want to do.

But, it was a surprise to us because they outnumbered us 64 to 36 in submarines and 20 percent more bombers capable of carrying nuclear missiles than we had. So, why should we believe that they had placed that much more reliance on land-based? But even after we gave in and said all right, let's discuss it all, they walked away from the table. We didn't.

TREWHITT: Mr. Mondale, I'm going to hang in there. Should the President's age and stamina be an issue in the political campaign?

MONDALE: No. And I have not made it an issue nor should it be. What's at issue here is the President's application of his authority to understand what a President must know to lead this nation, secure our defense and make the decisions and judgments that are necessary.

A minute ago, the President quoted Cicero, I believe. I want to quote somebody a little closer home, Harry Truman. He said the buck stops here. We just heard the President's answer for the problems at the barracks in Lebanon where 241 Marines were killed. What happened?

First, the Joint Chiefs of Staff, with the President, said don't put those troops there. They did it. And then five days before the troops were killed, they went back to the President, through the Secretary of Defense, and said please, Mr. President, take those troops out of there because we can't defend them. They didn't do it. And we know what's—what happened.

After that, once again our embassy was exploded. This is the fourth time this has happened—an identical attack in the same region, despite warnings even public warnings from the terrorists. Who's in charge? Who's handling this matter. That's my main point.

Now on arms control—we're completing four years—this is the first Administration since the bomb went off that made no progress. We have an arms race under way instead. A President has to lead his Government or it won't be done. Different people with different views fight with each. For three and a half years, this Administration avoided arms control, resisted tabling arms control proposals that had any hope of agreeing, rebuked their negotiator in 1981 when he came close to an agreement, at least in principle, on medium-range weapons and we have this arms race under way. And a recent book that just came out by, perhaps, the nation's most respected author in this field, Strobe Talbott, called "Deadly Gambit," concludes that this President has failed to master the essential details needed to command and lead us both in terms of security and terms of arms control. That's why they call the President the Commander in Chief. Good intentions, I grant, but it takes more than that. He must be tough and smart.

TREWHITT: This question of leadership keeps arising in different forms in this discussion already. And the President, Mr. Mondale, has called you whining and vacillating, among the more charitable phrases—weak, I believe. It is a question of leadership. And he has made the point that you have not repudiated some of the semi-diplomatic activity of the Rev. Jackson, particularly in Central America. Do you, did you approve of his diplomatic activity? And are you prepared to repudiate him now?

MONDALE: I read his statement the other day. I don't admire Fidel Castro at all. And I have said that. Ché Guevara was a contemptible figure in civilization's history. I know the Cuban state as a police state. And all my life, I've worked in a way that demonstrates that.

But Jesse Jackson is an independent person. I don't control him. And, let's talk about people we do control. In the last debate, the Vice President of the United States said that I said the marines had died shamefully and died in shame in Lebanon. I demanded an apology from Vice President Bush because I had instead honored these young men, grieved for their families and think they were wonderful Americans that honored us all. What does the President have to say about taking responsibility for a Vice President who won't apologize for something like that?

MODERATOR: Mr. President, your rebuttal.

REAGAN: Yes, I know it'll come as a surprise to Mr. Mondale, but I am in charge. And as a matter of fact we haven't avoided arms control talks with the Soviet Union. Very early in my Administration, I proposed—and I think something that had never been proposed by any previous Administration—I proposed a total elimination of intermediate range missiles where the Soviets had better than a, and still have better than a, ten-to-one advantage over the allies in Europe. When they protested that and suggested a smaller number, perhaps, I went along with that. The so-called negotiation that you said I walked out on was the so-called "walk in the woods" between one of our representatives and one of the Sovet Union and it wasn't me that turned it down. The Soviet Union disavowed it.

MODERATOR: Mr. Mondale, your rebuttal.

MONDALE: There are two distinguished authors of arms control in this country. There are many others, but two that I want to cite tonight. One is Strobe Talbott in his classic book "Deadly Gambit." The other is John Newhouse, who's one of the most distinguished arms control specialists in our country. Both said that this Administration turned down the "walk in the woods" agreement first and that would have been a perfect agreement from the standpoint of the United States and Europe and our security. When Mr. Nitze, a good negotiator returned, he was rebuked and his boss was fired. This is the kind of leadership that we've had in this Administration in the most deadly issue of our time. Now we have a runaway arms race. All they've got to show for four years in U.S.-Soviet relations is one meeting in the last weeks of an Administration and nothing before. They're tough negotiators, but all previous Presidents have made progress. This one has not.

MODERATOR: Miss Geyer, your question to Mr. Mondale.

GEYER: Mr. Mondale, many analysts are saying that actually our No. 1 foreign policy problem today is one that remains almost totally unrecognized. Massive illegal immigration from economically collapsing countries. They are saying that it is the only real territorial threat to the American nation-state. You yourself said in the 1970's that we had a "hemorrhage on our borders" yet today you have backed off any immigration reform such as the balanced and highly crafted Simpson-Mazzoli Bill. Why? What would you do instead today if anything?

MONDALE: Ah, this is a very serious problem in our country and it has to be dealt with. I object to that part of the Simpson-Mazzoli Bill which I think is very unfair and would prove to be so. That is the part that requires employers to determine the citizenship of an employee before they're hired. I am convinced that the result of this would be that people who are Hispanic, people who have different languages or speak with an accent would find it difficult to be employed.

I think that's wrong. We've never had citizenship tests in our country before. And I don't think we should have a citizenship card today. That is counter-productive. I do support the other aspects of the Simpson-Mazzoli Bill that strengthens enforcement at the border, strengthens other ways of dealing with undocumented workers in this difficult area and dealing with the problem of settling people who have lived here for many many years and do not have an established status. I further strongly recommend that this Administration do something it has not done. And that is to strengthen enforcement at the border, strengthen the officials in this Government that deal with undocumented workers and to do so in a way that's responsible and within the Constitution of the United States.

We need an answer to this problem. But it must be an American answer that is consistent with justice and due process. Everyone in this room, practically, here tonight, is an immigrant. We came here loving this nation, serving it and it has served all of our most bountiful dreams. And one of those dreams is justice. And we need a measure, and I will support a measure that brings about those objectives, but avoids that one aspect that I think is very serious.

The second part is to maintain and improve relations with our friends to the south. We cannot solve this problem all on our own. And that's why the failure of this administration to deal in an effective and good-faith way with Mexico, with Costa Rica, with the other nations in trying to find a peaceful settlement to the dispute in Central America has undermined our capacity to effectively to deal diplomatic in this, diplomatically in this area as well.

GEYER: Sir, people as well-balanced and just as Father Theodore Hesburgh at Notre Dame, who headed the Select Commission on Immigration, have pointed out repeatedly that there will be no immigration reform without employer sanctions because it would be an unbalanced bill and there would be simply no way to enforce it. However, putting that aside for the moment, your critics have also said repeatedly that you have not gone along with the bill, or with any immigration reform, because of the Hispanic groups—or Hispanic leadership groups, who actually do not represent what the Hispanic Americans want because polls show that they overwhelmingly want some kind of immigration reform. Can you say, or how can you justify your position on this, and how do you respond to the criticism that this is another, or that this is an example of your flip-flopping and giving in to special interest groups at the expense of the American nation?

MONDALE: I think you're right that the polls show that the majority of Hispanics want the bill, so I'm not doing it for political reasons. I'm doing it because all my life I've fought for a system of justice in this country, a system in which every American has a chance to achieve the fullness of life without discrimination. This bill imposes upon employers the responsibility of determining whether somebody who applies for a job is an American or not, and just inevitably they're going to be reluctant to hire Hispanics or people with a different accent.

If I were dealing with politics here, the polls show the American people want this. I am for reform in this area, for tough enforcement at the border, and for many other aspects of the Simpson-Mazzoli Bill, but all my life I've fought for a fair nation and, despite the politics of it, I stand where I stand, and I think I'm right. And before this fight is over, we're going to come up with a better bill, a more effective bill, that does not undermine the liberties of our people.

GEYER: Mr. President, you too have said that our borders are out of control. Yet this fall, you allowed the Simpson-Mazzoli Bill, which would at least have minimally protected our borders and the rights of citizenship because of a relatively unimportant issue of reimbursement to the states for legalized aliens. Given that, may I ask what priority can we expect you to give this forgotten national security element; how sincere are you in your efforts to control, in effect, the nation's states, that is the United States?

REAGAN: Georgie, and we, believe me, supported the Simpson-Mazzoli Bill strongly, and the bill that came out of the Senate. However, there were things added in in the House side that we felt made it less of a good bill; as a matter of fact, made it a bad bill. And in conference, we stayed with them in conference all the way to where even Senator Simpson did not want the bill in the manner in which it would come out of the conference committee. There were a number of things in there that weakened that bill—I can't go into detail about them here. But it is true our borders are out of control, it is also true that this has been a situation on our borders back through a number of Administrations.

And I supported this bill, I believe in the idea of amnesty for those who have put down roots and who have lived here, even though some time back they may have entered illegally. With regard to the employer sanctions, we must have that—not only to ensure that we can identify the illegal aliens but also, while some keep protesting about what it would do to employers, there is another employer that we shouldn't be so concerned about, and these are employers down through the years who have encouraged the illegal entry into this country because they then hire these individuals and hire them at starvation wages and with none of the benefits that we think are normal and natural for workers in our country. And the individuals can't complain because of their illegal status. We don't think that those people should be allowed to continue operating free, and this was why the provisions that we had in with regard to sanctions and so forth.

And I'm going to do everything I can, and all of us in the Administration are, to join in again when Congress is back at it to get an immigration bill that will give us once again control of our borders. And with regard to friendship below the border with the countries down there, yes, no Administration that I know has established the relationship that we have with our Latin friends. But as long as they have an economy that leaves so many people in dire poverty and unemployment, they are going to seek that employment across our borders. And we work with those other countries.

GEYER: Mr. President, the experts also say that the situation today is terribly different—quantitatively, qualitatively different—from what it has been in the past because of the gigantic population growth. For instance, Mexico's population will go from about 60 million today to 120 million at the turn of the century. Many of these people will be coming into the United States not as citizens but as illegal workers. You have repeatedly said recently that you believe that Armageddon, the destruction of the world, may be imminent in our times. Do you ever feel that we are in for an Armageddon or a situation, a time of anarchy, regarding the population explosion in the world?

REAGAN: No, as matter of fact the population explosion, if you look at the actual figures, has been vastly exaggerated—over-exaggerated. As a matter of fact, there are some pretty scientific and solid figures about how much space there still is in the world and how many more people can have. It's almost like going back to the Malthusian theory, when even then they were saying that everyone would starve with the limited population they had then.

But the problem of population growth is one here with regard to our immigration. And we have been the safety valve, whether we wanted to or not, with the illegal entry here; in Mexico, where their population is increasing and they don't have an economy that can absorb them and provide the jobs. And this is what we're trying to work out, not only to protect our own borders but to have some kind of fairness and recognition of that problem.

MODERATOR: Mr. Mondale, your rebuttal.

MONDALE: One of the biggest problems today is that the countries to our south are so desperately poor that these people who will almost lose their lives if they don't come north, come north despite all the risks. And if we're going to find a permanent, fundamental answer to this, it goes to American economic and trade policies that permit these nations to have a chance to get on their own two feet and to get prosperity so that they can have jobs for themselves and their people.

And that's why this enormous national debt, engineered by this Administration, is harming these countries and fueling this immigration.

These high interest rates, real rates, that have doubled under this Administration, have had the same effect on Mexico and so on, and the cost of repaying those debts is so enormous that it results in massive unemployment, hardship and heartache. And that drives our friends to the north—to the south—up into our region, and we need to end those deficits as well.

MODERATOR: Mr. President, your rebuttal.

REAGAN: Well, my rebuttal is I've heard the national debt blamed for a lot of things, but not for illegal immigration across our border, and it has nothing to do with it.

But with regard to these high interest rates, too, at least give us the recognition of the fact that when you left office, Mr. Mondale, they were 22 1/2, the prime rate; it's now 12 1/4, and I predict it'll be coming down a little more shortly. So we're trying to undo some of the things that your Administration did.

MODERATOR: Mr. Kalb. No applause, please. Mr. Kalb, your question to President Reagan.

KALB: Mr. President, I'd like to pick up this Armageddon theme. You've been quoted as saying that you do believe deep down that we are heading for some kind of biblical Armageddon. Your Pentagon and your Secretary of Defense have plans for the United States to fight and prevail in a nuclear war. Do you feel that we are now heading, perhaps, for some kind of nuclear Armageddon? And do you feel that this country and the world could survive that kind of calamity?

REAGAN: Mr. Kalb, I think what has been hailed as something I'm supposedly, as President, discussing as principle is the result of just some philosophical discussions with people who are interested in the same things. And that is the prophecies down through the years, the biblical prophecies of what would portend the coming of Armageddon and so forth. And the fact that a number of theologians for the last decade or more have believed that this was true, that the prophecies are coming together that portend that.

But no one knows whether Armageddon—those prophecies—mean that Armageddon is a thousand years away or day after tomorrow. So I have never seriously warned and said we must plan according to Armageddon.

Now, with regard to having to say whether we would try to survive in the event of a nuclear war—of course we would. But let me also point out that to several parliaments around the world, in Europe and in Asia, I have made a statement to each one of them, and I'll repeat it here: A nuclear war cannot be won and must never be fought.

And that is why we are maintaining a deterrent and trying to achieve a deterrent capacity to where no one would believe that they could start such a war and escape with limited damage. But the deterrent—and that's what it is for—is also what led me to propose what is now being called the Star Wars concept, but propose that we research to see if there isn't a defensive weapon that could defend against incoming missiles. And if such a defense could be found, wouldn't it be far more humanitarian to say that now we can defend against a nuclear war by destroying missiles instead of slaughtering millions of people?

KALB: Mr. President, when you made that proposal, the so-called Star Wars proposal, you said, if I'm not mistaken, that you would share this very super-sophisticated technology with the Soviet Union. After all of the distrust over the years, sir, that you have expressed towards the Soviet Union, do you really expect anyone to take seriously that offer—that you would share the best of America's technology in this weapons area with our principal adversary?

REAGAN: Why not? What if we did and I hope we can, we're still researching. What if we come up with a weapon that renders those missiles obsolete? There has never been a weapon invented in the history of man that has not led to a defensive, a counter-weapon, but suppose we came up with that. Now, some people have said ah, that would make a war imminent because they would think that we could launch a first strike because we could defend against the enemy. But why not do what I have offered to do and asked the Soviet Union to do? Say look, here's what we can do, we'll even give it to you, now will you sit down with us and once and for all get rid—all of us—of these nuclear weapons and free mankind from that threat. I think that would be the greatest use of a defensive weapon.

KALB: Mr. Mondale you've been very sharply critical of the President's strategic defense initiative and yet what is wrong with a major effort by this country to try to use its best technology to knock out as many incoming nuclear warheads as possible?

MONDALE: First of all, let me sharply disagree with the President on sharing the most advanced, the most dangerous, the most important technology in America with the Soviet Union. We have had, for many years, understandably, a system of restraints on high technology because the Soviets are behind us and any research or development along the Star Wars schemes would inevitably involve our most advanced computers, the most advanced engineering and the thought that we would share this with the Soviet Union is, in my opinion, a total non-starter. I would not let the Soviet Union get their hands on it at all.

Now, what's wrong with Star Wars? There's nothing wrong with the theory of it. If we could develop a principle that would say both sides could fire all their missiles and no one would get hurt, I suppose it's a good idea. But the fact of it is, we're so far away from research that even comes close to that that the director of engineering research in the Defense Department said to get there we would have to solve eight problems, each of which are more difficult than the atomic bomb and the Manhattan Project. It would cost something like a trillion dollars to test and deploy weapons. The second thing is this all assumes that the Soviets wouldn't respond in kind, and they always do. We don't get behind, they won't get behind and that's been the tragic story of the arms race. We have more at stake in space satellites than they do. If we could stop right now the testing and the deployment of these space weapons and the President's proposals go clear beyond research. If it was just research, we wouldn't have any argument, because maybe some day somebody will think of something. But to commit this nation to a buildup of anti-satellite and space weapons at this time in their crude state would bring about an arms race that's very dangerous indeed.

One final point: The most dangerous aspect of this proposal is for the first time we would delegate to computers the decision as to whether to start a war. That's dead wrong. There wouldn't be time for a President to decide. It would be decided by these remote computers. It might be an oil fire, it might be a jet exhaust, the computer might decide it's a missile and off we go. Why don't we stop this madness now and draw a line and keep the heavens free from war?

KALB: Mr. Mondale, in this general area, sir, of arms control, President Carter's national security adviser Zbigniew Brzezinski said, "A nuclear freeze is a hoax," yet the basis of your arms proposals as I understand them is a mutual and verifiable freeze on existing weapons systems. In your view, which specific weapons systems could be subject to a mutual and verifiable freeze and which could not?

MONDALE: Every system that is verifiable should be placed on the table for negotiations for an agreement. I would not agree to any negotiations or any agreement that involved conduct on the part of the Soviet Union that we couldn't verify every day. I would not agree to any agreement in which the United States' security interest was not fully recognized and supported. That's why we say mutual and verifiable freezes.

Now, why do I support the freeze? Because this ever-rising arms race madness makes both nations less secure, it's more difficult to defend this nation, it is putting a hair trigger on nuclear war. This Administration, by going into the Star Wars system, is going to add a dangerous new escalation. We have to be tough on the Soviet Union, but I think the American people and the people of the Soviet Union want it to stop.

MODERATOR: Time is up, Mr. Mondale. President Reagan your rebuttal.

REAGAN: Yes, my rebuttal once again is that this invention that has just been created here of how I would go about rolling over to the Soviet Union—No, Mr. Mondale, my idea would be with that defensive weapon, that we would sit down with them and then say, now, are you willing to join us? Here's what we can—give them a demonstration, and then say, here's what we can do. Now, if you're willing to join us in getting rid of all the nuclear weapons in the world, then, we'll give you this one so that we would both know that no one can cheat—that we've both got something that if anyone tries to cheat—but when you keep star-warring it—I never suggested where the weapons should be or what kind. I'm not a scientist. I said, and the Joint Chiefs of Staff agreed with me, that it was time for us to turn our research ability to seeing if we could not find this kind of a defensive weapon. And suddenly somebody says, oh, it's got to be up there—star wars—and so forth. I don't know what it would be, but if we can come up with one, I think the world will be better off.

MODERATOR: Mr. Mondale, your rebuttal?

MONDALE: Well, that's what a President's supposed to know—where those weapons are going to be. If they're space weapons, I assume they'll be in space. If they're antisatellite weapons, I assume they're going to be armed against any satellite. Now, this is the most dangerous technology that we possess. The Soviets try to spy on us—steal this stuff—and to give them technology of this kind, I disagree with. You haven't just accepted research, Mr. President, you've set up a strategic defense initiative and agency. You're beginning to test. You're talking about deploying. You're asking for a budget of some $30 billion for this purpose. This is an arms escalation, and we will be better off—far better off—

if we stop right now, because we have more to lose in space than they do. If someday somebody comes along with an answer, that's something else, but that there would be an answer in our lifetime is unimaginable. Why do we start things that we know the Soviets will match and make us all less secure? That's what a President is for.

MODERATOR: Mr. Kondracke, your question to Mr. Mondale?

KONDRACKE: Mr. Mondale, you say that with respect to the Soviet Union, you want to negotiate a mutual nuclear freeze. Yet you would unilaterally give up the MX missile and the B-1 bomber before the talks have even begun, and you have announced in advance that reaching an agreement with the Soviets is the most important thing in the world to you. Now aren't you giving away half the store before you even sit down to talk?

MONDALE: As a matter of fact we have a vast range of technology and weaponry right now that provides all the bargaining chips that we need, and I support the air launch cruise missile, ground launch cruise missile, Pershing missile, the Trident submarine, the D-5 submarine, the stealth technology, the Midgetman— we have a whole range of technology. Why I disagree with the MX is that it's a sitting duck. It'll draw an attack. It puts a hair trigger, and it is a dangerous destabilizing weapon. And the B-1 is similarly to be opposed because for 15 years the Soviet Union has been preparing to meet the B-1, the Secretary of Defense himself said, it would be a suicide mission, if it were built. Instead, I want to build the Midgetman which is mobile and thus less vulnerable, contributing to stability, and a weapon that will give us security and contribute to an incentive for arms control. That's why I'm for Stealth technology to build the Stealth bomber, which I supported for years, that can penetrate the Soviet air defense system without any hope that they can perceive where it is because their radar system is frustrated. In other words, a President has to make choices. This makes us stronger.

The final point is that we can use this money that we save on these weapons to spend on things that we really need. Our conventional strength in Europe is under strength. We need to strengthen that in order to assure our Western allies of our presence there, a strong defense, but also to diminish and reduce the likelihood of a commencement of a war and the use of nuclear weapons. It's by this way by making wise choices that we're stronger, we enhance the changes of arms control. Every President until this one has been able to do it, and this nation, the world is more dangerous as a result.

KONDRACKE: I want to follow up on Mr. Kalb's question. It seems to me that on the question of verifiability that you do have some problems with the extent of the freeze. It seems to me, for example, that testing would be very difficult to verify because the Soviets encode their telemetry. Research would be impossible to verify, numbers of warheads would be impossible to verify by satellite except with on-site inspection, and production of any weapon would be impossible to verify. Now in view of that, what is going to be frozen?

MONDALE: I will not agree to any arms control agreement, including a freeze, that's not verifiable. Let's take your warhead principle. The warhead principle, they've been counting rules for years. Whenever a weapon is tested, we counted the number of warheads on it, and whenever that warhead is used we count that number of warheads, whether they have that number or less on it or not. These are standard rules. I will not agree to any production restrictions or agreement unless we have the ability to verify those agreements. I don't trust the Russians. I believe that every agreement we reach must be verifiable, and I will not agree to anything that we cannot tell every day. In other words, we've got to be tough, but in order to stop this arms madness we've got to push ahead with tough negotiations that are verifiable so that we know the Soviets are agreeing and living up to their agreements.

KONDRACKE: Mr. President, I want to ask you about negotiating with friends. You severely criticized President Carter for helping to undermine two friendly dictators who got into trouble with their own people, the Shah of Iran and President Somoza of Nicaragua. Now there are other such leaders heading for trouble, including President Pinochet of Chile and President Marcos of the Philippines. What should you do and what can you do to prevent the Philippines from becoming another Nicaragua?

REAGAN: Morton, I did criticize the President because of our undercutting of what was a stalwart ally, the Shah of Iran. And I am not at all convinced that he was that far out of line with his people or that they wanted that to happen.

The Shah had done our bidding and carried our load in the Middle East for quite some time and I did think that it was a blot on our record that we let him down. Had things gotten better, the Shah, whatever he might have done, was building low-cost housing, had taken land away from the mullahs and was distributing it to the peasants so they could be landowners, things of that kind. But we turned it over to a maniacal fanatic who has slaughtered thousands and thousands of people calling it executions.

The matter of Somoza, no, I never defended Somoza. And as a matter of fact, the previous Administration stood by and so did I—not that I could have done anything in my position at that time. But for this revolution to take place and the promise of the revolution was democracy, human rights, free labor unions, free press. And then just as Castro had done in Cuba, the Sandinistas ousted the other parties to the revolution. Many of them are now the Contras. They exiled some, they jailed some, they murdered some. And they installed a Marxist-Leninist totalitarian Government.

And what I have to say about this is, many times—and this has to do with the Philippines also—I know there are things there in the Philippines that do not look good to us from the standpoint right now of democratic rights. But what is the alternative? It is a large Communist movement to take over the Philippines.

They have been our friend for—since their inception as a nation. And I think that we've had enough of a record of letting, under the guise of revolution, someone that we thought was a little more right than we would be, letting that person go and then winding up with totalitarianism pure and simple as the alternative and I think that we're better off, for example, with the Philippines of trying to retain our friendship and help them right the wrongs we see rather than throwing them to the wolves and then facing a Communist power in the Pacific.

KONDRACKE: Mr. President, since the United States has two strategic bases in the Philippines, would the overthrow of President Marcos constitute a threat to vital American interests, and, if so, what would you do about it?

REAGAN: Well, as I say we have to look at what an overthrow there would mean and what the government would be that would follow. And there is every evidence, every indication that that government would be hostile to the United States and that would be a severe blow to the—to our abilities there in the Pacific.

KONDRACKE: And what would you do about it?

MODERATOR: Sorry, sorry, you've asked the follow-up question. Mr. Mondale, your rebuttal.

MONDALE: Perhaps in no area do we disagree more than this Administration's policies on human rights. I went to the Philippines as Vice President, pressed for human rights, called for the release of Aquino and made progress that had been stalled on both the Subic and the Clark airfield bases.

What explains this Administration cozying up to the Argentine dictators after they took over? Fortunately a democracy took over but this nation was embarrassed by this current Administration's adoption of their policies. What happens in South Africa, where, for example, the Nobel Prize winner two days ago said this Administration is seen as working with the oppressive Government of that region, of South Africa.

That hurts this nation. We need to stand for human rights. We need to make it clear we're for human liberty. National security and human rights must go together, but this Administration time and time again has lost its way in this field.

MODERATOR: President Reagan, your rebuttal.

REAGAN: Well, the invasion of Afghanistan didn't take place on our watch. I have described what has happened in Iran and we weren't here then either. I don't think that our record of human rights can be assailed. I think that we have observed ourselves and have done our best to see that human rights are extended throughout the world.

Mr. Mondale has recently announced a plan of his to get the democracies together and to work with the whole world to turn to democracy. And I was glad to hear him say that because that's what we've been doing ever since I announced to the British Parliament that I thought we should do this.

And human rights are not advanced when at the same time you then stand back and say, "Whoops, we didn't know the gun was loaded," and you have another totalitarian power on your hands.

MODERATOR: In this, in this segment, because of the pressure of time, there will be no rebuttals and there will be no follow-up questions. Mr. Trewhitt, your question to President Reagan.

TREWHITT: One question to each candidate?

MODERATOR: One question to each candidate.

TREWHITT: Mr. President, could I take you back to something you said earlier? And if I'm misquoting you please correct me. But I understood you to say that if the development of space military technology was successful, you might give the Soviets a demonstration and say, "Here it is," which sounds to me as if you might be trying to gain the sort of advantage that would enable you to dictate terms, and which I would then suggest to you might mean scrapping a generation of nuclear strategy called mutual deterrence, in which we in effect hold each other hostage. Is that your intention?

REAGAN: Well, I can't say that I have roundtabled that and sat down with the Chiefs of Staff, but I have said that it seems to me that this could be a logical step in what is my ultimate goal, my ultimate dream. And that is the elimination of nuclear weapons in the world. And it seems to me that this could be an adjunct, or certainly a great assisting agent, in getting that done. I am not going to roll over, as Mr. Mondale suggests, and give them something that could turn around and be used against us. But I think it's a very interesting proposal to see if we can find first of all something that renders those weapons obsolete, incapable of their mission.

But Mr. Mondale seems to approve MAD—MAD is Mutual Assured Destruction, meaning if you use nuclear weapons on us, the only thing we have to keep you from doing it is that we'll kill as many people of yours as you will kill of ours. I think that to do everything we can to find, as I say, something that would destroy weapons and not humans is a great step forward in human rights.

TREWHITT: Mr. Mondale, could I ask you to address the question of nuclear strategy. Formal doctrine is very arcane, but I'm going to ask you to deal with it anyway. Do you believe in MAD, Mutual Assured Destruction, mutual deterrence, as it has been practiced for the last generation?

MONDALE: I believe in a sensible arms control approach that brings down these weapons to manageable levels. I would like to see their elimination. And in the meantime, we have to be strong enough to make certain that the Soviet Union never attempts this.

Now here we have to decide between generalized objectives and reality. The President says he wants to eliminate or reduce the number of nuclear weapons, but in fact these last four years have seen more weapons built, a wider and more vigorous arms race than in human history. He says he wants a system that will make nuclear arms wars safe, so nobody's going to get hurt. Well, maybe someday somebody can dream of that. But why start an arms race now? Why destabilize our relationship? Why threaten our space satellites, upon which we depend? Why pursue a strategy that would delegate to computers the question of starting a war.

A President, to defend this country and to get arms control, must master what's going on. I accept his objective and his dreams, we all do. But the hard reality is that we must know what we're doing and pursue those objectives that are possible in our time. He's opposed every effort of every President to do so; in the four years of his Administration he's failed to do so. And if you want a tough President who uses that strength to get arms control, and draws the line in the heavens, vote for Walter Mondale.

MODERATOR: Please, i must again ask the audience not to applaud, not to cheer, not demonstrate its feelings in any way. We've arrived at the point in the debate now where we call for closing statements. You have the full four minutes, each of you. Mr. Mondale, will you go first.

MONDALE: I want to thank the League of Women Voters, the good citizens of Kansas City and President Reagan for agreeing to debate this evening.

This evening we talked about national strength. I believe we need to be strong, and I will keep us strong. But I think strength must also require wisdom and smarts in its exercise—that's key to the strength of our nation.

A President must know the essential facts, essential to command. But a President must also have a vision of where this nation should go.

Tonight, as Americans you have a choice. And you're entitled to know where we would take this country if you decide to elect us.

As President, I would press for long-term vigorous economic growth. That's why I want to get these debts down and these interest rates down, restore America's exports, help rural America which is suffering so much, and bring the jobs back here for our children.

I want this next generation to be the best educated in American history; to invest in the human mind and science again, so we're out front.

I want this nation to protect its air, its water, its land and its public health. America is not temporary. We're forever. And as Americans, our generation should protect this wonderful land for our children.

I want a nation of fairness, where no one is denied the fullness of life or discriminated against, and we deal compassionately with those in our midst who are in trouble.

And above all, I want a nation that's strong. Since we debated two weeks ago, the United States and the Soviet Union have built 100 more warheads, enough to kill millions of Americans and millions of Soviet citizens.

This doesn't strengthen us, this weakens the chances of civilization to survive.

I remember the night before I became Vice President. I was given the briefing and told that any time, night or day, I might be called upon to make the most fateful decision on earth—whether to fire these atomic weapons that could destroy the human species.

That lesson tells us two things. One, pick a President that you know will know, if that tragic moment ever comes, what he must know. Because there'll be no time for staffing committees or advisers; a President must know right then.

But above all, pick a President who will fight to avoid the day when that God-awful decision ever needs to be made. And that's why this election is so terribly important.

America and Americans decide not just what's happening in this country; we are the strongest and most powerful free society on earth. When you make that judgment, you are deciding not only the future of our nation; in a very profound respect, you're providing the future—deciding the future of the world.

We need to move on. It's time for America to find new leadership. Please join me in this cause to move confidently and with a sense of assurance and command to build the blessed future of our nation.

MODERATOR: President Reagan, your summation, please.

REAGAN: Yes, my thanks to the League of Women Voters, to the panelists, to the moderator, and to the people of Kansas City for their warm hospitality and greeting.

I think the American people tonight have much to be grateful for: an economic recovery that has become expansion, freedom, and most of all, we are at peace. I am grateful for the chance to reaffirm my commitment to reduce nuclear weapons and one day to eliminate them entirely.

The question before comes down to this: do you want to see America return to the policies of weakness of the last four years, or do we want to go forward marching together as a nation of strength and that's going to continue to be strong?

We shouldn't be dwelling on the past or even the present. The meaning of this election is the future, and whether we're going to grow and provide the jobs and the opportunities for all Americans and that they need. Several years ago I was given an assignment to write a letter. It was to go into a time capsule and would be read in 100 years when that time capsule was opened. I remember driving down the California coast one day. My mind was full of what I was going to put in that letter about the problems and the issues that confront us in our time and what we did about them, but I couldn't completely neglect the beauty around me—the Pacific out there on one side of the highway shining in the sunlight, the mountains of the coast range rising on the other side, and I found myself wondering what it would be like for someone, wondering if someone 100 years from now would be driving down that highway and if they would see the same thing.

And with that thought I realized what a job I had with that letter. I would be writing a letter to people who know everything there is to know about us. We know nothing about them. They would know all about our problems. They would know how we solved them and whether our solution was beneficial to them down through the years or whether it hurt them. They would also know that we lived in a world with terrible weapons, nuclear weapons of terrible destructive power aimed at each other, capable of crossing the ocean in a matter of minutes and destroying civilization as we know it.

And then I thought to myself: what are they going to say about us? What are those people 100 years from now going to think? They will know whether we used those weapons or not. Well, what they will say about us 100 years from now depends on how we keep our rendezvous with destiny. Will we do the things that we know must be done and know that one day down in history 100 years, or perh·.ps before, someone will say: thank God for those people back in the 1980's, for preserving our freedom, for saving for us this blessed planet called earth with all its grandeur and its beauty.

You know, I am grateful for all of you for giving the opportunity to serve you for these four years and I seek re-election because I want more than anything else to try to complete the new beginning that we charted four years ago.

George Bush, who I think is one of the finest Vice Presidents this country has ever had, George Bush and I have crisscrossed the country and we've had in these last few months a wonderful experience. We have met young America. We have met your sons and daughters.

MODERATOR: Mr. President, I'm obliged to cut you off there under the rules of the debate. I'm sorry.

REAGAN: All right, I was just going to——

MODERATOR: Perhaps I should point out that the rules under which I did that were agreed upon by the two campaigns.

REAGAN: I know, yes.

MODERATOR: Thank you, Mr. President. Thank you, Mr. Mondale. Our thanks also to the panel, finally to our audience. We thank you and the League of Women Voters asks me to say to you: don't forget to vote on Nov. 6.

THE VOTES IN THE 1984 ELECTION

CANDIDATES FOR PRESIDENT AND VICE PRESIDENT
Democratic—Walter Mondale; Geraldine Ferraro
Republican—Ronald Reagan; George Bush

STATE	Dem.	Rep.	ELECTORAL VOTE D	R
Alabama.........	551,899	872,849	—	9
Alaska	62,007	138,377	—	3
Arizona	333,854	681,416	—	7
Arkansas	338,646	534,774	—	6
California.......	3,922,519	5,467,009	—	47
Colorado	454,975	821,817	—	8
Connecticut	569,597	890,877	—	8
Delaware	101,656	152,190	—	3
Dist. of Col.	180,408	29,009	3	—
Florida	1,448,816	2,730,350	—	21
Georgia	706,628	1,068,722	—	12
Hawaii	147,154	185,050	—	4
Idaho	108,510	297,523	—	4
Illinois...........	2,086,499	2,707,103	—	24
Indiana	841,481	1,377,230	—	12
Iowa	605,620	703,088	—	8
Kansas	333,149	677,296	—	7
Kentucky	539,539	821,702	—	9
Louisiana	651,586	1,037,299	—	10
Maine	214,515	336,500	—	4
Maryland	787,935	879,918	—	10
Massachusetts	1,239,606	1,310,936	—	13
Michigan	1,529,638	2,251,571	—	20
Minnesota	1,036,364	1,032,603	10	—
Mississippi	352,192	582,377	—	7
Missouri	848,583	1,274,188	—	11
Montana.........	146,742	232,450	—	4
Nebraska	187,866	460,054	—	5
Nevada	91,655	188,770	—	4
New Hampshire ..	120,347	267,050	—	4
New Jersey	1,261,323	1,933,630	—	16
New Mexico	201,769	307,101	—	5
New York	3,119,609	3,664,763	—	36
North Carolina ...	824,287	1,346,481	—	13
North Dakota	104,429	200,336	—	3
Ohio	1,825,440	2,678,559	—	23
Oklahoma	385,080	861,530	—	8
Oregon	536,479	685,700	—	7
Pennsylvania	2,228,131	2,584,323	—	25
Rhode Island.....	196,300	212,100	—	4
South Carolina ...	344,459	615,539	—	8
South Dakota	116,113	200,267	—	3
Tennessee	711,714	990,212	—	11
Texas	1,949,276	3,433,428	—	29
Utah	155,369	469,105	—	5
Vermont.........	95,730	135,865	—	3
Virginia	796,250	1,337,078	—	12
Washington	798,352	1,051,670	—	10
West Virginia	328,125	405,483	—	6
Wisconsin........	995,740	1,198,584	—	11
Wyoming	53,370	133,241	—	3
Total	37,567,331	54,455,093	13	525